Why Build Apartments?

The most straightforward of projects is, unfortunately, often the most difficult! Creating an apartment floor plan is as challenging as preparing the perfect spaghetti. The way you start is similar. For an apartment, you already know the spaces to include: entrance →1.2.3, hallway →1.2.4, bedroom →1.3.2, bathroom →1.3.5, living room →1.4.1, kitchen →1.4.2 and dining area →1.4.4. For the familiar spaghetti al pomodoro, you need a pot with salted boiling water, pasta, an onion, butter, and pelati tomatoes. For over thirty years, we have been trying to create the perfect apartment layout as well as the perfect everyday pasta dish.

We're interested in life, specifically the living that takes place in these apartments. Similar to a set in a theater, an apartment provides the setting for everyday life in all its facets. We place tremendous value on its infinite wealth, its variety. The idea of working like a director or choreographer to set up a cozy home fascinates us. That's why we enjoy building apartments. Drawing floor plans makes us happy. This passion for creating something special from the normal and banal is what drives us the most, day in and day out.

Housing construction is always linked to the needs of its residents, and therefore to the greatest possible responsibility. The direct impact on people's daily lives differentiates this type of construction project from many others and necessitates particularly careful planning. Mistakes can't be tolerated. If they occur, the consequences are disastrous, since apartment construction is always a long-term, costly investment. Once built, a floor plan with a defective layout remains in use for decades and has a long-term influence on the lives of its inhabitants. This is precisely why we, as designers, bear responsibility.

We design dwellings and we are ourselves dwellers—every day. For this reason, we're our own biggest critics. This direct connection to lived reality, which keeps our feet on the ground, is of vital importance in the profession of architecture. We not only bring the necessary creativity to bear, but also take the time to contemplate, let things take their course, and finally, examine what we have designed. Against this background, those banal household tasks that we too are familiar with, such as ironing a shirt, cooking, putting fresh sheets on a bed, or cleaning the bathroom, attain a new and satisfactory significance.

We are delighted that the majority of our buildings have been constructed in the immediate vicinity of our office. It is a privilege to be able to see, on our way to work or on the way home, our design ideas slowly taking shape, and to be

Creating an apartment floor plan is as challenging as preparing the perfect spaghetti.

Our practice is designing dwellings and we are ourselves dwellers—every day.

able to smell the wet concrete and touch the materials. We're thankful for this, too.

We established our office at the end of the 1980s, despite a downturn in the construction industry at the time. Following a ten-year learning phase with a lot of competition entries, some competitions where we placed first, only small construction sites, and formative years in assistant faculty positions at ETH Zurich, the tide began to turn at beginning of the new millennium. The goal announced at the time by Zurich's municipal government of building 10,000 apartments in ten years epitomized a boom in apartment construction that has continued to this day.

The Paul Clairmont apartment block → 2.2.1 and the James development → 2.2.2 —both in Zurich—allowed us to demonstrate our understanding of high-quality residential construction. These, and other construction projects, also formed a basis that has for years ensured our continued invitation to produce site studies. But while a bit of luck is necessary to be awarded a study commission or win a competition, it's necessary for other things, too. Working together with the building contractor through all phases of design and construction to achieve first prize while withstanding appeals and keeping to the budget at all times sometimes also requires a lot of good fortune. We have won first prize again and again. This continues to form a basis for our work, meaning that we constantly have floor plans in all phases of design on our desks.

Jakob Steib and Patrick Gmür found partners and, above all, friends in Michael Geschwentner and Matthias Kyburz, who have worked together with them throughout the years to design and realize these residential buildings. In 2020, we brought together our different ventures and merged offices under the admittedly rather long-winded name "Steib Gmür Geschwentner Kyburz Partner AG Architekten & Stadtplaner."

The ingredients we work with are spaces. But building apartments is not the only thing we have in common; we're also united through a passion for food. Around public holidays, we

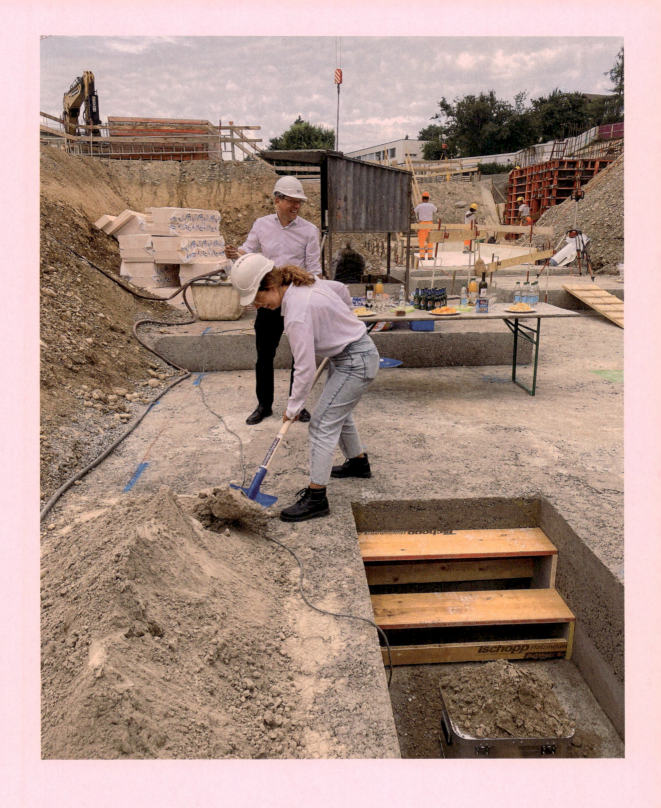

It is a privilege to be able to see our design ideas slowly taking shape.

Why Build Apartments? 9

even take a detour here and there to eat in a three-star restaurant. If we're honest, though, we prefer the simple, excellent meals you can find in a little trattoria. Designing apartments, and creating floor plans in particular, correlates to everyday meals like these. In both arts, we are constantly striving to improve.

This opulent box of five volumes with the title *Food for Architects* bears witness to our long-standing cooperation. The first volume brings together short, personal texts on the individual spaces of an apartment building and on other aspects of dwelling. Volume Two provides an insight into how our various working ventures developed into a joint office, and exhibits around sixty of our most significant buildings and projects. Volume Three presents a range of furnished floor plans, split into twelve chapters and including a detailed overview. To demonstrate the similarities between the perfect apartment plans and cooking the perfect spaghetti, several pasta recipes are also included in this book. The fourth volume is dedicated to apartment residents, since we are curious about how our designs have fared in practice. In the final volume of this "five-course menu," a roundtable discussion with our office partners addresses a range of additional topics that are important for our architectural practice. Above all, our enthusiasm for building residences remains a constant. This publication chronicles this enthusiasm and in particular exhibits our "one true love"—the floor plan—in all its facets.

Jakob Steib, Patrick Gmür,
Michael Geschwentner, Matthias Kyburz

This publication exhibits our "one true love"— the floor plan—in all its facets.

Why Build Apartments? 11

To Each His Room

The following texts deal with the topic of dwelling in a personal way. Based on my own observations, and experiences from our shared studio, they illustrate how residential construction is a passion that pulls together the different threads of our design work.

With constant curiosity and some luck, I have been able to practice architecture and urban development in various ways. Despite this diverse sphere of activity, my own interests always led me back to building residences. Large complexes and high-rise buildings with many floor plans, and many variations, testify to this true love. But my passion also extends to each individual room of the house. This is the focus of the essays in this volume.

I would like to thank my partners Jakob Steib, Michael Geschwentner, and Matthias Kyburz for their trust and good will. I very much appreciate that they have allowed me to write these contributions on behalf of the firm and to design the slipcase for these volumes. In doing so, I have been able to fulfil a long-held wish. Never would I have thought that our shared house had so many rooms.

Patrick Gmür

Contents

1.1   Love at First Sight p.14
→ In Front of the Building → The Entrance Hall
→ The Parking Garage → The Mailbox Area
→ The Bicycle Storage Room → The Stroller Room

1.2   Home at Last p.30
→ The Stairwell → The Elevator → The Entrance → The Corridor
→ The Hall → The Guest Bathroom → The Staircase
→ The Rooftop Terrace

1.3   A World of One's Own p.52
→ The Kid's Room → The Bedroom → The Dressing Room
→ The Storage Room → The Bathroom → The Guest Room
→ The Balcony → The Sauna

1.4   Day In, Day Out p.68
→ The Living Room → The Kitchen → The Pantry
→ The Dining Room → The Library → The Room with the Fireplace
→ The Study → The Music Room → The Conservatory
→ The Coworking Space

1.5   Ancillary Spaces p.90
→ The Attic → The Utility Room → The Hobby Room
→ The Workshop → The Basement → The Weight Room
→ The Laundry Room → The Pool → The Wild-Card Room
→ The Common Room → The Wine Cellar

1.6   Everything Is Interconnected p.108
→ The Cabinet of Curiosities

1.1 Love at First Sight

1.1.1	In Front of the Building
1.1.2	The Entrance Hall
1.1.3	The Parking Garage
1.1.4	The Mailbox Area
1.1.5	The Bicycle Room
1.1.6	The Stroller Room

1.1.1 In Front of the Building

Our apartments are always part of a building. This in turn is part of the immediate neighborhood, the district, and finally, the city. A competition or study commission is won through urban development and local planning solutions. The general location, the scale, the volume of the project and consequently its fine details, the incorporation of the project into the terrain, the provision of access to it, and the positioning of the entrance are all decisive issues. Therefore, as we draw up a concept for the building, we spend most of our time adapting it to the surrounding environment. Analyzing the location, with all its stories as well as the stories connected to the assignment, helps us get started with the design. We always perceive our constructions as part of the city. Although Aldo Rossi was no longer teaching when we were students at ETH Zurich, our professors and lecturers taught us his approach, and his studies of the city shape our understanding of architecture today.

Still, we're faced with the question of where an apartment begins. Does it begin at the apartment door, with the door handle? Or, is where you feel at home, and why, more important? When does a location become home—is it the country, city, or village in which we live? Our own four walls around us are important, but of course we need more than that to feel comfortable and at ease. Neighborhood and the immediate environment also play a role. Currently, the idea of the fifteen-minute city is being promoted for sustainability reasons. It suggests that living, work, shopping, and leisure time should all take place in our immediate vicinity, and facilities for these should be safe and easy to access. But it's not just the location that's important; the city is also made attractive by all the various things it has to offer. A balance between public, shared amenities with our life at home is crucial. This is why we are interested in transitions: the areas and zoning that lead from a public space and then a semi-public area to a semi-private building entrance, then your apartment, and finally, your own room.

Where does an apartment begin? At the apartment door? With the door handle?

Waiting area, Stockholm forest crematorium by E.G. Asplund, 1940.

The courtyard as a meeting-point for residents. Hirschi building, Adligenswil.

When it comes to choosing friends, people are careful. Neighbors are simply around. Community is a wonderful thing, but on the other hand, social monitoring is unpleasant. So it's important to plan how you'll get home, or your route to work, or the places where you'll spend your free time with care. Are there meeting places, and, at the same time, is there the option of avoiding them, or simply passing them by? The apartment and building function in the same way as village and city. There are different spaces, different routes, main paths, side paths, crossroads, and places to relax or just pass through. These are bright, secluded, green, or shaded, and they change depending on the time of year.

We always devote a lot of attention to exteriors. These are where the immediate neighborhood joins with the new building, conversion, or extension. When, years later, we visit our buildings and see that they have merged with the neighborhood through their use or through the planting of trees, or have even become established there, we have achieved our planning intentions. We call this goal "more city for the city."

We had the opportunity to build two apartment buildings → 2.4.8 in the Seebach area of Zurich. In this district, where the less privileged residents of Zurich live, the city is still as it once was, unassuming and normal. The competition brief was clear and straightforward: we had to realize as many affordable apartments as possible. Interestingly, the two plots of land are located across from each other. The public street, am Sandacker, both separates and connects them. Zurich building laws helped us resolve the main demand of the competition outlined above, but required two very different residential buildings. For reasons of space, the minimal required number of parking spaces is located in the basement of one of the buildings. This means that when some of the residents come home by car, they always enter the "wrong" building. This link, together with an extremely concise layout for the apartment floor plans, shapes the design. With their different entrances and staircases, the two apartment buildings extend over the public street in a spatial relationship. The colors of the street-side facades opposite each other underpin this special neighborhood and create a shared entrance.

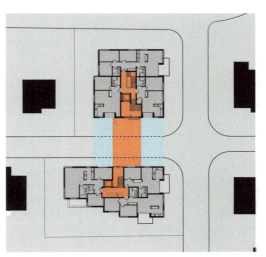

The stairwells link up across the street. MFH Sandacker, Zurich.

We always see our constructions as part of the city.

Love at First Sight 17

"But Miles to Go Is Miles Away"
Bruce Springsteen

The architectural profession is engaging and fulfilling. We can work on our projects endlessly. There is always something else to try out, and we're always thinking about the task and, in particular, possible solutions. Countless options are always available. Therein lies the challenge: to identify and implement the best of all these options.

From elite athletes, in particular Roger Federer, we have learned that rest, not training, is the most important thing. Since we have to make so many decisions, switching off and taking a break from work is crucial. Life and work are important to us. The path between these two worlds connects them. For some time now—the coronavirus pandemic certainly facilitated this—I've walked every day from home to work, and back in the evening, in all weathers.

The city—in particular the neighborhood—is our source of inspiration. When we walk, we see everything. I follow the curbs, feel the structure and quality of the surfacing, take note of how the water drains. I look at the trees, observe the play of light and shadow among the leaves, and perceive slight differences in temperature. I pay attention to interfaces and transitions. Doors and gates define and limit what is without and within. I study the facades of ordinary apartment buildings, thankful that they exude a degree of privacy. Luckily, the kitchen, bathroom, bedroom, and living room aren't always visible at first glance. How have the plinth details, wall construction, or roof edge been designed? How is the facade proportioned as a result? Which materials have been used to achieve a certain kind of feeling or hierarchy? What kind of atmosphere or mood emerges? Why do I like one building more than another, and what are the significant differences? At the same time, I get a sense of the spaces of the city. I size up the dimensions: height, length, width. How could an apartment floor plan work here? How wide is the sidewalk or the street, how much space is needed for the front of the building and the green area? I consider proximity and its relationship to open space. When is close actually close? I measure the environment as I learn. The insights are integrated into our projects.

Being familiar with some basic dimensions is especially helpful for apartment designers. How wide can a narrow door be, how high is the kitchen workspace, and how much room does someone need to make a bed? Working with these measurements affects your familiarity with the proportions of your own body: your gait, your eye height, the distance when you stretch out your arms. Le Corbusier's *Modulor* is still a useful reference point in this context today. There are different options for the stroll from my home to the office. Usually, I don't take the shortest route, but the most appealing one. As is well known, the journey is the goal. This ramble leads across the largest city cemetery in Zurich—today, it's also a maintained park. I treasure the expanse and the calm of this location, which offers time and space for me and my thoughts.

Walking and looking allows the new to emerge.

This artificial, yet natural landscape in the middle of the neighborhood offers many possibilities for simply wandering, or taking a looped walk. There are main routes, side paths, squares, crossroads, some monuments, chapels, statues, fallen angels, crosses and crucifixes, burial areas, graves as well as tombstones with candles and red eternal lights, groves of urns, elm-lined avenues, overhanging trees, small bushes, water reservoirs, and colorful wild meadows.

This walk leads through a city of the dead. It makes me contemplate the city of the living, and its planning. My wanders also lead me past the graves of acquaintances and friends. I greet them, and remember them. This path gets me thinking about death, our ever-present companion,

As I learn, I take the measure of the world.

every day. I attempt to be on good terms with it, and it certainly helps put everyday lives and stresses into perspective. Nature also reveals itself, demonstrating its changing nature at every moment. My way to work is illuminated differently depending on the time of day or year. What I can perceive at night is different, too. Darkness lessens the distractions. Only the essentials remain visible.

I perceive all this, while, as I walk, I'm preparing myself for my day at work. I design things and think about projects spatially or materialize them in my thoughts. During this reflective time, anything is possible: building codes, investors, costs, standards, and other obligations are far away. On the way home in the evening, too, many things fade out, can be put into perspective, or disappear altogether. Mostly, I am able to leave my daily work, with all of its questions and unresolved issues, behind.

My walking and observing enables me to create something new. It is often in this way—not at my desk or while sketching—that I have come up with solutions or interesting ways to test new design approaches in our projects, which we can then develop further together.

1.1.2 The Entrance Hall

The added height underlines the importance of the entrance. Hard Turm Park apartment and office building, Zurich.

Colors for a specific identity. James development, Zurich.

We believe that, just like in real life, when it comes to buildings there is also such a thing as love at first sight. But in reality, it's only ever other people who get smitten. We take the train alone, and travel halfway around the globe, but unfortunately, the only people who sit next to us are the ones eating bananas or smelling of garlic, whose behavior, noises, or odors don't exactly inspire the feeling of having butterflies in your stomach.

For us as architects, it is helpful when we keep believing in goodness and above all, fairness. We never give up the hope that luck will be on our side one day. Tirelessly, over and over, we take part in competitions and study commissions. We develop our designs further and work on variations in the constant hope that what we create will be recognized, and might even be loved from the get-go!

First impressions are decisive in terms of appealing to people or being rejected by them. What does this mean for our buildings? We believe that the design, the choice of material for the facade, the positioning of the entrance, and the entrance hall are significant factors. A residential building needs a spacious entrance area with plenty of natural light. With its dimensions, material ambience, lighting, acoustics, smell, and color scheme, this area sets the tone for the first point of contact to the building. At the same time, the foyer is one of the undefined spaces in a building. For this very reason, we are interested in this area of transition between indoors and outdoors, between public space and the privacy of an apartment.

Unfortunately, buildings in Switzerland do not traditionally have a foyer, even in larger complexes. In the USA, older buildings always contain a spacious lobby, complete with a smiling attendant who receives, greets, and bids farewell to the occupants, day or night. They are the good-hearted soul of the building, and people's first contact for questions and issues that arise. Packages, food deliveries, and registered mail are all delivered to the lobby attendant. They keep everything in view, which creates a sense of security. These residential buildings are welcoming. The entrance areas are carefully furnished with

We believe in goodness and fairness!

chairs, reading desks, and sofas. Here is where the visitor waits for their host, and here is where they say goodbye. Factors like these make a foyer part of the building's address. The culture of receiving and bidding farewell

Love at First Sight

requires spatial movement, as well as familiarity with fire safety regulations.

Today, we know how this kind of entrance contributes to the emergence of an identity. We design our residential buildings based on this knowledge. Entrance halls are core spaces in addition to apartment floor plans. We place focus on the entrance hall, resist cost-saving efforts, and do everything we can to ensure that each building is provided with a vestibule.

We are still proud today that we suggested a lobby concierge for the main entrance during competition stage for the former LUWA industrial site →2.2.2 in Albisrieden, Zurich. The first tenant was particularly supportive of this idea, and this led to us naming the complex "James." We were able to create a truly atypical entrance hall in terms of dimension and color scheme. The James development has a proper address with a spacious reception including a porter's lodge. It is still one-of-a-kind in Switzerland.

The entrance hall also functions as a meeting place. The mailboxes, parcel lockers, and direct access to the bicycle garage or the stroller storage room enable the inhabitants to meet. A bench invites people to relax. But an entrance area can be much more than this. It is always directly connected to all apartments: the stairways and the area in front of the elevators form a spatial link to the apartment entrances.

For the Paul Clairmont residential building, the entrance hall is a naturally illuminated "rue intérieure," which on the one hand provides access to various stairwells, and on the other is enhanced by studios that can be leased, a doctor's office, and a common room. Once a year, the inhabitants gather round a long dining table there to hold a party. Children love this space, which is defined as a stand-alone fire compartment. They can meet there, and thanks to the two entrance and exit points, the hall can be used as a bicycle course, or simply for getting around on scooters. Large, illuminated zoo images by Zurich photographer Georg Aerni decorate the entrance to the stairs. These percent-for-art images can also be used for navigation, so you might have a little kid telling people, "I live at the tiger"!

Our Am Rietpark residential complex →2.3.19 in Schlieren features two differently designed courtyards, which provide light for the entrance halls and connecting areas. These spaces are also separate fire compartments. This allows people to use the spacious, high-ceilinged entrance hall for events and parties, or to turn the space into a cinema or public viewing area for major sports events. All walls are painted with metallic colors, which lead to differently colored and numbered stairways.

The Obmatt duplex house in Adligenswil has table soccer in the communal entrance hall. A bench also encourages people to linger. This is joined to a platform that forms a base for cascading stairs that lead through

The entrance as meeting point. Sandacker apartment blocks and Casa Gálvez by L. Barragan, San Angel, Mexico City, 1955.

Sometimes, however, the favorable first impression that an entrance hall makes can inaugurate a life-long friendship.

Zoo images by Georg Aerni mark the stairwell entrances.
Paul-Clairmont-Strasse apartment building, Zurich.

A black ceiling, white walls, and the floor of natural green stone together with an extra-large mirror enhance the entrance area.
Am Rietpark apartment building, Schlieren.

the entire house while also connecting the entrance with the garden. A floor-to-ceiling window offers a view of the common front yard. Each unit in the building can be entered through a lobby area laid with colorful mosaic stones. Skylights illuminate the stairwell, rounding off the spatial experience of this transition area.

"I live at the vulture!" says the small child.

Since a day care center occupies the entire first floor of our family house in Langgrütstrasse → 2.4.3, Zurich, the foyer in this case emerges from the way the space is laid out: the staircase cascades to the entrance area. For a multi-family home on the neighboring street Langgrütweg → 2.4.4, which we designed at the same time, the foyer connects with a projecting roof built using specific materials to form a spatial sequence of differing areas.

In Imbisbühlstrasse, Zurich, by contrast, the entrance halls are located deep within the building. Pairs of staircases and a corresponding elevator are connected via interior, high-ceilinged spaces. Short, split-level staircases utilize the gradient of the ground. A *promenade architecturale* concept and a careful choice of materials additionally enhance these areas.

We know that not every encounter delivers love at first sight. Sometimes, however, the favorable first impression that an entrance hall makes can inaugurate a life-long friendship. In the best-case scenario, tenants will say that they never want to leave.

Love at First Sight

"Touched for the Very First Time"
Madonna

Few occupations are as diverse and multifaceted as that of the architect. Our tasks relate to the most different of areas. We plan and construct small houses as well as huge residential estates. We modernize and renovate old buildings. We find new uses for buildings. And we also consider districts, new neighborhoods, and urban regeneration. Context is of interest to us. We're able to find solutions for complex, ambitious tasks with many unknowns. And what's more, we implement these solutions as three-dimensional spatial designs

in our buildings, making them a visible and accessible part of the environment we construct. We are not specialists. When it comes to certain areas, we only know some things. That's what makes us curious, open, courageous, and audacious.

A plan is always the result of teamwork. Our design ideas and spatial concepts are dependent on other disciplines. Static force must be dissipated at the right locations using supports or load-bearing walls. Toilets, bathrooms, and kitchens should be intelligently located on top of each other. Plumbing, electrical, and heating engineers are responsible for the building services. Experts point us to sustainable materials. Building physics engineers calculate heating requirements and help us comply with innumerable standards. We fulfill building laws and regulations with the aid of solicitors and building authorities. Construction managers create schedules and calculate the construction costs, coordinate the builders, and supervise construction. Clients monitor their commission and how it is realized in terms of structure, space, and construction. But not even all this suffices for the creation of architecture.

Design is intertwined with complex searching and research, but also with rejection. Analyzing the task and the location helps us develop ideas that work with the context. Often, unfortunately, this doesn't happen right away. Ideas must be worked on and polished. Costs, building contractor requirements, legal stipulations, and construction requirements have a decisive influence on our designs. "Trial and error" describes our everyday life in a nutshell. "Kill your darlings!" is the name of our approach to design.

At the start of a project, however, we do our best to avoid thinking about all these things. We imagine something beautiful: for instance, the door handle of the entrance door. This brings everything together. It represents the threshold between inside and outside, public and private, city and home, and cold and warm.

The door handle is our first and last point of contact with home.

We open the door, and can enter and walk through our design. We stand in the rooms we have imagined, hear the echo of our voices, smell the timber, see the proportions and colors, and touch the materials with our hands. Light and shadow show us the way. The door handle is the first and last point of contact with our house. It makes our architecture, and all of our ideas, palpable.

1.1.3 The Parking Garage

For every project, schedule, or design plan that requires approval by a government body or legislature, the question of car parking will have been discussed in-depth by the time project costs are outlined, at the very latest. Every individual parking space can be related to costs, but is also a barometer for the current party agenda and political stance. After all, construction is a political act.

That the Green Party is against additional parking lots is logical. The FDP/Liberal Party is opposed to regulating parking lots, and says the free market should regulate this. Parties on the right are, on the one hand, in favor of extra parking spaces, since the Green Party

Construction is a political act.

and the Left Party are against them, but on the other, immigrants might also use new spaces, which counts against them. Alternative parties view parking lots as a symbol of unequal wealth and the chance to combat the much-lambasted SUV. The Social Democratic Party of Switzerland only supports more parking spaces if equal opportunities

Yellow paint to imitate sunlight.
James development, Zurich.

and solidarity are also advanced. The Centre Party advocates more options for car parking, if this strengthens the concept of the family as a whole.

Following the initial cost projections for a housing project, architects are invariably requested to find cost savings. We know that this is not easy. Houses can't do without bathrooms and kitchens. In any case, we adhere to the investors' specifications for room size in the apartments. Besides, we already factor in the most favorable market prices to our cost estimates. Our experiences, however, show that the basement stories and, thus, the underground parking areas offer considerable savings potential.

This is why we love designing optimized parking garages. Unfortunately, room grids and parking grids never fit on top of each other. In the case of high-rise residential complexes in particular, this means that directly transmitting the static forces for the transition from first floor to basement is not possible. Costly deflections for upper floor load bearing are necessary. For this reason, situating

The mirrored ceiling emphasizes the stairwells.
Imbisbühlstrasse apartment building, Zurich.

Love at First Sight

Since most investors view parking as an obligation rather than an opportunity for creativity, we make use of these freedoms.

parking areas next to a residential building is one of the most effective ways to reduce costs. However, this contradicts environmental guidelines regarding rainwater infiltration, and also means that trees cannot be planted. We view these very contradictions as an opportunity to flesh out specific, cost-effective, and architecturally appealing parking solutions.

We always take the time necessary to design the optimal, custom-fit parking garage. With their exhaust fume extraction systems, which can be used to channel daylight into the basement levels, acoustic requirements, service conduits, construction in exposed concrete, support pillars and beams, interesting architectural spaces are created—particularly in complexes with many apartments. Since most investors view parking as an obligation rather than an opportunity for creativity, we make use of this freedom to experiment with color, artificial light, and signage. The parking garage connects with building entrance areas via stairwells and elevators, which also opens up possibilities for design.

Integration of signage and pillars. Sandacker apartment buildings, Zurich.

1.1.4 The Mailbox Area

The mailroom as the building's actual address.
Hard Turm Park high-rise, Zurich.

With larger residential buildings, the repetitions are fascinating. When the windows and balconies are always arranged in the same way and are always identical, and the facades are constructed using the same materials throughout, a building conveys a certain tranquility and clarity. On the other hand, the repetition of these parts means that anomalies such as entrances are instantly recognizable.

In one small room, you get a visualization of just how many apartments there are.

The entrances for these buildings need to be clearly defined. Built in 1922, the Hornbaekhaus apartment building by Danish architect Kay Fisker in Copenhagen is a prime example of this architectural approach.

The mailbox area is a wonderful demonstration of the concept of repetition. The mailboxes themselves are standardized. They have a mail slot with a low-opening box, as well as a larger storage surface for small packages. When this individual element is then fitted and installed two hundred times in one small room, you suddenly get a visualization of just how many apartments there are. This space can also function as a social meeting point. It allows for initial contact between neighbors, which the seating also promotes. A careful choice of materials and colors can also add value. In addition to the personal address assigned to each apartment, the mailroom becomes the actual address for a residential building. In the Hard Turm Park high-rise building → 2.2.9 in Zurich, the entrance door to the elevator area, and thus the apartments, is located behind the mailroom.

Shopping habits have changed in the past years. Virtually anything can be ordered online. Particularly in larger buildings, this can lead to a veritable deluge of packages. As well as the postal service, all delivery companies drive to the main entrance, delivering orders with packages of all sizes that take up the same amount of space. Spacious parcel lockers have now been added to the mailboxes.

In the Am Rietpark residential complex → 2.3.19 in Schlieren, the mailbox area is accentuated with a suspended ceiling painted black. The area is additionally enhanced by a cupola inlaid with gold leaf and fitted with a ring-shaped LED strip light, and an asymmetrically positioned pillar. Recalling Art Nouveau buildings by the architect Otto Wagner from Vienna, the pillar is painted Schweinfurt green, which pairs well with the gold of the ceiling.

The golden cupola shows that this place is special.

Love at First Sight

"Go Your Own Way"

Fleetwood Mac

We are finding that the demands placed on us as architecture professionals are increasing, and we are also having to take on more responsibility. There are various reasons for this. Even investors delegate their own tasks and responsibilities to us, to some extent. We develop schedules of accommodation and review these using feasibility studies. We regularly participate in competitions. These lay bare the complexity of design and construction within an increasingly demanding environment. Even during the initial phase, we work together with more and more specialists. We coordinate these processes as a matter of course, which puts us among the last generalists. We are expected to develop the perfect solution while maintaining an overview of everything at all times.

We spend a large part of our weekly board meetings discussing what we have to and can achieve, together with ideas about what we actually want to do. These topics also raise certain expectations. But that's just like real life: expectations mainly exist in order not to be fulfilled. As a consequence, disappointment is commonplace in our job. It is important not to develop any expectations, if possible. This can be difficult, but it's easier to work this way, and far fewer conflicts emerge.

I've been into music since the mid-1970s. Just like architecture, music has changed; it follows current trends and is subject to the zeitgeist. Bands and musicians come and go. There are wonderful hit songs that are deeply etched in my mind and associated with specific memories. As I've grown older, my curiosity for discovering contemporary music has declined. Perhaps I just am not able to get into it. At the same time, I have a desire to be able to better understand the song lyrics of the musicians I idolized when I was younger.

Of the musicians I discovered during my adolescence, some have died, or the bands have broken up. Bob Dylan, Bruce Springsteen, Neil Young, and The Rolling Stones continue to release albums, and now and then these older gentlemen still go on tour. I follow their later work with interest. Mick Jagger still fulfills the expectations of his fans to this day. Even though he is almost eighty, he still jumps and dances around the stage like in earlier days. He's as fit as a fiddle. Neil Young remains unpredictable. Each one of his new albums brings a surprising new sound, ranging from grunge to country. His concerts are loud, raw, quiet, reflective, kind of angry, and full of energy. I am envious that at seventy-five, he's still got the zest for making so much noise. I also always enjoy listening to The Clash and Talking Heads—preferably at high volume.

Expectations are mainly there to go unfulfilled.

I still remember April 11, 1981. It was Bruce Springsteen's first concert in Switzerland. With a show that was over four hours long, he brought the house down in the sold-out Hallenstadion arena. He rocked that stage until he was completely exhausted. With a combination of his own songs and selected covers, his ability to skillfully extend songs with another refrain or a wild guitar solo, and the perfect accompaniment in the E Street Band, it was probably the best concert that I've ever seen, heard, and experienced. As I write, he's back on an extended world tour. He, too, still wants to bring his powerful brand of stadium rock to fans in arenas all over, and to meet their expectations.

In my view, Bob Dylan is the most interesting of all these elder statesmen. Whenever I've been able to, I've followed him on his *Never Ending Tour*. I've seen him in concert in Zurich, Basel, Lustenau, Sursee, Milan, Mainz, Montreux, Paris, London, Copenhagen, Oslo, Stockholm, Berlin, Huesca, St. Louis, Kansas City, and Tokyo. Each concert was unique in its own way, never the same, always full of surprises, and with no routine. Dylan's songs are his material. Like a sculptor, he works away at these to shape and reassemble them. He searches for the perfect, harmonious moment, when the melody, his voice, the lyrics, and his band's instruments come together in a way that makes time seem to stand still, reminiscent of his album title *Time Out of Mind*. Moments like these affect your heart and soul. Dylan has always gone his own way. Consciously and deliberately, he surprises us. Perhaps the reason why is that he's not fulfilling any expectations. This enables him to continue to create the unexpected, and still age gracefully. In 2016, he sold his archive to the Georg Kaiser Family Foundation in Tulsa, Oklahoma. Visiting the Bob Dylan Center, which opened there in 2022, illustrated to me how the singer works as he constantly searches for the right lyrics and the music to go with them. His *Bootleg Series Volumes* are a meticulous record of this research.

It is this ongoing process that intrigues me. In a similar way, I myself try, in my daily work, to stay curious and deepen my knowledge of everything. To identify the nature and the essence of a task, it helps to be independent, honest, open, and, above all, free of expectations.

1.1.5 The Bicycle Storage Room

All residential construction competition briefs call for bicycle storage rooms, so these must be planned and implemented accordingly. Aside from politicians, nobody takes an interest in these spaces and they are sometimes considered a tiresome obligation. Therefore, we use them, in the same way as parking garages, to quietly give our imagination free rein, and as an opportunity to try out unfamiliar things.

We are finding that the space requirements for bike parking are growing with each new design. One or two bicycles per bedroom are estimated today, depending on the municipality. For two hundred apartments, this amounts to approximately 800 bicycles, or even more. This doesn't yet factor in bike trailers or cargo bikes, which require a lot of space. More expensive models may also need to be locked in individual cabinets. Bicycle storage rooms should, of course, be located in a convenient location on the first floor so that people can easily use them and there is no need for expensive ramps to the basement.

"A building can only be as good as the contractor allows it to be" is a well-known saying. The James development project → 2.2.2 in Zurich bore fruit due to the harmonious relationship between the investor, construction management, reinsurer, and us, the architects. The secret to this collaboration was the Swiss Society of Engineers and Architects' (SIA) cost guarantee contract. Thanks to

We use the opportunity to try out new things!

this mutual and equitable agreement between the investor, the reinsurer, and our consortium of architects and construction management, we had a precise overview of costs at all times. The total sum was defined and contractually stipulated. Due to a bonus-malus clause, we were keen to keep to this amount. And we did—receiving the bonus!

The entire planning and construction period was characterized by sound, respectful cooperation. The collegial atmosphere allowed us to be wildly creative. For this massive complex with 275 new apartments—consisting of seventy-five different plan types, over 6,000 square meters of business and office space, a badminton hall with four courts, a bouldering gym, as well as suitably designed

Color studies and the finished bicycle storage room. James, Zurich.

Love at First Sight

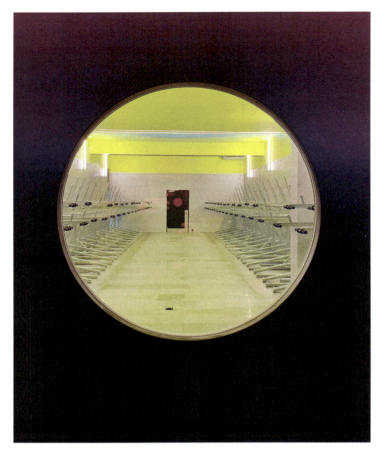

Almost like a church. Extra-high bicycle hall at the Am Rietpark apartment building, Schlieren.

On an average day, the bikes spread out around the entrance area.

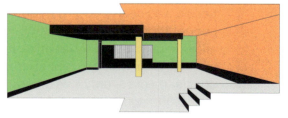

Color sketch for bicycle parking area. Apartment buildings on Alte Landstrasse, Kloten.

outdoor space—we used every opportunity to test the boundary between the spatial richness we wished for, and feasibility, including additional costs.

This motivated us to work together with the Swiss artist Peter Roesch to develop a bold color concept for all common access areas, the around 600 different bathrooms,

With its dimensions, it is more reminiscent of a club room or a dining hall.

and for the balcony soffits. As a basis, we used a Mexican color chart from the 1950s. I'd found this in Mexico City during a tour to discover more about Barragan. The colors changed as construction progressed. During the last stage, in particular, everything became more colorful and audacious. The bicycle storage room in the corner building, in particular, is a testimony to our joyful, colorful creative work.

We were also lucky with our cooperation on the Am Rietpark apartment building → 2.3.19 in Schlieren. During this project, too, the mutual trust of our partners meant we could implement a well-balanced color concept for the common entrance areas and staircases used by all tenants. We also used the design plan specification of the very high first floor for the bicycle spaces; the resulting four-and-a-half-meter high bicycle garage has very spacious and unexpected characteristics. With its dimensions, it is more reminiscent of a club room or a dining hall. There's something sublime about locking up your bike here after an exhausting ride, or a long day at work. As Bruce Springsteen puts it: "From small things, mama, big things one day come"!

1.1.6 The Stroller Room

With no windows, and mostly located next to the entrance, the elevator, or the foot of a staircase, the stroller room is a typically soulless, low-ranking space. These rooms are planned and constructed because they are legally required, and because entrance halls crammed with strollers are an annoyance for building superintendents in particular. For many, these "cumbersome things" mean chaos and noise. Banishing something we don't like out of sight is standard practice in our society. But it is precisely these unloved spaces that show that—despite much emphasis being placed on children being our future, and welcome and important—talk of creating child-friendly residential buildings is often only repeated for the sake of appearances. The reality tells us something different.

In one project, we planned bright, light-filled stroller rooms with direct outdoor access. Spacious, floor-to-ceiling windows were intended to create a positive mood. We additionally suggested installing colorful acoustic ceilings. Our idea was that these spaces could be used by the children as separate areas for playing when it was raining outside or in winter. We thought about how birthday parties could be held here, and how the concrete walls could be partially painted with black chalkboard paint that the kids could use for chalk coloring. We could already hear the happy voices and the cheerful noise from the space …

As we outlined this idea, which we found to be a good one, during the presentation, under the admittedly clumsy label "lawless zones," it was rejected immediately on the basis of the economic argument: "And who's going to pay for that?". The space was downgraded to a standard dark, because windowless, unpleasantly reverberant, and musty stroller room. It is precisely these kinds of spaces that deserve a lot more attention.

> **Banishing something we don't like out of sight is standard practice in our society.**

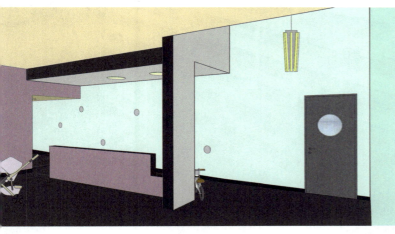

Studies for the stroller room as part of the spatial sequence. Entrance area of the Stelzen apartment buildings, Meilen.

Love at First Sight 29

1.2 Home at Last

1.2.1   The Stairwell
1.2.2   The Elevator
1.2.3   The Entrance
1.2.4   The Corridor
1.2.5   The Hall
1.2.6   The Guest Bathroom
1.2.7   The Staircase
1.2.8   The Rooftop Terrace

1.2.1 The Stairwell

When I was at university, I registered for a course taught by Heinz Tesar from Vienna, who was a visiting lecturer at the time. He had an original approach that differed from the positions on architecture, urban development, and detailing taught at ETH Zurich, which interested me. In all respects, Heinz Tesar was a remarkable character. For instance, I was intrigued by the fact he always wore the same black corduroy suit. Out of curiosity, I asked him why he did so, and his answer has stayed with me until this day: First, he found the suit comfortable, second, he never had to look for new clothes, because he could have the suits made to measure by a tailor. And third, the suit jacket had a very large pocket for his sketchbook, which he always carried with him. Any time I'm looking for my sketchbook—which I'm often on the hunt for—I recall this functional garment.

We listened to Tesar's critiques with great curiosity. We looked for the buildings he mentioned during discussions, and then studied them in the library. In this way, we discovered the works and theories of architects

Designing and detailing the safety barriers is above all fun!

that we weren't familiar with at the time. The study tour to Vienna he organized was a formative experience for me, and awakened an enduring fascination with the city. It was the reason why, after university, I went to Vienna and worked there in an architecture firm. In 2017, a visiting professorship at the Vienna University of Technology enabled me to experience, explore, and, above all, enjoy the city even more.

Tesar introduced me to the secrets of planning and constructing a stairwell. I have never forgotten my first ever interim review. I'd spent a lot of effort and many long nights looking for an urban planning solution to the brief we'd been assigned. But his first question was concerned with a completely different topic: "And how are you going to bring light into the stairwell?" In fact, I hadn't considered this at all. His answer informs my architectural way of thinking to this day: "Everything is possible, and permitted, in architecture today. But there's one rule you absolutely must observe: a stairwell needs natural light. And from now on, make sure to use the stairways for developing spatial concepts too!"

Modern apartment buildings are known to have strict limitations. An army of well-paid consultants monitor our plans. Building codes, standards, and guidelines help us fulfill all requirements. This is true for staircases, too. With the sheer number of rules, everything appears to be predetermined: the minimal stair width, the maximum length, the rise/run ratio, the slip resistance of the floor covering, the ease of maintenance of the materials, the lighting, the smoke extraction system, the dimensions in front of the elevator, but also the fall protection provided by the banisters and the continuous handrail, as well as the handrail's height from the finished floor.

These limitations intrigue us and challenge us. So, when viewing a completed building designed by my colleagues, I pay attention to the detailing of the stairwell and how it has been constructed. The way the handrail transitions into the straight line of the landing, and the way in which complex geometric requirements have been met, in particular, reveal how the architect has dealt with the material, the legal requirements, and the construction process on spatial terms. For me, this is where architectural ability and interests are manifest. I say to my colleagues, show me your stairwell and I'll tell you what kind of architect you are!

When variations in the slant of the handrail deliberately clash with the horizontal positioning of the landing, solutions emerge

Stairs as a spatial experience and one for the senses.

Home at Last 33

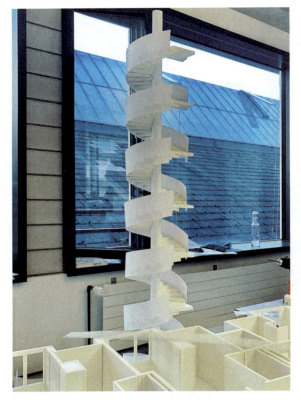

We build numerous variations on every stairwell.

that are abrupt, at times assertive, and contemporary. If the details have been worked out carefully and precisely, similar to how a watchmaker works, the designers are showing us that they're leaving nothing to chance. I encounter innovative approaches time and again. Like us, some view an everyday commission as offering the potential for developing architecture further.

We demonstrated that a stairwell can be more than just a vertical connective element with our accommodation buildings for students and the staff of the University Hospital in Zurich. A meandering, colorfully painted staircase runs diagonally through this eight-story building. This, which we have mysteriously dubbed a "Goethe staircase," serves as a standalone fire compartment, making it multifunctional. In addition to providing access, it functions as a meeting place, a location for collaborative learning, and even as a space for yoga.

As part of our "machine for living in" at the Am Rietpark residential complex in Schlieren, ten differently arranged stairwells connect 202 apartments. Two courtyards provide light for the spacious entrance halls and the corridors where the stairwells are located. Thanks to a color scheme with varying shades, every single stairwell has its own specific appeal. Despite their different colors, these bright connective elements combine to form a common spatial concept.

Show me your stairwell and I'll tell you what kind of architect you are!

"Find the Gap"

Jonny Cash

The majority of people who live in Zurich rent. This means that the majority of inhabitants take a strong interest in housing issues. At the same time, the quality of life for which Zurich is so renowned makes it highly attractive as a place to live. For several years now, the annual Mercer quality of living surveys have ranked it the second most livable city in the world. Obviously many people want to benefit from these qualities. One consequence of this is the ongoing acute shortage of housing. There are hardly any free apartments. That is one reason why many invest in housing construction. This is compounded by low interest rates, which promise a good rate of return, particularly in the real estate market. The result is a further heightening of investment pressures. Land prices are exploding. In recent times they have become so high that the pressure to cut costs both in terms of planning as well as construction is also constantly on the rise. As the largest landowner, the City of Zurich is able to reckon with cheaper land prices than other owners. At the same time, the City is obligated to adhere to high standards and also guarantee affordable rents.

Although almost everything is standardized and regulated when it comes to housing construction, these cost pressures mean that we architects are required to have our designs further checked and that every detail must be optimized. The search for gaps in the regulatory framework is becoming ever more challenging. A good example of this is in relation to staircase banisters. Because apartment and room sizes, the ways kitchens must be equipped, and the number of bathrooms are always predefined, and the legal requirements and standards are always the same, our staircase banister designs testify to the intensity of our engagement with the construction brief. Here we find an inconspicuous but important area where we can leave our own distinct architectural mark.

Being able to provide detailed and unique designs for building components that serve a primarily protective function is something that gives us a lot of joy!

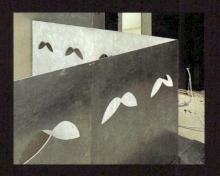

Modell Loeliger Strub architects.

The search for openings in the rules and regulations is getting more and more challenging.

1.2.2 The Elevator

When you talk to an elevator manufacturer during the tendering process, they say that anything is doable in terms of elevator cabin design. And when we receive offers from these companies, we notice that they all charge roughly the same costs. Then, when the contract is awarded and the detailed planning begins, things come to an abrupt halt. The bakelite paneling we designed specifically for the elevator cabins becomes industrially manufactured panels, with Bahama, sand, or Palermo beige as the surface color options. What's more, all the other parts are only available in shiny chrome. Just this picture alone gets us hearing the bland, unobtrusive tones of elevator music. Pure muzak!

There's not a lot of wiggle-room or opportunities for fun, so we concentrate our creativity on the entrance area.

We are increasingly finding that the implementation plans of our contractors do not match our own working drawings. The elevator shaft we have drawn is larger when built, the door opening smaller, or the control panel is on the wrong side. It's hard to get hold of the person responsible in the company, and they never call back. We discover that their design proposal for the elevator comes from a different contract, and was sent to us without any changes. All of a sudden, the interior cladding we ordered, the mirror we wanted, and the elevator cabin floor covering that matched the entrance hall and forecourt are also only available at a huge additional cost. The planner for the contracted elevator manufacturer doesn't have time to modify the implementation plans, either. This is because the elevator assembly is behind schedule on other construction sites, and the client there is sending the elevator manufacturer registered letters threatening to bill them with the resulting additional costs.

Under such circumstances, designing an elevator can be seen as a punitive task. But it doesn't have to be this way. This small space—the cabin—is interesting in itself, alone for the reason that it moves between the floors. Working with mirrors is also exciting. Experience shows that cabins are damaged a lot less when they include mirrors. Who wants to watch themselves as they wantonly make a scratch on a wall? As well as this protective measure, a mirror visually enlarges the small space of the cabin, and two mirrors

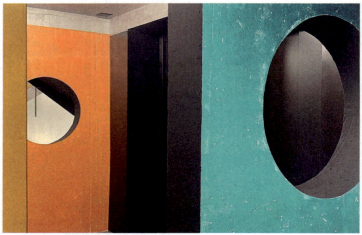

The area in front of the lifts extends the apartment entrances. Hard Turm Park, Zurich and Rietpark, Schlieren.

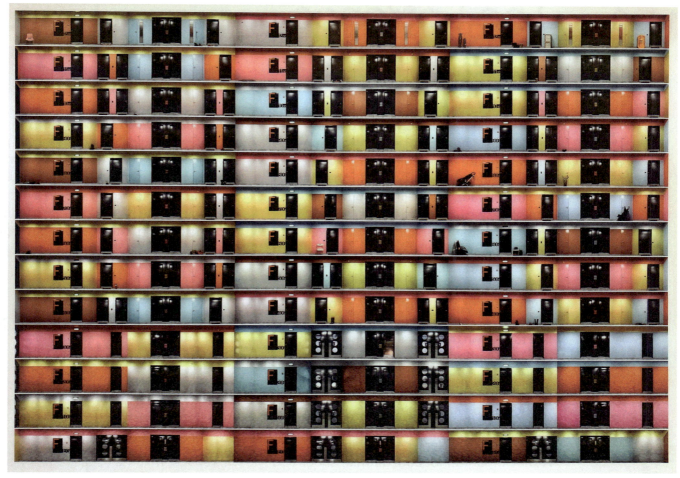

All lift spaces in the residential tower of the James development. Photos by Roger Frei.

Just this picture alone gets us hearing the bland, unobtrusive tones of elevator music. Pure muzak!

can even be used—here we should warn that this results in significant additional costs—to create the illusion of infinite depth.

Since designing and realizing an elevator doesn't offer much wiggle room, and it's not much fun overall, we like to reserve our creativity for the exterior. What do I see when the elevator door opens, or when I'm standing there waiting in front of it? For our Am Rietpark apartment block in Schlieren—an eight-story complex with ten stairwells—we had an almost room-high mirror mounted on each floor. Here, the residents can cast an eye over their appearance when they leave their apartment, and visitors can also take a quick look at themselves in the mirror before ringing the host's doorbell.

If an elevator opens directly into an apartment, it gives the impression of luxury. But it also means that these important places for social interaction are lost. The waiting area in front of the elevator reveals architectural opportunities that need to be seized and made the most of.

Home at Last   37

1.2.3 The Entrance

Sweet or sour, dry or wet, light or dark—the transitions between states are always the most interesting thing about them. Two different conditions create and enable new things. The entrance to an apartment is a location with these conditions. It connects the inside and the outside, the public and the private. It is the first room of a home that we enter, and the last when we leave. This characteristic is what makes it so important to us.

The entrance is where we take off our shoes, pull off a wet rain jacket, or slip into a warm winter coat to protect us from the cold outside. We receive guests and say goodbye to them in this room. It is a place of homecomings and welcomes, but also of farewells and partings. For this reason, it should not be too small in design. It's useful to include a closed coat storage unit, as well as a chair and a small storage tray for keys, wallet, and incoming and outgoing mail. A shoe organizer for both outdoor shoes and slippers helps prevent wear in this heavily used location. We therefore choose a robust, water-resistant floor covering that can be laid with ceramic tiles or stone slabs. A variation in materials sets the tone for the entrance. The coat closet is made of wood. When the closet is open, the various fabrics of the coats and jackets, together with the plastered wall surfaces, make an impact on the entrance area.

Usually, the entrance lies on the inward side. This has to do with efficiency in providing access to the apartment: when we enter apartments from the center of the building, circulation areas can be kept to a minimum. If this part of the plan is therefore unlit, it becomes important to think about artificial light and carefully choose the lighting.

This has the advantage that they can avoid being noticed by their parents.

This space, which is usually small, also offers designers the chance to utilize the ceiling area to create a particular atmosphere. For instance, in my own apartment I have deliberately lowered the ceiling and painted it black. This creates a lower space, and makes the rooms beyond it appear higher and more spacious.

The location of the entrance can also represent a specific way of dwelling. In a detached house or townhouse, the entrance is usually located beside the kitchen and the living area. Communal spaces have priority, while the individual bedrooms are situated on an upper floor. In the best-case scenario, there are stairs leading directly from the entrance area to the bedrooms. In his essay "Learning to Dwell," Adolf Loos encapsulates this idea as follows: "And with this I have come to the first point of what I would like to elaborate on. The individual in his own home lives on two floors. He clearly separates his life into two parts, into life during the day and life at night, and into dwelling and sleeping." (Adolf Loos, *Trotzdem 1900–1930* (in German), Innsbruck 1931.)

By contrast, from the entrance in an apartment you often first enter the private area with the bedrooms. This offers an advantage for teenagers coming home after going out on Saturday nights, since they can sneak right into their own rooms and avoid being noticed by their parents. A powder room with a sink can allow people to wash hands dirty from a day's work. A mirror is useful for checking one's own appearance, and a toilet situated immediately adjacent to the entrance increases its functionality and appeal.

I remember the entrance area of a neighbor's house from my childhood. The smell of the house always intrigued me when I was there, but it bothered me, too. And the entrance to the house was where I first noticed it. As I've been writing these texts, I have been wondering whether my own apartment carries a particular scent that my guests notice. It's possible.

It's a place of homecomings and welcomes, but also of farewells and partings.

lorful niches as connecting areas. Obmatt duplex, Adligenswil, with Helle Architektur, Zurich.

Home at Last 39

"Ghost in This House"

Alison Krauss

"Does the body have a soul?" How does this idea influence our designs, and how can we give a building—with all of its individual apartments—a distinctive spirit of its own? This is a question that preoccupies us and drives us on, inspiring us with the passion with which we design our floor plans and thus also our buildings as a whole.

Housing construction always involves multiple stakeholders. Some want to see a good return on their investment, others are advocates for affordable housing, and yet others are primarily concerned with the important goal of sustainability. But it is us as architects who are responsible for a building's atmosphere. Residents want to feel comfortable within their own four walls—as they well should. People used to refer to this sense of well-being by saying that a building was home to a friendly spirit.

Body and soul unite.

With the Roost development in Zug, we were able to visually implement this sensibility by means of a "Percent for Art" project undertaken by the Swiss artist Peter Roesch: each unit was given its own delightful spirit in the form of a colorfully painted porcelain animal. This enhanced each of the building's entrances. The spirit embodied in each of these figures awaits each resident and visitor as they enter the building. It greets and farewells all who pass. In addition, the small porcelain figures constitute a particular emblem for each part of the building as well as a distinctive form of address. As soon as I glimpse the lucky talisman, it immediately raises my spirits. I see it and I feel at home! In this way, body and soul unite.

And the house spirit greets the residents every day!

1.2.4 The Corridor

The food your mother made stays with you your whole life. It was the best! It always seems more delicious in retrospect; sometimes, you even dream about it. In a similar way, you can recall certain architectural spaces. What is interesting is that they are often pretty unspectacular.

I remember the corridor in my aunt's apartment in this way. She and her family lived in the former Hotel Musegghof in Lucerne, which had been converted into apartments. Since that time, this stately house has been divided down the center and contains two separate stairwells. Each section contains one very spacious apartment on each floor. My aunt lived on the top floor. The view of the city, with the lake, Mount Rigi, and Mount Pilatus in the background, was stunning. But my favorite part was the long, ultra-wide corridor of the former hotel. You could enter this space directly from the spacious landing.

I remember this corridor as being at least two-and-a-half meters wide. A bureau was located opposite the entrance door, which served as a storage surface and also displayed a gigantic mirror. At one end of this long space, there was a bulky brown cabinet that was used as a closet, as well as a door to my eldest cousin's bedroom. In the other direction, former hotel guest rooms and boarding house rooms lined both sides of the corridor. The long hallway ended with two doors to the kitchen and the bathroom. There was a little faux candle lamp in front of each door and a red-colored runner rug that emphasized the length of the corridor. Both the lamps and the rug kept the memory of the building's original use alive.

As kids, we utilized this grand space in different ways. Since all adjacent rooms were also connected with doors, there were even more ways to move from space to space. We played soccer there with my cousins, shot at small targets using air rifles, or just ran shouting and stamping though the apartment, chasing each other and then gathering back together again at this wonderful location to concoct new games.

The staircase lets light into the corridor that links the bedrooms. Hirschi building, Adligenswil.

In our apartment designs, we avoid corridors wherever possible.

The clearance space above the lift is also a skylight. Roost development, Zug.

Home at Last 41

Thanks to its extra width, the hallway is more than just a corridor. Langgrütstrasse apartment building, Zurich.

Despite this, we avoid corridors in our apartment designs whenever possible. When conceived merely as circulation areas, they swallow up valuable square meters of space. If a hallway is still required, we try to enhance its value in line with the memories I've described above. Additional furnishings such as bookcases, cupboards, and storage spaces add tremendous value to a space such as this.

Our experiences led us to design multi-family units for our complex in Langgrütstrasse, Zurich. Here too, the dimensions of the corridors turn them into spaces that can be furnished and used by the residents. When the doors to the bedrooms are open, this draws natural light into the extra-wide corridor.

The concept and the vision behind this generous hallway also aided us in designing the connecting areas for the Paul Clairmont residential building in Zurich →2.2.1. The entrance hall was transformed into a *rue intérieure*, with entrance and exit points at each end of the corridor. This long hallway, with a ceiling that is suspended to enhance the sense of space, does not provide access to bedrooms, but rather to stairwells, apartments, a multi-purpose room, as well as spaces that can be connected for use as studios or office spaces. But the fundamental principle remains the same. What we created was a shared space that can be used in a multitude of ways.

I remember this corridor as being at least two-and-a-half meters wide.

1.2.5 The Hall

The hall is a room that people pass through and spread out from. It allows residents to move around within an apartment. In most cases, all rooms are connected to the hall via doors, which makes for an interesting starting point.

The hall is the hub of the apartment. All paths intersect there. At the same time, depending on how the doors open, different spatial connections also emerge in accordance with the daily activities and habits of the residents. For this reason, we think about the dimensions and opening mechanism of every door. Is it floor-to-ceiling? Do double

Wide doorways illuminate the hall. James development, Zurich.

doors connect the hall to the living room, or to another room as well? Both the hall and the living room attain a further significance thanks to the wide opening of the doors. They can be used as a communal living, music, or TV room, or even as a reading room.

As a central area from which people spread out, the hall is usually located in the middle of the apartment. Illuminating the space can be challenging. Depending on the height of the double doors mentioned above, it's possible to draw daylight into the apartment's interior. If directly connected to the kitchen, the hall can be used as a dining area, if it's the right size. Since all the surrounding walls are most likely perforated by doors, furnishing the space can pose difficulties. A round table works well here; together with a hanging dining table lamp, it makes the space the core of shared apartment life.

For the James development → 2.2.2 in Zurich, we designed a kind of apartment → 3.2.3 in which a generously sized, multi-use space incorporates the idea of a hall. The roomy kitchen/dining area and an enclosed balcony run along the facade of the building in front of this space. The effect is incredible. The heavily-used kitchen receives plenty of natural light and is directly connected to the balcony, which is sheltered from the elements. The balcony in turn draws in light

The hall is the apartment's central hub.

to the open plan hall located behind it. A door opens to a small anteroom that provides access to private bedrooms and en suite bathrooms. An expanded area at the other corner of the room forms the entrance to the apartment. Directly accessible from this space is an additional room, which is a guest bathroom with shower. This arrangement means that the space can be used separately to the rest of the apartment.

We're fascinated by the potential contribution that a hall can make to a plan. Time and again in competitions, we've tried to explore this potential from the ground up. For the Waidmatt study commission → 2.4.1 in Zurich, we designed loggias with interior hallways that could also be used as living rooms. Giving this space multi-use functionality immediately transformed a four-room apartment into a five-room apartment. All rooms are roughly the same size. A well-furnished hall illuminated and ventilated via the loggia takes on the function of a corridor, and does not count as a room. Our plan did not completely win over the jury panel, unfortunately, and we placed third.

Home at Last 43

1.2.6 The Guest Bathroom

When we think about the most impressive guest bathroom we've ever seen, we think about Villa Mairea. This monument to modernity was built between 1938–39 by Aino and Alvar Aalto in Noormarkku, Finland for the couple Maire und Harry Gullichsen.

An entrance area with an inviting canopy and the entrance porch form a spatial unit positioned four steps below a separate living and dining area. The outline of the design follows the natural contours of the terrain. Oval wooden poles of different lengths and placed at varying distances accentuate the division of the space. This restricts the visitor's view of the living areas when they enter the building, while awakening their curiosity to explore them on the upper level.

At the side, a second narrow staircase leads directly to the dining area and a separate kitchen. Next to these stairs, there is a small office on the same level as the entrance hall. Narrow horizontal windows positioned high above the interior entrance door bring light into the high-ceilinged hall. A bench opposite the entrance door, a mirror with a shelf next to the wide staircase, as well as a

Unfortunately, the guest bathroom is now usually just a wet room.

selection of paintings and a mobile by Alexander Calder hanging from the ceiling additionally enhance the entrance area. The coat closet is situated in a low alcove with a slanted wall. A skylight follows this line, subtly illuminating the area in front of the mirror. A narrow door leads from this alcove to a split guest bathroom. A small room with a sink is connected to a separate toilet. These spaces are provided with daylight by small round skylights, which is a nice touch. If memory serves, there's a Picasso hanging at eye level when you're seated! The attention to detail is impressive on every level, and it sets an example for us.

Unfortunately, the guest bathroom is usually a wet room these days. The name alone tells us where the priority lies: users want to be able to clean the space thoroughly, quickly, and easily. The large-scale production of bathroom fittings and tiles means that bathrooms have become impersonal and replaceable. There's no individuality. At the same time, this is the only place that we visit alone and where we can enjoy solitude.

If memory serves, there's a Picasso hanging at eye level!

A lot of potential for creative design approaches.

This is why we call the bathroom the "quiet place," where the silence is what inspires us to reflect on things. We view these ruminations as being linked to our search for architectural quality. What initiates it, and how is it created? For apartment construction, quality is always linked to everyday use. But we need to identify exactly what everyday use means. A little bookshelf in the bathroom can alter the space and its original purpose. Or, like in the example above, pictures can transform the guest bathroom into a unique space.

Without a shadow of a doubt, Villa Mairea is an icon of twentieth century architecture. With its integration into the landscape, the translation of the design into a specific building structure and a multifaceted architectural

Hotel room at Hotel Volkshaus by Herzog & de Meuron, Basel, 2020.

concept, the carefully considered detailing, the chosen materials, the spatial richness, the arrangement of the plan to fulfill the complex schedule of accommodation, the tasteful furnishings as well as an impressive art collection, this house is one of our favorite reference points in terms of a holistic approach to a Baukultur of living. The atmosphere of the building adapts to all seasons, and it is a house for both winter and summer. Everything is coherent right down to the smallest detail, including the less important spaces such as the guest bathroom.

Bathroom in apartment building E.1027 by E. Gray, Roquebrune-Cap-Martin, 1929.

"Don't [Get Around Much Any]more" [Do That in]...

Nat King Cole

Architecture is complicated because it involves designing, engineering, and constructing elements that always contradict each other. Additionally, there is a need for improvisation on the construction site when something has been included by mistake, or forgotten about. Designing means spatially imagining the uses specified by the schedule of accommodation, and realizing these through sketches, plans, and finally, the construction site.

Architecture requires a lot of cognitive work. At the same time, we think with our hands. We carry a pencil with us, always hopeful of a moment of inspiration. Our profession is a combination of construction and improvisation. Unfortunately, the design and planning process never simply begins with a brilliant idea that can be implemented directly and smoothly. Designing is comparable to constantly practicing and planning so that at some point in the entire development phase you'll get a chance to be inventive. Having courage and the willingness to fail and gets things wrong is also part of the process. When you design, you make mistakes. And these mistakes are also part of the process. Only by continuously analyzing what we do can we progress. We value the luxury of being able to revise mistakes and false assumptions during the design process. We've learned to see something positive in every mistake we make. For us, mistakes are opportunities! And when we make the most of these opportunities, they lead to new and surprising discoveries that can only come about in this way. For this reason, we encourage our employees, as well as ourselves, to always take risks when designing. Particularly with highly defined construction projects that always have the same schedule of accommodation and require a mix of housing that is always similar, this free, inventive way of thinking is necessary to advance things a little.

Designers make mistakes. We see mistakes as opportunities!

1.2.7 The Staircase

A void becomes a space! We've learned from our structural engineers that in their minds, a staircase is always first of all a ceiling cut-out. This basic piece of knowledge is something we try to make use of: if we make these recesses larger than is strictly necessary for the staircases themselves, then that creates extra space. Thus we see every staircase as an opportunity to incorporate additional spatial qualities into our designs. In addition, we ensure that we never plan in a staircase next to a two-story space, because two ceiling cut-outs right next to each other are structurally unfavorable. If the constraints on the floor area permit, we always place the stair-well in the two-story hall. This allows for the space be walked through diagonally.

Unfortunately, the demands that operate in housing construction have changed in the past few years—and here, we're deliberately not using the language of "further evolution."

This allows for the space be walked through diagonally.

Today, a construction brief is rarely formulated in terms of intrinsically spatial qualities. Other concerns such as economics, environmentalism, the concept of circular building, construction laws, regulations, the optimization of space, minimal use of windows, facade greening, soundproofing, accessibility, housing mixtures, utilities, waste disposal, and staggered development are what now determine how contracts and commissioned studies are awarded.

The work of the juries making these decisions has also changed. The number of jurors on any given committee is continually increasing. Every area that is identified by a criterion is now properly examined and assessed by an appropriate specialist. Recently, I was on a jury with no less than sixty-five members. It was extremely difficult to compare

The hidden staircase as gallery.

Home at Last 47

The value of the everyday.

and discuss the different designs. But precisely this type of process is essential in being able to collectively figure out which project has best fulfilled all of the requirements considered together. We members of the jury are handsomely paid to give building contractors the best advice we can, both architecturally and in terms of urban development. The assignments are the same as ever, but the requirements are continually becoming more demanding and more complex, and also involve political considerations and expectations.

Today, a construction brief is rarely formulated in terms of intrinsically spatial qualities.

The goal of any competition or study commission is and remains the realization of a construction project. It is thus important that the expert judges that comprise a panel are experienced architects who are active in the field. A holistic understanding of construction is indispensable. We are convinced that more decisive than the previously mentioned requirements are the insertion of a building project into its urban environment, the use of the existing topography, the spatial qualities of the external spaces, the way it addresses its surrounds, the architecture, the logical, cogent combination of a building's different possible uses, and the way in which the design is implemented. Because what good is a sustainable building if it isn't functionally sound?

Back when we were studying, we learned that "it's always about space and spaces." This idea is still as central to our work as ever. It is for this reason that residential buildings that incorporate fascinating layout solutions are some of our most important reference points. We're always coming back to learn more from the split-level principle exhibited by Palace Gate, the stately apartment building designed by architect Wells Coates in 1939. The spatial layout, which comprises two one-and-a-half level living rooms and three separate levels for private bedrooms and bathrooms continues to fascinate us today, more than 80 years after it was built. We also find continual inspiration in Le Corbusier's maisonette apartments in the Unité d'Habitation in Marseille.

It is the different possibilities for ceiling height and the provision of a two-story space that really draw us in, even if apartments that extend across two or more floors are often viewed negatively these days. The reasons behind such criticism are varied. The requirement for a building that is as accessible as possible as well as the need for additional space for the staircases are two grounds on which such types are often questioned. The argument is often: this is too complicated, and too expensive!

The brief for the James development in Zurich included the maximization, within the bounds of the legally permissible, of the usable space. Only a complete utilization of all aspects of the site would make the project economically feasible. For this reason, when we were competing to win the project, we were already thinking in terms of especially wide buildings. We saw the deep plans as well as the inconvenient orientation of the building structures as an opportunity to create specific apartment typologies.

When it came to what we thought of as the "long building," we developed a structure that incorporated a range of different maisonette apartment types that intermeshed spatially and—crucially—would be oriented towards two sides. The maisonette apartments oriented towards the south-west are structured around a two-level balcony. These maisonettes cover two-thirds of the building's depth. The apartments on the somewhat less advantageous north-west side comprise the remaining third of the building and have been arranged in a line along the facade (see also the interview about Casa Manetsch in volume four →4.4). On this side, two-story living areas also give rise to a particular spatial quality. The staircase leads to an open deck which has a work area and continues on to two bedrooms. Set at a 90-degree angle to the living area on the lower floor, the upper space extends into the building and is well-oriented towards the side of the building that faces south-east, which means that it receives plenty of natural light. It is ultimately the staircases that allow residents to experience the three-dimensional qualities of their homes.

The semi-detached houses built in Adligenswil are organized around the stairwells. This upward-reaching space is the defining center of the overall structure. A number of different lines of sight further enhance the spatial experience. Besides the staircase, the entrance area with its wardrobe, the

It's always about space and spaces.

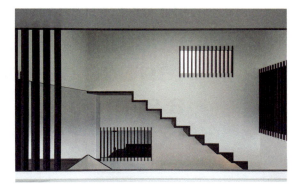

Negative staircase. Obmatt house with Helle Architektur.

space devoted to housework, the kitchen, the living room, the dining area, and the TV nook are all arranged in relation to this skylit space. The staircase to the rooftop terrace is visible as a negative form.

Creating living space across two floors allows for a simple, cogent organization of the primary uses. Such an approach allows for individual bedrooms to be located on one floor, while the more communal spaces can be placed on the other. It is these spatial possibilities that always give us reason to consider the potential of internal staircases. Our desire—even as we adhere to the implacable requirements that necessarily come with any residential construction project—is to design spaces that are special, surprising, and sound.

Villa Beer by J. Frank and O. Wlach, Vienna, 1930.

Home at Last

1.2.8 The Rooftop Terrace

As mentioned in the text on staircases, Le Corbusier's Unité d'Habitation in Marseille (1947–1952) remains an important reference point for our own housing designs. Alongside its striking and detailed architectural attributes, it also embodies an overarching idea of community living. Le Corbusier designed the "Unité"—which at the time corresponded to the idea of a building being "more than just a place to live"—with this clear vision in mind. As well as the communal floor, stores supplying daily necessaries, a hair salon, and a hotel, what really stands out about this building is the rooftop terrace, which is accessible to all residents. Without the architect's incredible power of imagination, the rooftop terrace's inclusion of a kindergarten, sculptural ventilation stacks, an open-air theater, sports facilities, and a running track, as well as a small pool for children would not have been possible.

Housing and commercial developments such as the Kalkbreite designed by the Müller Sigrist firm or the Zollhaus designed by Enzmann Fischer—both among the most discussed building projects in Zurich in recent years—have responded to a similar brief. The tender processes that preceded the construction of these projects were centered around the desire to create places that fostered communal inner-city living. It was precisely this requirement that provided architects with the opportunity to design innovative solutions: in essence, that the idea of community was prioritized over private interests. In such projects, there is a shared approach to providing generous interior and exterior spaces. The thoughtfully designed rooftop spaces are open to be used by everybody.

Private investors and bourgeois politicians often complain that such co-operative housing projects are given preferential treatment in publicly funded tender processes. It is said that they don't work from the same starting conditions. The difference, however, is one of atti-

The communally accessible rooftop terrace becomes a symbol of community!

Where the residents come together. Webergut redevelopment, Zollikofen.

50

tude: there is a nuanced yet crucial difference between a housing project being based on a social conception of living together or on the maximization of profits!

With our residential complex Am Rietpark in Schlieren, two staircases lead to a rooftop terrace accessible to all residents. Its atmosphere is defined by a very well-frequented pool. To ensure that this feature is actually used, the current water temperature is always displayed on an illuminated sign in the entrance hall.

With respect to the project in Zollikofen near Bern, we first won a study commission for the conversion of the former federal administrative court building from the Abendrot Foundation in Basel. The idea is to transform a massive office building, which we found a bit unfriendly, into an attractive housing community →2.5.4. The building's particularly deep layouts inspired us to develop special floor plans for the housing project that could also serve as communal spaces and places to work. The converted building is intended to function like a village: the "village square" is to exist in sections, and be spread across the entirety of the building. The stairwell will be an element that connects the different parts of the building, culminating in a rooftop terrace accessible to all, allowing all residents a wonderful panoramic view of the Bernese Alps.

Clear views of the Mediterranean. Hotel Parco dei Principi by Gio Ponti, Sorrento, 1960.

The terrace as rooftop garden. Apartment on Zurich's Gertrudstrasse, with Helle Architektur.

Is the housing project based on a social conception of living together or on the maximization of profits?

A pool with a view. Am Rietpark apartment building, Schlieren.

Home at Last

1.3 A World of One's Own

1.3.1   The Kid's Room
1.3.2   The Bedroom
1.3.3   The Dressing Room
1.3.4   The Storage Room
1.3.5   The Bathroom
1.3.6   The Guest Room
1.3.7   The Balcony
1.3.8   The Sauna

1.3.1 The Kid's Room

Our childhood bedroom is typically our first architectural memory of a space. I can still see in my head the window I'd peer through first thing in the morning when I'd wake up. This everyday moment has become lodged in my brain. To this day, I could walk blindfolded through my childhood room without bumping against a wall or window. I've interiorized the dimensions of the space for perpetuity.

The room's dimensions have remained the same. But as I've grown and developed, the space has changed accordingly. At first its only function was sleeping; later it became a play room; later still it became a small office, a recreation space, and a place of retreat. I remember all the fortresses I built and the battles I imagined, all the racetracks, all the hours I spent studying in there, sometimes learning useful things, sometimes not so

Suddenly, an unfamiliar pair of shoes beside the door means: "Do not disturb!"

useful. I bent my head over math homework, crammed for Latin, drafted essays and papers. As I used it, the room's furnishings changed: the bed grew longer and wider, a bookshelf was added. My first books laid the foundation for an ever-expanding library. The pictures and posters on the walls changed according to my phases. As we search for our personality, our childhood bedroom changes as well. Suddenly, an unfamiliar pair of shoes in front of the door means: "Do not disturb!"

You can plan an apartment, but you can't plan a life. We search for housing that fits with our life situations. People who live alone may rent themselves a one-bedroom apartment; if they start a relationship, maybe a two-bedroom. When children enter the picture, they all ideally get their own rooms. Suddenly the children are gone. They've moved out with the ex-partner and only visit once a fortnight. But it may very well happen that the new partner has three kids instead of two, and everyone moves into the apartment. A floor plan should be capable of responding to the most variable life situations. This is especially true of children's rooms, which quite possibly need to be the most flexible areas of an apartment, considering that the needs of children are constantly evolving.

We discuss plan designs in great detail with our staff. Over and over again, we redraw them, reimagine them. We think it's important to always conceive of spaces with furniture in mind. When we design a child's room, we think very precisely about where the bed might be located. Definitely not beside a cold exterior wall! The obligatory closet and desk are fundamental furnishings for us as well. We mull over the room's circulation: What's the most logical place for the door? How can you reach the window as directly and easily as possible while maximizing the play area, so kids don't stumble over Lego blocks or dollhouses in the dark? Not everyone understands why we develop our apartments using these kinds of mental exercises. For us, however, it's clear that precisely these kinds of everyday considerations help us to design a plan that suits all possible residents—especially children.

1.3.2 The Bedroom

Bedroom in apartment building E.1027 by E. Gray, Roquebrune-Cap-Martin, 1929.

Dreams often resemble stories. Which is why books belong in the bedroom. Not specialty books; profane works of fiction fit best. I'm thinking, for example, of books by Gabriel Garcia Marquez like One Hundred Years of Solitude, whose fantastical narratives help us to dream. At night, I always read in bed, hopeful that the story I'm reading will bleed into my sleep in unexpected ways. After all, slowly drifting off to sleep is one of the most beautiful moments of the day.

In the bedroom, this personal space, in addition to the bookshelf that exudes coziness, there should be a wall for art and a window

The bedroom is an underappreciated space.

with a view. We sleep better in cooler temperatures. What's important is that I can leave my fears, anxieties, and resentments at the door. Lying in the dark, I try to picture the artworks on the wall and imagine how they were made. I paint new faces on them, and by the time I've counted all the layers of paint on the wall, I'm already asleep.

The bedroom is an underappreciated space. Its function is clear and unambiguous. This is where we sleep. But aside from the bathroom with its toilet and vanity, the bedroom is the most intimate room of an apartment or house. When we sleep, we're vulnerable and exposed. The placement of the bed is critical. In this room, we want to feel safe and secure. So the particular place where we sleep should never be adjacent to a cold exterior wall.

Like our cars, our beds are constantly growing larger. But not our bedrooms, unfortunately. Because of this—though most importantly, because it's more stylish—our firm never designs beds wider than 1.4 meters. We think this width should suffice.

Somewhere in Uruguay. Bedroom for the night.

Bedrooms at Villa Tugendhat by L. Mies van der Rohe, Brünn, 1930.

But what do I see when I wake up and open my eyes? When I design, I try to imagine this picture. This makes me think of the story of Charlemagne's last few months alive. He spent his final days in the Jerónimos monastery of Yuste, near Jarandilla de la Vera in Extremadura, Spain, sick with gout. Since his room was beside the monastery chapel, he had the wall removed. From his bed, he could look directly at the altar. This not only enabled him to attend services; the new-found spatial connection also presumably brought him emotionally closer to God. You should never underestimate the role of the bedroom.

If a room has two doors, it will be better utilized, as it can also serve to connect other rooms or hallways. When it comes to bedrooms, it can be interesting to think deeper about their function. An elegant throw can transform a bed into a chaise longue; the room can be integrated into the apartment and make it feel larger. In our attic apartment on Zurich's Hinterbergstrasse, the bedroom is connected to the bathroom → 4.6 . The door is situated so that a direct line of sight is created from the tub to the bed. Additionally, two large sliding doors make the room part of an enfilade. The floor plan thus allows the space to be broken up into small, private compartments, or opened up to allow loft-style living.

Like our cars, our beds are constantly growing larger. But not our bedrooms, unfortunately.

"Shine a Light"
The Rolling Stones

It is a well-known fact that most aspects of designing a home are already determined before the process starts. Beyond its planned use, what shapes an apartment's plan are norms, developers' specifications, laws, and its orientation. The same applies to furniture, whose form and dimensions are similarly determined by function. Within this well-trod, often inflexible framework, bulbs and lamps can serve as a welcome addition, a creative loophole through which the space can be given an unexpected accent. Bulbs can function as light sources of the most varying kinds, while light fixtures offer an infinite variety of creative possibilities in their forms and applications. The way I see it, it's interesting for architects to design their own lighting—and it just makes sense. Especially in Nordic countries with their long, cold winter nights, it is no surprise that architects are active in this field and have made distinctive contributions.

When we think about residential interiors, lamps and light fixtures clearly number among the objects that make up a substantial share of home decor. As objects, they help to define a space during the day, while at night they become indispensable sources of light. They help create different moods in an apartment. Only through the interplay of light and shadow does a room acquire its own atmosphere.

Only through the interplay of light and shadow does a room acquire its own atmosphere.

Casa Galvez, San Angel, Mexico by Luis Barragan.

A World of One's Own

1.3.3 The Dressing Room

In today's times of reducing our personal footprint to achieve sustainability writ large, of constantly climbing rents and of justified demands for more affordable living space, it seems somewhat misguided to talk about dressing rooms in residential construction. This is a space that solves no urgent questions. Indeed quite the opposite: a walk-in closet, alongside a master bedroom and an en-suite bathroom, are reflective of an exclusive image of luxury living. Taken as a trio, they form an intimate spatial unit.

Recently, we went on an architecture trip. In the span of three days, we visited Villa Beer (1929–1931) by Josef Frank and Oskar Wlach in Vienna, Villa Tugendhat (1929–1930) by Mies van der Rohe in Brünn, and Villa Müller (1928–1930) by Adolf Loos in Prague. Seeing these twentieth-century architectural icons was a striking and highly instructive experience. The three villas, built more or less simultaneously, are all indebted to Modernism but represent different approaches to space: Loos implemented his spatial vision in Villa Müller; Mies designed a flowing spatial composition with a steel frame for Villa Tugendhat; while Josef Frank and Oskar Wlach lent Villa Beer a partly open spatial concept with differentiated circulation routes.

The apartment is our home. At best it functions—as Josef Frank wrote in his text "The House as Path and Place"—like a city, with public spaces for shared family life and for receiving guests. But it also features interstitial spaces and transitional zones; it separates day and night activities; it offers areas for private retreat and places only accessible to residents. The dressing room, in this sense, is among the most intimate of chambers. Frank designed Villa Beer accordingly.

Behind the notion of the dressing room is a luxurious conception of living. Clothes need their own space, because they too desire to be housed properly. Of course, in most cases, closets serve the purpose well enough. But a visit to Villa Müller reveals the staggering potential of a dressing room. In tandem with its perfect carpentry, its bountiful drawers, its nearly floor-to-ceiling mirrors that enable the contemplation of the selected clothes, the space represents a specific concept of Wohnkultur that has become scarce in our times.

As home builders, we need to take an interest in different values and inherited behaviors. We're constantly learning and

This is a space that solves no urgent questions.

attempting to understand how plans are designed and implemented. Architectural history opens up a broad and above all abundant field.

Beyond their spatial conceptions, these three buildings especially impressed us with their harmonious and skillful use of materials. The courage shown by the clients and the faith they placed in the four architects is similarly noteworthy. But worthy of the highest respect is the way they handled the appreciation they were given, and translated it into exceptional designs.

1.3.4 The Storage Room

In my parents' house, there was a "cagibi." As a little child, the expression was a mystery to me, and for that reason alone the room had something of a magical aura. Later on, I learned that my mother had brought home this French word for "storage room" after a year studying abroad.

The cagibi measured two by two meters. It had a specific smell. During the day it was lit by a small skylight, always shut since it was beyond reach, at night by a naked bulb. The pull switch was a white cord dangling in the middle of the room. As a little boy, this cord was too high to be operable. So after dark, I would try to avoid the barely accessible closet and all the knickknacks stuffed inside. In my childhood imagination, inconceivable things transpired in this forsaken place. My assumption was that, like the cellar, it was a lair frequented by goblins, ghosts, and evil hungry creatures who had it in for me. Sometimes, if I listened closely, I could hear creepy and inexplicable noises that only amplified my childish fears. I only entered accompanied by my mother—she would go first, while I'd hang back and use her as a shield.

It was the mid-1960s. In England, the Beatles were enjoying their meteoric rise and, thanks to my older sister, they were a major presence in our house as well. I proudly boasted a Beatles haircut. In the little cubbyhole there was a Hoover vacuum whose handle, perched at the perfect height, served as my imaginary microphone. Thanks to its little wheels, the vacuum was even mobile.

My assumption was that, like the cellar, it was a lair frequented by goblins, ghosts, and evil hungry creatures.

"We all live in a yellow submarine, a yellow submarine, a yellow submarine," I would warble, replaying on an endless loop the first single I'd been gifted as a five-year-old. When no one was looking, I would transform into a rock star.

Equally fascinating for me was how many things my mother managed to stockpile in the little room. Whenever I was invited to a friends' birthday party, she'd find the perfect gift inside. The closet was significant for our household—the home for any item not used on a daily basis. But even objects that no longer served any purpose would find their way into this ever-more-bursting hideout. When designing apartments today, we try to apply what I learned back then: if possible, every apartment should have its own cagibi.

Office in a government building by Le Corbusier, Chandigarh, 1958.

A World of One's Own   59

1.3.5 The Bathroom

These days, all construction processes—from space allocation to the choice of building materials—are meticulously analyzed and optimized. While this can bring certain limitations, we also feel that it harbors opportunities for innovations in residential construction. Precisely because one of the strengths of architects is that we think in both possible and impossible combinations—a skill practiced daily while obtaining an architecture degree—this approach sometimes leads us to new, unexpected solutions.

Bathrooms have evolved considerably over the years and will continue to do so in the future. Water-repelling panels have grown larger and larger, while fittings are increasingly mass-produced. The mirror cabinet long ago became a standardized product. To save space, shrunken shower booths have replaced the cozy tub. Today, the bathroom is a wet room that can be prefabricated on the cheap if it's repeated in enough copies of the same form.

For our Langgrüthof apartment building →2.5.5 in Zurich, we worked alongside the developers and specialists to design a prefabricated bathroom made of wood. One interesting question that arose was how and when during the construction process the finished cabins should be installed. Naturally, we were also concerned with ensuring adequate fire and noise protection, as well as the long-term accessibility of the installation shafts. On top of this, the structural integrity of the cells needed to be maintained during transport.

We had already sketched out and implemented this idea once before when designing buildings for students and staff of the University Hospital Zurich in the neighborhood of Binz—the bathrooms were produced and cleaned in Berlin, then transported on trucks to Zurich. The efficient unloading and installation then took place at the construction site. The bathroom doors were only unlocked and opened during the final inspection of the building. Everything—down to the toothbrush holder—was in place and ready to use. Since the principle behind the buildings is akin to that of a hotel, all the bathrooms are connected to a wastewater heat recovery system that can be operated in a sustainable fashion, without fossil fuels. So far, so good!

Today, the bathroom is a wet room.

We travel often, and at night we'll check into an ordinary hotel somewhere, where the bathtub might stand beside the bed, or the shower is only separated from the sleeping area by a glass wall. Apparently, nobody is bothered by this interpretation of sleeping and hygiene. All of a sudden, it's possible to conduct recreation, work, sleeping, and bodily hygiene in a single room. Imagine the opportunities this would open up for affordable residential construction—why not design a kitchen with a bathtub inside it? Or combine bedroom and bathroom into a single spatial unit? Only the toilet needs to be its own separate little chamber. A window and direct sunlight can turn a bathroom into a pleasant space. Seemingly, we've stumbled into a creative loophole. Maybe we should start calling them "washrooms" again, to lend the space its appropriate weight.

Colors are capable of transforming such functional rooms, of elevating them through

The bathroom as part of the adjoining bedroom.
Villa Tugendhat, L. Mies van der Rohe, Brünn, 1930
E. Gray, Roquebrune-Cap-Martin, 1929.

"Metaphysical horror!" Bim Coiffeur, song by Mani Matter.

Why not design a kitchen with a bathtub inside it?

Two bathrooms. Sägestrasse development, Kreuzlingen, and Hirschi building, Adligenswil.

simple means and lending them their own atmosphere. In the James development in Zurich, we played with this principle in all the bathrooms of the seventy-five different apartment types. The point of departure was six colors that always go together → 4.4 → 4.9 . Every bathroom was assigned three colors, with wall and ceiling colors always alternating. The ceiling color of the main bathroom matches the color of the underside of the balcony opposite. The results were striking and encourage identification with the space; the tenants really love these individualized bathrooms.

We also designed colorful bathrooms for the apartments of the Hirschi building → 4.11 and the Obmatt duplex, both in Adligenswil. These receive additional daylight via narrow two-story shafts, which are also painted. The atmospheric richness is striking.

An oversized mirror, rather than a standardized, prefabricated mirror cabinet, can sometimes be of service. Its spatial impact can be surprising—a small room doubles in size, becoming considerably more attractive. In such cases, we make sure to provide the required lockable storage space elsewhere, for example underneath the wash basin.

For our two apartment buildings on Sägestrasse in Kreuzlingen, we clad the showers in large-format polished granite panels. The mood of these bathrooms was immediately altered, transforming the mundane space into something special.

We know that there are three spaces that are decisive for renting out an apartment: the kitchen, the balcony, and the bathroom. But the latter can be more than just a room for your daily ablutions.

"The City We Want"

Dwight Yoakam

As director of Zurich's City Planning Office, the revision of the city's building and zoning code was not my most interesting, but certainly my most complex assignment. Some people regarded every single building restriction as a loss of revenue. Others wanted more urban density—but not without taxing the added value, insisted the left and the greens. Planners desired more creative freedom and a simplified building code. Many Zurich residents were simply sick of nonstop construction and the changes associated with it; they wanted old building substance to be better protected. "Stop climate change now" was a fully justified demand, even then. Another change that the legal overhaul was supposed to encourage was shifting commuters from their individual motor vehicles toward public transit. On top of all this, the urban character and architectural quality of the city and its buildings needed to be reinforced. And it goes without saying that, simultaneously, strict legal equality and security had to be ensured for everyone. All preexisting federal and cantonal regulations as well as federal court rulings needed to be complied with as well.

When I was given the assignment by the City of Zurich, my lack of knowledge on the subject proved to be helpful. Otherwise, the impossibility of handling such a monster task would have likely had me throwing in the towel straight away. In the work-intensive period that followed, I often spent evenings lying in the hot water of my bathtub. I would close my eyes and think: "What sort of city do we want? What would happen if there were no building regulations? If they were reimagined from the ground up? What rules are unavoidable for building and planning?" I dreamed of a building and zoning code for Zurich that could fit on an A4-sized piece of paper. Unfortunately, the bath water always got cold before I could come up with conclusive answers. Today, after many years of intensive building experience in Zurich, I'm more convinced than ever that a great deal could be accomplished through radical simplification of the building code and more exacting requirements regarding urban planning and architectural quality.

I learned a great deal about the advantages of our excellent, functioning Swiss legal system. To shepherd the new building and zoning code through the special parliamentary commission as well as through the municipal council—the legislative branch—we needed to find a weighty topic on which all political parties could take a stand. With the "Zurich basement," which was excluded from a building's floor space ratio, we found a suitable legal provision to serve as a basis for debating at length most of the demands mentioned above. The proposal was to ban this "Zurich basement" in the future. The media storm of indignation that swept over us was correspondingly intense.

The vehemence of the outrage was decisive, because just like in real life, the discussions also opened up certain opportunities. Our solution, likewise invented in the bathtub, was as simple as it was surprising: in order to avoid losing the right

to utilize this extra basement story, we convinced politicians to raise residential zones by a single floor. At the same time, the unattractive "Zurich basement," always half-buried in the ground, was banned. Permitted building heights were adjusted so that no additional stories were possible beyond that. Building owners were not granted any additional utilization rights. But they received, alongside planners, more leeway in their designs.

Today, the revised regulations have facilitated more interesting sectional solutions, as one is no longer restricted to working with minimal story

What sort of city do we want? Urban and architectural qualities are decisive.

heights. One major advantage of this is that, on ground floors, builders can offer oversized rooms and thus more public functionality, which makes neighborhoods livelier and more livable. Building code should exemplify the city we want to live in. What should be decisive are urban and architectural qualities.

In the process, I learned that it can be helpful to generate something like feigned pain. All the arguments about the "Zurich basement" made it possible to slip other legal alterations into the slipstream of the deliberate outrage cycle. In addition, I learned how relaxing a warm bath can be.

1.3.6 The Guest Room

An apartment has many tasks to fulfill. It offers protection from the elements. It provides security, facilitates the storage and preparation of food, the looking after of one's personal hygiene. It offers space for creative latitude, for self-presentation—and for the receiving of guests. Many of us welcome family members and friends inside our own four walls. Hospitality is an important aspect of our culture, with a long tradition. Even if nowadays we don't generally host strangers, receiving and entertaining friends and offering

Hospitality is an important aspect of our culture, with a long tradition.

them a place to spend the night if need be is part of everyday life. In affordable housing construction, however, there isn't enough space for an additional guest room. This is where the sofa comes in handy, or a convertible children's room capable of housing in-laws, cousins, or old university friends for a few nights. If a guest room is possible, it can be designed in such a way that it functions like a hotel room inside a house or apartment. A separate entrance, its own bathroom, or possibly even a small kitchenette can enable guests to enjoy an independent and peace-ful stay.

We're more interested in exceptions than mass-produced articles. We feel a bit like truffle-hunting dogs. Especially in the highly standardized residential construction sector, we're always searching for creative loopholes. A major part of our design process is studying and discussing planned or finished reference buildings designed by colleagues or predecessors. Again and again, we try to figure out the secrets of an apartment through its floor plan or sections. Sometimes, its qualities are only revealed through a personal visit. Seeing an inhabited apartment in particular can provide insights into its everyday use.

On a research trip to Portugal, we had an opportunity to visit some single-family homes and other buildings by Álvaro Siza, thanks to one of his former employees. The trip to Casa Vieira de Castro left an especially powerful impression. Siza worked on the residence for over ten years. Every detail has been deeply mulled over, down to the toilet brush designed specifically for the house. The depth of its details and its spatial qualities are unbelievable. Some aspects only became comprehensible thanks to explanations from the owner. For example, Siza accepted the commission only under the condition that he had a free hand in the design. This is the only way to make sense of the bedroom fireplace, which is found in a guest room. The owners, studying the architect's plans, were curious as to why there'd be a fireplace in such an unusual location. They told him they didn't need an open chimney in the room. To which Siza replied that he'd come visit after the villa's completion only if he could sleep over and there was a fireplace in the guest room.

I don't know for certain if the anecdote is true. But I assume Siza had a precise conception of a bedroom with a fireplace. Interestingly, it angles away slightly from the guest bed. Daylight falls on the reading chair from behind through a balcony window. In my imagination, I picture Siza sitting in this room, sketching in one of his notebooks, the open fire blazing before him and warming him up.

1.3.7 The Balcony

Cozy corner and balcony, a spatial unity.
Paul-Clairmont-Strasse apartment block, Zurich.

As it winds around with its projections forward and backward, it functions like an oversized accordion.

For us planners, many aspects of residential construction are predetermined: the number of sinks and kitchen elements, whether to have showers or bathtubs, the width of hallways, the maximum size of a room, the most economical claddings, the quality of a window, the relationships between closed wall surfaces, the number of installation shafts and their accessibility. In order to achieve cost certainty, all this is demanded as early as the competition stage. At the same time, the land price, or its share in total costs, is a fixed predetermined figure that we cannot influence.

Likewise, legal stipulations are constantly affecting new areas. The requirements, needs, and desires of residents are constantly changing. Things like the reduction in working hours, climate change, the introduction of daylight saving time and the increased hours of daylight that went along with that, as well as other societal changes mean that, with each new project, we need to start from scratch searching for creative latitude.

Although balconies have been built thousands of times and their functions, uses, and sizes are well-known, they've proven to be a multi-faceted aspect of construction with interesting creative potential. A balcony thrives on the oppositions between inside and outside, warm and cold, protected and open, wet and dry. A balcony belongs to an apartment and yet it's located beyond its four walls.

At the outset of designing the Paul Clairmont apartments in Zurich, we asked ourselves a naive question: When does a balcony become a "proper," usable balcony? By this we meant what dimensions, what length and width? The brief was to design generous family apartments →4.2. Therefore, we decided that the balconies should be accessible to small children. We imagined kids making figure eights with their tricycles unimpeded. With resulting dimensions of four by six meters, we found the answer to our self-imposed requirement.

This was the basis on which we developed our design. The idea wasn't to create a building with two-story balconies based on existing examples; our aim was to achieve a balcony depth of four meters while still getting daylight into the attached living room. From this challenging premise, we planned the two-story balcony levels that define the building in accordance with the stipulations of the building code, the competition program, and the structural possibilities.

Truth be told, getting a handle on the various interconnections took over a year of intensive work. We discovered that the key lay in how each unit's living rooms were aligned—together with the kitchens, these each form a spatial unity that runs lengthways along the facade. The length of this living area is precisely the length of three bedrooms of a standard four-and-a-half-room apartment. Additionally, to create a two-story balcony space that guarantees enough light for the room behind it, the kitchens needed to switch sides with each story.

A further challenge was integrating the five-and-a-half-room apartments demanded by the competition program into this spatial system. By thrusting two additional rooms into a bay-window-style avant-corps and developing two specific bedroom configurations, we were able to meet this requirement while complying with the necessary restrictions caused by the added height and length.

But another challenge was the visibility problem posed by neighboring apartments. High windows or glazing with privacy films solved this issue for the kitchens while providing them with natural light. As for neighbors on the same floor, boundaries are defined by deep cupboards that simultaneously function as storage for tools and garden furniture.

We were able to realize the building affordably thanks to an innovative structural design by the Zurich engineering firm Lüchinger + Meyer. The stairwells are designed as rigid cores. The floor slabs are supported by prefabricated columns. A jointless, load-bearing concrete facade surrounds the entire structure. As it winds

A small child should be able to make an uninterrupted figure eight with their tricycle.

The balcony idea defines the expression of the facade. James development, Zurich.

Triangular balconies, too, are easy to make use of. Hard Turm Park apartment and office building, Zurich.

A World of One's Own

Balcony partitions resembling Schiller curls. Reitmen development, Schlieren.

Leafy balcony as a reference-point for the Paul-Clairmont-Strasse apartment block, Zurich. Seida building by Francesc Mitjans, Barcelona, 1962, and Carrer de J. S. Bach building by José Antonio Coderch, Barcelona, 1955.

around with its projections forward and backward, it functions like an oversized accordion: depending on the temperature, it expands and contracts. Its form means that it doesn't require any expansion joints. The concrete facade's sculptural shape, defined by its play of light and shadow, also influenced the building's color concept, which comprises exclusively gray tones mixing different levels of black and white.

After this experience, we've pushed the idea of two-story balconies further and further in subsequent projects. In the corner building of the James development in Zurich-Albisrieden, for example, we combined them with spatially optimized three-and-a-half-room apartments. In Zurich's Hard Turm Park office and residential building, the triangular balconies that rotate out of the building's rectangular layout—which are very usable, by the way—respond to the unfavorable orientation of the apartments. Spatially fascinating apartments are created by the combination of a wide variety of apartment types with the alternation of living rooms on every floor necessitated by the two-story outdoor spaces. Thanks to the oversized balcony heights, even small trees can thrive, making an important contribution to the building's microclimate.

When does a balcony become a "proper," usable balcony?

1.3.8 The Sauna

"It's the little in-between spaces that make up an apartment!" a colleague told me as we bent our heads over the designs for an apartment building in Zurich. Our task was mundane and familiar: stick to the program on the bottom, freestyle on the top. In three-and-a-half-room apartments there isn't a square centimeter to spare, while attics can play with the slope of a building's roof, enabling extra spaces that can be used as entrance areas, walk-in closets, interstitial spaces, or storage areas. Inside the same building, what gives apartments differing qualities are precisely these small rooms, the elements that can really set a plan apart.

The sauna belongs to this spatial category. People familiar with Nordic Wohnkultur, who've had the pleasure of experiencing it in everyday life, won't want to miss out on the benefits of a sauna. Sweating and icy cooling off are good for the body. Regular sauna

The sauna encourages reflection.

use protects you against colds and illness. The heat helps you relax. Time in the sauna lends itself to philosophizing. The steam room's tranquility encourages concentration on, and reflection about, yourself. In addition to the wood-clad sauna room, it's important to have a space for relaxation. Of course, a rooftop terrace can serve the purpose. What's a more harmonious way to end the week than taking Sunday evening to wrap yourself in a wool blanket and stare into the starry night sky with a knitted cap on your head?

Up where the winters are still proper winters, on the border between Norway and Sweden, there's a lovely little hotel. Naturally, it's situated beside a pristine lake. The rooms are homey and cozy, very Scandinavian in their furnishing. Only local food is served, which means there's always (only) reindeer and char. Eating breakfast, you can watch the chef trudge through the snow of the frozen lake. With a saw, he bores a hole in the ice. A few minutes later, he returns with fresh-caught fish. It's available in countless variations, alongside the reindeer meat, as a main course or appetizer.

The unspoiled nature, with countless kilometers of trails, is ideal for cross-country skiing. But the best moment arrives after the exercise. On the lake, there's a separate

building, a little lonely almost, with a sauna. Warming up there again, really sweating it out, and then kicking a hole in the ice with your bare foot and cooling off in the cold water, before retiring to the little relaxation room and watching the winter twilight descend at three in the afternoon—is a truly regenerative, sensual experience.

We're aware that saunas require energy. Maybe that's why nowadays there's such a thing as sauna shame. We prefer to treat it like food: every now and then, we eat something unhealthy, something it would be better to avoid. But that's precisely why we enjoy it!

A World of One's Own

Smile, breathe and go slowly.

1.4 Day In, Day Out

1.4.1 The Living Room
1.4.2 The Kitchen
1.4.3 The Pantry
1.4.4 The Dining Room
1.4.5 The Library
1.4.6 The Room with the Fireplace
1.4.7 The Study
1.4.8 The Music Room
1.4.9 The Conservatory
1.4.10 The Coworking-Space

1.4.1 The Living Room

The English word "living room" is more fitting, more precise somehow, and much broader in its meaning than the German Wohnzimmer. "Living room" suggests that – in this room – anything is possible and much is allowed. That is why the living room reveals itself as the most challenging room in an apartment. While the use of the other rooms is clear and pre-determined, the good old parlour does not carry a precise idea of its use or a specific activity that is carried out within it. Hence, we often ask ourselves what living means today. Our experience shows that this room is mostly used for watching television. A sofa, one or two comfortable armchairs, a small side table for the remote control and programme guide, and the oversized television set make up the most common furnishings.

Every few months for more than thirty years, we've been submitting a competition entry or a study commission. Recently, the briefs have become more and more demanding and comprehensive. Architects are asked to find a suitable and cost-effective answer to all kinds of questions even in the competition phase. Interestingly, the main task—designing good housing—is never or only briefly described. Usually what is specified is the size of the apartment, the number of bathrooms, and the number of rooms.

During the tender, the preliminary examination, and the judging, countless experts provide input. Red, yellow, and green points are bountifully awarded in relation to each of the specifications. The buildings should follow the topography, address their

These days living rooms are multi-purpose spaces.

surroundings in a logical way, and be constructed in a sustainable, resource-saving, and recyclable way. In addition, we are also invited to present our design in BIM and show a facade section at a scale of 1:20 – as proof we can build. If a contractor or investor is very particular, they even specify in advance how many elements a kitchen may have depending on the number of rooms. Likewise, the size of the two bathrooms is precisely defined. Perhaps last but not least, what is sought after are functional and well-furnished apartment layouts.

With regard to quality of life, there are no concrete requirements. The assessment is left to the judges and the commissioning parties. It is, therefore, all the more important that they have a certain amount of experience

Let us sit on these chairs and chat and discuss!

A wall full of memories.

Now and then we allow ourselves to dream of cultures of dwelling from the past. We are fascinated by how Le Corbusier lived, and we admire the generosity of the living rooms in Luis Barragán's designs in Mexico City. The architecture, the proportions of the rooms, and the choice of furniture and hung art form a coherent unity there. For us, such examples are still a formative point of reference.

With regard to quality of life, there are no concrete requirements

in housing construction. It helps to know all the tricks of the trade and to be able to apply this knowledge when judging the entries. In addition, furnished floor plans are easier to assess than empty rooms, even if you have a good feeling for room sizes.

Therefore, we consider early on where the sofa and TV could be placed, how to move around the living room, where a convenient place for the reading chair could be found, where a bookshelf could be placed, which lines of sight are attractive, what access to the balcony, the kitchen, or the entrance looks like, and where a play corner for the children could go. We also make sure that the room has two walls that can be furnished well, which we affectionately call the "cozy corner."

It's incredibly interesting to us to see how our living rooms are used once someone has moved in. During the design process, we might have been able to anticipate some variations in how people arrange the space, but others surprise us. Vagueness is a potential. These days living rooms are multi-purpose spaces: from working to practising yoga—everything has to be possible. We've also encountered a complete bicycle park with eight bikes belonging to a family of four or half a pet shop with all kinds of reptiles, lizards, and lemurs in what we had carefully planned as living rooms.

The same use, different atmospheres. Casa Prieto López by Luis Barragán, Jardines del Pedregal, Mexico City, 1951, and Villa Tugendhat by Ludwig Mies van der Rohe, Brünn, 1930.

Day In, Day Out

"Light My Fire"
The Doors

Even as a little boy, I was fascinated by the open fireplace in our house. I could sit in front of the flickering flames for hours, poking firewood, only to be amazed at where the log burst fastest into flames. But the fireplace wasn't the only place I "played with fire." When I caused a small forest fire after a long dry spell and ran home with scorched hair, my mother wisely gave me the single of the Mani Matter song "I han es Zündholzli azündt" ("I lit a match"). Since that watershed moment, I've been more careful with fire – but the fascination for fireplaces has remained.

When I think of an open fireplace today, I remember the floor plan of the small summer house Erik Gunnar Asplund built for himself on the archipelago outside Stockholm in 1930. I imagine the blazing fireplace on cold Nordic nights, and how the warmth, and the smell, of the fire slowly spread through the house.

It is not only the striking form of the fireplace that appeals, but also its position on the floor plan. To connect the inner world with the surrounding natural environment, the vacation home has five entrances and exits. It skilfully follows the natural terrain. The layout reacts to the topography with steps. The interesting thing about this little house is how the daily functions are divided up: the kitchen with a dining area is at one end, the living room—which is set off at a slight angle—with the spacious fireplace at the other. We have adopted this arrangement in our apartment on Hinterbergstrasse. It makes the apartment seem larger, which becomes used more evenly as it always has to be walked through.

In Asplund's case, the corridor also provides access to two differently-sized bedrooms. These differ in ceiling height, with the larger one also having a higher ceiling. Along this corridor is also the dining area, which interestingly has two entrances and exits: one leading to the back of the building and the other to the west-facing covered veranda, where the entrance is. This room is connected to the living room. The entrance area overlooks the living area, which is four steps lower. The brick steps transition seamlessly into the open, semi-circular fireplace, which deviates slightly from the orthogonal grid to reveal the slight axial rotation of the room. The fireplace thus becomes the hinge, the spatial joint of the house. At the same time, the offset opens up an L-shaped outdoor area protected from the sea breeze, which in turn defines the particular look of the main entrance.

Compared to the modest size of the house, the fireplace is huge. A curtain and a sofa form a unit together with the open fireplace. A side table and two chairs, all designed by Asplund, show how the great architect imagined the quiet evenings in the circle of his family.

Open fireplace in Stennäs vacation home by E.G. Asplund, Sorunda, near Stockholm, 1937.

Since that watershed moment, I've been more careful with fire.

1.4.2 The Kitchen

Cooking needs workspaces.

Even if something is good, it can always be better. This is the conviction of sushi master Jiro Ono, who runs a nondescript restaurant with just ten seats, four levels below ground in an underground station in Tokyo, in the 2011 film Jiro Dreams of Sushi by David Gelb. At the time, this micro-restaurant was considered the best sushi restaurant in the world and was decorated with three Michelin stars. The documentary is impressive because it shows what it takes to create the best sushi. Jiro Ono believes that it takes a lifetime of work.

Even if something is good, it can always be better.

At the time of filming, he was 85 years old. Of course, it also takes the best and freshest ingredients.

The little tricks that Jiro reveals in the interview are striking: for example, he hands each guest a glass of water while they wait, without asking. He does this to see which hand the guest uses to take the glass, so that he can serve his sushi creations for left- or right-handed people accordingly. The master varies the size of these depending on the guest's estimated body weight. Even though the chef has been preparing sushi for 70 years and always seems to be doing the same thing, it's the small, fine, and decisive details that count. In the documentary, you can sense the humility and the satisfaction in the daily work that fulfils Jiro, but also the knowledge that nothing is ever flawless.

When I design, I remember this film, because the schedule of accommodation for an apartment is also always the same: a kitchen, one, two, three, or four bedrooms depending on the size, one or two bathrooms, a dining area, and a living room. Nevertheless, we develop each plan very carefully from scratch. We love this work because it is

Day In, Day Out

Urban cooking in Hard Turm Park high-rise, Zurich.

Washing up with a view of the lake. Roost development, Zug.

Small window openings as pass-throughs for the balcony. Imbisbühlstrasse apartment building, Zurich.

about dealing intensively with daily life in its normality.

Probably the scope for variation when designing a kitchen is as minimal as when designing a bathroom. Standardized elements and procedures shape the organization and appearance. Kitchens seem interchangeable, and in fact visits to newly constructed apartment buildings by our colleagues reveal fundamental similarities and affinities in the layout and appearance of these spaces.

Today, the kitchen is often a "food station"

Nevertheless, it is always interesting to design a kitchen—we ourselves like to cook and we think of this space as about pure living. We want to create pleasant working conditions. We're not interested in haute cuisine, but in good everyday cooking.

Dining kitchen, Alte Landstrasse development, Kloten.

1.4.3 The Pantry

With the ability to shop twenty-four hours a day, seven days a week, the good old pantry has become somewhat redundant. The tendency to heat up ready-made products is also not helping. But there is hope! If we consider sustainability holistically, changing eating habits is an important contribution. It is not obvious why—to take one example—we go to so much expense to transport kiwis from New Zealand. Preferring regional products is certainly the right thing to do. The trend to pickle vegetables, bake bread, ferment foods, store spices, or dry fruit also requires a small pantry.

In our office, we maintain a virtual supply room: every Friday morning, the four partners meet in the large meeting room to discuss all our projects with the staff in this setting. The work is presented and critiqued. In joint discussion rounds we develop ideas, research, and exchange. Deliberately, there are no rules, everything is allowed. However, the discussions are minuted. This allows us to build up a stock of ideas.

For more than thirty years, the majority of our commissions have been the result of successful competition entries. We often have not just one, but two or three study commissions on our desks at any one time. It is important for us to continuously engage with current issues in housing construction. Thanks to comparisons with our colleagues, we learn. Daily training is essential.

Over the years, we've acquired our own design strategy. We start every competition with a so-called zero project. This shows us the challenges of the location, the brief, the building code, the granularity, the addressing, the phasing and the development, giving us hints about the housing mix and the design of the outdoor space. One or both of the responsible partners bring this first draft to our Friday discussion group. Sometimes something new suddenly emerges. We go on tangents and develop new floor plan ideas seemingly out of nowhere. We follow the desire to dare the impossible. We put together unfamiliar sequences of rooms as a creative response to building regulations. We think about what would we would consider to be "decent" room sizes, room heights or layout possibilities. Most of the time, the plans that result are unusable. Nevertheless, we keep them stored away in our minds.

From the simple question 'How deep can a floor plan be?' we developed both the residential building on Imbisbühlstrasse →2.2.6 in Zurich and the Hard Turm Park high-rise →2.2.9. We get inspired by working on briefs such as building on a noisy north-facing slope

Our ideas have no expiry date and our pantry is always bursting at the seams.

with the frontage on the wrong side. Our submission to the Birnbäumen competition in St. Gallen →2.2.4 —which didn't win, unfortunately—was based on this principle. Even if our entry isn't selected, we hang on to rejected housing ideas like those. We carefully store them in the architectural pantry of our office. These rough diamonds rest there and wait for a hopefully more successful use in the next zero project.

For years, for example, we've been looking at new solutions for a pergola development and the corresponding innovative apartment plans. Unfortunately, without success – but we keep at it and are convinced that the time will come! Our ideas have no expiry date and our pantry is always bursting at the seams.

1.4.4 The Dining Room

"For us, the greatest innovation imaginable in residential construction is a sliding door between the kitchen and dining area!" With this pithy statement, we started our collaboration with the client after winning the competition for the James development in Zurich. Eight years later, on completion of the three residential buildings, we handed over 75 very different apartment types to the investors, distributed over 274 apartments. From small studios to studios with living areas, from maisonette apartments to spacious retirement communities, we designed floor plans to meet the needs of a wide range of inhabitants.

How was it possible to persuade our clients to accept such a variety of types? Of course, we were lucky, and over the course of the collaboration we were able to convince them of our abilities. For example, the first landlord encouraged us to dare to do something special with each floor plan. An important idea was to also attract prospective tenants to Zurich-Albisrieden who had previously lived in the central Seefeld district or well-heeled Zürichberg, which is to say, in upmarket residential areas. Our thinking was that we wanted to convince potential tenants with additional features as well as with floor plan proposals that deviated from the usual. Countless revisions, clarifications and models on a 1:20 scale formed the basis for this. To illustrate the scale, we used photographs

Our biographies no longer run in a straight line.

of the clients. In addition, during the presentations we endowed them with fictional biographies related to the apartments. Whenever they looked at the models, they saw themselves in the leading role, living an interesting and unusual life. Let's face it: who among us wouldn't want to live in an oversized flat and cook appropriate dishes for their guests on Saturday night in a Jamie Oliver kitchen? Or who wouldn't like to be able to ride their Harley Davidson right into their oversized, loft-like living room?

With these stories and the corresponding floor plans, we deliberately moved away from common standards. These are often based on rigid images and ideas of how people live: here the closed kitchen, there the dining area. The fact that sleeping is done in the bedroom and the bathroom is used for hygiene no longer needs to be mentioned.

Is the use of an apartment still so clear-cut today? Our biographies no longer run in a straight line. There are breaks and changes, in our relationships as well as in our professional careers. A floor plan must be able to react to this. We therefore wanted to create different possibilities for the diverse beings we are: there are apartments in which the kitchen is arranged in the middle like a workshop manager's office. The dining area can there-

The dining table is the heart of an apartment.

fore be both on the same side as the living room and in an adjoining room. Suddenly there is a real dining room. But with its direct access to the bathroom, this same room can also be used as a bedroom, with a simple connection to the kitchen.

Our relationship to food has also changed. Today, the kitchen is often a "food station," used mainly for spontaneous meals at different times. A joint meal with the whole family has to be arranged and planned far in advance. Or there is a rule that the family eats together on Sunday evenings.

Nevertheless, the dining area remains one of the most important places in the home. The table and the chairs symbolise community and hospitality. This is where we eat, talk about our day, discuss things, make decisions, and entertain guests. We laugh and drink. So, the room should be well furnished. Circulation around the table

The table and the chairs symbolize community and hospitality.

must be unhindered. If the area is too open, we feel uncomfortable. It is important to have a feeling of security and spatial support, for example by means of an enclosed corner. The table needs to be a certain size, but not too big. The lighting above the table creates the desired atmosphere. The light should not be too bright, but also not too dim, because people like to see what they're eating.

Dining areas in two homes by Luis Barragan. Casa Gálvez, San Angel, Mexico City, 1955, and Casa Prieto López, Jardines del Pedregal, Mexico City, 1951.

Friday evening aperitif between dining room and veranda.

Day In, Day Out 77

1.4.5 The Library

A library is also a space of contemplation.

A bookseller friend of mine, who owns an antiquarian bookshop, told me the story of a solvent customer who bought old books from him by the meter. The fact that there were rarities worth thousands of francs among them apparently did not move him. This suggests that the buyer had not acquired the books primarily for reading, but rather wanted to create a library in his new house with which to impress his guests. Books testify to the knowledge of the owner. Moreover, books on a shelf radiate something homely.

Books have fascinated me ever since I learned to read. As a child, I put every book on

Books testify to the knowledge of the owner

the shelf and was proud when my library grew by an inch or two. Books from the library or borrowed from friends were never my thing. I wanted to own them myself. Besides fiction, I'm interested in technical literature and cookery books. Even today, I am not able to pass by a bookshop without saying hello—from the inside. My library has grown over the years—also because I have never been able to give a book away and always buy more books than I can ever manage to read!

That's why focusing on a few architects, authors, and specific cookbooks helps me. For example, I only buy a cookbook if I discover a few recipes in it that I don't know and would like to cook again. In fiction, I focus mainly on authors whose work makes me think. In specialist literature, I follow the works of certain architects over years or even decades. I own all the publications I have been able to acquire by Alvar Aalto, Le Corbusier, Álvaro Siza, Herzog & de Meuron, Sigurd Lewerentz, Louis Kahn, and Erik Gunnar Asplund. Visiting their buildings goes without saying and has also been the motivation for various trips.

A library reveals a lot about its users. It provides information about their interests, thought, and actions. This is why the famous photographs of Le Corbusier at his desk are so valuable: they are not only snapshots, but also reveal the writings he was grappling with and that influenced him.

The written word also stands for memories and documents what has happened. In the same way, we see an apartment as a compendium of a person's life. For us, it is a spatial vessel in which the idiosyncrasies of the residents can manifest themselves. Open shelves are wonderful storage areas for all the little holiday mementos and collections of personal interests. Books, records, CDs, art objects, found objects, stones, pottery, flower vases, memorabilia, and much more can be laid out and displayed on them.

"Grand Confort"
Le Corbusier

Reading is one of my favourite pastimes. There are always piles of books and magazines next to my armchair. Almost every Saturday I go on the same tour of the city, visiting different bookshops. I carry the new acquisitions home and deposit them on the ever-changing tower of books next to my Grand Confort armchair by Le Corbusier.

As an apartment becomes lived in, through its furniture, specially hung art, the materialization, and lights, individual spaces are created over time. They are closely linked to personal habits. They are often areas where people like to relax and enjoy the security of their own four walls.

Most of the time, when I come home, I sit down in my worn-out armchair. Straight away, my cats come to me. They greet me, first sitting on the backrest and then making themselves comfortable on my lap. Their purring relaxes me and is immediately transmitted to me. I often sit there for a moment before I take a book and leaf through it, then start reading at random. This is also where all my architecture magazines are. I have been subscribing to them since I first began my architecture degree. The periodicals alone fill linear meters of bookshelves.

I'm convinced that an essential character trait of an architect is curiosity. This trait always drives me to discover new things. At the same time, I'm concerned with the question of how far knowledge helps or hinders architectural work. Isn't it an advantage in a design to find new and surprising solutions, thanks to not knowing? I remember the nonchalance with which we, as young architects, threw ourselves into competitions, and the pleasant naivety with which we drafted solutions back then. Surprisingly, it was precisely this attitude that led to our successes in competitions.

An essential character trait of an architect is curiosity.

1.4.6 The Room with the Fireplace

Alcove with fireplace at Villa Beer by J. Frank and O. Wlach, Vienna, 1930.

Fireplace at Villa Müller by A. Loos, Prague, 1930.

Is it appropriate to write about this room? There are currently practically no vacant apartments in the larger Swiss cities. A lack of vacancies means having no choice when looking for a new place to live. Rising rents are another challenge. Land costs and rampant inflation are making building even more expensive. Finding a suitable home is becoming an ordeal.

Any mention of housing calls up certain expectations and ideas. To inhabit a private sanctuary is a basic right. We dream of

We dream of loft-like halls or cozy rooms.

loft-like halls or cozy rooms. It is precisely in this context that the fireplace room holds significance: it represents our longing for a home that is cozy and secure. No wonder, because harnessing fire was crucial to the development of humankind. With this step, we were able to create an essential difference between ourselves and other primates. A fire protects, gives warmth, creates light in the dark night, and changes our food by preserving it or making it edible in the first place. The hearth formed the center of our dwellings from the beginning. That is why we still have the need for an open fireplace today.

From time to time I stay overnight in Stuttgart, being a member of the city's design advisory board. The people of Baden-Württemberg are very cost-conscious—also when it comes to choosing a hotel. An affordable room near the train station is always booked for me. In this functionally optimized room, there is of course a TV. Whenever I check in downstairs at the reception, the screen is switched on in my temporary abode upstairs, showing an endlessly blazing fire. Even if the materials are clean and their texture—for example as imitation wood—cannot hide the fact that they are made

Keep the fire burning.

of plastic, the endless loop of the virtual fire is supposed to simulate an image of coziness and security. Besides this unpleasant artificiality, the typical crackling and the specific smoky smell of a real fire are missing. Normally, I immediately switch off the annoying picture. Curiously, however, I wondered if this fire would change, as a real one would, leaving behind only embers at dawn. "Keep the fire burning," I thought to myself once and left the TV on all night. When I woke up in the morning, the fire was blazing just as it had been when I fell asleep.

We all have memories of a fire burning in a hearth. We associate it with cozy get-togethers with friends, with quiet contemplation and staring into the flames, or with the cozy heat after an exhausting and cold day of skiing on vacation. It is such moments of relaxation that make us dream of a "cozy" fireplace room. That's why an apartment is more than just an investment property. It's our task and responsibility as architects to develop floor plans that allow space for the personal and specific needs of the occupants. The fireplace stands as a symbol of this desire. Ultimately, it is also about dignity.

The other day I was on a jury for the planning of well over two hundred apartments. On the one hand, a renowned architectural firm had the jury impressed by a very coherent urban planning proposal; on the other, the floor plans presented were disappointing. In every apartment and in all plans of every floor, the toilet bowl was located on the axis of the drawn-in dining table. In everyday use, and even more so when there are visitors, this is an unpleasant situation. With this arrangement, going to the bathroom becomes a challenge. In my opinion, this is a no-go. Housing is also about values. Perhaps the word is poise. In any case, you don't need a fireplace room for that.

Quiet reflection by the hearth.

Day In, Day Out

1.4.7 The Study

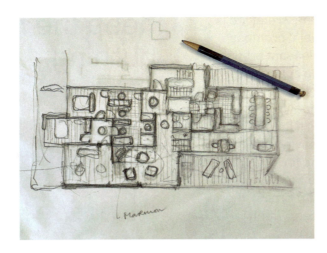

Up to the age of fifty-five, architects are considered young; after that, our experience sets us apart. That's at least what we have learned. The question whether we creatives are helped more by youthful ignorance or by many years of immersion in architectural practice cannot be answered conclusively. The crucial thing is just to always let our curiosity guide us and drive us further. It helps to be your own biggest critic and to always question your own work. When designing apartments, routine, a broad general knowledge, and life experience are undoubtedly useful. Being able to put the rooms of an apartment into a coherent relationship has a lot

Designing housing is grueling work.

to do with combinatorics. Our wealth of experience means we have countless variations on every solution at our fingertips. We also use our skills to analyze the strengths and weaknesses of a floor plan sketch.

Designing housing is grueling work. It takes time, tireless application to the task and, above all, patience to get all of the conditions—the functional processes, circulation, and proportions between the rooms, the connection between indoor and outdoor space, the statics, building services, shielding against noise, fenestration, lighting and views, the spatial diversity, possible lines of sight, and use of materials, the location of sockets and light switches, and the color scheme—to jell. If the client appreciates these efforts then we feel doubly motivated.

Tracing paper, a soft pencil, and a scale ruler are our trustiest design tools. We do our searching and thinking with our hands! Perhaps this way of working reveals that we're almost ready to be put out to pasture. However, we notice that when designing with the mouse and the corresponding drawing programs, which can be scaled at will, it's impossible to get an intuitive feel for dimensions and proportions.

When developing a plan, quiet and concentration can be beneficial. Unfortunately, an architect's good ideas rarely occur to them during working hours. That's why we all make space for a studio space at home. We sit there, ponder, and brood over our drawings and sketches. We draw on reference works, study competition entries from our colleagues, and lose ourselves in our extensive architectural libraries. We often think that drawing, designing, and studying layouts is similar to daily sports training. Just like a chess player, practice gives us the ability to test the suitability of plan ideas two, three, or four moves in advance.

Years of application, focus, and specialization have given us the not-always-pleasant ability to spot mistakes immediately. Sometimes this seems like an occupational disease. Having received a jury's preliminary examination report, on leafing through it I discover the problems immediately. We also quickly notice deficiencies during project development in the office. But we're subtle in how we make suggestions for improvement, because we have a deep appreciation for the work of our colleagues.

The Covid-19 pandemic changed the world of work. Suddenly, working from home became possible, perhaps even welcome. Hopefully, this will have an effect on how hous-

The miscellany of everyday life and selected furnishings and lights produce a creative work atmosphere.

ing is built. In recent years, we've had to optimize floor plans more and more—which is to say, make them smaller. It is precisely a study or an appropriately usable niche that can increase the attractiveness of an apartment and thus its long-term rentability.

It helps to be your own biggest critic.

Day In, Day Out

1.4.8 The Music Room

In the spring of 2014, The Hare with Amber Eyes, a touching book by Edmund de Waal, took me to Odessa, in Ukraine. At that time, Russia annexed Crimea, but no one foresaw the destructive war that is now raging. I sought out and visited the birthplace of the Jewish Ephrussi family, which served as the origin of the book. The stately home is in the immediate vicinity of the even more famous Potemkin Stairs, which connect the city center with the harbor. The tapered design of the stairs produces an impressive perspectival effect: if you stand on the top landing and look down, the staircase appears short and steep. Looking up from below, it appears to be infinitely long. The lines of the staircase edging let the vanishing point end in the infinity of the firmament. The staircase leads to the sky.

However, it was the walk through the city center that became etched in my memory. The temperature was mild, though the harshness of the Ukrainian winter still hung in the air. All the trees were still leafless. Buildings erected around 1900 dominated the look and atmosphere of the city. The opera house rose above everything, as if it was the city's crown. Time seemed to have stood still. Many windows were open. Numerous melodies radiated from the buildings surrounding this cultural monument. Fascinated, I listened to someone practicing a certain passage of a piano concerto over and over again. Opposite, a singing teacher was rehearsing an aria with her pupil. Further down the street, someone was honing their guitar playing. Soft music filled the city.

Unfortunately, we have never been able to design a music room in our work as architects. Our residential buildings, mostly committed to affordable housing, have to do without this luxury. Since my visit to Odessa, however, I have had a wish to be able to

It is a space for peace and contemplation.

plan and build such a room one day. I can already imagine it: similar to the body of a double bass, my music room would be completely lined with wood—walls, ceiling, and floor. I would use the same types of wood as are used for the instrument—spruce, maple—and as for special parts such as the fingerboard, the higher and lower saddles—black ebony. It would be important to me that the paneling has the same colors as the double bass. I imagine the numerous lacquered wood patterns to achieve the intended mood. A wide variety of carpets with different colors and patterns would cover the floor. A shiny black concert grand piano would stand in the center of the room. A bookshelf filled to the brim with illustrated books and other volumes, LPs, and CDs would complement the furnishings. There would also be a stereo system with inconspicuous built-in speakers. The room would have both a comfortable sofa for listening to music or reading and a side table made of a noble natural stone. The lighting and the choice of light features would also be carefully considered, no doubt including the table lamp designed by Álvaro Siza and the A808 floor lamp with the shiny golden

Music room at Villa Beer by J. Frank and O. Wlach, Vienna, 1930.

Dreaming of a White Christmas. Grand piano at Graceland, Elvis Presley's home, Memphis, Tennessee.

lampshade by Alvar Aalto. A larger, friendly-looking armadillo from my collection would guard this room. A mysterious painting with bold colors by the Swiss painter Peter Roesch would adorn the wall.

A large panorama window opens my fantasy room to the outside world. Your gaze reaches out into nature. In my imagination, not a single human intervention can be seen. Over an untouched valley with a wild river, my eye wanders into the distance to mountain slopes covered with deciduous trees. I see the reddish-brown spectacle of the leaves turning in an intense "Indian summer," the wintery, snow-covered fairy-tale landscape, the delicate light green of the first spring leaves, and the lush green of the summer forest before me. To complete the cliché of this ideal room, the owner plays *Trois poèmes d'amour* by Erik Satie on the grand piano.

A music room should be a tranquil retreat. It is a space for peace and contemplation. It would do us good to have such rooms. The music collection carries our life story. Each purchase represents a period of our life. The interesting thing about music is that we associate it with feelings that can resurface when we listen to it later. Often certain experiences are associated with a song, be they painful or marked by happiness. Music, like architecture, is an expression of the zeitgeist.

But we always let it rip during a competition!

No wonder that in our memory certain competitions and individual songs belong inseparably together. Preferences can change, some favorite bands remain. But we always let it rip during a competition!

Cash only. Soundtrack to a competition submission!

Day In, Day Out 85

"Cosy Corner"

Arthur Rüegg

When we design an apartment, we start from our own ideas about living. These largely correspond to a general average, since we know that we're normal sorts of people and a bit boring. It is precisely this realisation that helps us. Even though we've been studying floor plans in depth for years, it is our everyday experiences within our own four walls that guide us. The daily, self-critical reflection on our own actions supports us in the design of our apartment floor plans. We leave out everything we dislike, and we assume that much of what we love will also be liked by the tenants, who are always unknown to us. Our staff are often amazed at how we explain our floor plan sketches to them and how easily we are able to explain them from our own everyday living experiences. In this sense, we are real practitioners!

Every apartment should offer its occupants the greatest possible freedom to furnish it according to their own ideas and to use the rooms accordingly. However, this doesn't mean that we, as architects, are relieved of our tasks and duties. It is our responsibility, for example, to position the doors in order to make sure that the rooms can be furnished in as many ways as possible. A door that opens in the wrong direction is a nuisance. A missing entrance is unforgivable. We detest a single-line kitchen unit on the exposed back wall in the living room–kitchen area, because the person cooking always turns his or her back to the others in an unfriendly manner. A direct line of sight from the dining table to the toilet bowl is equally unacceptable.

To check this, every now and then we draw in the relationships between the circulation areas and the furnishable ones. Each floor plan is transferred several times to the next largest scale and, in particular, gets equipped with the appropriate furniture. Selected furniture, books, pictures and trinkets are what make an apartment cozy. To do this, they need the appropriate space. So, we try to arrange a "cozy corner" in each of our apartments. By this we mean a corner formed by two windowless walls at right angles to each other. Such a "cozy corner" can be well furnished and gives a feeling of security.

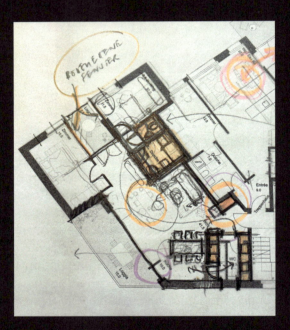

We know that we're normal sorts of people and a bit boring.

1.4.9 The Conservatory

The conservatory provides not only the residents but also us designers a welcome free space. Its use is only clearly defined in winter: similar to a greenhouse, it serves as a sanctuary for temperature-sensitive plants. The room is cool with a damp smell. When it gets warmer, the plants can move back into the garden or onto the balcony. The conservatory then becomes an empty room, looking for a new, temporary use in the warmer seasons. In spring and summer, sometimes until late autumn, it can be used as a sheltered outdoor space thanks to sliding doors or movable glazing.

We love images of orangeries filled to bursting, but we also know the conservatory as a cozy reading corner or airy breakfast room whose light furnishings are reminiscent of a holiday home. The flooring is always robust and not affected by water. Thanks to the different materials, such an oasis differs from the rest of the home.

We have had the opportunity to build several high-rise residential buildings. One question always influenced our design process: what is more likely to affect the stability of a high-rise building in Zurich, the wind or a possible earthquake? A wind tunnel test with a 1:50 scale model of our project for the Hard Turm Park high-rise at EPFL Lausanne showed us that a hurricane-like westerly wind would have a stronger influence on the statics—and in particular the stability—of the building than an earthquake. The indications of where the wind can cause dangerous vortexes and turbulence were also interesting.

During the construction of the James high-rise residential building → 2.2.2, we looked in detail at different means of providing shade and protection from the sun. The main issue was what wind speeds they could withstand. Around the year 2000, an average of ten to fifteen days with wind speeds of over 30 km per hour were forecast in Zurich. Due to global warming, the number of such days has more than doubled annually. From this we concluded that protruding

The conservatory is a place where cacti can pass the winter, home-made pasta be left to dry, or breakfast be eaten.

The conservatory provides a welcome free space.

Day In, Day Out 87

Glazed veranda at Villa Tugendhat by Ludwig Mies van der Rohe, Brünn, 1930.

The most interesting aspect of a conservatory is that it only has a specific use in the cool seasons.

third story and we arranged two-story, all-round conservatories on every fifth floor as climate buffers and multipurpose meeting zones and break areas. Thanks to these generous, green conservatories, the high-rise building was given its own expression, which took its cues from the architectural scales of the surrounding neighborhood.

Derived from the idea of the conservatory, each apartment in the planned high-rise building Uetlibergstrasse →2.4.5 is to have a spacious glazed room. This connects the individual apartments with the immediate neighborhood. The alcove can be assigned to the living area and used by the residents entirely according to their needs.

balconies on high-rise buildings in our city are unsuitable and limited in their use. We adapted our floorplans accordingly. Above a certain height, it is also unpleasant to stand close to the window. The void spreading out in front of you can produce vertiginous feelings. Therefore, in a high-rise building, it is very good to live, eat, or sleep on a second level inside the apartment. The ancillary rooms, such as the bathroom or the kitchen, can be located along the outer walls. Wind-protected conservatories can take the role of balconies and multipurpose intermediary spaces.

For a commission to design a sustainable office tower, we used our experience of prefabricated residential construction: four solid concrete cores with lifts and emergency exit stairs, arranged in the corners of the plan, provided access to the flexibly usable office spaces. On every fifth floor we proposed a table construction, also made of concrete. The four floors in-between were to be built out of prefabricated wooden elements once the skeletal structure was completed. This construction allowed us to make the fourth floor column-free. In addition, an interior, double-story hall could be offered on each

An extra-high conservatory with numerous possible uses. Competition for an office block.

1.4.10 The Coworking-Space

Suddenly it's there—a new space! It is called a coworking space. It's so up-to-date that there's no German term for it yet. We have only just heard and read about it. It is representative of the rapidly changing tasks in our architectural office. We no longer build apartment buildings. Our buildings function like small villages. Dwelling, cultivating a community, and working—these uses are mutually dependent and belong together.

In the area between Fellenbergstrasse, Langrütstrasse, and Langrütweg, we were fortunate enough to be able to plan and construct our idea of a post-density neighborhood. In addition to more than 100 affordable family apartments, we were able to complete a neighborhood bakery with a café and ballroom, a day-care center for children, and a small production space for a window factory that provides more than twenty jobs. A residential building with exclusively three-and-a-half- and four-and-a-half-room apartments is under construction, while another with seventy apartments diversified into more than fifteen different types is in the final planning stage. It will also house a common room and a coworking space. Of course, in collaboration with landscape architects, we attach great importance to diverse, natural outdoor spaces: a small stream has been opened up, a pond will make an important contribution to combating the summer heat, and a legally required enclosure for the entrance to the parking garage will additionally enhance the surroundings as a colorful garden.

We, too, study the current statistics on population development in the city of Zurich. The trend towards smaller households is continuing. Two-thirds of the population now live alone. This population segment therefore accounts for most of the planned apartments. In the Langgrüthof apartment building →2.5.5, we are trying to respond to this development. Compact small apartments make up the majority of the newly-required housing. The functionally perfectly organized motorhome serves as a reference here. Kitchens and toilets are prefabricated in wood.

To enable residents to work comfortably in their home offices, the tightly planned accommodation is supplemented with a spacious coworking space. Located directly at the main entrance, it offers well-equipped workstations, an additional meeting room, a server room and a printer room, a kitchenette with a coffee machine, and small, acoustically well-insulated cubicles for confidential discussions.

When we design, we are not only concerned with the question "How will we live tomorrow?" It is just as important for us to create "more city for the city"! It looks as if the coworking space is the latest building block.

To make the apartments, which are organized analogously to a motorhome, function even better, they are supplemented with a coworking space.

Entrance area with coworking space for all residents. Langgrüthof apartment building, Zurich.

It's just as important for us to create "more city for the city"!

Day In, Day Out 89

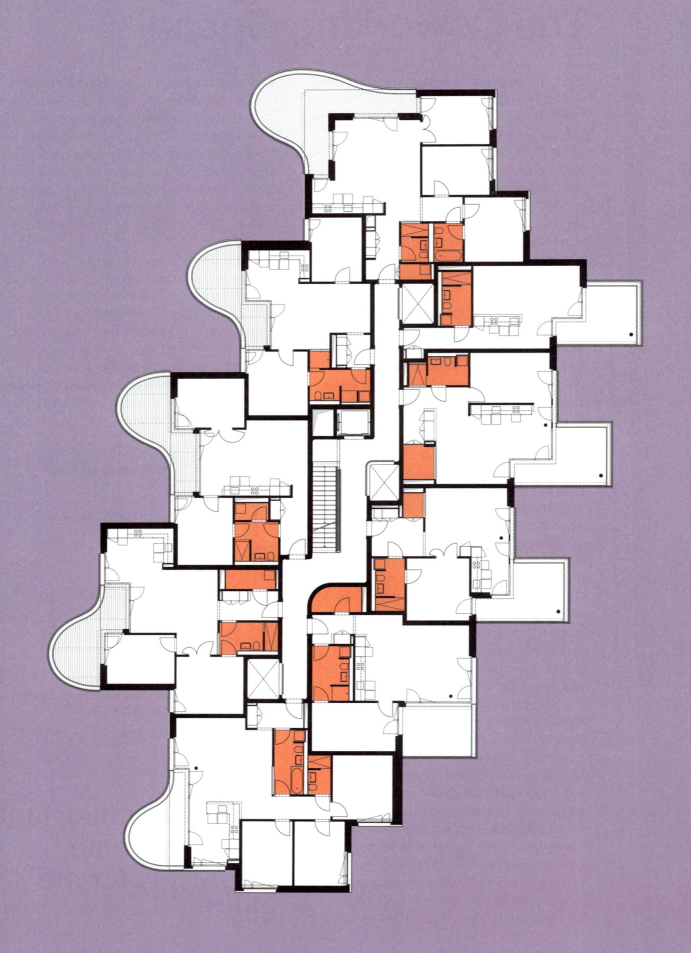

1.5 Ancillary Spaces

1.5.1   The Attic
1.5.2   The Utility Room
1.5.3   The Hobby Room
1.5.4   The Workshop
1.5.5   The Basement
1.5.6   The Weight Room
1.5.7   The Laundry Room
1.5.8   The Pool
1.5.9   The Wild-Card Room
1.5.10   The Common Room
1.5.11   The Wine Cellar

1.5.1 The Attic

I have been drawing for as long as I can remember. I've always wanted to keep improving this craft. So I began to deal with spatial representations and perspectives and continued to practice my sketching. For this and other reasons, I decided to study architecture at ETH Zurich after graduating from high school.

I was lucky: Prof. Ernst Studer, who had just begun his professorship, had a design assistant by the name of Kaschka Knapkiewicz. She had just returned from London. As the first assistant to the then-unknown Zaha Hadid, she had designed and drawn the winning entry for the Peak in Hong Kong. Of course, I had never heard of Zaha Hadid or this important competition, but Kaschka kept telling us students about those heroic times. At some point—because I was so curious—

It was as if a flash of lightning had gone off in my head.

Old doors from Jaguars, found in an attic.

she gave me a small publication about this project idea as a present. It was as if a flash of lightning had gone off in my head: an unknown world opened up to me. For hours I studied the masterful, explosive drawings and tried to imagine spaces that could correspond to all those strokes.

I remember another formative experience from my student days. During a lecture at ETH, a famous architect from Basel explained that it was impossible for him to design a house with a slanted roof. This was the time of the internationally celebrated "Swiss boxes." One material, one detail, which could meet all requirements—that was our architectural ideal at the time. The statement of that architect really got to me. As a student and a future architect, I was also concerned with all those non-rectangular spaces under the sloping roofs.

Today, the attic is a dying space. It is located under the sloping roof, and provides useful space for the things we don't need every day, such as our winter clothes, or it serves as storage for all the things that we once loved and therefore don't want to pass on or throw away. Most often, the attic is not a finished, inhabitable space, nor is it insulated. In summer, the space heats up, and in winter it is bitterly cold. Together with unused clothes and shoes, discarded furniture, old files and folders, memorabilia and dusty toys, an attic is characterized by a specific smell that is deeply imprinted in our memory.

As a former member of the historical monument preservation committee in the City of Zurich, I had the opportunity to visit dozens of such attics. In addition to the smell, which was always peculiar, these attics revealed wonderful wooden constructions with corresponding details. The civil engineer Jürg Conzett, also a member of the committee, always enthusiastically explained to us the structural significance of each individual beam. It was during such visits that I learned a lot about tensile and compressive forces, and I would marvel at how skillfully the loads were transferred to the walls and columns below. Despite evidence of a high level of craftsmanship, economic pressures usually meant that the entire potential floor space of a house needed to be used and monetized. Meaning that existing attics are converted into apartments.

The building code sometimes inspires the creation of generous rooftop terraces.

In-between spaces in Le Corbusier's Palace of Justice in Chadigarh are used for storage.

Additionally, our building laws—which always make sure not to disadvantage anything or anyone—allow the design and construction of apartments by setting back the roof in the attic. This ensures that a building with a flat roof is not disadvantaged compared to one with a pitched roof. As roof trusses were mostly used as leftover spaces, they do not count as floor space. Therefore, a second attic floor, which is often possible with a pitched roof, may not be converted to living space.

Today, the attic is a dying space.

Rigorous regulations regarding the maximum permitted size of skylights are also intended to prevent this.

In nineteenth-century stately homes, the servants' rooms were located under the roof. Later, in the modern era, these were made into storage spaces and laundries for the tightly laid-out, functionalist apartments below. The attic also served as a heat and cold buffer for the floor below. Today, we take pleasure in the facades of such buildings. Since these supplementary spaces have modest windows, the building can culminate in a relatively closed facade. Roofs covered with brown tiles remind us of a deeply imprinted archetype of a house.

On the top floor, the legally required setbacks allow for generous rooftop terraces. In addition, the interior rooms, such as bathrooms, can be attractively lit with skylights. Furthermore, attic apartments usually differ from the apartments below, which are always the same. The location under the sky together with a magnificent view has come to be associated with a certain social status. These roof suites are therefore furnished with more expensive materials, and the rent is correspondingly higher. And who doesn't want to live in a privileged position on the top floor of a building!

Ancillary Spaces

1.5.2 The Utility Room

Two plaid shirts that aren't from Hannes B.

For over thirty years, I have exclusively worn plaid shirts. Maybe I like the squares because I am one, but it might also be because I found the ideal place for me: Hannes B.'s store in the Münsterhof in Zurich. Hannes Bühler was a wonderful fashion designer. Over the years, each of us developed a high estimation of the other. I bought all his plaid shirts—every

Maybe because I am a square.

collection—summer and winter. Now I have a genuine collection of these items. Wearing the checkered, patterned clothes became an obsession. I have never thrown away a "Hannes B. shirt" or put one in a donation bin. All the scuffed and worn-out pieces lie freshly washed, ironed, and carefully lined up in various closets in my apartment.

Hannes had once confessed to me that at every textile fair he went to in Italy, he thought of me when choosing his fabrics. He always chose wonderfully patterned checks on sumptuous fabrics to tailor his elegant shirts. I never had to try one on. Twice a year he would call me in. In his store, the entire collection of all the new plaid shirts would be waiting for me. It became a habit on my Saturday walk through the city, after visiting the architecture bookstore, to make a short detour to the Schipfe district to say hello to him.

Homes have a lot to do with habits and with everyday activities. It is part of my morning ritual to iron my shirt after taking a shower. My apartment is designed and planned accordingly: yes, I have a utility room with a shower in it! Only when I put on this freshly washed shirt does my working day begin.

Ironing shirts has become a fixed habit for me, just as morning yoga is for others. During this first activity, which takes place at dawn, I think about what awaits me that day. Now and then, in that moment, I even get an idea for one of our projects.

Early morning thoughts are still pure and untroubled.

94

"Curiosity Killed the Cat"

Curiosity Killed the Cat

When we draft apartment designs, we create scripts in our heads for both extraordinary and ordinary everyday situations. When we revise our designs, we discard most of our ideas: sometimes because they don't work, are too complicated, or because the bathrooms on different floors do not align with each other and the mass does not match the specifications. Designing means discarding. At least that's what we've learned.

Since design takes a lot of practice, I have redesigned my own apartment several times, each time together with my partner. Designing for yourself combines everything that makes our profession so wonderful. As I go through the process, I have an image in my head that corresponds to a life situation I have not yet experienced, and of course the picture I paint completely outstrips my financial means. Step by step, I approach these images, implement them spatially, give them material form. It's a truly beautiful thing. Naturally, I'm always asking myself as I go how I want to take care of my everyday needs: How do I want to cook, how do I want to wake up, where will I hang my pictures, how will I organize and store my books, where should I put my extensive CD collection, what do I want to see when I eat, is the bathroom more than just a functional space, and how and where do I store my plaid shirts? What furniture do I want to surround myself with? What atmosphere do I want to live in, what is it like during the day, on a cool, damp Sunday in November, and what is it like at night? What materials and colors can I use to achieve this mood? How do I want to light the rooms? What kind of lights will I need to do this? All of these questions, along with many others, are important—and can be solved through the design process.

When I come home these days, my cats are waiting for me. Often, they're sitting directly behind the

Each cat takes ownership of the space in their own way.

door. I always imagine them staring at the blue-black door panel for hours on end—but they probably just hear my footsteps and then move into this position, which gives me such a guilty conscience that I feed them immediately. Every now and then, the two siblings squat on the narrow balustrade in the two-story room. Greeting me joyfully with their big eyes.

Cats are fascinating pets. They make the place feel more homely. It is interesting that the addition of these living beings changes the mood of an apartment. Each cat takes ownership of the space in their own way. They have their favorite spots, which can change from day to day. They like to have a clear view of everything, so they look for elevated spots. Which is why they like to squat on the stacks of books in my house. Cats love warmth. They appreciate a stone floor heated by the sun. And, of course, it's so nice when they're waiting for you at home in the evening—even if it is just to get fed.

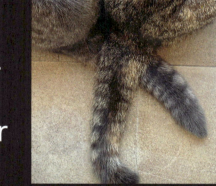

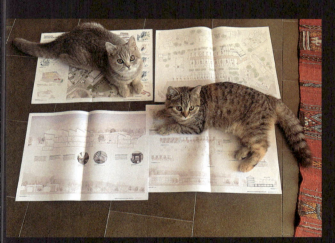

Ancillary Spaces 95

1.5.3 The Hobby Room

"Are you happy?" This question—preferably asked on a rainy, cold, and damp Monday morning in November—is familiar to all our staff. But it is a serious question. The happiness of our staff is just as important to us as our satisfaction with our own lives. We all strive for it. Happiness in life depends on various factors, such as family, friendships, love, career, finances, and housing. These are all aspects we can partly influence ourselves, but which partly depend on our environment and society.

Nowadays, everyone wants to live their dreams. As architects, we have the privilege of our profession also being a vocation. There are few fields of work these days that are as diverse and multi-layered as architecture. Our occupation demands that we be generalists, not specialists. An understanding of the whole is indispensable. Daily learning and professional development are essential. We need architectural fodder! In addition to professional knowledge, literature, music, painting, handicrafts, cooking, traveling, art, sports, or theater help to feed our intellectual hunger—we are always on the hunt for surprising answers to the questions that occupy us.

In this sense, our office is our hobby room. "Everything is interconnected!" This key insight of Alexander von Humboldt shapes our understanding of the construction of housing.

When we were planning the James development →2.2.2 in Zurich, we spent a lot of time looking at possible uses for the ground floor. The mighty footprint of the buildings did not make it any easier. We considered what we ourselves liked, while also considering what was insufficiently represented in Zurich. We developed the idea of building a badminton hall on the first basement level of the "corner building," which would be accessible from the inner courtyard. We contacted the operators of the only badminton facility in Zurich at that time. A preliminary contract was quickly drawn up with the investors. Today, we play badminton at least once a week and whack the shuttlecocks around. We now have a second hobby room just around the corner from our office!

Nowadays, everyone wants to live their dreams.

Our hobby room: the badminton court at the James development, Zurich.

1.5.4 The Workshop

During the second half of the twentieth century, in the newly built single-family houses out in the suburbs on the outskirts of Swiss cities, it was common practice to build a workshop in the half-buried basement, right next to the parking space in the garage. Now it was not the case that all these fathers of middle-class families were suddenly obsessed with some specific hobby or another. It was just that usually, the area of the

People get together to cook, celebrate, converse, share, and mend.

garden-level floor—consisting of the entrance, the kitchen, the dining room, the living room, and a small office—was larger than the basement needed to be, with the laundry, the provisions compartment in the air-raid shelter, and the parking space for the car. So there was room for a workshop or a hobby room to be added.

With the concept of big home improvement stores only beginning to emerge in Switzerland, it was a time when you did certain jobs yourself. This included things like fixing household appliances and patching the inner tubes of bicycle tires. The garden shed, the chicken coop, or the soapbox racer were also planned and built yourself. Most of the time, the workshop was the realm of the men. The roles were clearly assigned. Hammers, saws, drills, files, screwdrivers, Allen keys in various sizes, chisels, spirit levels, pliers, socket wrenches, brushes, putty knives, folding yardsticks, and knives were carefully lined up on the wall, often according to size. A workbench with a vice occupied the center of the room. Despite the best intentions—and partly because of the encroachment of television on daily life—this room began to lead a lonely existence, and so the workshop became the hobby room. Under the strictest guidance and supervision of the father, sons from a certain age would build a Märklin model railway. Or Carrera slot car races were held, in which the idols of the time—Jo Siffert, Clay Regazzoni, Jochen Rindt, and Jacky Stewart—were emulated.

Times have changed. Today, the single-family home has become unaffordable on an average, middle-class income. Furthermore, this form of housing is ecologically questionable. The neighborhood turns out to be monotonous and a tad boring. Shopping options and cultural events are few and far between, the bus stop is too far away, and the public transport timetable, despite steady improvements, still leaves much to be desired.

On the other hand, cities today have become attractive. There are apartments to suit every life situation, the variety of bars and restaurants is overwhelming, the cultural events are diverse, medical care is guaranteed day and night, childcare is constantly being expanded, the education system fulfills every wish, and there are facilities for every sport you can imagine. The public transportation network is so good that every place in the neighborhood, in the city, the region, even in Switzerland can be reached quickly and easily. Communal living is also in vogue. People get together to cook, celebrate, converse, share—and even mend things. Which has led to a renewed need for communally used and operated workshops. There is an increasing demand for high-ceilinged rooms that can be tailored to a range of uses.

Ancillary Spaces

"Sweet Dreams (Are Made of This)"

Eurythmics

Participating in competitions and tenders is essential to our firm. Virtually all of our projects have come from winning these kinds of competitions. We lose a whole lot more than we win. Most of our friends are excellent architects. And then there is a whole new generation on the rise that is looking to develop innovative approaches to pressing issues, such as circular architecture or holistic conceptions of sustainability. We know that it takes more than luck to win a competition. It has made us appropriately humble.

We lose a whole lot more than we win.

Although we have already competed in what feels like 300 competitions, each time is different. We loathe routine. In order to promote the right mindset for competitions, we set up our own competition studio. It is located on the same floor as the main office. It can only be entered via the elevator lobby and two fire doors that are always closed. The studio is located in a bare-boned room, with only a few tables for the computers and for model building, a couple of partitions for pinning up sketches and plans, and a fair amount of creative chaos. This workshop is our space for experimentation. All thoughts are welcome here—even the impossible and the unrealizable. Making Atelier Süd a "lawless" space.

In the studio, we search and struggle for the best solutions. We have learned to take certain risks. "Top or flop" is as much part of our competitive wisdoms as "trial and error" or "kill your darlings." Despite knowing that our office can only survive in the long-term by winning competitions, it's important that this work remains enjoyable. The debilitating pressure to win the next tender has never been helpful.

When we began drawing our competition submissions on the computer, we always used previous work for the basic layout. At the end of one submission process, we suffered a bit of a mishap: we didn't notice that the site plan and the figure ground plan of the previous design were still drawn into the final submission. The project description also referred to the previous competition, which had not yet been decided. When we realized what had happened, we immediately placed the faulty entry in our "broken dreams" category.

So you can imagine our surprise and joy when we found out that we had we won the tender anyway. The project feedback in the jury's report was fantastic. The person who wrote it really had to do some verbal gymnastics: "For all the apparent incomprehensibility of the submission in the site plan, the clever and well-thought-out apartment plans are truly surprising. The facades and their constructive implementation also pleased the jury, even if they have little to do with the site." Rarely have we laughed so hard when reading a jury report!

Ever since then, we have meticulously checked our plans the night before submission. Partly because we have heard similar competition stories from friends who are also architects: once, during the final check, friends of ours realized they had placed their design on the wrong side of the street—i.e. outside of the perimeter of the site.

We loathe routine.

In a stressful all-nighter, they had to amend all the plans. Unfortunately, the building they'd designed only had enough space on the plot in a rotated and mirrored version. Funnily enough, they also won the competition despite this contretemps.

1.5.5 The Basement

It helps if, as an architect, you have a good sense of space. A vivid imagination is also useful. This is something we all had when we were small children. The basement of our parents' house was populated with all kinds of shady characters, nasty good-for-nothings, dreaded bogeymen, disgusting fiends, unpleasant figures, bloodthirsty vampires, slimy critters, dangerous brutes, and other scary monsters. Heavily armed with nothing but a stick, we ventured into the basement—always with the utmost caution, silent, and ready to race back up the stairs in an instant. We groped for the light switch with our fingers, thinking we could still feel the moist breath of one of these creatures—but whenever we turned on the light, the abhorrent beasts had already disappeared!

Doors for cellar monsters.
Sandacker apartment buildings, Zurich.

We quickly learned that these monsters are afraid of the light.

We quickly learned that these monsters are afraid of the light. Which is why, whenever we can, we still try to incorporate daylight into our basement designs. Clever layouts make it possible to channel light under the ground. We want to avoid leftover spaces, instead seeking to give these rooms specific, architectural features. Normally, clients are not interested in these spaces. They just want the legal conditions to be fulfilled. But that's why we view these basement floors as a chance to be creative. Of course, we're aware that you can burn a lot of money down there. That is precisely why we design them extremely carefully and take care not to create any unnecessary spaces. Another exciting question is how these spaces can be used in new ways, without them being included in the floor space ratio and thus competing with rentable spaces.

In our Tiny Homes project, we channel daylight into the basement through the stairwell, which is located directly next to the facade. Meaning this space can suddenly be used as an additional gym, a laundry, a study, or even a guest room.

Over the course of our lives, we accumulate more and more things that we are unwilling to throw away for a variety of reasons. We need storage space for all these things. Thus, a basement compartment is first and foremost a compact storage space which can be filled surprisingly easily—and densely!—over the years. Sometimes moving house is a good thing. But sometimes, clearing out the basement can lead to nasty surprises. We find things that we would have rather not found, things we didn't want to be reminded of. Or we find moving boxes that have been stored untouched in the basement since we last moved in and whose contents we never missed. A sure sign that it's time to get rid of them.

Ancillary Spaces   99

1.5.6 The Weight Room

The weight room is used for individual physical training, especially for building muscle. Only once, during the conversion of a stately villa, have we had the opportunity to plan and implement a gym. Floor-to-ceiling mirrors and a well-kept wooden parquetry floor, together with the permanently mounted wall bars give the place an appearance resembling a gymnasium. Just that the telltale aroma of a well-used gymnasium, familiar to all of us, is fortunately missing.

It's not the individual that matters, but the team. Only together are we strong.

Personal fitness equipment.

Daily workouts are a lonely affair. Discovering a foreign city on an early-morning jog, on the other hand, is a genuine treat. We are also enthusiastic tennis and badminton players. Speed, agility, technique, endurance, and concentration are all crucial for winning points, along with strength and general fitness. The social aspect is another benefit. Which is why we prefer team sports. It's not the individual that matters, but the team. Only together are we strong. But for that, you need social skills. After all, "teamwork makes the dream work!"

This is one of the reasons why we prefer to design communal spaces, laundromats, coworking spaces, or entrance halls for our housing developments that can also serve as meeting places. We are fascinated by how communities are created. We want buildings that don't just offer individual residences but also spaces for encounters. We want the residents to know each other. We fear nothing more than the anonymity of monotonous housing developments. That is why the relation to the street, the entrance areas, stairwells with daylight, and the immediate surroundings—in short, all the communal areas—are particularly important to us. They determine our designs. Our ideal is the urban village.

In our fathers' houses, the weight room lives a rather underwhelming existence. Perhaps because the range of equipment at the local gym is more varied, broader, and sophisticated. In addition, at the gym, you can train together with like-minded people. This brings us back to the idea of community and to our personal conceptions of how to determine the hierarchy of the rooms in our home.

1.5.7 The Laundry Room

Laundry without a weekly schedule. James development, Zurich.

On our travels, every now and then we come across old washhouses. They were always places of cooperation and communication. This is where you could catch up on the latest neighborhood gossip—but they were also sites of social control. Thankfully, this is a thing of the past—as is the strenuous physical labor.

These covered and open-air washhouses undoubtedly awaken a longing for a bygone time in us. We wish that the laundry room could also be a place for casual encounters today without becoming a scene for neighborly quarrels because of the strict rules that have to be observed. In our busy daily lives, there is usually no space or time for a good old chat. At the same time, loneliness is on the rise. Among other things, belonging somewhere means living in a building with neighbors you know. Having a laugh together, talking about your worries or borrowing tools, helping each other, perhaps taking turns to look after each other's children, cooking together, or seeing each other while you do the laundry—all of these things enrich our lives.

When we design larger housing developments, we want to facilitate these kinds of social meeting places. The laundry room, as an artificially lit, obligatory room somewhere on the third basement level is our nightmare. We envision flexible spaces in central locations, facilitating a wide variety of communal spaces that can be used as needed. Maybe you meet your neighbors there, but maybe you don't.

The laundry room can be additionally enhanced with home workspaces, allowing you to use the coworking space next to the laundry while you wait for your washing to finish. Positioning the laundry by the main entrance, with access to the garden, is just as suitable as up in the attic. Combined with a community terrace, maybe even an outdoor kitchen, this becomes a pleasant space. We know that such spaces don't bring any extra return on investment, but it does promote a sense of community.

At the James development, the laundry is located near the reception area. The space is also accessible from the car-free common outdoor area. It is possible to install a coffee vending machine. Each apartment is assigned a locker for the washing powder. A washing

Maybe you meet your neighbors there, but maybe you don't.

machine and tumble dryer can be rented as a unit. In the center of the colorfully painted room there is a chrome steel work surface—ideal for folding your laundry on the spot rather than having to do it in your apartment.

The room was tastefully furnished. So carefully, in fact, that the furniture was surreptitiously removed shortly after the apartments were occupied! In retrospect, perhaps the idea that the single residents of the high-rise would meet in the laundry room was too optimistic. Nevertheless, it certainly sees plenty of use. The investor had to purchase 275 fewer washing machines and tumble dryers. We were able to use these savings for more robust kitchen appliances and the complex color scheme. So everyone wins.

"What a Wonderful World"

Louis Armstrong

For us, spaces and colors belong together. However, especially when it comes to building rental apartment blocks, it is understandably best to offer rooms that are as neutral as possible. Which means missing out on a lot of opportunities for creativity. But even then, an apartment does not only consist of white walls and ceilings: flooring, kitchen worktops, tiles, door frames, baseboards, windows, electrical switches, fittings, handles, curtain rails, and bathroom fixtures all differ in color and material composition. The task is to combine them harmoniously. This is where working with colors begins for us.

I like to visit museums. I am interested not only in the exhibitions showcasing the work of an individual artist, but also in the collections, especially Modernist paintings. I stand in front of the paintings and take them in. Why do some paintings affect me more than others? Is it the subject matter or the use of color? Over the years, I have trained myself to have a good memory. When we discuss color concepts in the office, I am good at remembering images, their colorfulness, color combinations, and the different hues. "Look at the paintings by Blinky Palermo at the Dia Art Foundation in Beacon, New York State!"—I advise a co-worker, and they immediately have an idea of what I'm talking about.

We are not interested in the individual hue but in the atmosphere that can be created with this simple and inexpensive medium and its interaction with the other building materials. Thanks to colors, elements can be combined or spatial relationships can be built within an apartment. A vibrant paint job changes the room. A light-blue ceiling makes it wider and larger. Painting a wall brown moves it closer. Furthermore, the

The secret life of colors.

intensity of color can clarify spatial hierarchies: intense hues, for example, are suitable for public spaces; pastel colors for adjoining rooms such as bathrooms; and delicate, only lightly colored shades for the common rooms in an apartment.

Bruno Taut chose his colors according to daylight. He thus painted the east facades with "cool" shades that correspond to the pale morning light, and the west facades with "warm," reddish colors reminiscent of the rays of the evening sun.

An important reference for us is the Thorvaldsens Museum (1838–1848) in Copenhagen by Michael Gottlieb Bindesbøll. Here, an enfilade connects all the exhibition spaces. Each room has its own specific color scheme. It is interesting that the coloring doesn't compete with the sculptures on display, but that both the artworks and the colored rooms gain from the pairing.

Is it the subject matter or the use of color?

Whenever I'm in Copenhagen, I visit the museum. I wander from room to room, each time trying to fathom the effect and mood of the complex color combinations.

During our travels, we've noticed that the color schemes of cities and villages bears a relation to their geographical location. Pastel shades dominate the Nordic cities. It has to do with the flat angle of the sun. In the tropics, on the other hand, where the light is harsh and unmerciful, strong and bold colors predominate.

1.5.8 The Pool

One component of happiness comes from living in appealing surroundings. In addition to versatile floor plans, this requires spaces and places for the community. It is very important to us that residents identify with their homes. When planning the James development, for example, we were able to convince the client to leave an old factory building standing. Today, it serves as a very busy climbing gym with a restaurant that can be used in a variety of ways.

We were confronted with similar issues when planning a building with apartments and commercial units opposite the Rietpark in Schlieren → 2.3.19, a Zurich suburb. Using a considered design plan, we were able to convert a former industrial area into a residential district. An attractive park runs the entire length of the district, providing a unifying feature. In order to guarantee the desired urban planning and architectural qualities, a competition was held for each building site. But what could make an urban building block of this kind socially unique?

We were already a long way through the design and execution planning of our building when we decided, together with the client, to build a swimming pool accessible to all residents on the roof of the central, connecting section, which divides the building into two differently designed and used inner courtyards.

We tackled this additional task with a great deal of joy and creative energy. The additional weight created by the mass of water was particularly challenging, especially due to the underground garage, which had already been fully planned. In the spacious entrance hall, unusually positioned support beams carry the additional load. The pool is accessible via two staircases, and in contrast to the colorful vertical connections, it is kept neutral in color.

The blue pool, the brown boards, the white, elevated fence, and the sky form the backdrop for this summery aquatic atmosphere. The social space, which has been very well-received by the tenants, receives a splash of color from the individual towels and clothes. Swimming early in the morning before work or having an aperitif together with the new neighbors on a balmy summer evening while letting your legs dangle in the water—what more could you want? Living in an apartment building can be more than just renting a roof over your head!

The shared swimming pool brings people together!

Swimming as a treat for all residents. Am Rietpark apartment building, Schlieren.

Ancillary Spaces

1.5.9 The Wild-Card Room

We all know those situations you just can't plan for: your husband snores, your daughter is going through puberty, your son's first girlfriend moves into the already reduced bedroom area, your partner wants to write and offer yoga classes. The solution to all these potential conflicts? The wild-card room (Jokerzimmer)! This term has only emerged over the past few years in Switzerland. But the problems it solves have been around forever. However, spaces that could be rented when the need arose were called studios or Schaltzimmer (extra rooms that can be incorporated into more than one apartment), or you just had to relocate to a small commercial space with a bathroom.

In larger building complexes, these kinds of rooms, which are as flexible as possible in their usage, are undoubtedly useful. They are ideal for half-grown-up children or a partner who wants more freedom and independence in certain life situations. The rooms can also be used for hobbies and, after the arrival of a little one, for grandparents who move in for a while to help the new parents.

As the name suggests, the wild-card room is a jack-of-all-trades—spatially though, it's uninteresting, because it is always just a square box. Its versatility is also its weakness: since it has no specified use, these rooms often lack any character of their own. It is up to us architects to find a spatial response to the emptiness of such rooms.

In the Paul Clairmont apartment building → 2.2.1 in Zurich, a *rue intérieure* suffused with natural light provides access to all the stairwells, a number of small apartments, and eight wild-card rooms. To ensure that the total permitted building height is not exceeded, the ground floor is partially buried—what's known as a "Zurich basement," which were still allowed at the time of the build. This means that these areas don't count toward the floor space ratio. After intensive discussions, we were able to convince the developer to offer studios and commercial spaces here—which today would be called wild-card rooms. Since we chose to create a closed base for this facade for architectural reasons, the rooms, which are located in the protruding sections of the building, are lit from the sides. This also provides the necessary escape routes for the rooms, as well as smoke extraction for the parking garage. Le Corbusier called this kind of problem-solving a *solution élégante*, in which several problems can be solved simultaneously through one architectural feature.

Architecture and zeitgeist belong together. That is why architecture always reacts to changes in society. New forms of cohabitation are currently being explored, such as Zurich's Hallenwohnen (loft-style living inspired by the city's squats), large shared apartments and cluster living, temporary living spaces, housing for the third phase of life, multi-generation households, car-free living, student living setups, self-designed living, or tiny houses. All of these ideas are united in their intention to build affordably and sustainably. A stripped-back aesthetic underscores the robustness of the spaces. The goal is for the occupants to make the spaces suit their needs. Individual living spaces are intentionally scaled down. The focus is on community and sharing.

This room is a jack-of-all-trades.

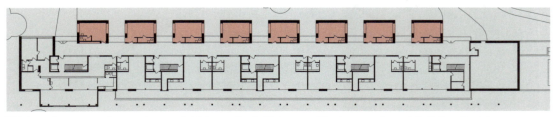

Wild-card rooms enhance the *rue intérieure*. Paul-Clairmont-Strasse apartment building, Zurich.

1.5.10 The Common Room

Cities are synonymous with diverse forms of cohabitation. So when we hear the word common room, we first think of the city. The idea of a meeting place in a larger residential complex is more of a secondary association.

In any design, fitting into the location is central. If the layout of the surrounding streets and infrastructure is not resolved, we cannot design apartment floor plans. Lines of sight, as well as the arrangement of public spaces and their functional organization on the ground floor are crucial for working out the building's relationship to the neighborhood and the outdoor spaces. Our residential buildings are supposed to fuse with the neighborhood. The existing and the new belong together. We strongly believe that a certain harmony is important here. Every apartment is part of the city, and the city is part of every apartment.

The arrangement of public spaces on the ground floor is crucial.

Housing cooperatives usually offer their residents a common room. With their kitchens and bathrooms, these rooms make an ideal place to celebrate a special occasion or hold meetings. Unfortunately, such rooms are mostly made using neutral materials, and equipped with standard, inexpensive, stackable furniture and kept all white—reminiscent of function rooms in public institutions. They lack an inviting atmosphere with any character of their own. This is not unlike the children's playgrounds that are built to fulfill legal requirements for new housing developments. Of course, it makes sense to provide areas for children to play undisturbed. But when you walk through a newly built residential development and see the lack of love with which

The city we want. Local bar as meeting place at Brüderhofweg development, Zurich.

Ancillary Spaces 105

Neighborhood store and common room.
Reitmen development, Schlieren.

Neighborhood bakery. Fellenbergstrasse development, Zurich.

these facilities are planned and kitted out, it breaks your heart.

When I was responsible for urban planning at the City of Zurich's City Planning Office, I quickly learned that money always finds a way: with private investors, it was always clear from the start that they wanted to plan and build something special. Never did a developer come to me and say: "now let's build something really bad for once!" This means that the primary task of urban planning is to provide for the community and to create appropriate places and spaces. In this sense, public space became my main field of work.

My goal has always been to create a revitalized, safe, and livable city for all residents. To achieve this, thinking of the public uses of the ground floor of a building is crucial. At the same time, things should be as

"Now let's build something really bad for once!"

flexible as possible. Some spaces need to be left open, because not everything can be planned, or because some of the ideas for a design can't be (fully) implemented. There needs to be room for something new to emerge, something unknown. There is no finished or final urban plan. With these ideas in mind, we were able to enter into negotiations when it came to defining competition programs or the city's position in private tenders.

Of course, we always supported the planning of common spaces. High-ceilinged spaces on the ground floor help to create these kinds of places, which are so important to the community. When they combine well with the outdoor space, it's not just the tenants who benefit, but the entire community. A city dominated by community is the only sustainable city.

1.5.11 The Wine Cellar

Our life as architects is easier and more pleasant if we cultivate a positive attitude to our working routine. It helps to approach the job with optimism and joy. We mostly see the glass as half full. We take the same view of the wine cellar—if it's well stocked, we're content. This is the only room in our building that has a certain hidden addictive potential. It is without architectural or spatial ambitions. Usually located below ground level, its most important characteristic is a consistently cool temperature. Purely a space for storage, it needs no windows. Its contents are in any case more important than its form! Just as furniture and decor breathe the soul into an apartment, so a cellar needs its bottles. One client even told us that the wine was the nucleus of his home.

Like the preparation of spaghetti, wine has certain similarities with the housing construction. In both cases we're fascinated by diversity. It is dull to always drink the same wine. The same goes for designing floor plans. Forever drafting the same apartment might be economical and guarantee that projects will come in under budget, but such monotony would certainly be tiresome.

If every bottle of wine is unique, then every apartment is also different from all the others. Thanks to an initial situation that always varies, every single apartment is always a unique case. Familiar old questions require answers that are innovative, customized, and specific. There are always differences—whether they concern the placement within the plan of a floor or on different floors. Perhaps it is just the view that differs, but every small detail can provide an opportunity. It is in fact not the case that we're able find these slight but subtle differences more quickly or easily after a glass or a bottle of wine. On the contrary, one can never be sure that something decisive in the design of an apartment building hasn't been forgotten or overlooked. Although building—or rather, the process of building, in which a building rises up, step by step, out of the earth—is an unbelievably lovely moment, I often hesistate to visit a construction site. Because there are always two ways to implement any detail: it can be done correctly or incorrectly. My years of experience have taught me that, unfortunately, the latter is often the case. Even when everything has been drawn and dimensioned in plan and section and provided with the corresponding elevation labels, the plan is rarely executed in the way we've stipulated.

A visit to the construction site also provides unforgiving proof of whether or not we designers have thought every room and detail through to its ultimate conclusions. That's another reason why I avoid our construction sites as best I can. If my presence is requested anyway, this mostly means that there's a problem. Luckily there are usually multiple options for solving it—which is another reason I'm always reassured by the fact that the wine cellar is well stocked and not half empty.

This is the only room in our building that has a certain hidden addictive potential.

Ancillary Spaces 107

"Everything is interconnected!"

Alexander von Humboldt

When we finish our residential buildings and hand over the apartments to our clients, they are clean, empty, and usually still soulless. It is always a special feeling to walk through the rooms we have designed. All the considerations and decisions that were made come back to us and can now be reviewed on a 1:1 scale. We pause. We enjoy this moment, having worked toward it for so long. Unfortunately, we also notice our mistakes, inaccurate executions, or arbitrary changes ordered by god-knows-who. For example, the sockets placed annoyingly in the middle of the wall, making it impossible to position furniture and hang lamps or photos.

Each completion also means saying goodbye to a design and its material implementation. In most cases, it takes years to get from the initial idea to the construction of an apartment building, and finally to the point where the residents can move in. At that moment, a very personal relationship and bond ends. Besides all the joy about what has been achieved, there is melancholy: the last stroll through an apartment ready for occupancy leaves us with the pain of parting, because we know that we will probably never visit it again.

Now the apartments belong to the new owners or tenants. It is only now that we find out whether our apartments can be used and furnished well, and whether—the best-case scenario—they will become a home that will be loved over time. We architects should become imperceptible after the handover. The architecture should recede into the background, becoming a shell for the life and memories of the new occupants.

I am fascinated by the furnished rooms of an apartment. I learned from my teacher at ETH Zurich, Arthur Rüegg, to always pay attention to the background in photographs of apartments: the arrangement of the furniture, the fixtures and fittings, the pictures on the wall, the carpets, the books on the shelves, the found or collected items positioned around the room—all these things reveal entire lives. The interests and passions, the thoughts or attitudes of the occupants become visible, testifying to their way of living. Pictures of this kind fascinate or leave us perplexed, because we might have our own ideas about this person and about what their home might look like. At the same time, such documents show the real lives of these people.

I like to listen to the songs of Tom Petty. Coincidentally, I once saw an interview with him recorded in his house. However, in my opinion, his home furnishings do not match his music: his songs rock, their lyrics are convincing. But his house reflects familiar, stuffy ideas. It is soulless and impersonally furnished. I was also disillusioned and perplexed by my visit to Elvis Presley's Graceland in Memphis, Tennessee. Except for really weird wallpaper in one of his bathrooms, I couldn't find a single item that I would have liked to put in my apartment.

The architecture should recede into the background, becoming a vessel for the life of its occupants.

TV and living room at Graceland, Elvis Presley's home, Memphis, Tennessee.

Since our firm works almost exclusively on apartment buildings, it stands to reason that we should be intensely concerned with our own living environments. All four partners are fortunate enough to own their own homes and to be able to redesign, remodel, and furnish them according to their own ideas.

In my apartment, for example, I have installed about 160 meters of storage shelving and bookshelves. These are where my memories are collected. Some of the most fruitful trips I've made have been to Mexico. On my first road trip in the late 1980s, I purchased a beautifully painted armadillo carved from wood. I showed it to my mother. From then on, she's gifted me an armadillo for every birthday and every other chance she gets, laying the foundations of my armadillo collection, which consists mainly of old folklorically painted critters from the area around the Mexican city of Oaxaca. The uniqueness of this curious hobby leads to me receiving gifts of anything armadillo-related from friends and acquaintances. As part of my collection, I own cookbooks with recipes on how to prepare such an animal, old prints, two taxidermied specimens—which I named loosely after the most famous Mexican architects "Barragan" and "Legorreta"—artifacts made of wood, stone, papier-mâché, and metal. I also own painted armacillos by artists such as Regina Götz (Vienna) and Zilla Leutenegger (Zurich). I am also a patron of the only animal rehabilitation clinic in the world for armadillos who have been injured by cars in Mendoza, Argentina.

Sometimes, when I listen to loud music in my apartment, I have the feeling that these silent animals start dancing on the shelves. In reality, these "armadillos" are just souvenirs from my travels and gifts from my friends. What is a farewell for one person, is for another a new start in a new apartment.

1.6.1 The Cabinet of Curiosities

All the rooms and elements described in this volume form part of our home. Large and small rooms alternate, narrow passageways with suspended ceilings follow airy, high-ceilinged rooms. Niches and bookshelves provide storage areas for found objects and mementos. Staircases connect the floors and create diagonal views. A gallery provides a line of sight into the distance. The conservatory, lush with cacti and citrus trees, connects two rooms. A long dining table encourages people to sit down and eat a meal together and have a discussion. A sofa awaits the residents

Here they sit and talk about the joys and sorrows of everyday life.

in front of the fireplace. Here they sit and talk about the joys and sorrows of everyday life. The well-organized kitchen makes the prospect of preparing meals alluring. Collected devotional objects adorn the wall of the pantry. Pots, pans, plates, glasses, and pieces of ceramics are piled up on open shelves. Cookbooks testify to the interest in good food.

The guest bathroom has a golden ceiling. Pictures decorate the walls of the powder room. A corner mirror enlarges the space. The bathtub with a bench is ready for a quiet Sunday morning. A favorite chair, placed at an appropriate spot, tells its story. Bestsellers, great big tomes, reference books, magazines, and other publications are piled up everywhere, waiting to be read and studied. Comfortable armchairs form a circle and welcome visitors, just as a small guest room awaits family members and friends from abroad.

In the bright utility room, the ironing board is on hand. Shelves bulging with books, old records, and CDs, together with the two-tone painted baseboards, connect the rooms of the apartment. Oil paintings, prints, drawings, and photographs from a variety of eras, by artists from around the world, decorate the walls and tell of the interests and desires of the residents. Indirect light gently illuminates the space at night, supported by carefully chosen lights.

The intimate and cozy bedroom finds its spatial conclusion in the dressing room. Exquisite curtain fabrics filter the daylight. Freshly framed art awaits its ideal place on one of the walls, which are arranged by theme. A staircase leads to the rooftop terrace. An outdoor kitchen means you can dine there under a pergola covered with foliage. Curtains help to create an open-air room for the summer, while at the same time protecting the shower from prying eyes.

Each door, cabinet opening, and drawer has its own different and carefully selected knob or handle. The carpentry is painted with subtle, lime-green oil-based paint, the bluish ceilings call to mind the sky and make the rooms seem more spacious. Carpets mark out special places. Custom-fired tiles with drawings by Ivaro Siza decorate the bathroom and shower. Brightly painted mythical creatures, carved from wood, peek out from niches and shelves. Different shells and stones tell stories of hikes along seashores, through unknown forests, and up massive mountains.

All this represents a lived culture of home decor. The four walls do not belong to the architects who designed the house, but to the people who live in it. They tell their story and house their memory. Like the rings of a tree trunk, the rooms are filled with new memories every day. The home bears witness to the richness of life, and means living and belonging in one. We see every home as a cabinet of curiosities. Only when someone has taken ownership of it, when it is inhabited in the truest sense of the word, have we done our job well.

An apartment is always also a collection of rare items and curiosities.
Chamber of Art and Curiosities, Frans Francken II, around 1620/1625.

"Everything is Interconnected!" 111

Food for Architects
Volume 1: In Our Father's Houses Are Many Rooms

Published by: Steib Gmür Geschwentner Kyburz Partner
Texts: Patrick Gmür
Editor: Christoph Wieser
Translation: Ryan Eyers, Hanna Grześkiewicz, Marc Hiatt, Rob Madole, and Gráinne Toomey for Gegensatz Translation Collective
Proofreading: Marc Hiatt and Joel Scott for Gegensatz Translation Collective
Design and layout: Sibylle Kanalz, Jürg Schönenberger, Nora Spaniol
Image processing: Karin Prasser
Photo credits: Steib Gmür Geschwentner Kyburz, except for those by Georg Aerni p. 17, 19 b.; Nicole Deiss p. 64 b.; various others, including Roger Frei p. 33; Roger Frei p. 11, 19 t., 20, 23 b., 25, 27 b., 36, 35, 37, 39 t., 41, 57 t., 61 b., 65, 74, 77, 96; Zeljko Gataric p. 35, 51 b., 102, 103; Annette Helle p. 100; KHM-Museumsverband, Wien p. 111; Kunst Guido Nussbaum p. 52, 114; Kunst Hans Schärer p. 119; Kunst Peter Roesch p. 68, 115; Kunst Pierre Haubensack p. 118; Kunst Sabina Gmür p. 116, 117; Menga von Sprecher p. 38, 39 b., 49 r., 51 m., 67, 93; Rita Palanikumar p. 54, 98; Saskija Rosset p. 105; Beat Schweizer p. 101; Christoph Wieser p. 72; Seraina Wirz p. 106 t.
Printing and binding: DZA Druckerei zu Altenburg GmbH, Thuringia

© 2023 Steib Gmür Geschwentner Kyburz Partner and Park Books AG, Zurich
© for the texts: the authors

Park Books
Niederdorfstrasse 54
8001 Zurich
Switzerland
www.park-books.com

Park Books has received support from the Federal Office of Culture with a general subsidy for the years 2021–2024.

All rights reserved; no part of this publication may be reproduced, stored in a retrieval system or transmitted in any form or by any means, electronic, mechanical, photocopying, recording, or otherwise, without the prior written consent of the publisher.

ISBN 978-3-03860-360-3

This book is volume 1 of Food for Architects, a set of five volumes in a slipcase which are not available separately.

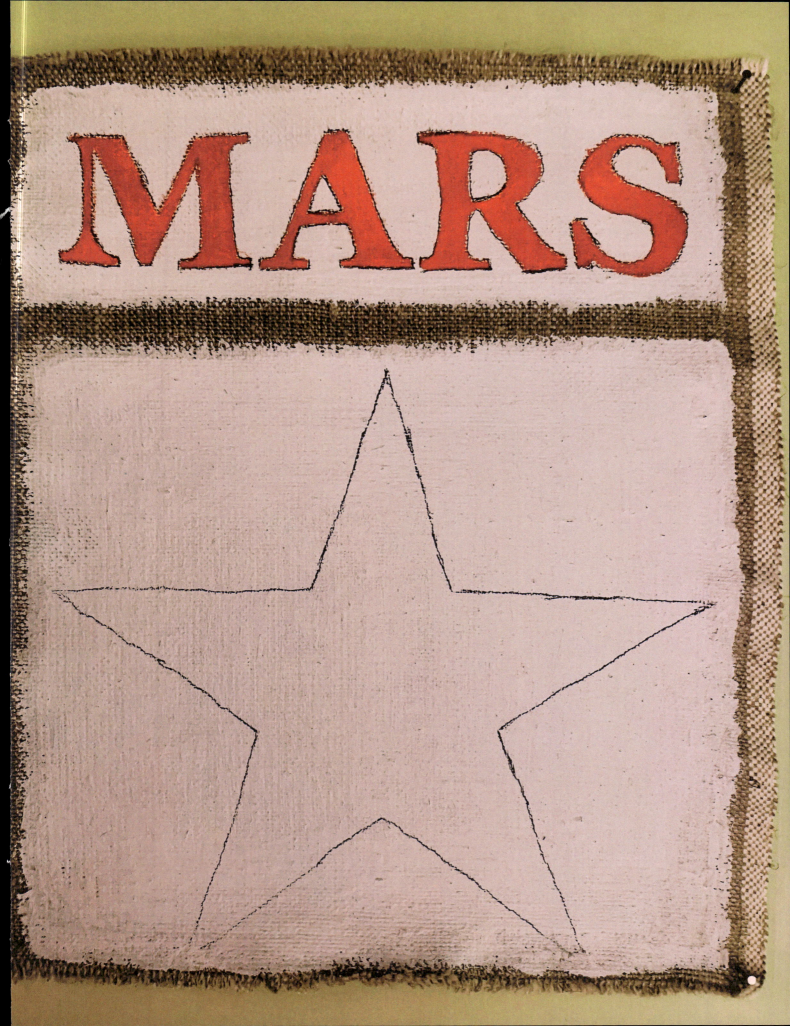

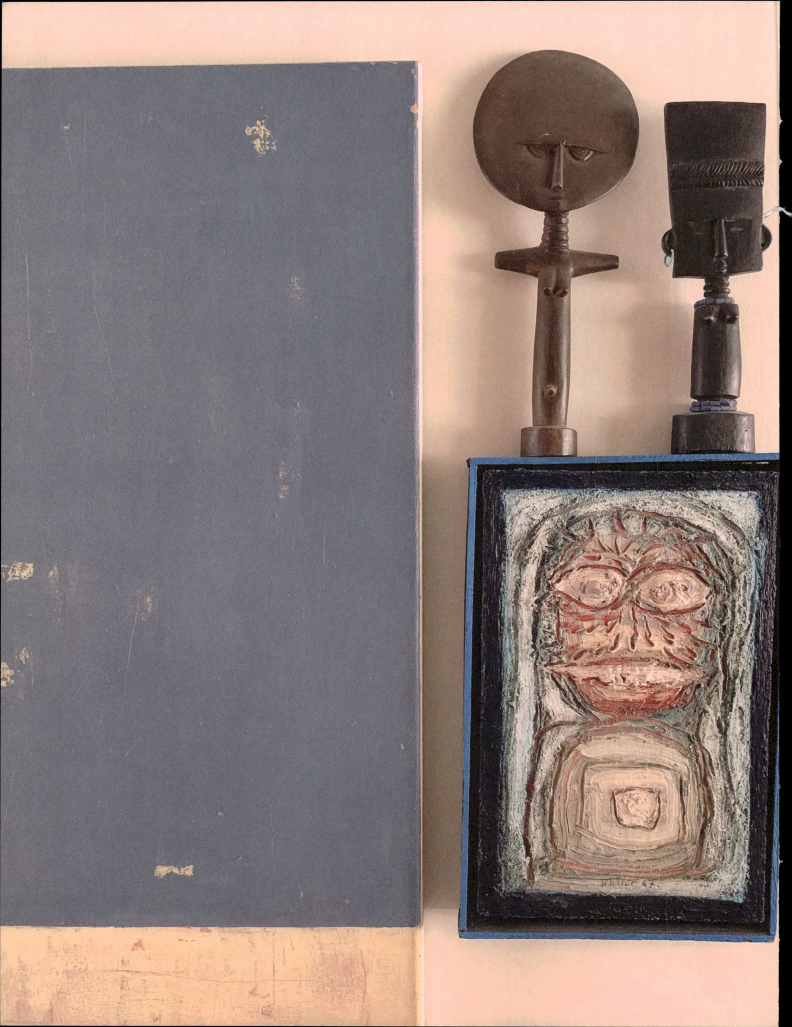

Not One Office, but Several

How should one go about writing the story of an architectural firm that doesn't match the traditional sense of the term, but which has always consisted of various fluctuating constellations, of individual firms and different modes of collaboration? Let's give it a shot: the Steib Gmür Geschwentner Kyburz Architekten AG (SGGK), founded in Zurich in 2020, is like a large coat. That is to say that it functions as an umbrella which organizes the professional activities of the four friends Jakob Steib, Patrick Gmür, Michael Geschwentner, and Matthias Kyburz to facilitate their collaboration and maximize the possible synergies without encroaching upon each individual partner's freedom. This format allows them to work in different combinations on projects of varying magnitude. The common denominator is residential construction in all its facets: from compact, affordable rental housing to sprawling, high-end living, from individual buildings to residential complexes, from urban houses to buildings in rural environments.

First Steps
Jakob Steib founded an architectural firm of his own in 1987, which still operates parallel to his other activities. At that time, Steib was also an assistant to Arthur Rüegg, the well-known professor, Le Corbusier specialist, and Chair of Architecture and Construction at ETH Zurich. Patrick Gmür was also involved in the teaching at ETH, but the two young architects had already met each other earlier—more on that later. Steib's first landmark construction, the Weizacker residential building, was undertaken as a collaboration with his parents, Wilfrid and Katharina Steib from Basel.

Since 1997, Jakob Steib has been teaching at the Zurich University of Applied Sciences (ZHAW) in Winterthur. While working there, he became acquainted with Matthias Kyburz, a student he would come to hold in high regard. Steib offered him an internship position. Further assignments followed during the semester breaks. The chemistry was right, so Kyburz became a permanent member of staff after finishing his diploma in 2005, and in 2013 became a member of the management team at Jakob Steib Architekten (JSA).

We are organized to facilitate collaboration and maximize the possible synergies without encroaching upon each individual partner's freedom.

```
1987   |   |   1990   |   |   |   |   1995   |   |   |   |   2000   |   |   |   |   2
```

Jakob Steib Architekten   MK internship   MK permanent position

Gmür & Steib
Architekten

Gmür Lüscher Gmür Architekten   RL leaves
                        MG internship   MG permanent position
                                                           Patrick Gmür Architekten

MK: Matthias Kyburz
MG: Michael Geschwentner
PG: Patrick Gmür
RL: Regula Lüscher
◆ milestones

| | | | 2010 | | | | 2015 | | | | | 2020 | | | 2023 |

MK managing director

PG leaves

Steib & Geschwentner Architekten

MK managing director

Steib Gmür Geschwentner Kyburz (SGGK)

PG leaves

G partner

Gmür & Geschwentner Architekten

PG joins

Not One Office, but Several

Sometimes, surprising proposals like this result merely from luck and coincidence. What's important is remaining open, so you can recognize an unlikely solution.

Meanwhile, in 1989, shortly after graduating from ETH Zurich, Patrick Gmür had also embarked on the path of self-employment, in his case with Regula Lüscher Gmür, his wife at the time. They started with a small commission, but it soon fizzled out and remained incomplete. Regula Lüscher Gmür had completed an internship at the W + K Steib office during her studies, which is where Patrick Gmür and Jakob Steib first met. But the two of them didn't start collaborating until end of the 1990s, first sporadically, then on a more regular basis.

The Gmür Lüscher Gmür (GLG) architectural firm took part in numerous competitions. As an up-and-coming architectural firm, they also quickly began receiving invitations to various competitive design processes. In addition to residential buildings, they designed schools and nursing homes. Through their acquaintance with Karl Josef Schattner, then a visiting

Urban Planning, and Michael Geschwentner took the reins and carried the business forward under the new moniker Gmür & Geschwentner Architekten (GGA).

Joint Experiments

In an urban planning competition for the Talwiesen neighborhood in Zurich, which was announced in 1998, three firms were shortlisted, including those of Jakob Steib and Patrick Gmür. The two agreed that if one of them were to win, they would still involve the other. Unfortunately, this never came to fruition, since the third competitor won the bid for the project.

But this never came to fruition, since the third competitor won the bid for the project.

professor at ETH Zurich, they stumbled upon a competition in Pleinfeld, Bavaria, to design a family recreation center. The study commission was carried out in collaboration with Beat Waeber, now Waeber Dickenmann Architekten. Michael Geschwentner was also involved as an intern. He met Patrick Gmür in his second year of studies while Gmür was teaching under Arthur Rüegg. Gmür was also Rüegg's research assistant. In 1998, Geschwentner was hired at the Gmür Lüscher Gmür architectural firm.

That same year, Regula Lüscher took a job at Zurich's Office for Urban Planning, so the company was renamed Patrick Gmür Architekten (PGA). Like Matthias Kyburz, Michael Geschwentner had already become a partner several years earlier, after having long been a member of staff. He held this position at PGA from 2006 to 2009. The office structure would soon undergo another change: Patrick Gmür was appointed director of the Office for

Another opportunity for collaboration arose soon after in the form of a competition for an office building in Zurich West. Additional joint experiments followed. After winning second place a few times, they won two bids in 2000: one for a school building in Hittnau and one for the Paul-Clairmont-Strasse residential building in Zurich. This building, with its characteristic two-story, staggered balconies, made a splash and became an early milestone for the two architects.

But why develop joint projects when each of the offices were flourishing on their own? The initially informal collaboration, which became more official in 2002 under the name Gmür & Steib Architekten (GSA), gave both firms a lot of room to maneuver. They used this leeway to pursue promising design concepts, sometimes taken to the extreme, and experiment with plans, approaches to development, urban design models, and many other aspects.

Not One Office, but Several   9

They formed an amoebic vessel, an audacious architectural enterprise: the hedge fund as a business model, so to speak. In the end, it all panned out. Failures encouraged them to come up with new designs. They developed joint projects in shared spaces to streamline the planning processes: for example, the Paul-Clairmont-Strasse residential building was planned on the top floor of a property that hosted Patrick Gmür's office, and was not far from Jakob Steib's office. Michael Geschwentner and Matthias Kyburz first met at this location when one borrowed an NCS color fan and apparently never returned it. After completing the James development, Patrick Gmür, Michael Geschwentner, and the staff of Gmür & Steib Architekten (GSA) moved into the spacious premises on Flüelastrasse, home to the firm to this day. Jakob Steib remained at Wettingerwies with his own office, Matthias Kyburz and other members of staff.

New Roles, New Organization
After becoming director at the Office for Urban Planning, Patrick Gmür had to renounce all his involvements at the firm at the end of 2009. However, the successor company retained his name due to the ongoing projects his firm undertook. It was called Gmür & Geschwentner Architekten (GGA), reflecting Michael Geschwentner's new role. At the same time, Patrick Gmür also left the joint venture with Jakob Steib, so the name became Steib & Geschwentner Architekten (SGA). From 2009 onwards, Michael Geschwentner led one firm together with Jakob Steib and was de facto the sole responsible partner in the other. Matthias Kyburz took on increased responsibility as well. He continued to work at Jakob Steib Architekten (JSA), but was also involved in GGA and SGA projects, which motivated him to relocate to Flüelastrasse.

The final stage of the James development was completed in 2009, and more large-scale projects followed in its wake. More and more staff were hired to handle the mounting workload. The increasing demands placed on the firm, many of which pertained to the organization of planning, execution, and competitions, occasionally unnerved the now approximately sixty employees. Another challenge was explaining to the wider world why there were two companies (GGA and SGA) when both are located on Flüelastrasse and their architectural style seemed virtually indiscernible. How does

Jakob Steib's office fit into this matrix? Which partner is responsible for which employees? The complexity of the interlocking office structures came to a head around 2015.

Four Friends, Common Interests
In October 2016, after seven years as director of the Office for Urban Planning, Patrick Gmür returned to life as an independent architect. He returned to Flüelastrasse as a partner and co-owner of Gmür & Geschwentner Architects + Urban Planners (GGAS). This change of legal framework was accompanied by a clarification when it came to matters of substance. The new beginning provided the four friends—Matthias Kyburz's leading role as a member of the management of Steib & Geschwentner Architects (SGA) had been explicit since 2015—with an opportunity to reformulate their individual and shared goals. A commission for Gmür & Steib Architects (GSA) which had been dormant since 2008 was also relaunched, breathing new life into the firm. While they continued to be ambitious, they were more circumspect regarding their participation in competitions or similar procedures, the workforce was reduced, and the offices were pared down. These efforts led to the founding of Steib Gmür Geschwentner Kyburz Architects (SGGK) in 2020. GGA and SGA will continue to operate in the background until all liabilities for defects have expired. Jakob Steib's firm also still operates.

from a distance, and a shared, solidified position emerges, providing the basis for subsequent collaboration. Having this constant "moose test" drives the projects forward by improving them, which also makes it easier for staff members to identify with them. Everyone works to strengthen the collective. But each of the four partners remains true to themselves, since the workplace ethos encourages this, and the mutual trust is so great that diverging perspectives serve as an impetus for further development. That might just be the secret of their collaboration.

This volume is divided into five chapters, each of which traces the development of various working groups and office structures and brings together the most important buildings and projects.

Christoph Wieser

The four architects are equal partners.

The four architects are now equal partners. The perks of this arrangement become apparent in the weekly meetings, in which designers present ongoing projects and discuss them with the company owners: everyone can contribute their individual strengths, the partners who are not directly involved in a particular project can provide critical feedback on the designs

Contents

2.1   How It All Began (1990–1999) p.14
2.2   Early Milestones (2000–2008) p.24
2.3   Multi-Track Operations (2009–2015) p.56
2.4   Reaching New Heights (2016–2019) p.102
2.5   United Forces (2020–2023) p.130

2.1 How It All Began

In 1987, Jakob Steib founded his own architecture firm in Zurich, becoming the first of the four longtime friends to do so. The firm, Jakob Steib Architekten (JSA), still exists today. Two years later, Patrick Gmür also started his own business in Zurich with Regula Lüscher Gmür, his wife at the time.

While Jakob Steib started out by collaborating informally with his parents, Wilfrid and Katharina Steib, and others in Basel, the architecture firm Gmür Lüscher Gmür (GLG) was launched to participate in competitions. When Regula Lüscher left the firm in 1998 to take up a job at the Office for Urban Planning in Zurich, it was renamed Patrick Gmür Architekten (PGA). Michael Geschwentner joined the team that same year. Matthias Kyburz started out as an intern—at Jakob Steib's office, however—becoming a fully-fledged staff member there in 2005.

2.1.1 Weizacker Apartment Block

When an architect designs their debut project, there is always the risk that they will smother it with ideas and that this excessive flair will be detrimental to the architecture itself. But such issues are nowhere to be seen in the design of this building. Far from it: thanks to its clear and legible architectural expression, the Weizacker building radiates a pleasant calm. In the relatively open surrounds of a typical Winterthur suburb, the row of apartments nestles elegantly against the slope. The subtle slant of the roofline, the pronounced stair tower, and the structural design of the facade at the foot of the slope create a striking architectural identity and tie the terraced elements together into a single form.

The large building is comprised of several smaller apartments. Inside, stacked maisonettes fuse the privacy of a single-family home with the feeling of a tight-knit housing community. The apartments can be accessed via an enclosed courtyard on the first floor or an open circulation deck on the roof. The driving force behind the spatial concept is the dramatic landscape, which is brought to the fore in the longitudinal section. The plan follows a clear organizing principle that interacts with the complex cross section, creating a variety of interior spaces. This is particularly evident in the penthouses, in which the building's terraced volume becomes noticeable in the form of split-level apartments with extra high ceilings, evoking the feeling of a unique way of living.

Address
Weizackerstrasse 25, Winterthur

Architecture
Jakob Steib Architekten (JSA)

Type of commission: Direct commission
Planning and execution: 1990–1992
Schedule of accommodation: 11 apartments
Client: Winterthur Lebensversicherungen

Apartment plan
→ 3.5.1
→ 3.5.2

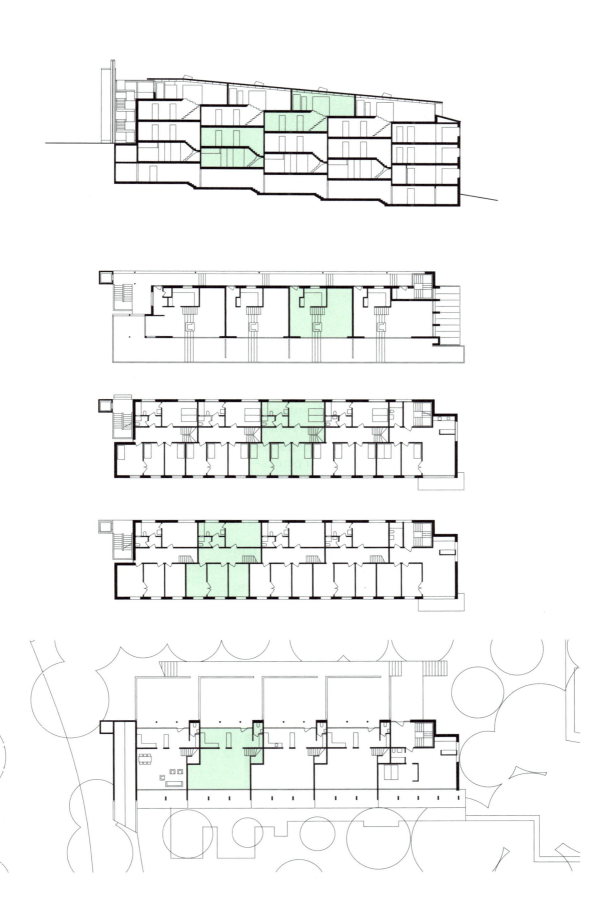

ground floor – first floor – second floor – top floor

2.1.2 Hinterfeld Apartment Block

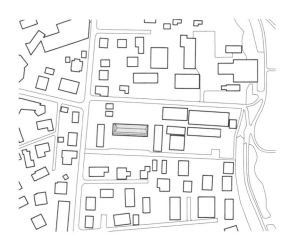

The distinctive north–south orientation of the property provides the leitmotif for the design idea. On the north side, a protective hard brick facade with crisply punched-out windows envelops the volume, which presents a completely different appearance when viewed from the south. From the latter perspective, the paneling—made up of large cedar planks—exudes a calm, dignified homeliness, which distinguishes the building from the architectural hodgepodge typical of a suburban residential neighborhood.

The meticulous execution of the wooden paneling gives the large building the appearance of a carefully crafted piece of furniture.

A long canopy binds the expansive volumes and forms the counterpart to the brick wall, which marks the outer boundary of the building in the form of a garden wall, then transitions to an outdoor corridor, and finally concludes in an emblematic chimney.

The complex spatial organization of the apartments is translated into a spacious architectural language that lends a special flair to the suburban rental apartment building. Two-story outdoor spaces combined with rooftop patios and large windows eclipse the small-scale interiors. Each apartment has a private outdoor space that is closely integrated into the spatial organization of its plan. The building has an intricate circulation system composed of compact staircases and an access corridor which emphasizes the concept of individual housing units in a large suburban building.

Address
August-Cueni-Strasse 1–9, Zwingen

Architecture
Jakob Steib Architekten (JSA)

Type of commission: Direct commission
Planning and execution: 1993–1995
Schedule of accommodation: 15 apartments
Client: Max Scherrer AG, W. and K. Steib

Apartment plans
→ 3.1.1

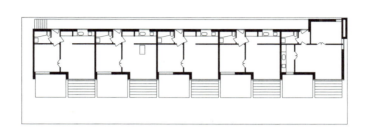

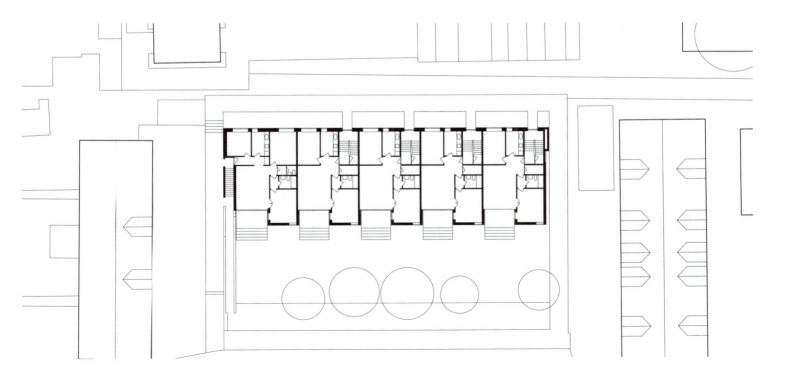

ground floor – first floor – second floor

How It All Began 19

2.1.3 Heimeli Apartment Blocks

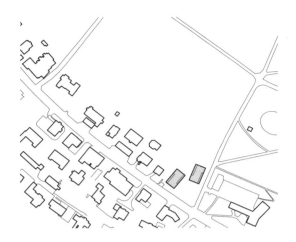

The design for two residential houses on Zürichberg—a wooded hill overlooking Lake Zurich—is rooted in a time that marks the beginning of a new era in Zurich's housing construction. Housing construction was once a neglected task that promised little prestige and often resulted in drab architecture defined solely by its function as an investment. At the beginning of the 2000s, a new interest emerged in a specific housing culture that expressed social change and prioritized spatial concerns.

This competition entry, which celebrates the individuality of the apartments while preserving the unity of architectural expression, must be understood in this context. The two houses form a pair that boldly occupies a protruding section of the plot and extends the prevailing small-scale building pattern.

Each apartment receives a share of the garden with its own entrance and access to the top floor, which offers a magnificent view of Lake Zurich. Such features allow all apartments to benefit equally from the unique qualities of the location.

Paired, interlocking maisonette apartments, accessed via a Venetian staircase, traverse the building volumes diagonally, tapping into the spatial potential of the simple cubes. The straightforwardly systematic approach exhibited in the plan is revealed in the section drawings as a complex spatial figure that wrests an unexpected explosive power from a mundane architectural brief.

Address
Susenbergstrasse 84/86, Zurich-Fluntern

Architecture
Gmür Lüscher Gmür Architekten (GLG)

Type of commission: Study commission 1998
Planning and execution: not executed
Schedule of accommodation: 8 apartments
Client: private

Apartment plans
→ 3.5.3

0 5 10   ground floor – upper floor – top floor

2.1.4 Kurfirstenstrasse Apartment Block

The apartment complex with seven individual condominiums is situated on a moraine hill above the left shore of Lake Zurich. The natural features of the plot, the optimal arrangement of the interior spaces, and the stipulations of the commission—apartments which emphasize individuality and privacy—result in a multifarious cube which makes restrained use of the building materials. The main hallmark of the building is the way in which living areas and bedrooms alternate from floor to floor.

This design principle enables the living rooms to have ample space, with three-meter-high ceilings, while the bedrooms have a conventional height. The simple arrangement and stacking of different spatial strata—visible in the plan—generates a complex and diverse living environment that interacts symbiotically with the architectural style.

The shifting location of the living spaces and the slight variation in floor plans on each story provide the motifs for shaping the building volume and the sculptural design of the facade. The thick cladding in which the "Kurfürst" is clad illustrates the principles of stacking and interleaving, individuality and privacy. At the same time, the robust coherence of its overall form prevents the large building from disintegrating into its constitutive parts. The finely tuned gradations, the carefully placed punched windows, and the consistent use of the dark brick veneer lend the vibrant cubic volume a tasteful English modesty.

Address
Kurfirstenstrasse 18, Zurich-Wollishofen

Architecture
Jakob Steib Architekten (JSA)

Type of commission: Direct commission
Planning and execution: 1999–2000
Schedule of accommodation: 7 apartments
Client: Condominium owner

Apartment plans
→ 3.2.1

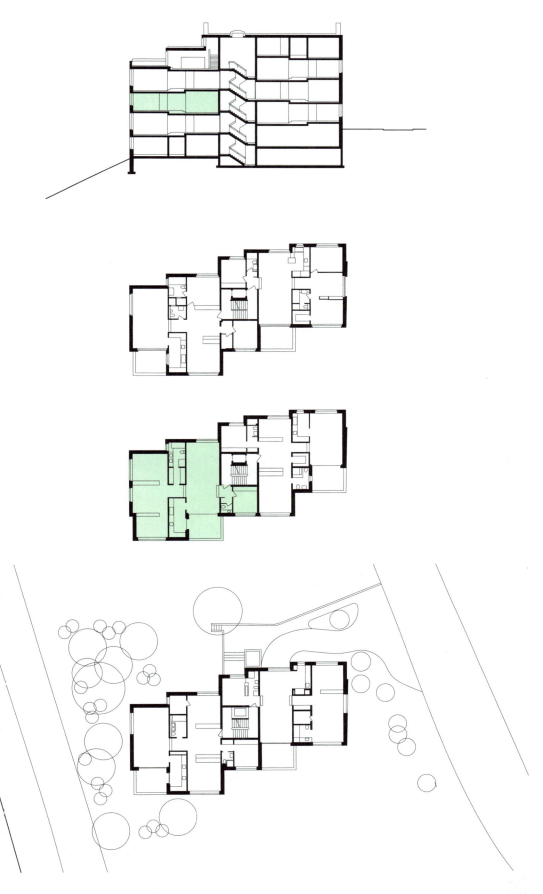

ground floor – first floor – second floor

2.2 Early Milestones

With the Kurfirstenstrasse residential building and the James development, both in Zurich, Jakob Steib and Patrick Gmür were both able to complete key projects shortly before and after the turn of the millennium. At the time, the two of them had never officially worked together before, although they had teamed up to enter into several competitions starting in the late 1990s.

This loose, enjoyable, experimental collaboration took place parallel to the work they did at their own firms, and led to the construction of the Paul-Clairmont-Strasse residential building in Zurich, among others. The collaboration was later formalized with the creation of Gmür & Steib Architekten (GSA). The building attracted a lot of attention and is now recognized as an early milestone of their partnership. Incidentally, Michael Geschwentner and Matthias Kyburz first met each other during the planning for this project after one of them borrowed an NCS color fan and apparently never returned it.

2.2.1 Paul-Clairmont-Strasse Apartment Block

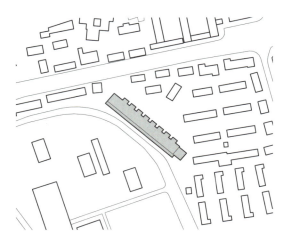

The initial idea of the design was to discover a novel dimension in the private outdoor space of each apartment. The balconies were transformed into unusually spacious patios, which, stacked but also offset from one another, form a system of two-story rooms that allows ample light to stream into the apartments, despite their sizable depth of four meters. The result is a frontal annex, which provides the apartments with a spatial buffer against the massive volume of the nearby Triemli Hospital. To make the patios private, the kitchen extends out into the overhead space of the apartments below, causing a domino effect in the plans that informs the spatial pattern of the building.

Room towers complement and articulate the northern side of the robust structure, whose silhouette is activated by the staggering of its heights. Floor-to-ceiling double doors work perpendicular to the horizontally oriented structure of the rooms, breaking it up. This detail connects the living spaces that face west, towards the light, to the city view on the other side of the building.

On the ground floor, the staircases are connected to a naturally lit *rue intérieure* which can be accessed through a shared entrance. Studios flank this access corridor and reinforce the prominence of the communal entrance level. At the head of the building, a kindergarten with a play yard forms a public entrance.

Address
Birmensdorferstrasse 467, Zurich-Wiedikon

Architecture
Gmür & Steib Architekten (GSA)

Landscape architecture
Regula Hodel

Type of commission: Invitation to compete for project tender 2000
Planning and execution: 2002–2006
Schedule of accommodation: 49 apartments, children's daycare center, studios
Client: Rotach housing cooperative

Apartment plans
→ 3.3.1
→ 3.3.2

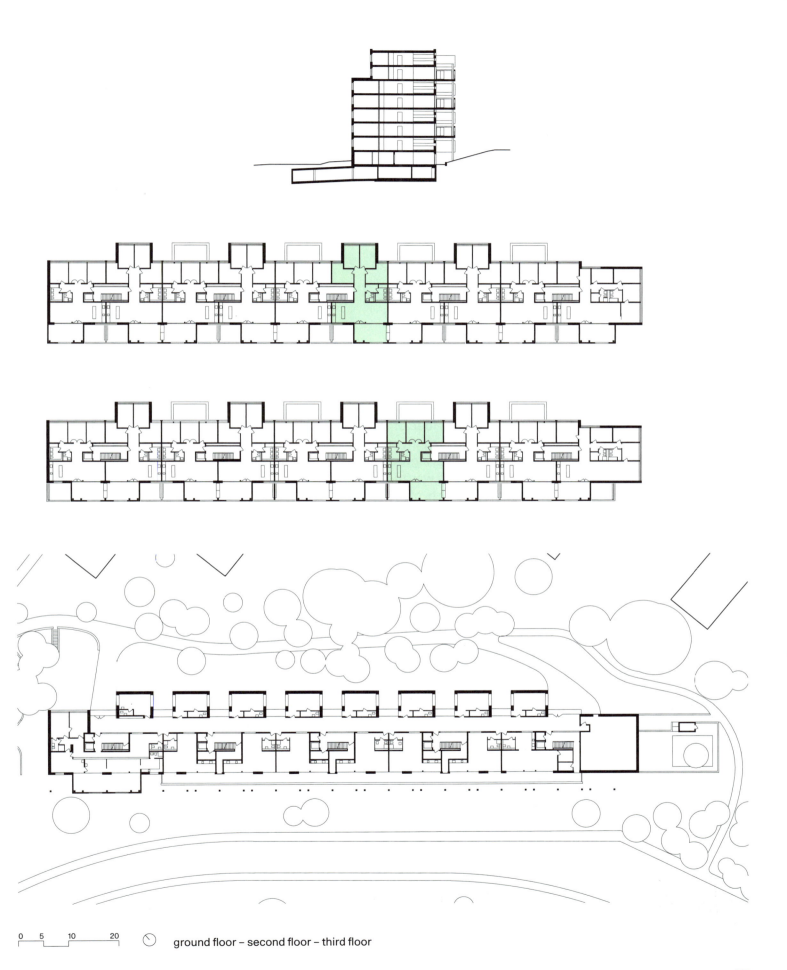

ground floor – second floor – third floor

Early Milestones

2.2.2 James Development

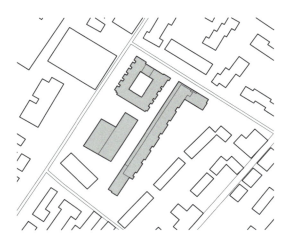

There are many respects in which James is a pioneering example of housing construction in Zurich. It has set a precedent with the diversity it showcases in urban planning and apartment typologies, and its idea of "dwellings with services" has also caught on. What is now perceived as an essential ingredient in any prosperous neighborhood was then a major venture project on the outskirts of the city, in an inhospitable former industrial precinct dominated by large office buildings and empty, open spaces.

Building in existing structures was still yet to become a hot topic, which makes it all the more gratifying that the converted industrial hall with a restaurant and climbing gym has become one of the neighborhood's major drawcards. Not only that: the first floor boasts a variety of recreational uses—including an indoor badminton court and a daycare center—which enliven the urban space and make James an important part of the urban development.

The story of housing diversity can be told in a similar manner: if in the 1990s Zurich's housing construction was characterized by a cynical profit-driven uniformity, James heralded a transition and a rethink. Given the social developments of the time, housing began to be construed as the expression of individual attitudes and biographies inflected in personal ways. The seventy-two different types of apartments distributed across 283 units testify to the extensive research that went into preparing the building, all driven by curiosity and inventiveness.

Address
Flüelastrasse 21–27, 29, 31 a–d, Anemonenstrasse 40 a–h, Zurich-Albisrieden

Architecture
Patrick Gmür Architekten (PGA)

Landscape architecture
Vetschpartner

Type of commission: Study commission via invitation 2001
Planning and execution: 2002–2009
Schedule of accommodation: 283 apartments, 6400 m2 commercial space
Client: Turintra AG c/o UBS Fund Management (Switzerland) AG

Apartment plans
→ 3.1.2
→ 3.1.3
→ 3.2.2
→ 3.2.3
→ 3.2.4
→ 3.3.3
→ 3.3.4
→ 3.3.5
→ 3.3.6
→ 3.3.7
→ 3.9.1
→ 3.12.1
→ 3.12.2
→ 4.4
→ 4.5
→ 4.8
→ 4.9

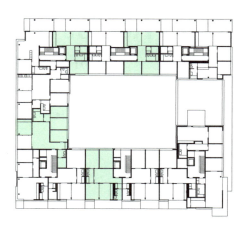

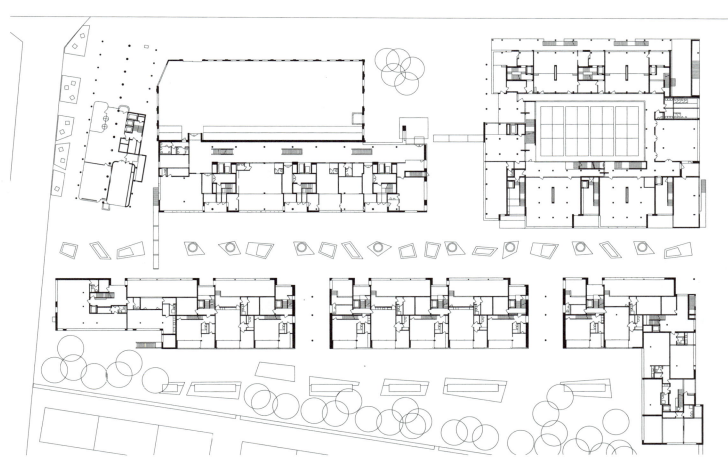

ground floor – regular floor

Early Milestones

2.2.3 Roost Development

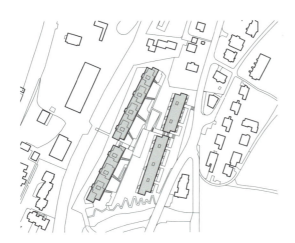

Affordable housing with a view of the lake! What sounded like a utopia in the low-tax canton of Zug became a reality thanks to the perseverance of two housing cooperatives and having the Canton of Zug take over the official role of developer. Four elongated volumes follow the sloped terrain and form a spacious residential area. Balcony decks spanning the entire length of the buildings embody the design idea, which reflects the location by the lake and the green environs.

Despite budgetary constraints, the buildings maintained high standards thanks to their simple structure and the repetition of defining features. The ventilated facade, the double-sided access concept which gives each apartment a two-sided orientation, and the high-quality interior finish testify to the effort to make the most of a limited budget and still achieve a high-quality, durable finished product. The apartment plans adhere to a classic zoning of individual and communal spaces that accommodates the needs of families. The apartments on offer are complemented by maisonettes with garden patios and spatially opulent top-level apartments with skylights and two-story bathrooms. The exterior appearance of the apartments is covered by white corrugated Eternit panels, which, in combination with the striped fabric awnings and the pastel-colored metal railing, creates a Mediterranean atmosphere. The residents regularly hold events in the community hall and form a close-knit community.

Address
Fridbachweg 1–3, 11–17, Zug

Architecture
Gmür & Geschwentner Architekten (GGA)

Landscape architecture
Vetschpartner Landschaftsarchitekten

Type of commission: Study commission 2002
Planning and execution: Two stages: 2004–2007, 2010–2013
Schedule of accommodation: 110 apartments, multi-purpose room
Client: City of Zug, AWZ (General Housing Cooperative Zug), GEWOBA (Cooperative for Non-Profit Housing)

Apartment plans

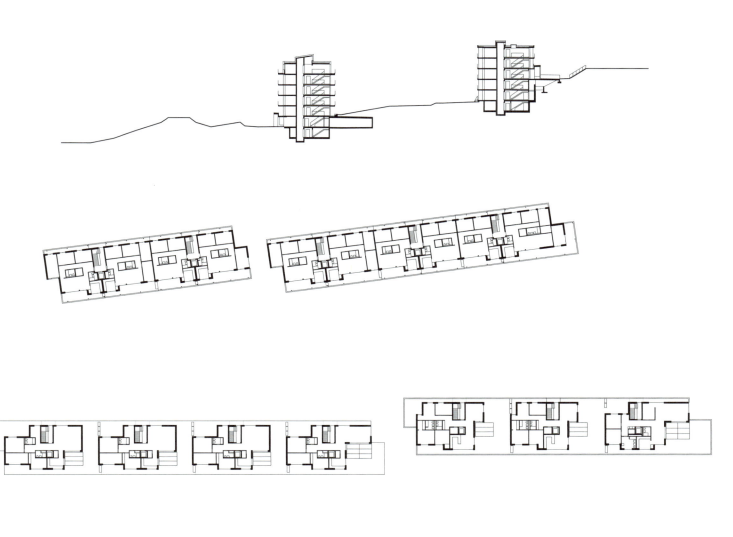
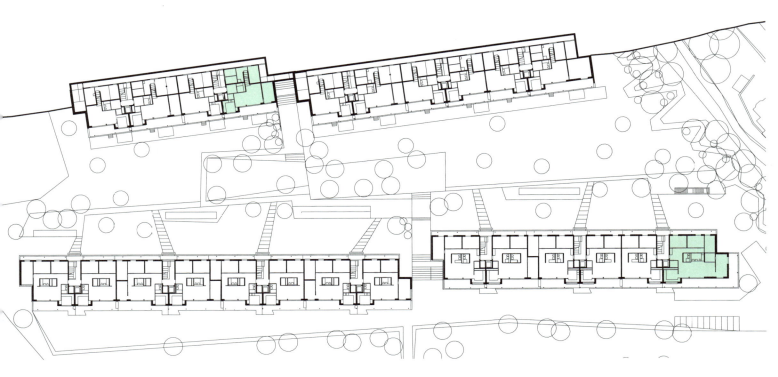

garden floor – top floor

Early Milestones

2.2.4 Birnbäumen Apartment Blocks (Building site 1)

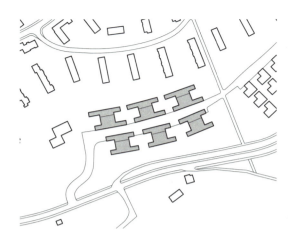

The design idea was driven by the steep slope, the fact that the building was oriented in the "wrong" direction, namely, to the north, and the enticing view of Lake Constance—the Mare Nostrum of eastern Switzerland. The obvious idea of building terraced rows was not viable. Linear blocks would have carved up the valuable landscape, while point blocks tend to create a disaggregated collection of individual buildings. The solution for this project consisted in synthesizing all these options, creating a distinctive and innovative building type whose spatial arrangement dovetails with the existing construction in the area, provides optimal sunlight to and views from each apartment, and showcases the natural landscape.

An elongated base sprawls across the terrain, anchoring the buildings in the ground and hosting the access area as well as the bedrooms. Wings on stilts extend out from the core, housing the living areas, which—thanks to the clever height gradation—enjoy a view of Lake Constance and catch the sun from behind. Parking is tucked into the slope along the road.

The basic concept can best be gleaned from focusing on individual sections: the underground volume is minimized to leave the natural terrain as intact as possible and to preserve the orchards as much as possible. The buildings are compact, fitting a significantly higher number of apartments into the landscape compared to the competing structures. In this respect, the design anticipates issues that are more relevant today than ever before.

Address
Meienbergstrasse, St. Gallen

Architecture
Gmür & Steib Architekten (GSA)

Type of commission: study commission 2004
Planning and execution: not carried out
Schedule of accommodation: 66 apartments
Client: Helvetia Patria Insurance

Apartment plans
→ 3.12.3

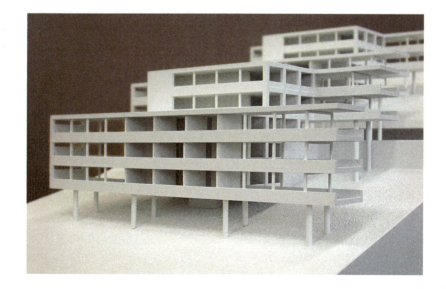

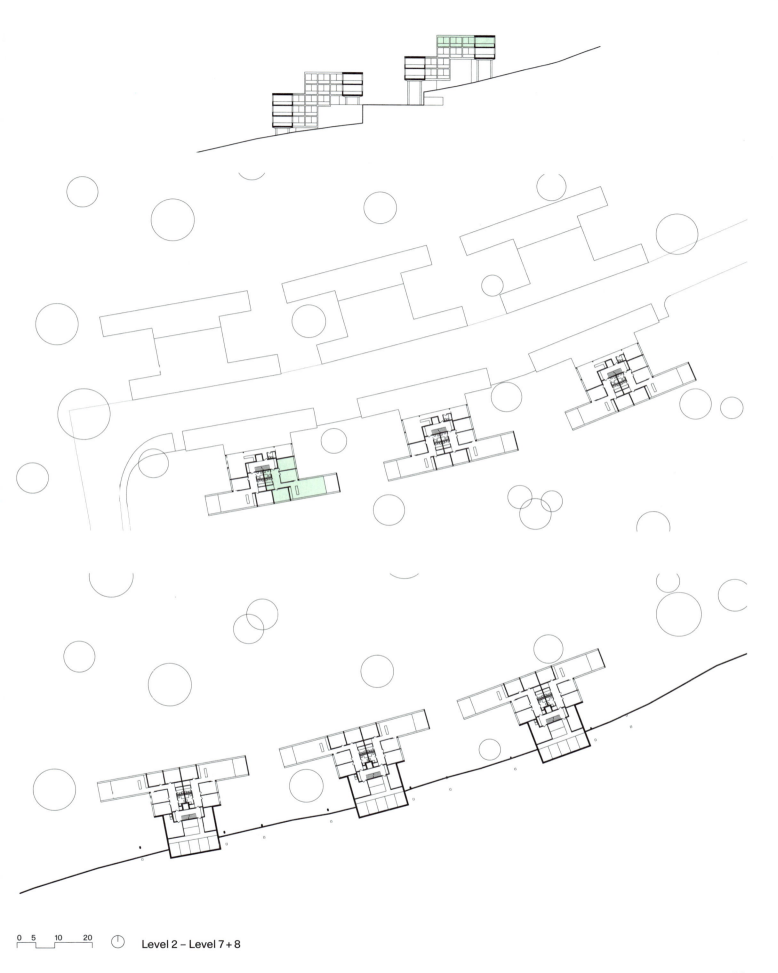

Level 2 – Level 7 + 8

Early Milestones

2.2.5 Im Forster Apartment Blocks

The main attraction of the site is a pristine, gently sloping meadow with a view of Lake Zurich. On the summit of the meadow, a country house from the 1930s recalls a time when Zurichberg formed a continuous landscape that had hardly been developed. This special scenery has been taken as the architectural motif for three apartment buildings: expansive building wings sit on sculpturally modulated pillars that gently dot the terrain and allow the meadow to flow beneath the buildings. The tactfully staggered placement of the building volumes and the piers which extend in alternating directions offer each of the apartments a spectacular view of Lake Zurich and a profound spatial immersion in the landscape.

The internal structure of the volumes is simple yet at the same time complex: on each floor, apartments with different layouts converge around a staircase and, starting from the core, snake out in all directions towards the view. The spacious internal pathways lead through generous foyers flanked by floor-to-ceiling double doors, and finally come to a halt in the living room, which hangs like a sidecar on the building's central nucleus.

The theme of upscale middle-class living is incorporated into various aspects of the design. A driveway serves as an arrival point as well as a prelude to a grand staircase with floating steel stairs and exquisite natural stone floors. A light brick facade evokes cozy Nordic living.

Address
Mittelbergsteig 4–10, Zurich-Fluntern

Architecture
Jakob Steib Architekten (JSA)

Landscape architecture
Schweingruber Zulauf Landschaftsarchitekten

Type of commission: study commission 2004
Planning and execution: 2009–2011
Schedule of accommodation: 27 apartments, 3 studios
Client: represented by Immopoly Zurich

Apartment plans
→ 3.12.4
→ 3.12.5

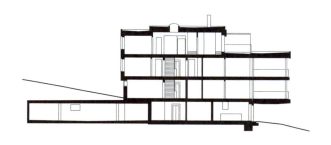

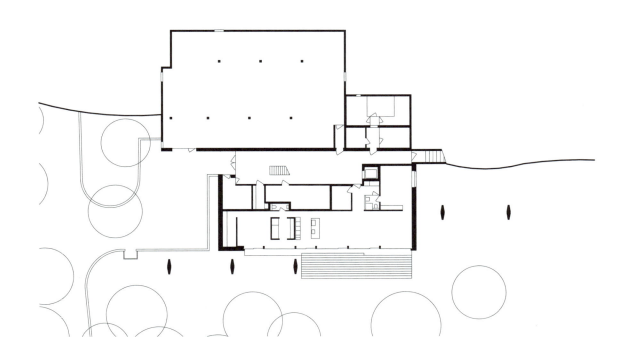

0 5 10   ground floor – second floor (floor plan detail)

Early Milestones   35

2.2.6 Imbisbühlstrasse Apartment Block

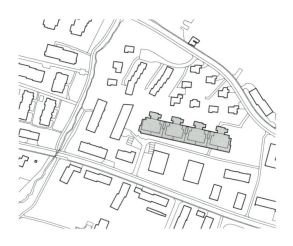

In retrospect, the competition project for the residential development on Imbisbühlstrasse appears to be a daring experiment from the firm's "Sturm und Drang period"—one that breaks new ground in residential construction. The design is characterized by a maximally experimental spatial approach, which demonstrates that apartments can have both shaded areas and brightly lit rooms, as long as the room height and floor plan design are consonant with the lighting. The one-and-a-half-story residential halls are located in the belly of the deep building volume and are indirectly illuminated on both sides of the facade through the offset stacking of spatial layers.

The design, which was unprecedented for its time, was clearly inspired by Loos's spatial plan. At the same time, iconic architectural works such as the Halston townhouse by Paul Rudolph in New York are a point of reference for this spatial experiment. The architectural appearance of the building derives its elemental power from an idea that drives the sectional pattern and informs every aspect of the design. The building responds to the spatially arbitrary character of the residential precinct with an imposing volume that provides the neighborhood with an ordering focal point.

Although it won the competition, the client requested that the design be toned down. In an initial revision phase, the unbridled exuberance of the original idea was restrained slightly by muting some of the features of the central living halls. Room layers staggered by a half-story were tactfully woven into the spatial structure, and the living halls now extend all the way to the facade. Despite additional tweaks made to simplify the design, the final product managed to preserve the idea of central living halls and rooms with high ceilings.

The final design demonstrated that even a building with a depth of thirty meters can be tackled with the right means. With three-meter-high ceilings, the apartments have unconventional proportions, which are impressively showcased in the large living halls and spacious balconies. Tower-like clusters of rooms are adjoined to the living halls, allowing light to seep into the depth of the apartments through an expansion joint. At both ends of the building, stacked maisonette apartments with conventional room heights frame the building volume, while the top-story apartments benefit from the staggered volume's shifting floor level, owed to the topography of the site.

The well-defined partitioning of the apartments into private and communal areas meets the needs of families who enjoy a living environment that feels metropolitan while being located in a green residential quarter. Spacious entrance halls clad in natural stone exude a grandeur not to be expected from the small-scale residential environment. Several steps were taken to make the spatial idea palatable to the local housing market. Nevertheless, the project represents the revived spirit of experimentation in Swiss residential construction in the 2000s like no other.

Address
Imbisbühlstrasse 106–114, Zürich-Höngg

Architecture
Gmür & Steib Architekten (GSA)

Landscape architecture
Schweingruber Zulauf Landschaftsarchitekten

Type of commission: study commission 2003
Planning and execution: 2004–2008
Schedule of accommodation: 52 apartments
Client: Swiss Re Company Ltd., Zurich

Apartment plans
→ 3.6.1
→ 3.6.2
→ 3.12.6
→ 3.12.7

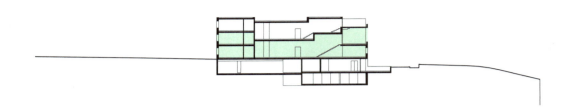
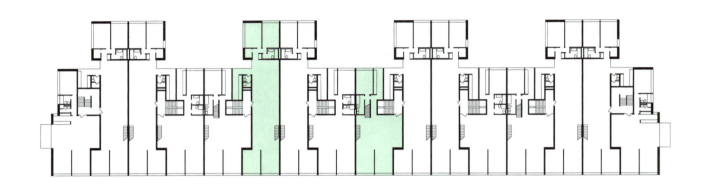
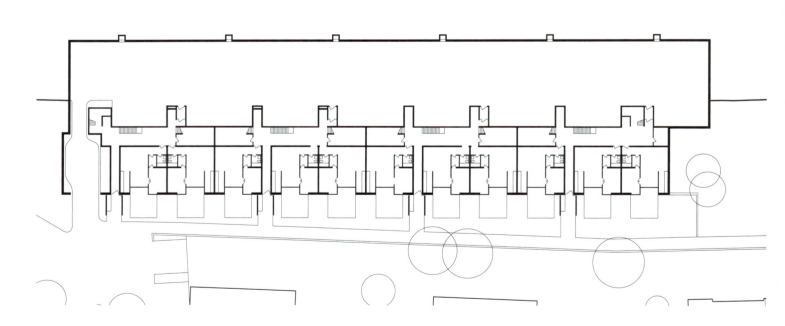

0 5 10 20   competition entry: ground floor – first floor

38

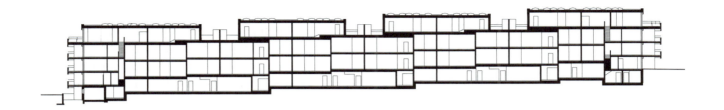

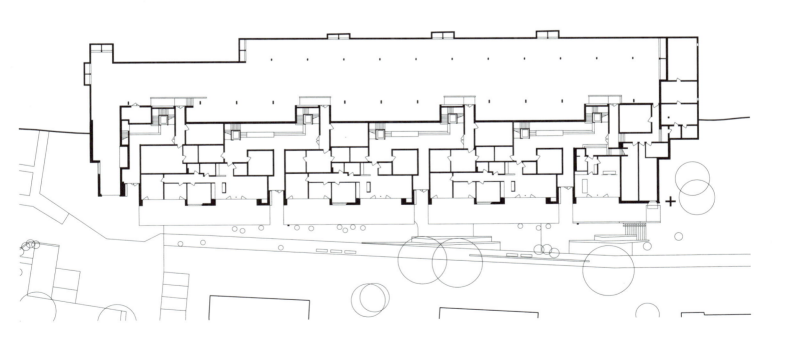

revised design: ground floor – first floor

Early Milestones

2.2.7 Büelen Apartment Blocks

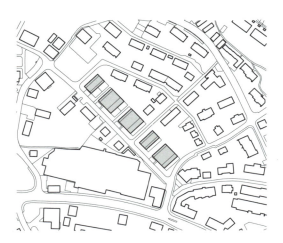

Competition projects can be roughly divided into two categories: the first is based on an idea founded in urban planning, while the other emerges out of a distinctive approach to living arrangements. The buildings in the Büelen neighborhood in Zurich's lakeside municipality of Wädenswil belong to the second category. They take on a building type that is perhaps the most difficult because it is unspecific: apartment buildings in a built-up area. The buildings line the street along the sloping terrain and are provided with direct access routes. The elongated geometry of the site made this the most sensible placement.
The design has no intention of being sophisticated, and aims instead to blend in with the existing neighborhood buildings and maintain a casual feel, as per the aforementioned approach to residential construction. This design integrates different types of apartments into the volumes. Maisonettes with garden plots flank the building and are combined with elongated, interconnected floor plans and expansive top-floor apartments to create a new variation on the apartment building theme.
In the top story, skylit kitchens, internal circulation, and surprising visual connections enhance the spatial concept.
The ground floor is outfitted with open, space-efficient carports. They save costs, reduce excavation, prevent the need for complicated ramp systems, and allow more space for the garden. The raw concrete facades emphasize the crisp geometry of the buildings, which appear extravagant as objects yet blend seamlessly into the surroundings.

Address
Büelenstrasse 4, 8–10, Dahlienstrasse 2, Weststrasse 9, Wädenswil
Architecture
Gmür & Steib Architekten (GSA)

Type of commission: Project competition 2005
Planning and execution: 2006–2008
Spatial preogram: 38 apartments
Client: Tenant Building Cooperative Wädenswil

Apartment plans
→ 3.6.3
→ 3.10.1

basement floor – ground floor – upper floor (floor plan detail)

Early Milestones

2.2.8 Kurlistrasse Apartment Block

The genre of the terrace house has been the subject of debate in recent decades, having become a symbol of the gradual destruction of the natural suburban landscape. The generic stacking and tiering of apartments on the sloping terrain leads to anonymous and expressionless clusters of buildings, which often face the street with a garage that detracts from the front yard. The exception confirms the rule: six of the nine residential units on Kurlistrasse are combined via a communal access area, which forms the backbone of the sophisticated sectional concept. Residential levels staggered by a half-story ascend in the opposite direction to the slope and allow the apartments to dovetail with the private outdoor spaces, which remain hidden behind the raised living spaces and thus enable the creation of an adequate facade.

The tiered living levels also produce two surprising spatial effects: light falls at a comfortable angle deep into the apartments, and the view from inside is directed diagonally towards the sky. The sense of living oscillates between two states: the bedrooms, lowered half a level, face the patio and offer a homely intimacy, while the living spaces, raised by the same amount, have an unobstructed view. The architectural expression foregrounds the spatial division of the units, which are separated by expansion joints and carefully fitted into the small-scale setting.

Address
Kurlistrasse 33–35, Winterthur

Architecture
Jakob Steib Architekten (JSA)

Type of commission: Direct commission
Planning and execution: 2005–2006
Schedule of accommodation: 9 apartments
Client: Lorenz Reinhart

Apartment plans
→ 3.9.2
→ 3.9.3

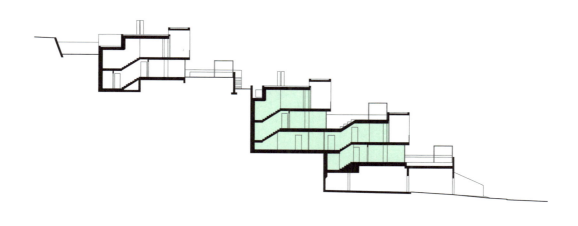

Level 0 – Level 3 (floor plan detail)

2.2.9   Hard Turm Park High-Rise

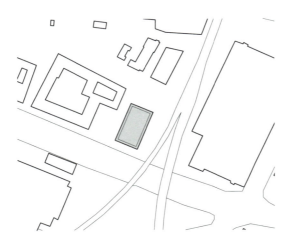

At a turbulent but stunning urban juncture in Zurich's rugged west, the robust cuboid with harmonious proportions in a ratio of 3:5:8 coalesces with the Toni-Areal tower and the Migros distribution center high-rise slab to form a magnificent ensemble in the urban setting.

The horizontally banded facade with distinctive bay windows depicts the inner structure of the house on the building envelope and shows its purpose: "people live here!" The apartments interact with the urban space, the building has room to breathe and appears accessible. Living in a high-rise is not an empty promise—it is the driving force behind the design idea. The interior is oriented outward: cockpit kitchens, seating niches in the bay windows, and bathrooms with a view of the Alps are arranged like front row box seats. The living areas, on the other hand, are cozy retreats in the interior of the building. There is a diverse mix of apartments in the tower: small and multi-room apartments, flats with a depth of thirty meters and two-story living halls, and at the very top, maisonette apartments all join to create vibrant living worlds. The lower half also has a four-star hotel with 196 rooms, a ballroom, conference rooms, and offices. The ground floor and the surrounding urban space benefit from being able to access this space. A perforated metal screen, called "Röckli," veils and calms the functionally heterogeneous plinth area of the building and offers passers-by shelter from the elements at the foot of the high-rise.

Address
Pfingstweidstrasse 98, 100, Zurich

Architecture
Gmür & Geschwentner Architekten (GGA)

Landscape architecture
Vetschpartner Landschaftsarchitekten

Type of commission: International project competition 2007
Planning and execution: 2010–2013
Schedule of accommodation: 121 condominiums, four-star hotel with 196 rooms, restaurant, café, conference rooms, ballroom, offices
Client: Pfingstweid Consortium, Zurich

Apartment plans
→ 3.4.4
→ 3.7.1
→ 3.7.2
→ 3.7.3
→ 3.7.4
→ 3.7.5

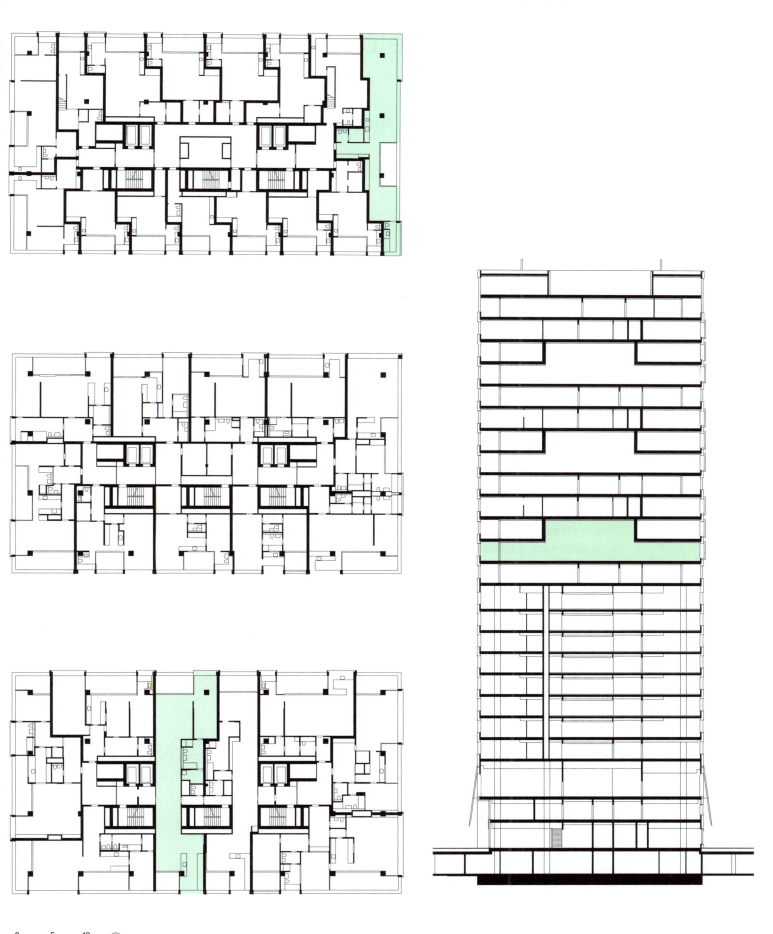

13th floor – 16th floor – 24th floor

Early Milestones 45

2.2.10 Altwiesen Development

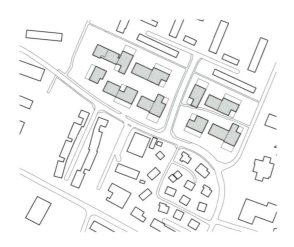

Given the increases in population density affecting many areas, the garden city model is in need of an update. That being said, merely increasing the height and width of buildings while retaining the same design model makes little sense, as this does away with the expansive green spaces that help to define the garden city.

This project in Zurich's Schwamendingen district takes a different approach: it combines row houses typical of the neighborhood with dense high-rise buildings and combines them into a new building type. Schwamendingen's green surrounds embrace the buildings and embed the houses in the neighborhood. There are no residual areas or green spaces separating the buildings, since the precious land is already put to intensive use. Private gardens, communal green spaces, and an elongated open space at the heart of the complex form a single structure with a variety of open spaces.

The buildings line the inner perimeter of the development, which forms the backbone and houses all the entrances to the development. The result is a lively neighborhood, which, by Swiss standards, possesses an unusual simplicity that is more reminiscent of Amsterdam than Zurich.

The 290 apartments contain around seventy-eight different floor plans. At the intersection point with the high-rise buildings, the terraced houses boast of an astonishing spatial opulence and sophisticated sectional ideas. Moreover, the setbacks on both sides of the upper floors of the high-rise buildings create apartments with large terraces and views of the landscape.

Address
Heerenschürlistrasse 1–9, Altwiesenstrasse 323–377, Zurich-Schwamendingen

Architecture
Gmür & Geschwentner Architekten (GGA)

Landscape architecture
Studio Vulkan, Lukas Schweingruber

Type of commission: Study commission 2007
Planning and execution: 2008–2016
Schedule of accommodation: 290 apartments, daycare center, assisted living, community room
Client: UBS Fund Management (Switzerland) AG, Basel

Apartment plans
→ 3.5.5
→ 3.5.6
→ 3.5.7

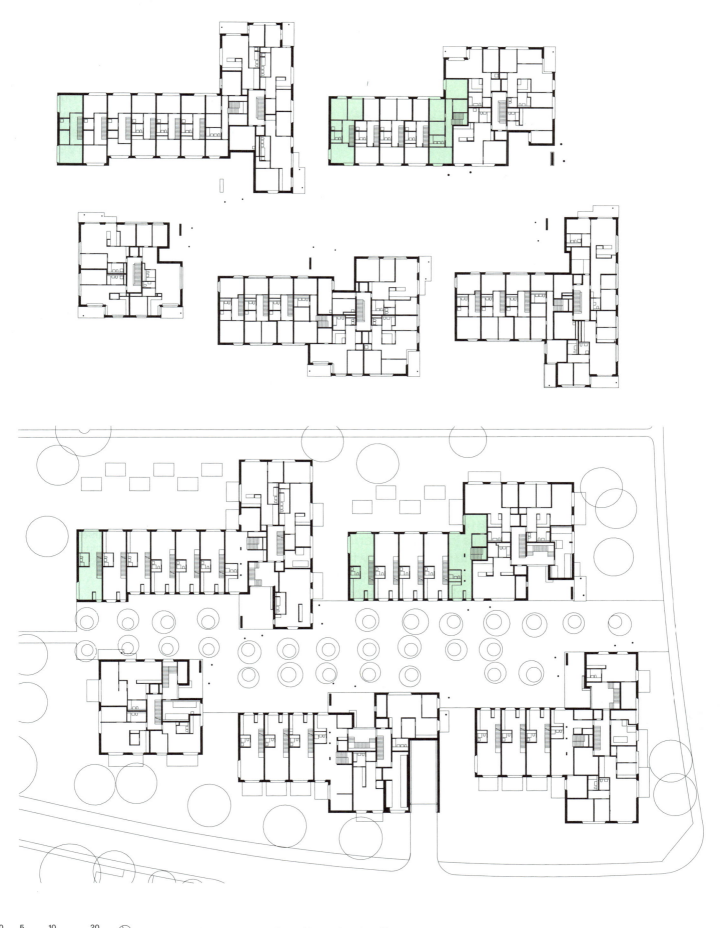

ground floor – regular floor (floor plan detail)

Early Milestones

2.2.11 Brünnen Development (Building site 11)

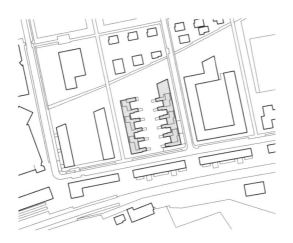

The urban development plan for Bern-Brünnen sorts building plots by layout type. The seemingly uniform pattern of the neighborhood is held together by a central park strip. Rather than urban density, a rather idiosyncratic equilibrium is achieved which oscillates between an anonymous suburban idyll and typical Swiss garden-patio living. This environment requires a bold residential concept to tap into the hidden potential of the site and create a new identity.

A layer of rooms with a joint balcony forms a protective envelope facing the street, while the living rooms facing the courtyard create an open platform with stacked balconies that extend out into the green space. The park strip juts into the courtyard and is integrated into the apartments. The arbor becomes a tree-house and a viewing platform over the dense greenery of the park. Spacious entrances, specialized shared rooms with private bathrooms, and a zoning into individual and communal areas emphasize the functional component of the apartments. The spectacular "residential piers" or "finger docks" outfitted with kitchen lookouts and balcony loggias, on the other hand, make for a special experience that has little in common with the "home cooking" that is otherwise on offer at this location. The path leading from the protected private bedroom to the open viewing station among the greenery offers an unexpected spatial dramaturgy on Bern's largely unassuming periphery.

Address
Riedbach-, Colombstrasse, Gigonweg, Bern-Brünnen

Architecture
Patrick Gmür Architekten (PGA)

Landscape architecture
Katja Albiez Architektur und Landschaft

Type of commission: Invitational competition 2007
Planning and execution: not executed
Schedule of accommodation: 66 apartments, 8 studios
Client: Baufeld 11 development consortium

Apartment plans
→ 3.12.8

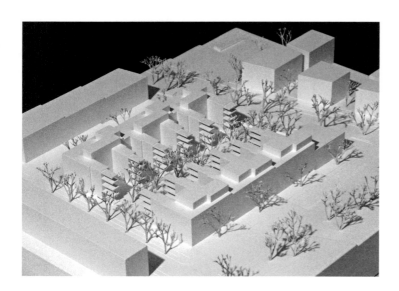

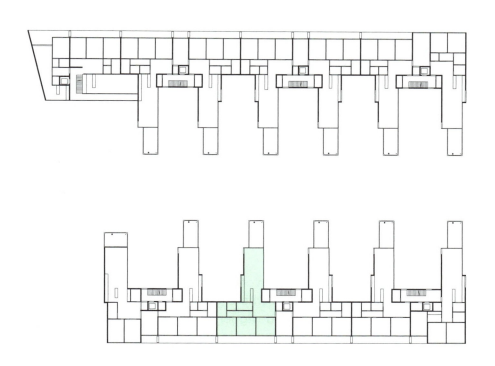
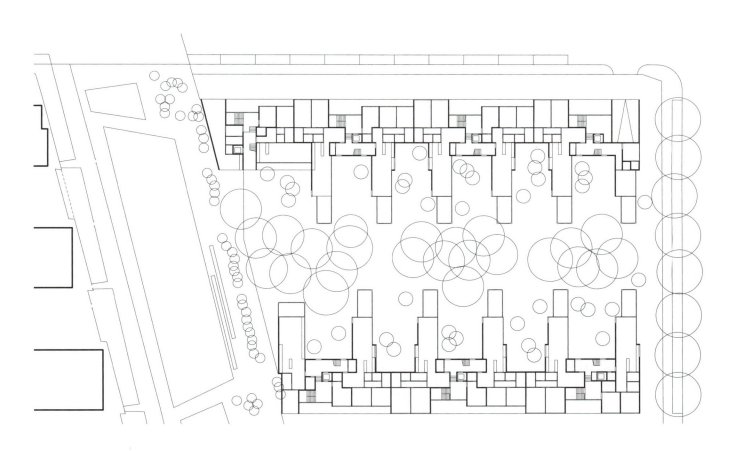

0 5 10 20   ground floor – first floor

Early Milestones 49

2.2.12 Alte Landstrasse Apartment Blocks

As often happens, the force of this design comes through strongest where its parameters radically restrict the designer's freedom. The steep slope, oriented in the "wrong" direction, in addition to the rigorous height restriction imposed by local regulations forced the volume into a tight corset. Despite the limitations placed on the amount of digging and re-molding that could be done on the terrain, the maximum living space still had to be wrung from the plot. A breakthrough was achieved with a complex sectional pattern that follows both the topographical conditions as well as the building regulations.

Like icebergs, each building reveals just the tip of its volume. The rest is submerged underground and receives daylight through all kinds of spatial tricks and techniques, such as skylights, roof incisions, and even the underside of a staircase. Some of the more extraordinary apartments have living rooms with ceilings over four meters high and provide diagonal visual orientation across several terraced living areas with a spectacular view of Lake Zurich. Bright natural stone floors and brightly painted surfaces diffuse light throughout the apartments, creating a peaceful ambience in the shady rooms. The staggered building silhouette repeats the theme of the section and tactfully integrates the houses into the landscape. The glazed garden landing makes it so that the upper floors appear to be hovering above the terrain. Bronze-colored aluminum bands span the buildings, which are oriented towards the view like periscopes.

Address
Alte Landstrasse 214–218, Kilchberg

Architecture
Jakob Steib Architekten (JSA)

Type of commission: Direct commission
Planning and execution: 2007–2011
Schedule of accommodation: 13 apartments, 3 separate rooms
Client: private, represented by MS Bautreuhand AG

Apatment plans
→ 3.4.1

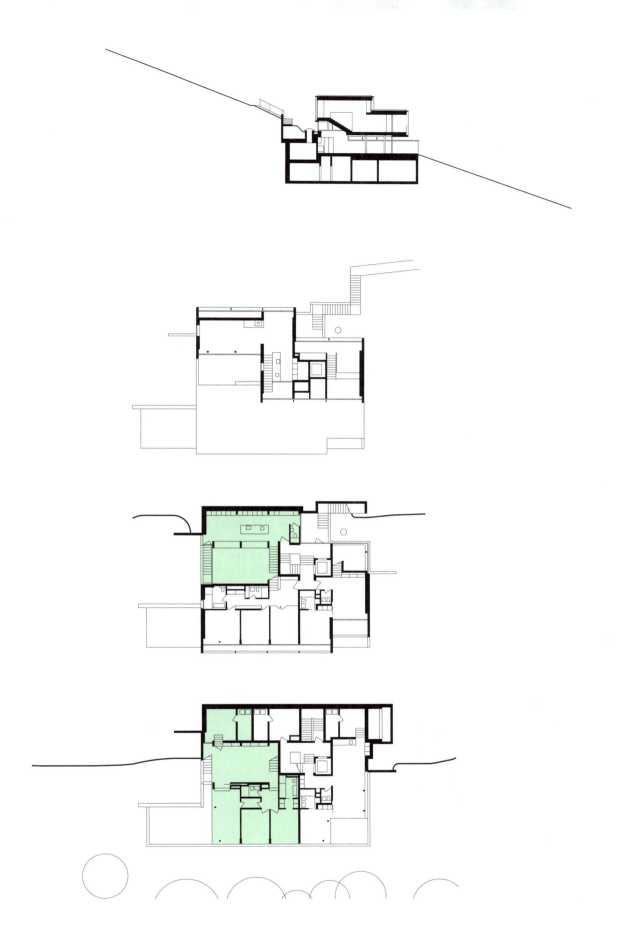

ground floor – first floor – second floor (floor plan detail)

Early Milestones

2.2.13 Rütihof Apartment Blocks

The plateau high above Lake Zurich offers a unique view and the finest conditions for upscale living in a prime location. The resolute privacy of the apartment buildings matches the prevailing atmosphere in the neighborhood. Yet at the same time, certain design elements emphasize the communal aspects, such as the three apartment buildings grouped around a central garden, which—on both a spatial and an atmospheric level—draws arriving visitors into the center.

The garden is located on the roof of the parking garage, which is recessed by half a level and situated between the two levels. This reduces the amount of excavation needed while simultaneously creating a special line of approach that gives each apartment an individual entrance. As a result, there is no need to provide each building with its own staircase, since all apartments can be reached directly from the communal garden via gently ascending and descending outside steps. A new type of housing is created by linking the privacy of single-family houses with the sociable lifestyle found in residential areas.
The plans serve to emphasize the striking view: the elongated living rooms stretch towards the lake and culminate in a large balcony which frames the vista. The most salient architectural features are defined by horizontality. Overhanging roofs, balconies that jut far out, soffits made of intricate wooden slats, and stepped weatherboard facades cultivate an appearance reminiscent of Frank Lloyd Wright's prairie houses.

Address
Rütihofstrasse 29, Uerikon

Architecture
Jakob Steib Architekten (JSA)

Type of commission: Study commission 2007
Planning and execution: 2008–2011
Schedule of accommodation: 12 apartments
Client: Dieter Wartenweiler

Apartment plans
→ 3.9.4

ground floor – upper floor

Early Milestones

2.2.14 Neufrankengasse Apartment Block

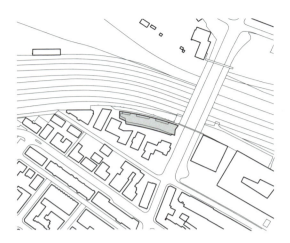

The competition on Neufrankengasse provided the opportunity to implement a long-standing spatial idea. The design was modeled on Frank Lloyd Wright's Price Tower, with its triangular balconies, supplemented by our experiences designing the Paul-Clairmont-Strasse residential building. The sophisticated layered structure of the building incorporates double-height spatial patterns into the plans. The walls change direction with a "windshield-wiper movement," producing wedge-shaped intersections.

The triangular shape has a decisive advantage over rectangular double-height spaces: the volumetric requirements for the luxury of an extra-high room are halved. The resulting spatial dynamism is dramatic! The gaps at interstitial points draw light into the interior of the volume and create a unique spatial experience with an ambiance that is somewhere between a studio and a loft apartment.

The creation of this specific atmosphere wasn't unmotivated—it takes its impetus from the setting itself. The exposed location directly adjacent to the railway track, the access portal provided by the Langstrassen underpass, and a dissipating tendency typical of the perimeter of a block are the urban factors that contribute to the uniqueness of the property. The top-floor apartments are deliberately set apart from the others. Their open plans contain rooms which reach a height of three meters, creating ideal conditions for a life-work combination befitting their situation overlooking Zurich's rooftops.

Address
Neufrankengasse 10 a, Langstrasse 151, Zurich

Architecture
Gmür & Steib Architekten (GSA)

Type of commission: Study commission 2008
Planning and execution: not carried out
Schedule of accommodation: 26 apartments
Client: SBB Immobilien

Apartment plans

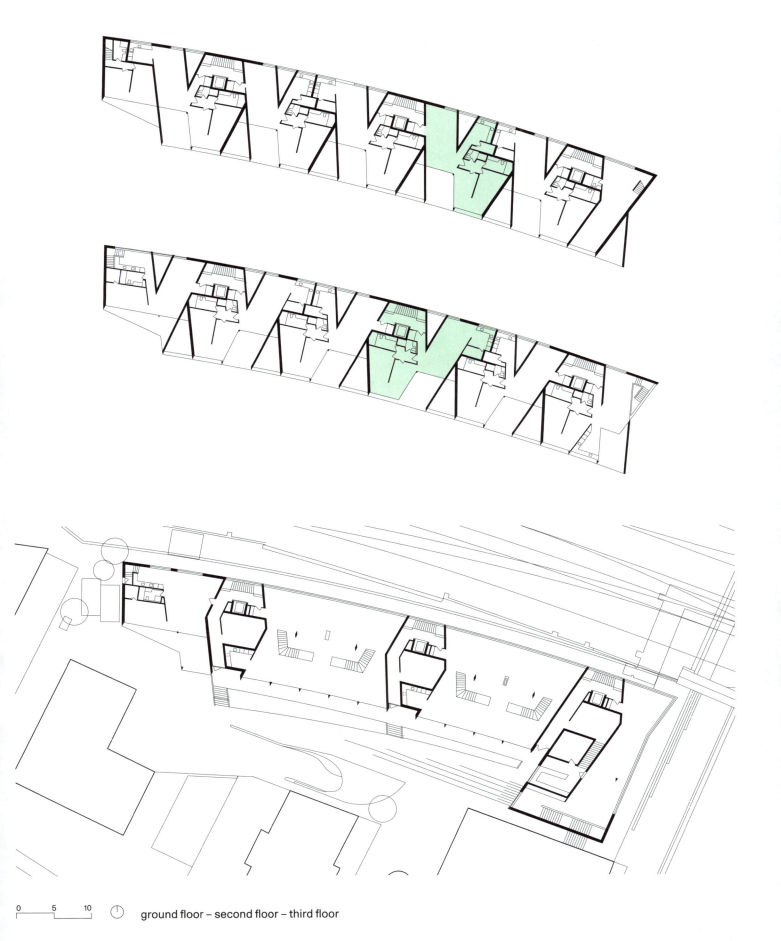

ground floor – second floor – third floor

Early Milestones

2.3 Multi-Track Operations

In 2009, the office was restructured once more. Patrick Gmür was appointed director of the Office for Urban Planning in Zurich, which obliged him to resign from all other positions. As a result, Michael Geschwentner assumed a new role: Patrick Gmür Architekten (PGA) was renamed Gmür & Geschwentner Architekten (GGA), and the sporadic collaboration between Patrick Gmür and Jakob Steib solidified into Steib & Geschwentner Architekten (SGA).

Over the years, Matthias Kyburz took on more and more responsibility as well—first as part of the management team at Jakob Steib Architekten (JSA), and then from 2015 on, at Steib & Geschwentner Architekten (SGA) as well. Numerous large-scale projects were completed during these years. All aspects of the operations became increasingly complex, not least due to the increasing number of employees and the parallel firm structures.

2.3.1 Am Rietpark High-Rise

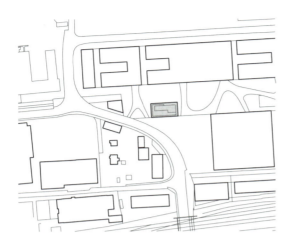

"Melrose Place"—the name says it all: this high-rise celebrates a utopian image of apartment living. Inside, it boasts an innovative paradigm for housing which offers optimized living space tailored for contemporary urban nomads inclined to seek out a pioneering style of life on Zurich's outskirts. While this concept may sound commonplace today, it was groundbreaking in 2009, promoting dense, customized living in a place whose historical urban identity had yet to be established.

Despite its towering height, the building remains well grounded, with commercial spaces on the first two floors connected to the outdoor space via an external stairwell. These spaces are surmounted by stacked and nested residential levels with extra-high interior spaces that lend the compact apartments a luxurious spatial atmosphere. To avoid sacrificing valuable living space for the vertical space, the room above is located in an intermediate position—with a ceiling height of 183 centimeters, it can be used as a bedroom or chill-zone.

The apartments are both lofty and spatially complex, and wind around the vertical volumes resulting in a smorgasbord of different niches which can be furnished in different ways. Spacious bathtubs, sleeping nooks in the heart of the apartment, and living spaces carved out of the deep interior of the building create an eclectic living environment that mirrors the internationality of the residents. The roof is accessible to people in the community. A jogging track and a swimming pool crown the building, bringing a light Californian vibe to Schlieren.

Address
Goldschlägiplatz, Schlieren

Architecture
Gmür & Geschwentner Archtekten (GGA)

Type of commission: Study commission 2009
Planning and execution: not carried out
Schedule of accommodation: 85 apartments, commercial space
Client: Halter AG

Apartment plans
→ 3.7.6
→ 3.7.7

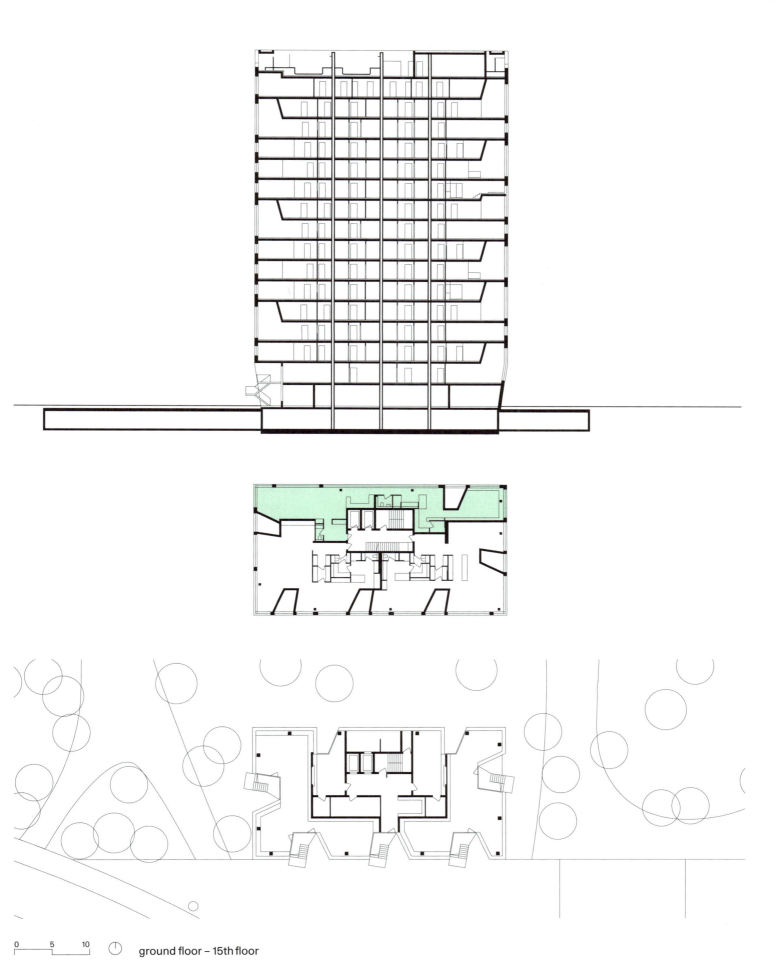

ground floor – 15th floor

2.3.2 Park Residence

An existing ribbon development culminates in these apartment buildings, which are directly adjacent to the spacious Eulachpark, after which they are named. The two buildings define a courtyard and are lodged in the surrounding park. To accentuate this scenery, the buildings are situated on a slightly elevated mezzanine platform. This has the additional effect of preserving the privacy of the apartments without encroaching upon the park's public character.

According to the floor plan, these apartments are rotated at an angle to the footprint of the building. This rotation creates spacious triangular balconies on both sides of the apartments, framed by striking balustrades. The apartments, accessible from two sides, are arranged in pairs and grouped around an internal triangular loggia, which reaches three meters deep at its apex. Here, each of the apartments soaks in ample daylight, and just around the corner the neighboring apartment begins.

In contrast to the compact "nighttime area," the "daytime area" has an open layout consisting of a spacious living and dining zone which spans all twenty-plus meters of the building. The rotation of the apartment makes it look as if the apartment is even longer. The basic features of the building lend it a subdued appearance which is brought to life by the interplay of light and shadow on the voluminous facades, and enhanced by a high-contrast color scheme.

Address
Hegifeldstrasse 10 und 10 a, Am Eulachpark 2–12, Winterthur

Architecture
Jakob Steib Architekten (JSA)

Landscape architecture
HAGER, Landschaftsarchitektur AG

Type of commission: Direct commission
Planning and execution: 2009–2011
Schedule of accommodation: 78 apartments
Client: L + B AG

Apartment plans
→ 3.9.5

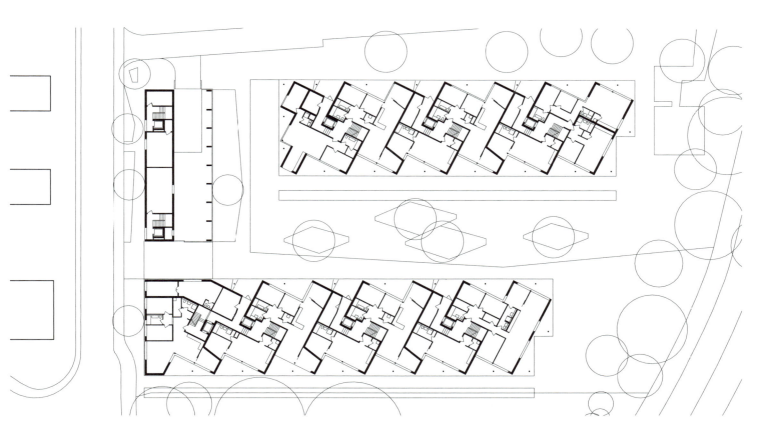

0 5 10 20   ⊖   ground floor – regular floor

Multi-Track Operations 61

2.3.3 Bombach Development

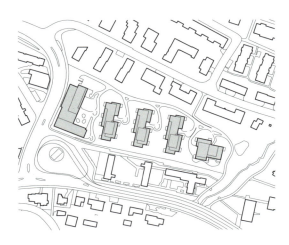

The atmosphere on the outskirts of the city was long dominated by the noisy transport node at Frankental—the last stop on the line. This all changed once the Höngg housing cooperative replaced the existing residential buildings, enabling a denser inhabitation of the area.

In a prime city location, a small village has popped up. Peering over the Limmat valley, 162 affordable apartments, two double kindergartens with after-school care, a large supermarket, various office spaces and studios, senior living communities, as well as two recreational rooms enrich the neighborhood and make Frankental an urban location around a city square. Four large, albeit compact buildings create expansive open spaces. This was pulled off by grouping as many apartments as possible around a staircase.

The main design feat of the project is that the buildings—each of which contains seven apartments—succeed in carving out commodious proportions from the open space.

Each floor of the building forms its own little community which reflects the tenant structure of the cooperative.

The plans revolve around diagonally arranged sequences of rooms which move from the staircase through a spacious entrance area to the living room and kitchen with a balcony. The houses rise towards the valley, yet compared to the smaller houses nearby, they seem to recede into the sloped terrain. Stacked and dovetailed maisonette apartments with patios ride piggyback on the building on the square, at the head of which small apartments are accessible via an arcade and are directly connected to the supermarket on the ground floor.

Address
Frankentalerstrasse 20, Schwarzenbachweg, Zürich-Höngg

Architecture
Steib & Geschwentner Architekten (SGA)

Landscape architecture
Albiez de Tomasi

Type of commission: Study commission 2010
Planning and execution: 2011–2017
Schedule of accommodation: 162 apartments, retailer, daycare center, 2 double kindergartens, recreational rooms, studios, offices
Client: Building and Housing Cooperative Höngg

Apartment plans
→ 3.5.8
→ 3.9.6
→ 3.10.2
→ 3.11.1

ground floor – second floor (floor plan detail)

Multi-Track Operations

2.3.4 Brünnen Development (Building site 12)

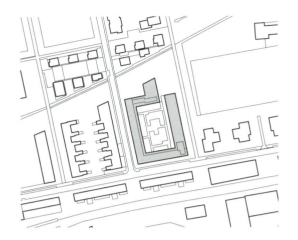

The development plan for the outskirts of Bern lays down a strict block-perimeter pattern, with courtyards opening up to a park-like green area. While it may look good at a first glance, closer inspection raises the question of whether there is enough density or public facilities for an urban atmosphere. This comes as no surprise, since these buildings are located in a peripheral area characterized by a congenially ordinary, rural atmosphere. The design adapts to this environment with an open courtyard and a public square with a recreation room and ateliers at the head of the building. The path through the courtyard leads past terraced houses that take up the ground floor living typical of the neighborhood with a suitable apartment typology. In this way, the courtyard is linked with the public space, enhancing the urban structure. The front yard of the row houses imbues the courtyard with a special flair and a distinctive identity. In addition, the row houses offer an unexpected spatial diversity in terms of their section designs, lending a special touch to the suburban-house-with-a-garden type.

The project offers a variety of differently designed apartments, creating a lively mix. All of the apartments are highly accessible, with each staircase serving up to five apartments, which produces unique spatial arrangements that fit together in a complex puzzle.

Address
Colombstrasse 24, 39–41, Riedbachstrasse 78–82, Bern

Architecture
Gmür & Geschwentner Architekten (GGA)

Landscape architecture
Albiez de Tomasi

Type of commission: Study commission 2010
Planning and execution: 2010–2013
Schedule of accommodation: 97 apartments, studios, recreation room
Client: Swatch Pension Fund, Biel

Apartment plans
→ 3.5.9

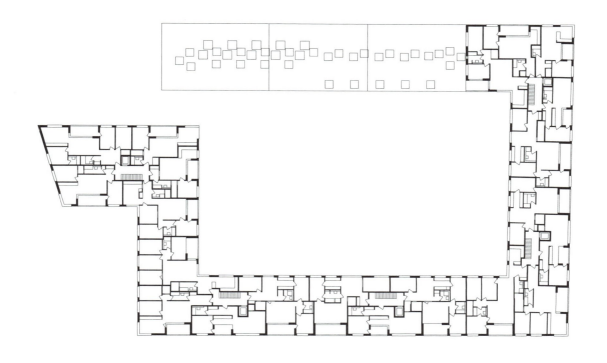
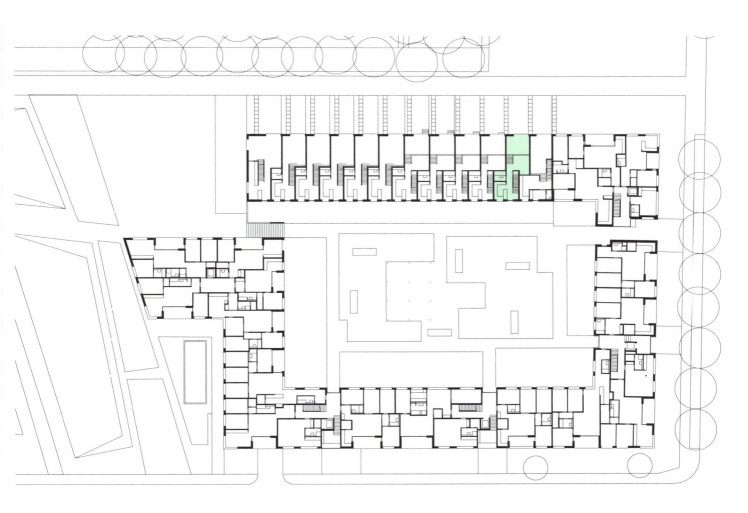

0 5 10 20   ground floor – top floor

Multi-Track Operations 65

2.3.5 Fellenbergstrasse Development

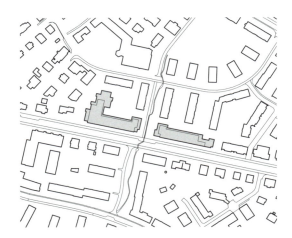

You wouldn't be able to tell just by looking at them, but the two apartment buildings have to meet various requirements in an ambitious location: the town planning level requires a clear design for the street space, while the rear garden area must be tailored to the small scale of the neighborhood. Meanwhile, the south side of the building requires protection against noise.

On the street side, the project responds to these imperatives with calm facades featuring ribbon windows, behind which—despite the stringent noise restrictions—there are living spaces and generously glazed conservatories. These give the buildings a lively and inviting appearance. Towards the garden, the elongated volumes gradually step downwards, approaching the size of the neighboring buildings and giving the luscious garden area an intimate feel.

The apartments benefit from the dynamic shapes of the buildings, which allow for a variety of different floor plans. From the "snorkel apartment" to circular plans and maisonette types, to terraced apartments whose ceilings are one-and-a-half-stories high—everything that upscale floor planning has to offer is included. The building as a whole is draped in a subtle coat of light-colored plaster with a brush-stroke texture, which, thanks to an added sprinkling of fragments of glass, sparkles seductively in the sunlight and has led the children in the neighborhood to refer to the buildings as "glitter houses"—much to the delight of the cooperative!

Address
Fellenbergstrasse 258–280, Zurich-Albisrieden

Architecture
Gmür & Geschwentner Architekten (GGA)

Type of commission: Study assignment 2010
Planning and execution: 2012–2016
Schedule of accommodation: 76 apartments, commercial space
Client: GEWOBAG – Trade Union Housing and Building Cooperative Zurich

Apartment plans

→ 3.4.5
→ 3.10.3
→ 3.10.4

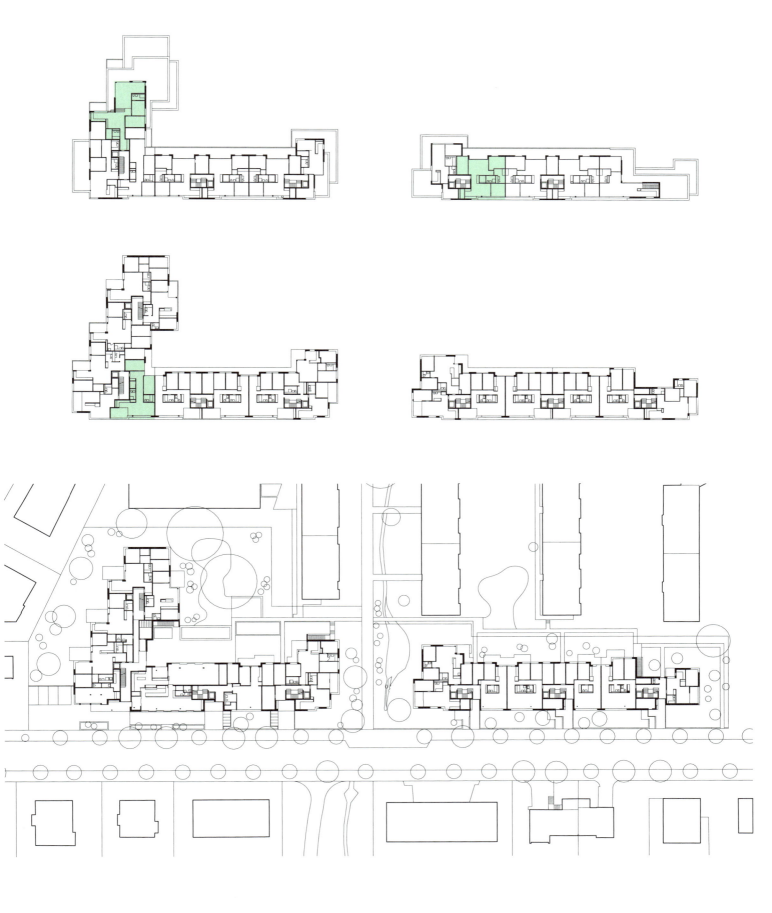

ground floor – second floor – top floor

Multi-Track Operations

2.3.6 Scheffelstrasse Apartment Block

The plot is located in the immediate vicinity of Bucheggplatz in the heart of Zurich-Wipkingen. The noise from the traffic junction to the north has a significant impact on the location. The long, narrow shape of the lot made navigating the building code quite tricky. The building type, built perpendicular to the slope, adapted cleverly to the situation with protrusions and recesses: from the street, the building appears as a coherent unit, but from the perspective of the garden, the complex appears to be broken up into several structures. With its plethora of small alcoves, it echoes the scale of the adjacent estate.

Some sections of the building floor are stepped ever so slightly downwards to accommodate the sloped landscape. The slanted roof ties the building sections back together into a cohesive form, making space for extra-high rooms in the penthouse level and the floors immediately below.

All the apartments are designed as a single spatial continuum which could easily be converted into loft-like apartments by doing away with the walls. The balconies and terraces are turned away from traffic and towards the west, into the open spaces of the neighborhood. To the east, triangular bay windows extend into the street space and open up the view from the apartment kitchens towards the lake. The accentuated gradation of the building volume grants all apartments a downhill view, effectively mitigating the narrowness of the site's geometry.

Address
Scheffelstrasse 39–43, Zurich-Wipkingen

Architecture
Jakob Steib Architekten (JSA)

Landscape architecture
Regula Hodel

Type of commission: Project competition 2010
Planning and execution: 2011–2013
Schedule of accommodation: 20 condominium apartments, 2 studio spaces
Client: BSZ Real Estate AG

Apartment space
→ 3.9.7

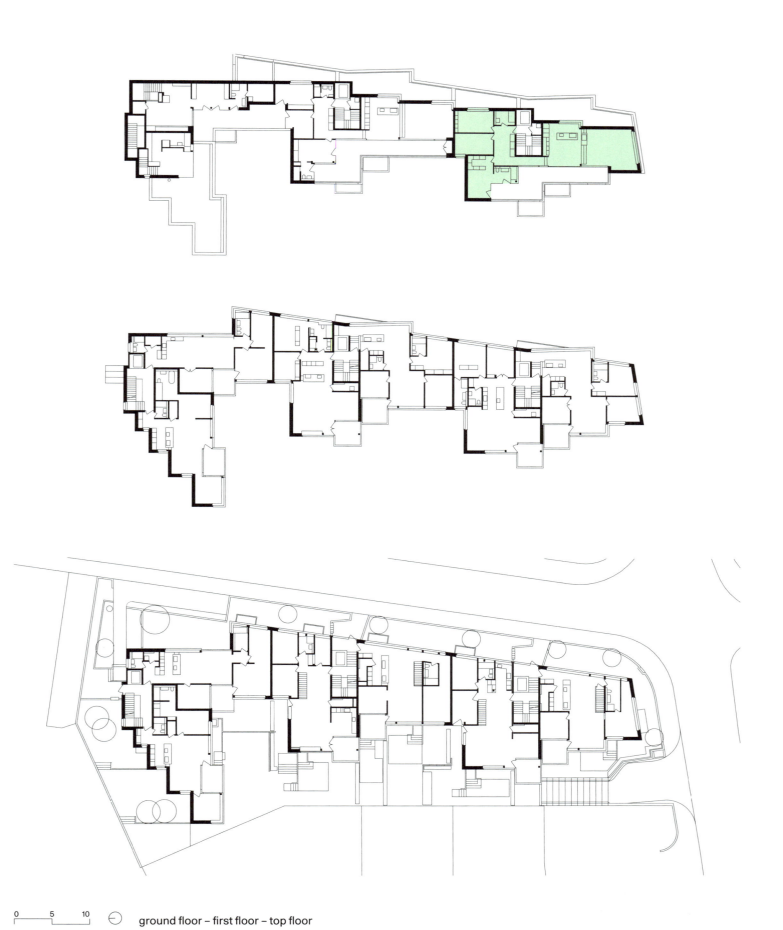

0 5 10   ground floor – first floor – top floor

Multi-Track Operations

2.3.7 Meisenrain Studios

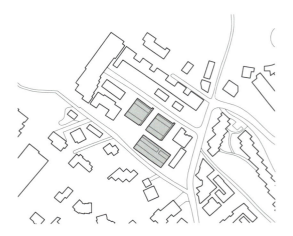

Studio living has a long tradition in Gockhausen. Once upon a time, the dreamy village in a forest clearing between Zurich and Dubendorf was an epicenter of Swiss-inflected Nordic modernism and a popular place to live for artists and architects. Numerous remarkable buildings testify to the spirit of the 1950s and 1960s. Amidst this historical environment, an existing estate was supplemented and expanded with studios that combine living and working.

Each of the individual units is accessible through private, enclosed gardens, either directly from outside or—like the upper floors—via an external ramp. The private front yards serve not only as access courtyards but also as buffers between outdoor and indoor spaces, making the residential areas feel even more intimate.

The modular studio apartments can be combined into larger units as needed. The plan follows a simple spatial principle with a series of parallel walls that emphasize the connection of the apartments to the courtyard garden. The full spatial splendor is once again revealed in the sectional design. Apartment layers that are offset by half a level and skylights in the roofs create a spatial atmosphere that is conducive to the spirit of the studio apartments.

Address
Binzen-, Nussbaumstrasse, Gockhausen

Architecture
Jakob Steib Architekten (JSA)

Landscape architecture
Nipkow Landschaftsarchitektur

Type of commission: Direct commission
Planning and execution: 2011–2014
Schedule of accommodation: 29 studio apartments
Client: SENN BPM AG, St. Gallen

Apartment plans
→ 3.12.9

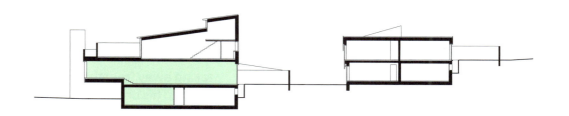

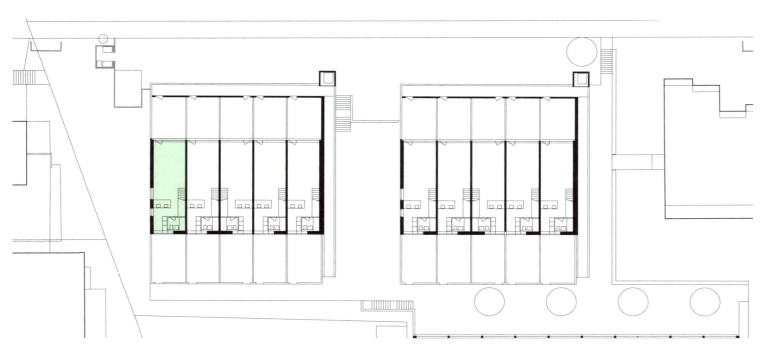

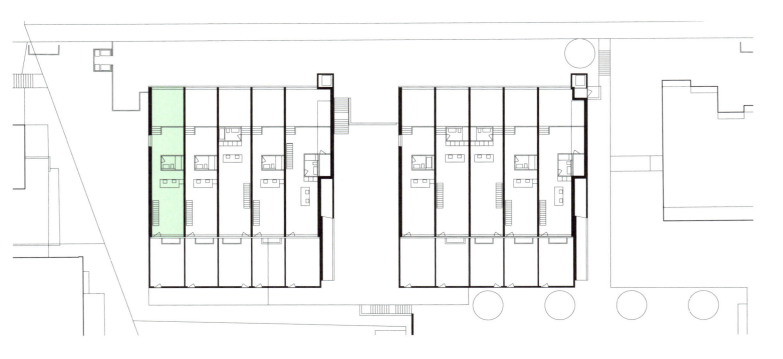

0 5 10   ground floor – upper floor (floor plan detail)

Multi-Track Operations

2.3.8 Claridenstrasse Development

The location on a relatively steep hill allows for a split-level access to the two large buildings, creating interlocking floor plans. The basic figure is formed by the intersection of two rectangles. The resulting volumes contain six exterior and two interior corners, which give the apartments an unexpected spatial opulence despite their compact organization. In addition, the width and depth of the volumes produce valuable space in the upper levels, which are used for special penthouse apartments.

The plans are based on a compact arrangement of living rooms and spaces, which wrap around a central bathroom. An enfilade connects the rooms and allows for interesting paths within the apartments without taking away from the usual amount of walking space. This creates a surprising spatial abundance from the concise plans.

The third building mimics the small-scale housing structures of the neighborhood. Two stacked maisonette apartments with their own entrances cleverly adapt to the terrain and, thanks to the ingenious sectional design, create a single-family home feeling in a row house format. The plan for parking was way ahead of its time. Outdoor parking spaces are arranged along the access road, which makes efficient use of the slope. This is just one of the ways the project conserves resources.

Address
Alte Gfenn-/Claridenstrasse, Dübendorf

Architecture
Steib & Geschwentner Architekten (SGA)

Type of commission: Invited competition 2011
Planning and execution: not carried out
Schedule of accommodation: 50 apartments
Client: Swiss Re Pension Fund, Zurich

Apartment plans
→ 3.1.5
→ 3.1.6
→ 3.1.7

ground floor –second floor

2.3.9 Brüderhofweg Development

Our research into "dense" buildings with several apartments each, which began with the Bombach residential development, culminates in Brüderhofweg. Its crowning achievement is its efficient and economical access concept. But even more important is the lively sense of community built on each of the floors, which fosters connection among the residents. And yet these compact buildings have still more to offer. Even though they utilize the full extent of the property, they maximize the open space by maintaining a moderate height. The surrounding green spaces are arranged according to the proportions of the original building and disguise the fact that the new one is much denser and hence introduces a new planning scale. The facades are attuned to this idea. A warm gray painted stucco plaster accompanies the colored windows and the natural stone base, creating a familiar mood.

The rest is top-notch craftsmanship, such as the floor plans, which are arranged like the pieces of a puzzle and give the large volumes a structure that is finely articulated. The apartments have a diverse spatiality and a strong connection to the outdoor space. And what does the neighborhood gain from all of this? A lot: in addition to affordable housing, the project included apartments for the elderly, a neighborhood restaurant, a multipurpose hall, and a daycare center. Nestled in the lush garden, a cluster of small studios completes the project.

Address
Brüderhofweg 5–10, 13–20, 26–45, Anna-Heer-Strasse 2–4, Zurich-Affoltern

Architecture
Steib & Geschwentner Architekten (SGA)

Landscape architecture
Albiez de Tomasi

Type of commission: Competition 2011
Planning and execution: 2 stages, 2012–2021
Schedule of accommodation: 288 apartments, restaurant, multipurpose hall, daycare center, community spaces, studios
Client: Frohheim Housing Cooperative, Zurich

Apartment plans
→ 3.2.6
→ 3.2.7
→ 3.11.2
→ 3.11.3

ground floor – regular floor (floor plan detail)

Multi-Track Operations

2.3.10 Holunderhof Development

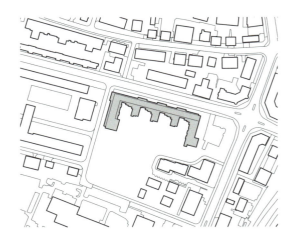

On the busier streets in Zurich, finding ways to minimize noise is a crucial factor in urban design. The project on Holunderweg provides one example of how a bold, dynamic urban design gesture can respond to this dilemma by creating different conditions on each of the four sides: a U-shaped volume encloses the street space and creates a green inner space to the south that is sheltered from the noise.

The large courtyard requires that the longitudinal building have an efficient organizational structure so that the open space that is gained does not come at the expense of cost-effectiveness. A row of staggered wall panels creates a large facade that hosts apartments with variegated depths. The rooms and living spaces are intricately nested together. This trick creates a workaround to the noise pollution, making it possible to invigorate the streetscape by adding living spaces.

An intricate split-level building masks the sloping terrain, which is only revealed on closer examination of the section. A gently slanting roof tempers the tiered building volume and unites the subdivided volume into a single large building. The two side wings of the building are reserved for ground-level living. Maisonettes with double-story kitchens provide sufficient intimacy in the west wing, while the east side responds to the urban neighborhood with stacked row houses and a system of access balconies.

Address
Regensbergstrasse 191–203, Holunderhof 1–8, Zurich-Oerlikon

Architecture
Steib & Geschwentner Architekten (SGA)

Landscape architecture
Rotzler Krebs Partner

Type of commission: Invited competition 2012
Planning and execution: not carried out
Schedule of accommodation: 101 apartments
Client: Non-Profit Housing Cooperative Röntgenhof, Zurich

Apartment plans
→ 3.10.5
→ 3.10.6

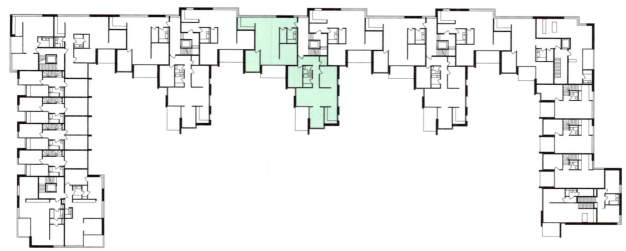

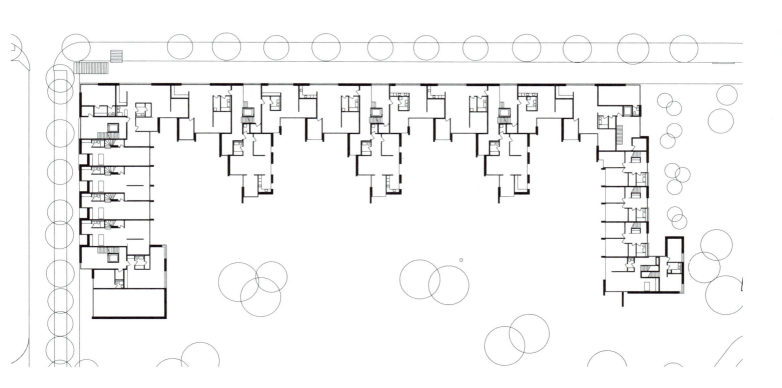

ground floor – regular floor

Multi-Track Operations

2.3.11 Schweighof Development

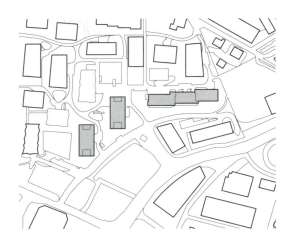

The design plan envisaged a uniform collection of point blocks with featureless spaces in between. The lack of an identity from an urban planning perspective was to be offset by distinctive architecture and a rich living environment. Fortunately, in the end, both the client and the jury were convinced that the three houses—two point blocks and one long one—ought to include maximum spatial and typological diversity.

The two blocks are clad with vertical facades which make them look taller. The apartments just beneath the top floors benefit from interior spaces that reach up through the attic level like a submarine periscope, capturing light from above. The rest of the top floor is filled with interior patios. This made it possible to add more space to the volumes by building out the attic into a fully-fledged floor, despite its reduced size in accordance with the building code. The resulting apartments have a rather peculiar shape that sets them apart from the conventional offerings in the neighborhood.

The two-story outdoor spaces contribute to the spacious appearance of the buildings. The long building is made up of row houses which are stacked two or more stories high. The lower units have garden access, while the upper units have two-story interior spaces and loggias. The house is accessible directly from the ground floor or via an outdoor corridor, which encourages circulation between the neighborhoods and provides access to the open space.

Address
Schweighofplatz 3, Schweighofstrasse 8–12, Schweighofweg 14, Kriens

Architecture
Gmür & Geschwentner Architekten (GGA)

Type of commission: Invited competition 2012
Planning and execution: 2013–2018
Schedule of accommodation: 133 apartments, community space
Client: SUVA, Lucerne

Apartment plans
→ 3.3.8
→ 3.4.6
→ 3.4.7
→ 3.4.8
→ 3.5.10
→ 3.11.4

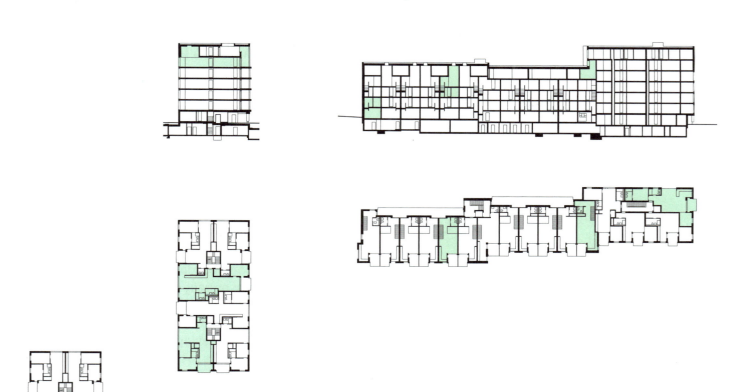

0 5 10 20   ground floor – third floor

Multi-Track Operations 79

2.3.12 Apartment Block in the Aeschbach Quarter

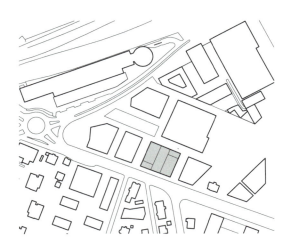

A new district is being built in Aarau. The development plan was predetermined, as were the volumes, which left little leeway for a specific residential idea. The U-shaped building in particular presents a challenging starting point, since it was primarily built to accommodate an urban planning concept rather than the demands of sound internal organization.

While this appeared to be a disadvantage, it also created an opportunity to tackle the bulky volume with a special housing design: two facing balcony systems provide access to small apartments while creating a communal area on each floor. These exceptionally deep galleries, connected via an external corridor, provide ample outdoor communal space. The roof of the connecting the floor that forms the bottom of the U is used as a garden which links the two parts of the building. Despite the tight budget, the design plan made extensive use of colors to create an architectural identity that adequately expresses the diversity of the residents.

The second building, on the other hand, aims to offer an equally diverse communal area centered around a staircase. The robust polygonal structure of the building makes it possible to fit seven apartments on each floor which—thanks to their precise positioning in the plan—take on a very unique shape.

The facades were required to be clad in clinker bricks, which gives the two buildings a fundamentally light tone with a Nordic feel.

Address
Buchserstrasse 9/11, Aarau

Architecture
Gmür & Geschwentner Architekten (GGA)

Landscape architecture
Studio Vulkan

Type of commission: Direct commission
Planning and execution: 2012–2018
Schedule of accommodation: 79 apartments, commercial spaces
Client: Mobimo Management AG, Küsnacht

Apartment plans
→ 3.9.8
→ 3.9.9
→ 3.9.10

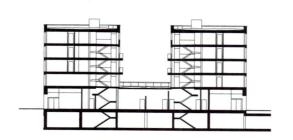

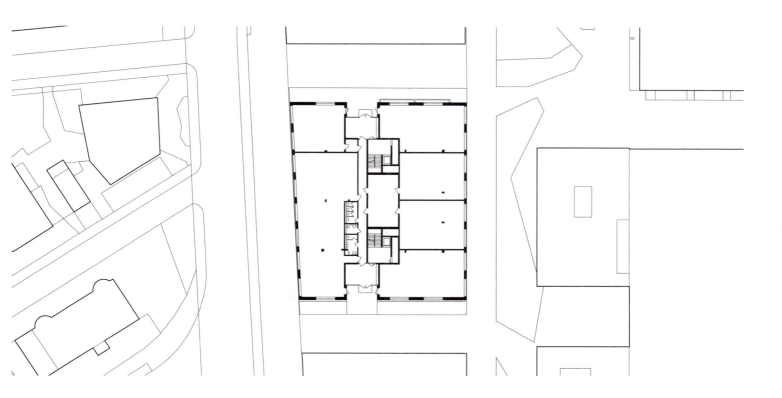

 ground floor – first floor

Multi-Track Operations 81

2.3.13 Hard Turm Park Apartments and Offices

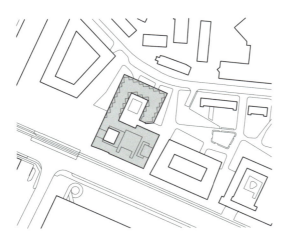

The design plan for this building had narrowly defined, contradictory requirements: the need to make full use of the surrounding urban space made a single volume seem ideal, while the bipartite spatial program made the separation of the building into two units seem more practical. For this reason, "conjoined twins" were created, which shape the urban space as a combined unit while maintaining their own distinct architectural identity. When viewed from Pfingstweidstrasse, the building appears to be an office space, while the other, residential side of the building includes a noise-protected courtyard.
The office building has an H shape which soaks up valuable daylight from all sides and allows the offices to mesh seamlessly with the urban space. Thus while office buildings often appear to be sealed-off spaces, the design plan here allows for maximum interlinking with the outside world. A large entrance hall and a public café make the street level more vibrant. The residential building is located on the northern half of the site. Because this positioning optimizes the amount of sunlight that hits the building, the apartments are oriented towards the south. For this reason, the apartments were built with an exceptional degree of interior depth and space, fostering a cozy living environment despite the building's density. Having two different floor types alternating one on top of the another makes for magnificent two-story balconies which let a lot of light into the apartments and shape the external appearance of the apartment building.

Address
Förrlibuckstrasse 223–229, Pfingstweidstrasse 110, Zurich

Architecture
Gmür & Geschwentner Architekten (GGA)

Landscape architecture
Vetschpartner Landschaftsarchitekten

Type of commission: Direct commission
Planning and execution: 2012–2017
Schedule of accommodation: 108 apartments (rental and owner-occupier), office spaces for 1000 workplaces, staff restaurant, public café, museum of finance, conference rooms, auditorium
Client: Hardturm AG, Zurich

Apartment plans
→ 3.3.9
→ 3.3.10
→ 3.3.11
→ 3.5.11
→ 3.6.4

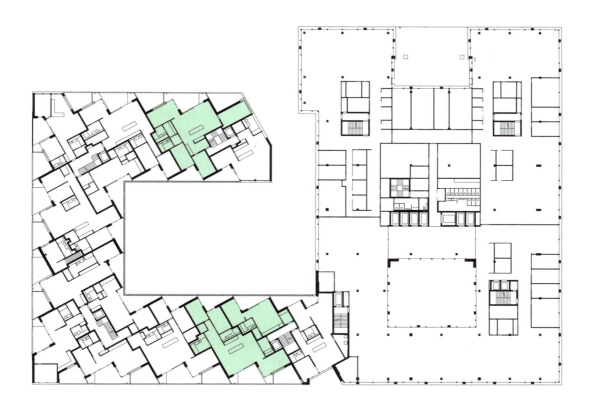

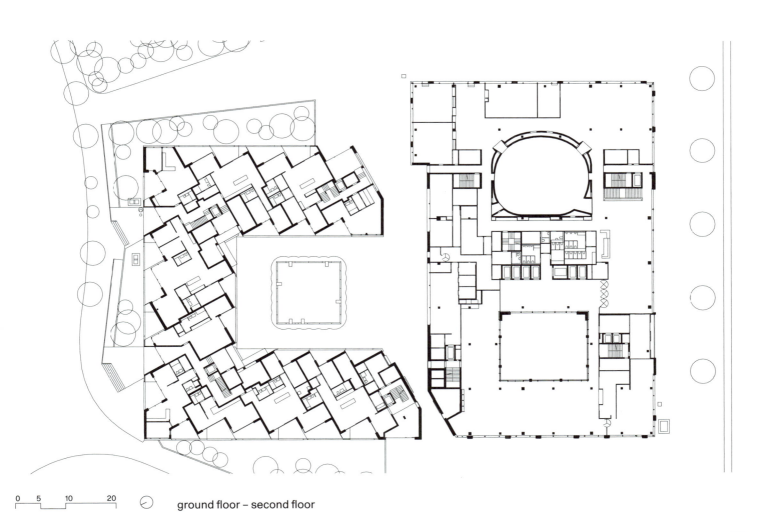

0 5 10   20   ground floor – second floor

Multi-Track Operations

2.3.14 Binz 111 Apartment Blocks

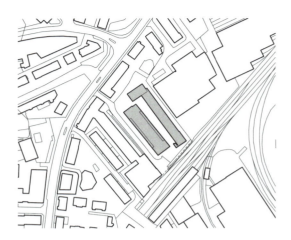

Considering the history of the site, it was a requirement of the program to respect the spirited urbanity of this sensitive location. The apartments for students and the staff of the University Hospital of Zurich replace a former paint factory in the second tier of an industrial area directly adjacent to the railway tracks. The factory was occupied for several years and was thus politically charged.

The challenging location determines how the two buildings are arranged. The plaza facing Uetlibergstrasse carves out a striking space on which the building entrances and a restaurant are located. The building makes several important contributions to the neighborhood, including its eclectic blend of international residents and the public ground floor which contains studios, a restaurant, community rooms, and a laundry room. Every last detail of the buildings is well thought out, making them both raw and colorful, playful and austere. Unnecessary elements were omitted, saving money and reducing CO_2 emissions. Colors are used as a cost-effective design element which amplifies the spatiality and gives the buildings a special identity, while breathing a homely atmosphere into the "refined shell."

The nucleus, or soul of the large building is the "Goethe staircase": a diagonal staircase that crosses through the entire building, infusing the rigorous grid with a surprising spatial opulence. Prefabricated restrooms, the single-brick facade, and a simple structural design helped keep costs low, making for affordable housing.

Address
Uetlibergstrasse 111, Zurich-Wiedikon

Architecture
Gmür & Geschwentner Architekten (GGA)

Landscape architecture
Nipkow Landschaftsarchitektur

Type of commission: Study commission 2012
Planning and execution: 2013–2018
Schedule of accommodation: 272 studios, 40 shared apartments, restaurant with bar, studios, community rooms
Client: Stiftung Abendrot, Basel

Apartment plans
→ 3.11.5
→ 3.11.6
→ 3.11.7

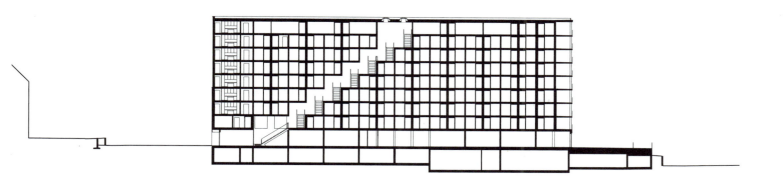

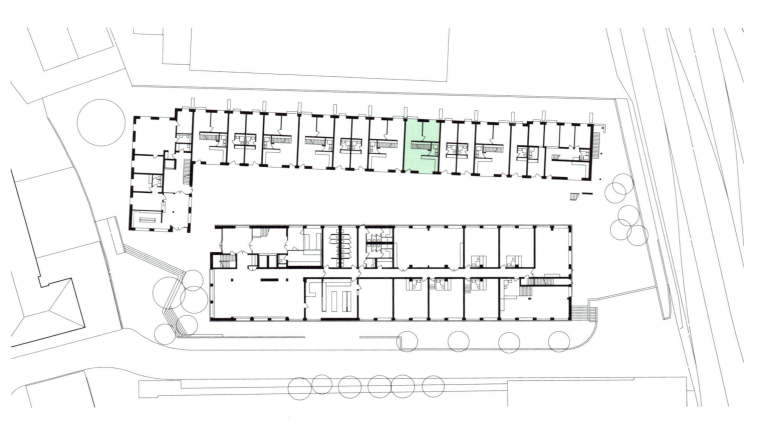

ground floor – second floor

Multi-Track Operations

2.3.15 Steinach High-Rise (Saurer WerkZwei)

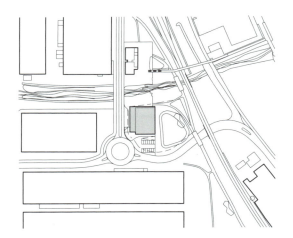

Steinach is an idyllic village in a rural area directly on Lake Constance. Why build a high-rise here of all places? The answer is gleaned by looking at Arbon, the neighboring canton. On a site where Saurer once manufactured its trucks, there has emerged a dense, mixed-use neighborhood with an urban character. The high-rise building marks the limit of the urban precinct and the transition to the residential areas of Steinach.

The modest footprint of the high-rise building leaves space for an expansive public park that connects with Steinach Bay. But while the public ground floor of the high-rise building contributes to the revitalization of the unused space, its mere presence at such a serene location inevitably caused a stir in the neighborhood, raising questions about how welcome the building would be. To help ease tensions, the roof was made available to the public, making its beautiful panorama view an asset to the neighborhood as a whole. A multipurpose room with a kitchen and a terrace overlooking Lake Constance were available for rent.

The flexibility of the building's structure allows for several different apartment types. They change their spatial organization depending on the location and orientation and fan out towards the view, which is captured by ribbon windows. The diversity of apartment styles makes the high-rise building accessible to everyone. Despite the benefits it offered to the surrounding neighborhood, the high-rise building was entrenched in a long-standing political debate, and was never built.

Address
Haupt-, Bahnhofstrasse, Steinach

Architecture
Gmür & Geschwentner Architekten (GGA)

Landscape architecture
Studio Vulkan

Type of commission: Study commission 2013
Planning and execution: not carried out
Schedule of accommodation: 80 apartments, commercial spaces, offices
Client: HRS Real Estate AG, Frauenfeld

Apartment plans
→ 3.7.8
→ 3.7.9

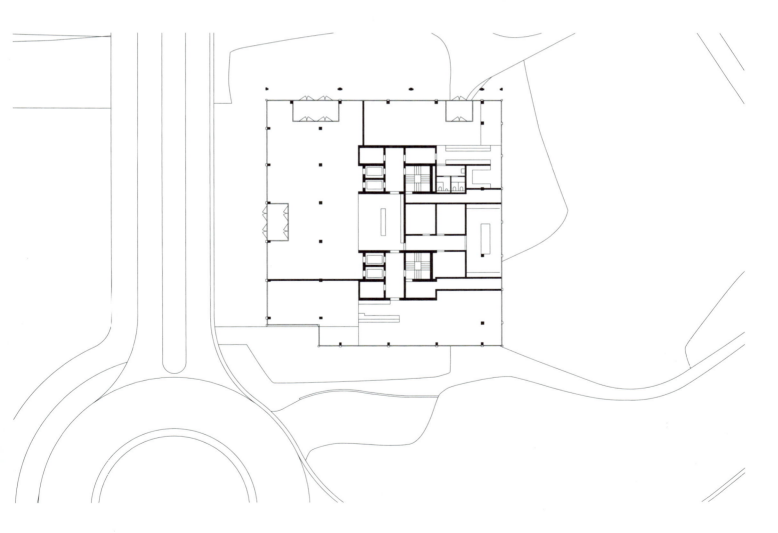

0 5 10   ground floor – 18. floor

Multi-Track Operations 87

2.3.16 Kleeweidstrasse Development

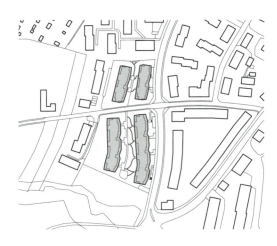

Expect the unexpected! This could be the title of the story of the study commission for this development in Zurich's Leimbach neighborhood, where the jury's decision—based primarily on marketing considerations—had to be corrected afterwards. Why? The project initially awarded first prize placed volumes across the slope, working against the terrain and significantly interfering with the natural course of the landscape. In contrast, the building volumes proposed by us, placed lengthwise along the slope,

adapted to their urban environment by leaving the terrain in its original state, complimenting the street space, and creating a green residential area that fits in with the open spaces in the rest of the neighborhood. All of this ensures that the buildings maintain a close connection with the natural environment.
The apartment layouts in our proposal, which were based on a standard type, were criticized for overemphasizing the central living hall. We based this design off Steiger Crawford's Doldertal apartments, which, thanks to the star-shaped arrangement of rooms around a living hall, gives the floor plan an extraordinary spatial transparency. Of course, in the competition project, the obligatory fireplace was a classy ornament to the living hall, and tapered, Italian-style walls helped the space flow smoothly. Yet all of this was probably too much of a good thing for the marketing professionals to appreciate. A round of revisions in the competition helped improve the project substantially, making it more appealing to the majority of the jurors. In the end, it won the bid. Our beloved living halls were sacrificed to make room for new ideas that ultimately optimized the design. The plans follow a simple but effective spatial principle: at the ends of the buildings, the apartments benefit from the availability of the added corner space and from the different views into the green spaces. In between, each stairwell serves three apartments. The space in these apartments is laid out stepwise, partitioning the living space in a way that emphasizes the diagonal. The main hall has been reinterpreted as a spatial cascade, allowing for several different uses. The shaded center of the living spaces serves as a secluded retreat—only the fireplace from the original study commission is missing.
The building's dynamic shape reflects the principles of the plan. The volume's protrusions and alcoves divide the facades, split up the length of the large volumes, and lend the building a dynamic appearance. The buildings widen at the ends, emphasizing the facades on the short sides, which complete

the articulation of each volume. The roof projects prominently, and rests on shear walls that support the attic volumes, which are arranged like porcelain dishes on a tray. The earth-colored mineral stucco blends with the terrain, while the white-painted attic floors create a Mediterranean atmosphere.

Address
Maneggpromenade 140–156, Kleeweidstrasse 40–45, Zurich-Leimbach

Architecture
Steib & Geschwentner Architekten (SGA)

Landscape architecture
Nipkow Landschaftsarchitektur

Type of commission: Study commission 2013
Planning and execution: 2016–2021
Schedule of accommodation: 129 apartments, community space
Client: Zürich Lebens-Versicherungsgesellschaft AG and Zürich Anlagestiftung

Apartment plans
→ 3.2.8
→ 3.2.9
→ 3.2.10
→ 3.11.8

Multi-Track Operations

competition entry: ground floor – first floor

revised design: ground floor – regular floor

Multi-Track Operations

2.3.17 Zollstrasse Ost Development

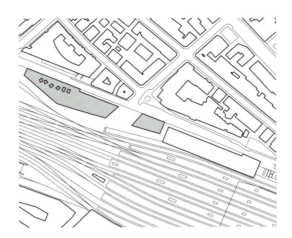

The exposed location sits directly adjacent to the railway tracks. Its remarkable depth was large enough to accommodate a type of residential building that is idiosyncratic and capable of capturing the unique atmosphere of the location. Like many other buildings in the neighborhood, the volumes take their shape from the geometry of the site itself and the nearby street. Thanks to the maximized dimensions, the building manages to provide the requisite accommodation with one floor fewer than it would otherwise need. As a result, all apartments have a truly unusual ceiling height of 3.3 meters! This starting point paves the way for special apartment floor plans with impressively large balconies, rooms arranged one behind the other, lavish bathrooms, and sprawling kitchen islands. The polygonal shape of the plots allows the plans to fan out, incorporating angled walls that lend each apartment a unique spatial identity. Large living areas wind through the massive buildings like light tunnels, and provide shelter from the hustle and bustle of the railway nearby.

The spacious facades are influenced by the oblique geometry of the plan. An intense play of light and shadow accentuates their pronounced plasticity, revealing an independent and striking architectural style. The development plan links the new buildings with the style of city development common in the late 19th century. Their architectural design echoes the colorful buildings that line the railway yard.

Address
Zollstrasse 27–53, Zurich
Architecture
Gmür & Geschwentner Architekten (GGA)
Helle Architektur

Type of commission: Project competition invitation 2013
Planning and execution: not carried out
Schedule of accommodation: 139 apartments, studios, commercial, restaurant, bar
Client: SBB Immobilien

Apartment plans
→ 3.6.5
→ 3.12.10

ground floor – first floor – fifth floor

Multi-Track Operations

2.3.18 Reitmen Development

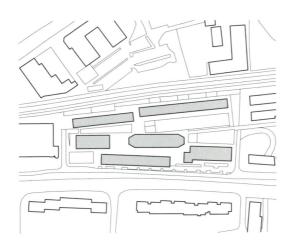

On the outskirts of Schlieren, a cluster of six houses was built based on a design by Haerle Hubacher Architects, two of which were planned by us. The fruitful collaboration created not just a residential development, but in many ways a new and vibrant neighborhood. The ground floor helps revitalize the urban space by offering a wide range of services that are both public and communal.

While each house has a unique architectural identity, the concrete base covered in glossy paint, the balanced palette of colors, and the open spaces link the volumes together. The green apartment building derives its architectural motifs from its exposed location next to the railway tracks. It appears long and slender with a comfortable depth and dynamic plans, large balconies on one side, and a majestic facade facing the tracks. Balcony partitions resembling Schiller curls, balustrades that look like membranes of a speaker, spiral staircases descending into the courtyard, and a strong green color scheme make up its distinctive architectural appearance.

The yellow house on the street filters out the noise with a bulky layer of balconies made of site-cast concrete. The high railings and the robust gallows structure made of concrete wall panels block the noise and provide structural efficiency. They shape the building's fortress-like appearance and give the apartments an unexpected spatial coziness which evokes the feeling of patio living.

Address
Badenerstrasse 90–92, 104–108, Schlieren

Urban design
Haerle Hubacher Architekten

Architektur Haus 1, 2 + 6
Steib & Geschwentner Architekten (SGA)

Landscape architecture
Raderschallpartner

Type of commission: Study commission 2014
Planning and execution: 2015–2020
Schedule of accommodation: 60 apartments, commercial space, studio and community room
Client: Turidomus Investment Foundation, represented by Pensimo Management AG

Apartment plans
→ 3.10.7
→ 3.10.8

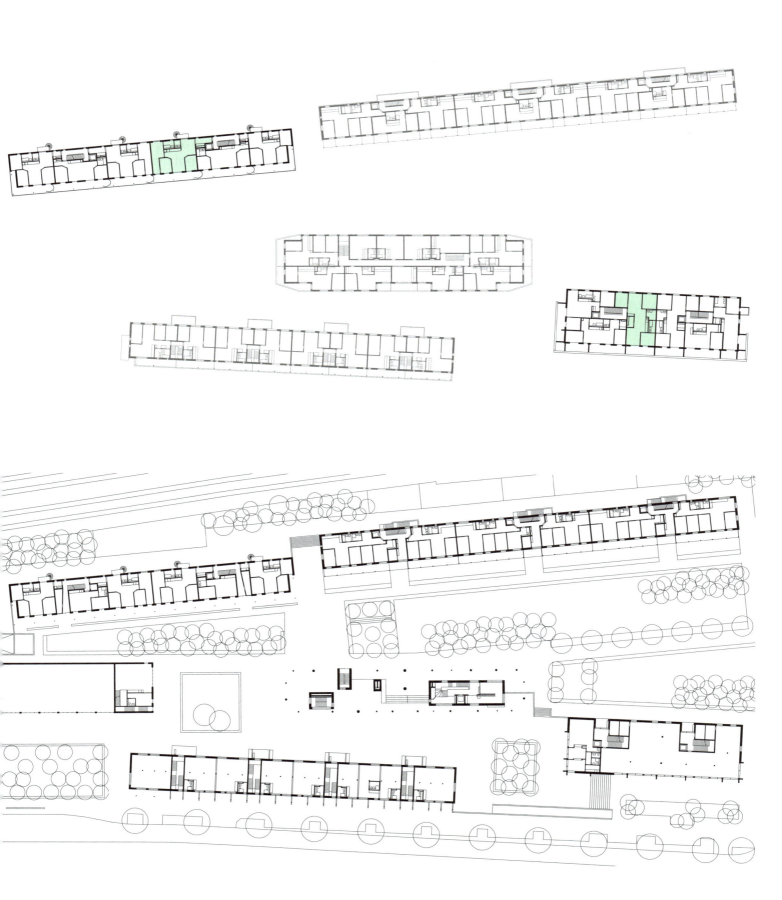

ground floor – regular floor

Multi-Track Operations

2.3.19   Am Rietpark Apartment Block

A new residential district with over 600 apartments is built on a former industrial site in Schlieren! Robust blocks gather around a spacious park, which forms the spatial backbone. The blocks are accessible from one side only, from Brandstrasse. How does one access the second and third buildings? By the exceptionally expansive access and circulation system, which provides the large building with a central entrance of ten staircases and has opulent four-meter-high ceilings, as well as a cascade of naturally lit inner streets, paths, and squares.
The heart of the superblock is a hall designed to host community events. Two lushly vegetated courtyards provide interior daylight and shape the spatial atmosphere on the ground floor. A rich palette of diaphanous metallic colors and dark-painted ceilings creates a subdued "underwater atmosphere." The midnight blue and champagne-colored facades complement the special color scheme.
The 200 apartments are densely organized and, as always, have a diversity of spatial layouts. Two-story interior spaces enhance the apartments in the central section, effectively compensating for the limited view. The crowning finale is on the roof: a pool with a sun deck, open to all residents. Up top, the vibe is different—reminiscent of somewhere in the south, far removed from the bustling commuter traffic outside the front door.

Address
Brandstrasse 21, Schlieren

Architecture
Gmür & Geschwentner Architekten (GGA)

Landscape architecture
Balliana Schubert

Type of commission: Study commission 2014
Planning and execution: 2015–2020
Schedule of accommodation: 202 apartments, office and commercial space, swimming pool
Client: Helvetia Insurance, Zurich

Apartment plans
→ 3.1.8
→ 3.4.9
→ 3.4.10
→ 3.11.9

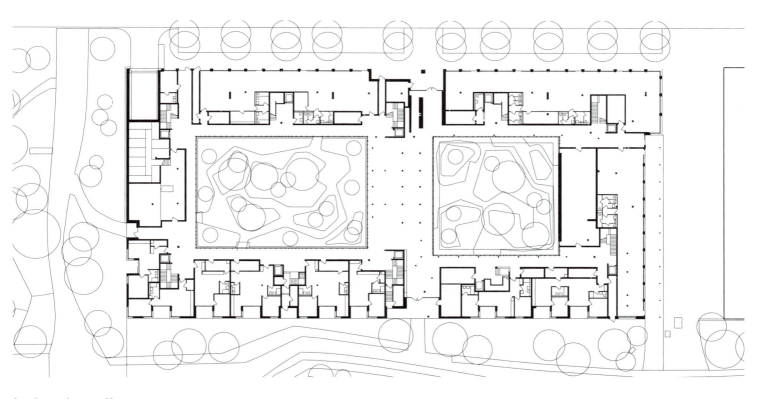

ground floor – fourth floor

Multi-Track Operations

2.3.20 Lauriedhofweg Development

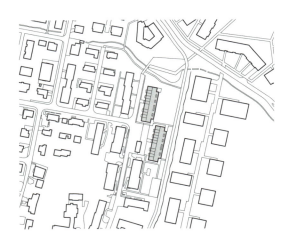

The housing cooperative called for compact and affordable apartments. Given this, the residential aspect of the design was prioritized, while with stoic sangfroid the urban aspect was more or less adapted to the signature of the existing area with the addition of two simple, spatially offset buildings.
In creating a volume that is even smaller than the spatial constraints (which in any case are tight), the available square meters are turned fully into living space: all individual rooms are directly accessible from the central living room. At the same time, the living area, including the kitchen, is limited to a necessary minimum. The freed-up space is put towards an additional room. With this, the three-and-a-half-room apartment becomes a four-and-a-half-room apartment, allowing the residents to cope with changing living circumstances within the same four walls. This system is only possible thanks to the access provided by an outdoor corridor. An adjoining conservatory provides privacy while also serving as an entrance, outdoor space, and spatial buffer zone for the adjacent room. The architectural expression of the two buildings is characterized by the leafy access balcony and the way in which the new building enriches the existing ones, which receive an architectural "update." The pitched roof appears as a delicate and elegant sheet metal structure, which maintains a sense of familiarity without the bulkiness of tiled roofs.

Address
Lauriedhofweg 8-20, Zug

Architecture
Steib & Geschwentner Architekten (SGA)

Landscape architecture
Regula Hodel

Type of commission: Project competition 2015
Planning and execution: not executed
Schedule of accommodation: 38 apartments
Client: Housing Cooperative Heimat, Zug

Apartment plans
→ 3.11.10
→ 3.11.11

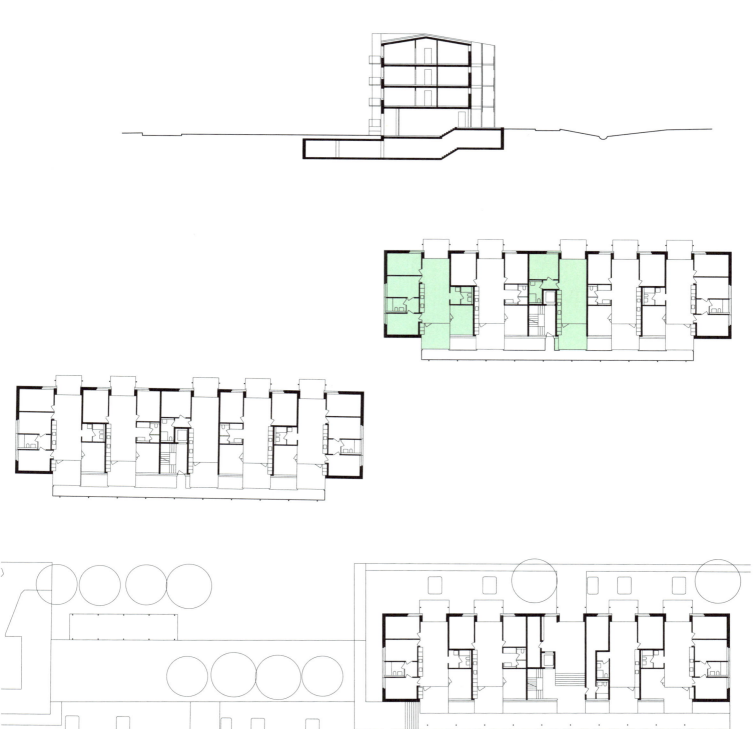

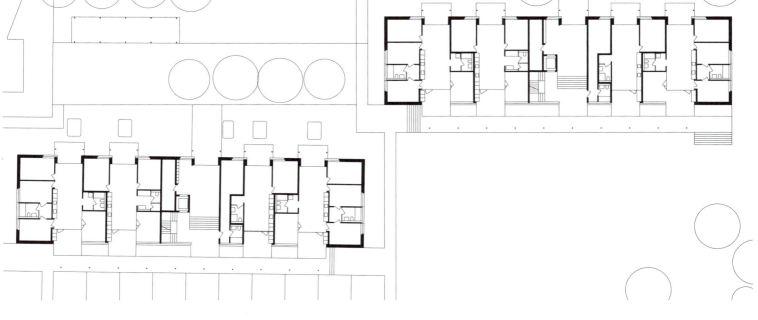

first floor – regular floor

Multi-Track Operations

2.3.21 Parkside Apartment Block (Saurer WerkZwei)

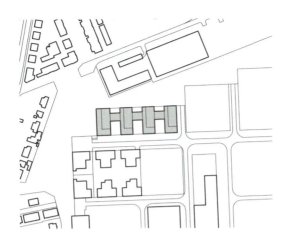

On the Saurer WerkZwei in Arbon, the narrow building space as well as its location next to the park required a meticulously designed building type. While most of the neighboring residential buildings take shape around a courtyard, such an arrangement would have been ill-suited for this particular plot. The proposed building shape with six outward-facing alcoves makes full use of the space defined by the legal stipulations on building on the perimeter of a lot and proves to be an effective structure for well-oriented housing with easy access.

The interior is inverted: all sides of the apartment participate in the public space and bring the large building into dialogue with the surrounding buildings. Two entrance portals—each with an open hall—connect the two courtyards, providing views along the north–south axis. The special building form provides an ideal starting point for the development of apartments with an idiosyncratic spatial identity. The building at the head of the development faces the park, and expands the selection with large apartments suitable for shared use.

The facade design works with the idea of neighborly proximity. High-level ribbon windows shield the rooms and create a pleasantly subdued daylight atmosphere, while the narrow, floor-to-ceiling windows provide selected viewing angles. This motif sets the industrial tone of the facades. Bright, cream-colored profiled sheeting contrasts with the dark, ribbon windows, accentuating the facade.

Address
Giessereistrasse 16–22, Arbon

Architecture
Steib & Geschwentner Architekten (SGA)

Landscape architecture
Krebs Herde

Type of commission: feasibility study 2015
Planning and execution: 2015–2018
Schedule of accommodation: 74 apartments, community room
Client: Cooperative Baufreunde, Zurich

Apartment plans
→ 3.11.12

ground floor – regular floor – top floor

Multi-Track Operations

2.4 Reaching New Heights

After serving seven years as director of the Office for Urban Planning in Zurich, Patrick Gmür returned to self-employment in October 2016. This provided an opportunity for the four friends to rethink their individual and shared professional goals.

They had already relocated their offices to the James building in 2009 with the intention of making operations simpler. Jakob Steib held onto his studio at Wettingerwies. Since then, joint projects are discussed and worked on at Flüelastrasse. During these years of consolidation, the focus on residential construction continued uninterrupted. There were experiments with new floor plans, urban design models were invented, and work on different high-rise buildings continued. The resumption of a project that Gmür & Steib Architekten had set aside in 2008 also helped breathe new life into the firm.

2.4.1 Developments 5–7, Waidmatt

This project responded to a rare brief, provided by a housing cooperative: to construct affordable apartment buildings at various locations in a neighborhood in Zurich's Affoltern. The conditions for each of the building plots were unique, both in terms of their size and the quality of their location. The design idea made these special circumstances into an opportunity to develop a tailor-made solution for each building site.

The aim is for the new buildings to incorporate themselves into the neighborhood rather than emerge as a stand-alone development. The motto is: keep building the city! Each building block takes into account the conditions of its specific location and produces an architectural expression of its own, tailored to its specific features and the particular spatial program.

The diversity in the housing on offer—from compact apartments to row houses with gardens to community-oriented gallery apartments—emerges spontaneously. This strategy of "analytical urban planning" allows the new buildings to tactfully and gradually weave themselves into the neighborhood, which ensures that the buildings are received favorably by the local residents. The open space plays a unifying role, connecting the buildings with each other and embedding them within the neighborhood. The communal facilities reflect this idea and are related to the surrounding design.

Address
In Böden, Wehntaler-, Riedenhaldenstrasse, Zurich-Affoltern

Architecture
Gmür & Geschwentner Architekten (GGA)/ Helle Architektur

Type of commission: Competition 2016
Planning and execution: not carried out
Schedule of accommodation: 260 apartments and single rooms, kindergarten, commercial space, neighborhood meeting place
Client: Waidmatt housing cooperative, Zurich

Apartment plans
→ 3.2.11
→ 3.2.12

ground floor – first floor (floor plan detail)

Reaching New Heights

2.4.2 Reussbühl Ost Development

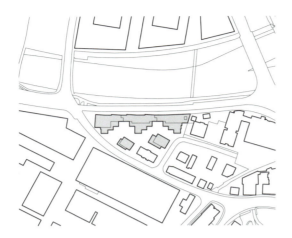

For connoisseurs of the Swiss music scene, the first thing the name Reussbühl brings to mind is probably the musician Hösli, who sang about the working-class suburb of Lucerne before his tragic, premature death. This location is subject to noise from nearby traffic and complex regulations for keeping the heavy vehicle traffic flowing. Still, this area—which despite its congestion is still important for the city—has many aspects which make it appealing, such as its immediate proximity to the Emme River.

The project was part of a larger development plan which included this prominent urban location. Our concept was to place a long building alongside the street space which would prevent noise from reaching the garden, which is home to two point blocks belonging to another owner. The narrow backbone of the long building is modulated by three finely gradated bulges in the building volume, which extend the facade as much as possible as it approaches the noise-protected side to the south.

A staircase provides access to six apartments, which nest into each other intricately and fan out towards the facade to capture as much light as possible. Special apartments with slim proportions are arranged along the street, stretching out to breathe the air in the courtyard, which is shielded from the noise. As a result, the living rooms and kitchens are located on the distinctly modernist-looking facade on the street side, which they endow with life, the noise restrictions notwithstanding.

Address
Reussbühl-, Reusszopf-, Hauptstrasse, Luzern

Architecture
Steib & Geschwentner Architekten (SGA)

Landscape architecture
Nipkow Landschaftsarchitektur

Type of commission: Study commission 2017
Planning and execution: not carried out
Schedule of accommodation: 94 apartments, kindergarten
Client: Reussbühl Ost joint venture

Apartment plans
→ 3.10.9
→ 3.10.10
→ 3.10.11
→ 3.10.12

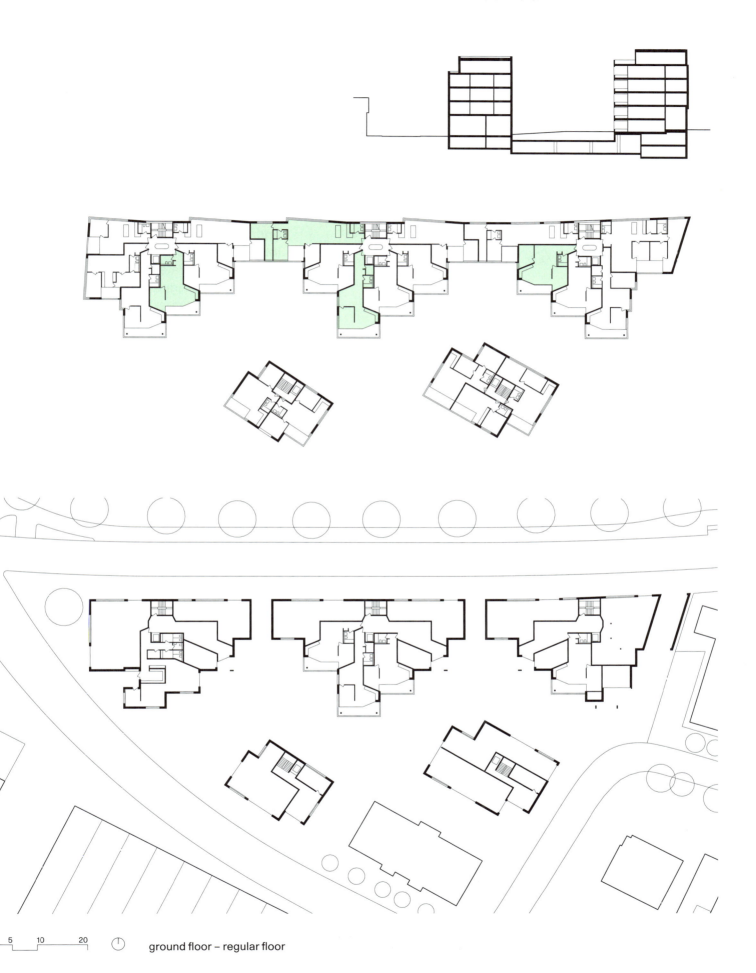

ground floor – regular floor

Reaching New Heights

2.4.3 Langgrütstrasse Apartment Block

The client's desire to build as many affordable and high-quality family apartments as possible in the heart of Zurich-Albisrieden was at odds with the building regulations of this location, which invoked almost every paragraph of the building code. "Form follows law and tougher than the rest," would be an adequate summary of this building. As is so often the case, these complex requirements also created unique opportunities for solutions.

At the house's center of gravity, a full seven floors rise up in a staggered manner, creating different floors with different plans. This diversity is owed to the building regulations. The angled design creates a spacious outdoor area for the daycare center on the ground floor. This facility helps orient the building towards the street, emphasizing its central location in the neighborhood. To resolve the conflict that a central staircase would have created in the plan of the daycare center, the staircase cascades from the ground floor to the first floor, revealing a striking entrance that extends diagonally into the interior of the building.

The richly decorated brick facade envelops the sculpturally designed building in solid, sophisticated attire. The large balconies facing Langgrütstrasse testify to a confident appearance that reflects the self-image of the robust housing cooperative.

Address
Langgrütstrasse 132/134, Zurich-Albisrieden

Architecture
Gmür & Geschwentner Architekten (GGA)

Landscape architecture
Vetschpartner Landschaftsarchitekten

Type of commission: Direct commission
Planning and execution: 2017–2022
Schedule of accommodation: 23 apartments, daycare center
Client: GEWOBAG, Zurich

Apartment plans
→ 3.6.6

108

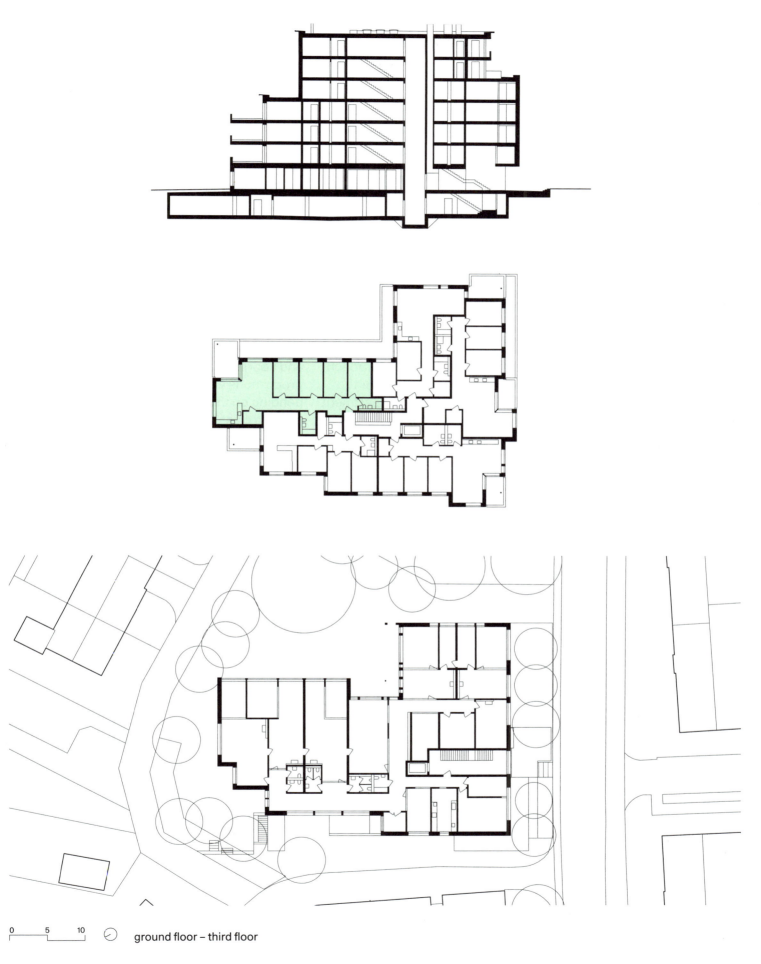

ground floor – third floor

Reaching New Heights

2.4.4 Langgrütweg Apartment Block

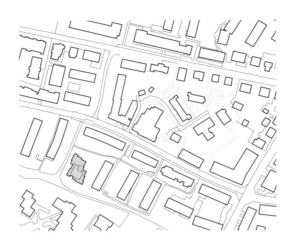

Continuing to develop the district: the Albisrieden trilogy has taken a respectful approach to developing the neighborhood in order to create new, affordable housing. The apartment building on Langgrütweg represents a provisional conclusion to this endeavor. It is part of a site development that takes place under a legacy regulatory framework and as such must be connected to the house on Langgrütstrasse, even though the urban planning context makes this difficult: while one building is located on a residential street, the site on Langgrütweg sits on the edge of a park-like corridor. This green space gives the site a unique ambiance, which is reflected in the design idea.

All apartments have a strong link to the outdoor space and—thanks to the intricately articulated structure of the volume—benefit from the special location. Balconies jut far out over the space below, both strengthening and elaborating the design concept of the building, which echoes the partner building on Langgrütstrasse.

The carefully crafted brickwork drapes across the facade, showcasing the skill that went into construction and offering a visual representation of the housing cooperative, which sees itself as a people-first organization. Various iterations of finely chiseled borders enhance the window size and adorn the facades, which show different proportions and a varied appearance depending on the viewing angle. The apartments follow a classic spatial principle which has clear zoning and is practical for everyday living.

Address
Langgrütweg 21, Zurich-Albisrieden

Architecture
Gmür & Geschwentner Architekten (GGA)

Landscape architecture
Vetschpartner Landschaftsarchitekten

Type of commission: Direct commission
Planning and execution: 2017–2024
Schedule of accommodation: 24 apartments
Client: GEWOBAG

Apartment plans
→ 3.9.11

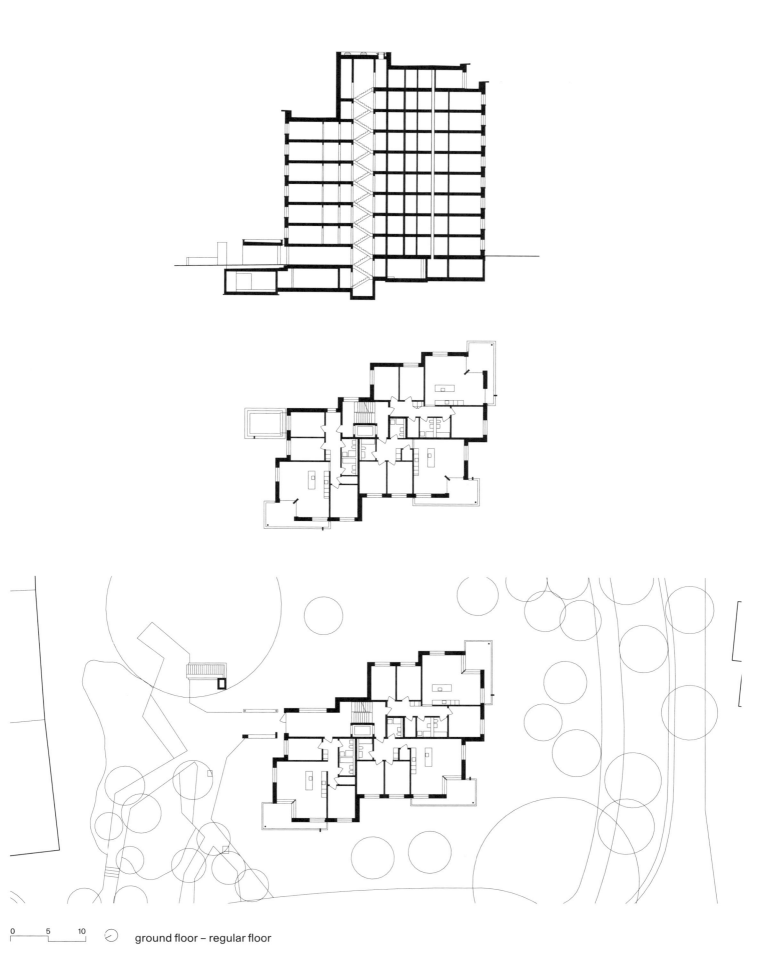

ground floor – regular floor

Reaching New Heights 111

2.4.5 Uetlibergstrasse High-Rise

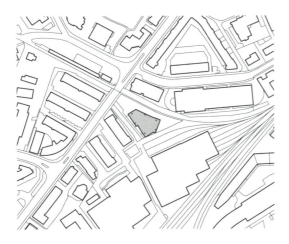

High-rise apartment buildings have once again become a trend in Zurich ever since the renaissance of this architectural form in the early 2000s. Yet few of these buildings prove to be impressive, since the building type rarely manages to adequately mesh with the concept to produce a thought-through architectural form. In particular, how these residential high-rises contribute to the revitalization of urban space is rarely discussed. The design ideas often limit themselves to experimenting with the facade design.

This is why it's important to have a good design team. The high-rise building on Uetlibergstrasse appears as a tall apartment block. The building exemplifies a new idea of "living above the roofs," which is implemented with a specific floor plan: the bay windows, fitted with dining areas protrude like large eyes that glow at night and mark the final destination of the internal traffic-pattern. The dining rooms vertically connect to glazed corner towers, which define and characterize the volume of the building architecturally.

The specific concept and the spatial design to which it gives rise create a distinctive architectural form with a strong identity, embedding the high-rise building in immediate surroundings as well as the larger vicinity. The building's strong visual cues are articulated in a striking manner. The most distinctive features of the building's frame are the plinth, the pilasters, and the cantilevered roof. The balustrade bands, fitted between the bay windows, are equipped with slanted solar panels.

Address
Uetlibergstrasse 65/67, Zurich-Wiedikon

Architecture
Gmür & Geschwentner (GGA)
Jakob Steib Architekten (SGA)

Landscape architecture
Regula Hodel

Type of commission: Direct commission
Planning and execution: 2018–2027
Schedule of accommodation: 57 apartments, commercial space
Client: Alfred Müller AG, Baar

Apartment plans
→ 3.7.10
→ 3.7.11
→ 3.7.12

ground floor – regular floor – top floor

Reaching New Heights

2.4.6 Tiny Homes, Forchstrasse

The trend towards increasing population density has long since reached the outskirts of urban areas. In these areas, open space is increasingly coming under pressure and being degraded into bland interstitial space. Their formal character is dictated solely by building codes. The plot on the congested Forchstrasse in Zollikon consolidates a specific housing concept into a spatially and socially dense neighborhood that accentuates the street space and creates a small-scale living space with squares, paths, and stairs.

The "Tiny Homes" make the living areas as compact as possible while also maximizing the homely ambiance. The path to each apartment, the quality of the outdoor space, the orientation, the shape of the rooms, and the proximity to the neighboring houses all figure heavily in the design concept. Four buildings host a total of thirty-nine apartments, all of which have garden patios, direct access to the basement level, or a two-story structure. An astonishing variety of apartment types, all stacked on top of each other under one roof, manage to squeeze into a very tight space. The use of building materials was pared-down, consisting of exposed concrete and profiled sheet metal panels. Together, they give off a Japanese delicacy and emphasize the unity of the building volume. The expressive roof landscape resembles origami figures and gives the building a distinctive architectural form. Folds on the top floor create complex spaces with overhead lighting and movable walls.

Address
Forchstrasse 100, Rietholzstrasse 2, 2 a + 2 b, Zollikon

Architecture
Jakob Steib Architekten (JSA)

Landscape architecture
Albiez de Tomasi

Type of commission: Study commission 2018
Planning and execution: 2019–2024
Schedule of accommodation: 39 small apartments
Client: UTO Real Estate Management AG

Apartment plans
→ 3.12.11

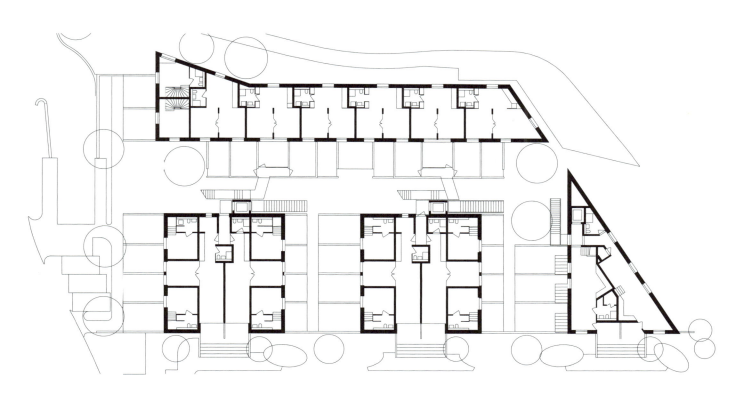

ground floor – first floor

Reaching New Heights

2.4.7 Hirtenweg Development

The urban plan and architectural idea for this one-of-a-kind location were derived from its direct proximity to the impressive Hörnli cemetery and the vast family gardens. The unassuming and functional appearance of the existing apartment buildings served as an opportunity to develop a serene, garden-oriented architectural language that makes meticulous and efficient use of the available resources.

The new development is positioned such that it reiterates and complements the existing arrangement of blocks of houses while simultaneously achieves an optimal expansion of the building site in the north–south direction. The strict geometry of these buildings informs the spatial structure of the apartments. Cascading exterior staircases provide access to the efficiently organized interior spaces, which are even smaller than the strict spatial constraints would have them. This makes for affordable housing. None of this takes away from the spacious impression that the apartments make, most clearly exemplified in the living rooms which receive natural sunlight from two different sides. To maximize the slender appearance of the building volumes, the staircases and balconies are located on the exterior. This design feature adapts the new apartments to the existing buildings, integrating them as seamlessly as possible into the neighborhood. Gently sloping gable roofs emphasize the suburban character of the houses, which are built from wood.

Address
Hirtenweg 16–28, Riehen

Architecture
Steib & Geschwentner Architekten (SGA)

Landscape architecture
Albiez de Tomasi

Type of commission: Comprehensive competition 2018
Planning and execution: not executed
Schedule of accommodation: 42 apartments
Client: Canton of Basel-Stadt

Apartment plans
→ 3.11.13
→ 3.11.14
→ 3.11.15

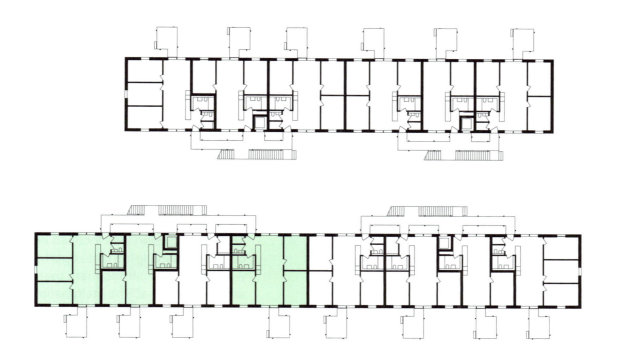
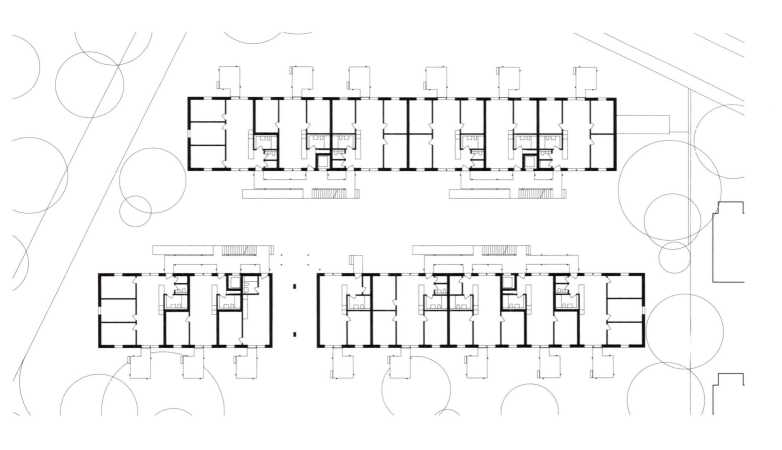

0 5 10   ground floor – first floor

2.4.8 Sandacker Apartment Blocks

Two plots on the street had extra space which had to be utilized, and this space was used to build affordable housing. Two tailor-made buildings were built with surgical precision—"form follows law"! Paradoxically, it was useful to eliminate one full story, since this created two wide volumes that could be efficiently configured with three apartments across as well as additional living space on the top floor.

Several architectural methods were used to synchronize these two mismatched siblings. Raw materials, windows that wrap around the corners, and bright red handrails create a kinship between them. The entrances to the two volumes are directly opposite each other, separated by the street. The deeper building casts a faint blue shadow on the longer one, which faces its counterpart with an oriel.

The client's vision was focused around compact and spatially intricate apartments that would exude an atmosphere that is both cozy and conventional. The staircases, on the other hand, have plenty of flair: a shimmering gold and silver coat covers the crude concrete surfaces, staggered artificial stone slabs sweep the stairs upward, and immense air spaces punctuate the volumes, showering the staircases with daylight. There are many special effects embedded in the architectural design, which pay homage to the art of H.R. Giger, the famous former neighbor.

Address
Sandacker 14 +15, Zürich-Seebach

Architecture
Gmür & Geschwentner Architekten (GGA)
Jakob Steib Architekten (JSA)

Type of commission: Fee-based submission with project idea 2018
Planning and execution: 2019–2023
Schedule of accommodation: 24 apartments
Client: Habitat 8000 AG

Apartment plans

→ 3.9.12
→ 3.11.16
→ 3.11.17

ground floor – regular floor – top floor

Reaching New Heights

2.4.9 Zwhatt Site High-Rise

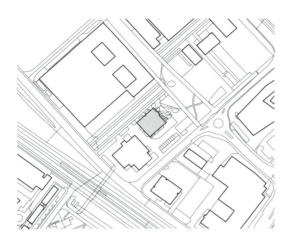

A high-rise building made of single-wythe masonry! A daring idea, which had to wait a long time to become the guiding principle for the construction of this special residential high-rise in the thriving small town of Regensdorf on the outskirts of Zurich. The development plan stipulated clear guidelines both for where to place the building and for its approximate dimensions.

The design is primarily driven by the construction concept: a reinforced concrete frame with slim dimensions is filled out with single-wythe masonry, which, clamped between the ceilings, acts as the building envelope. This method of construction is unmatched in its efficiency and simplicity. As soon as the shell was completed, the interior finish was ready to be applied. The extremely slim, monolithic structure reduces the number of layers needed, thereby conserving resources. Thanks to its compact design, the CO_2 balance is comparable to that of a wooden construction, with the crucial difference that the fire safety requirements and load bearing system can be handled much more easily and cost-effectively. The architectural expression of the walls is part of the design, since the construction idea and architecture depend on one another. One special feature is the staggered balconies, which maximize the wiggle room in relation to the cubic index and create two-story patios. Compact plans allow for ample flexibility, which can be maximally utilized thanks to the way the frame is constructed. The colors indicate a desire for a vernacular architectural design in a suburban context.

Address
Regensdorf

Architecture
Gmür & Geschwentner Architekten (GGA)

Landscape architecture
Lorenz Eugster Landschaftsarchitektur

Type of commission: Study commission 2019
Planning and execution: not executed
Schedule of accommodation: 156 apartments
Client: Pensimo Management AG

Apartment plans
→ 3.7.13
→ 3.7.14

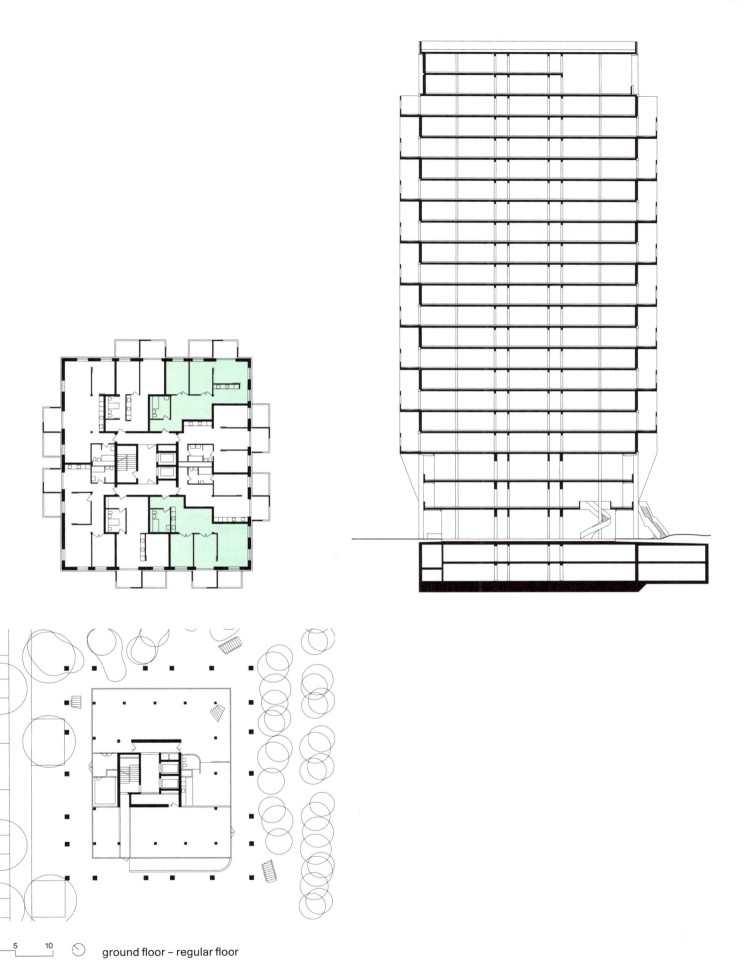

ground floor – regular floor

Reaching New Heights

2.4.10 Alte Landstrasse Development

While this location was once defined by an unwelcoming parking lot wasteland cut into the slope, today three squat buildings create a bountiful, fluid green space. By making the buildings compact and dense, like well-stuffed suitcases packed with deftly interlocking apartments, the battered landscape has been restored to its original topographic form. The protrusions and recesses of the buildings embellish the facade, which provides excellent lighting for the apartments and a host of different views of the open space, while also breaking up the visual impression that the buildings make, and lending the facades plasticity and dynamism. The main access corridor—whose exceptional spaciousness is reinforced with light wells that capture light from the roof and transport it to the basement like a periscope—is an intriguing aspect of the compact buildings in the development, each of which contains multiple units. Up to nine apartments gather around the sprawling stairwells, which have varying ambiances thanks to the fact that each building has a unique color scheme. The passion that informed the design permeates the apartments via colorfully tiled bathrooms and elegant natural stone floors. The facades made of two-toned green ceramic panels reproduce the spatial relationship of the buildings on the facade and merge the houses with the rich green of the surroundings like steamships in the fog.

Address
Alte Landstrasse, Kloten

Architecture
Gmür & Geschwentner Architekten (GGA)

Landscape architecture
Manoa Landschaftsarchitekten

Type of commission: Direct commission
Planning and execution: 2019–2024
Schedule of accommodation: 108 apartments
Client: UBS Fund Management AG, Basel

Apartment plans

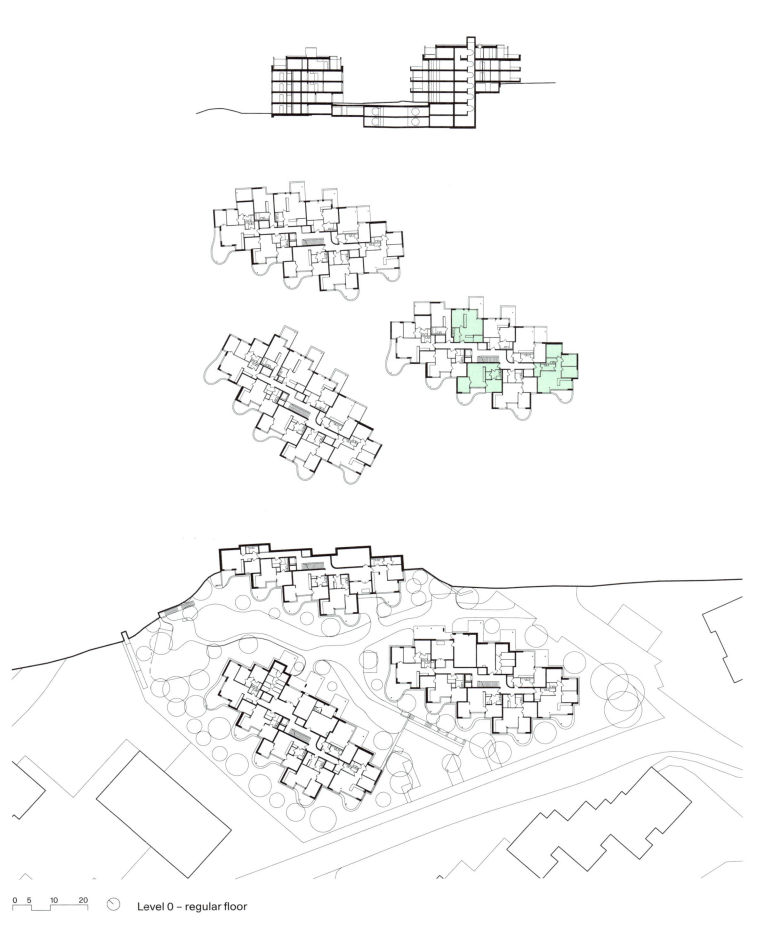

0 5 10 20 Level 0 – regular floor

Reaching New Heights

2.4.11 Sonne Development

The task was challenging: six owners with different interests had to team up to create a plan that would unlock the potential for developing this well-connected location. If any location ever cried out for denser habitation, then it was this one! The development concept makes the most of this situation by turning the neglected rear side of the existing buildings into a public entrance.

Four polygonal shaped volumes are assembled around a public area that complements and enhances the range of open urban spaces. The neighboring buildings have access to the new courtyard, which creates common ground to cushion the jarring transition between the differing street levels.

The spatial arrangement of the volumes lends each house a unique shape. The outcome is an urban ensemble that consciously defies the idea of a development and yet connects the previously unrelated buildings into a neighborhood block, without impinging on the autonomy of the individual property owners. Commercial spaces are arranged along Gersagstrasse, activating the street space in anticipation of the planned expansion of Gersag train station. Two-story loggias crown the houses and indicate the presence of exceptional apartments. On the other levels, the plans are characterized by a fluid sequence of spaces and a variety of views and visual relationships that the unusual shape of the buildings encourages.

Address
Gersagstrasse/Gerliswilstrasse, Emmenbrücke

Architecture
Gmür & Geschwentner Architekten (GGA)

Landscape architecture
Stephan Köpfli

Type of commission: Study commission 2019
Planning and execution: not executed
Schedule of accommodation: 180 apartments
Client: Steiner Invest

Apartment plan
→ 3.2.13
→ 3.2.14
→ 3.2.15

0 5 10 20   ⊖ ground floor – top floor

Reaching New Heights 125

2.4.12 Chirchbüel Apartment Blocks

The site is marked by its stunning location above Chirchbühlweg, nestled in a densely vegetated green space that looks out onto the Alps. The architectural concept had to address the stringent requirements for noise protection and the challenging topography and integrate these into the design in a sensible manner. There was also the opportunity to upgrade the square in front of the community center.

The plot, located close to Forchstrasse, appears as an open-space expansion of the cemetery and the community center. The topography is intensely dynamic, owing to the incision of the Schulhausbach stream. With its open building structures, the project proposal respects the urban character of the site in terms of scale and height. Two buildings, staggered in location and height, gently blend into the terrain and form a permeable open space with a clear entrance. The interior landscape is gently manicured, and a free-standing grid of pathways cuts through it to provide access to the buildings and connect the observation point with the play and recreation area.

The plans derive their spatial pattern from the staggered arrangement of the building volumes: protrusions and recesses create a multi-sided orientation, which allows the living areas to be tucked behind the first layer of rooms, making the volumes more compact. The apartments, which are exposed to the noise, are equipped with so-called "snorkel rooms" which curl around a second room and provide internal circulation.

Address
Chirchbüelweg, Zumikon

Architecture
Gmür & Geschwentner Architekten (GGA)

Landscape architecture
Nipkow Landschaftsarchitektur

Type of commission: Investor competition 2019
Planning and execution: not carried out
Schedule of accommodation: 70 apartments, commercial
Client: Zurlinden Housing Cooperative, Zurich

Apartment plans
→ 3.10.13

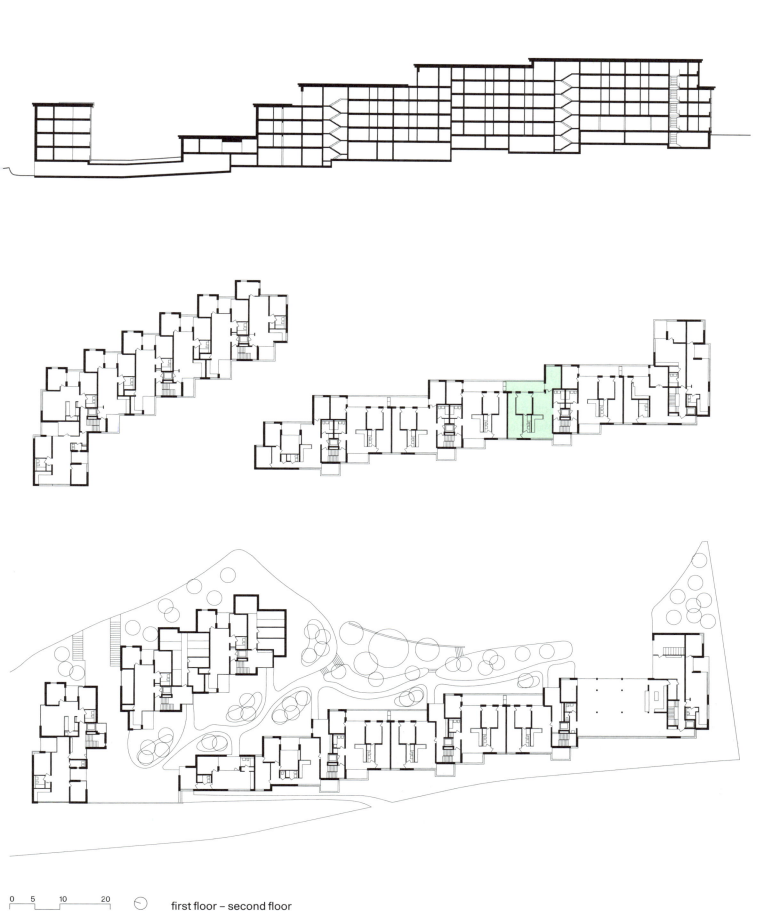

first floor – second floor

Reaching New Heights

2.4.13 Stelzen Apartment Blocks

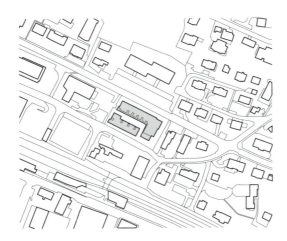

The fact that these buildings are located right next to the train station makes them an ideal urban focal point that enriches life in the village and offers accessible and affordable housing. Two differently shaped buildings define a publicly accessible space that opens to the west towards the church square and forms the heart of the complex.

The low building on the south side of the site—whose low profile admits plenty of light into this courtyard—has two faces: on the ground floor facing the street, commercial spaces are open to the public, and the atrium apartments on the floor above create a semi-public open space. The large L-shaped house encloses the courtyard and completes the ensemble on the side facing the upper street. The section reveals the source of the access concept, which adjusts to the steep slope with two different building depths: a single staircase connects entrances to the building on three different levels, thereby linking the apartments together into a single community. The spatially complex traffic pattern, full of surprising interior views and well-illumined spaces, winds through the house and forms two side arms, which—in the shape of a gallery and a corridor—provide access to a row of small apartments.

The goal of housing a diversity of residents is reflected in the range of apartments, which are typologically heterogeneous despite the relatively modest number of units. Atrium apartments make a second appearance on the roof of the larger building, another factor that ties the two buildings together.

Address
Stelzenstrasse, Meilen

Architecture
Gmür & Geschwentner Architekten (GGA)

Landscape architecture
Nipkow Landschaftsarchitektur

Type of commission: Study commission 2019
Planning and execution: 2020–2024
Schedule of accommodation: 32 apartments, 12 commercial spaces
Client: Non-profit Housing Meilen AG

Apartment plans
→ 3.10.14
→ 3.11.20
→ 3.12.12
→ 3.12.13

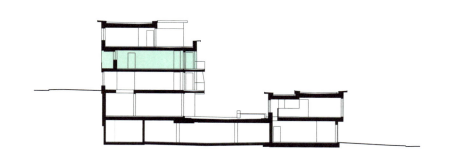

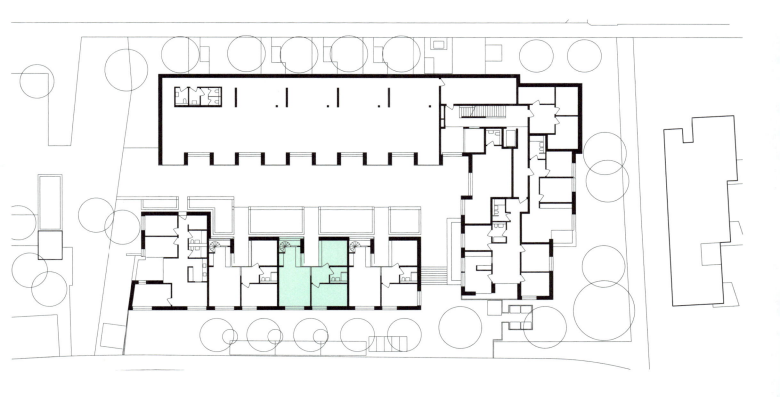

0 5 10   courtyard floor – second floor

Reaching New Heights 129

2.5 United Forces

The reorientation was also an opportunity to simplify the office structure. This was important, since at times it had been tricky to explain why there were two firms (GGA and SGA) whose architectural languages were nearly identical. All these factors ultimately led to the founding of Steib Gmür Geschwentner Kyburz Architekten (SGGK) in 2020. GGA and SGA will continue to operate in the background until all liabilities have expired. Jakob Steib's firm also remains in existence.

At the joint firm, the four architects are equal partners. The working environment at SGGK encourages each person to bring their individual strength to the collective without encroaching upon the freedom of the others. In addition to this, special emphasis is placed on the mutual trust which allows and even fosters differences as one of the many beneficial aspects of collaboration.

2.5.1 Eich-/Birken-/Lagerstrasse Development

Increasing the density of the built environment in a rural context calls for special design strategies. It is not cities that finds themselves in an urban planning crisis so much as the urbanized villages that have merged into a contiguous residential carpet. That's because the heterogeneous prototype for residential developments is undergoing an unchecked transformation in many places. There is little to indicate that the process of integrating new buildings into the existing fabric is being undertaken with the requisite care.

The five buildings on this site intend to solve this issue for this particular location. Although their volumes exceed the usual footprint for the neighborhood, their heights vary—depending on location and orientation—within an acceptable range. The number of floors is reduced on the buildings near the single-family houses and then increases again towards the north. In terms of external architectural design, the slightly inclined pitched roofs in different configurations are designed to match the neighboring buildings.

Despite the fact that they take up only a small amount of space, all apartments have a spacious feel that results from the diversity of room proportions and interior views. One distinctive feature is the large storage rooms required by building ordinances, each of which is positioned such that it can be used in multiple ways as a niche within the living space: as a workspace, guest room, or small library. In many cases, this storage room can be outfitted with a window, allowing it to be used as an extra bedroom. In this way, a strange legal requirement becomes a new design feature.

Address
Eich-, Birken-, Lagerstrasse, Neuenhof

Architecture
Steib Gmür Geschwentner Kyburz Partner (SGGK)

Landscape architecture
Nipkow Landschaftsarchitektur

Type of commission: Study commission 2020
Planning and execution: 2021–2024
Schedule of accommodation: 112 apartments, community room
Client: Logis Suisse AG

Apartment plans
→ 3.10.15

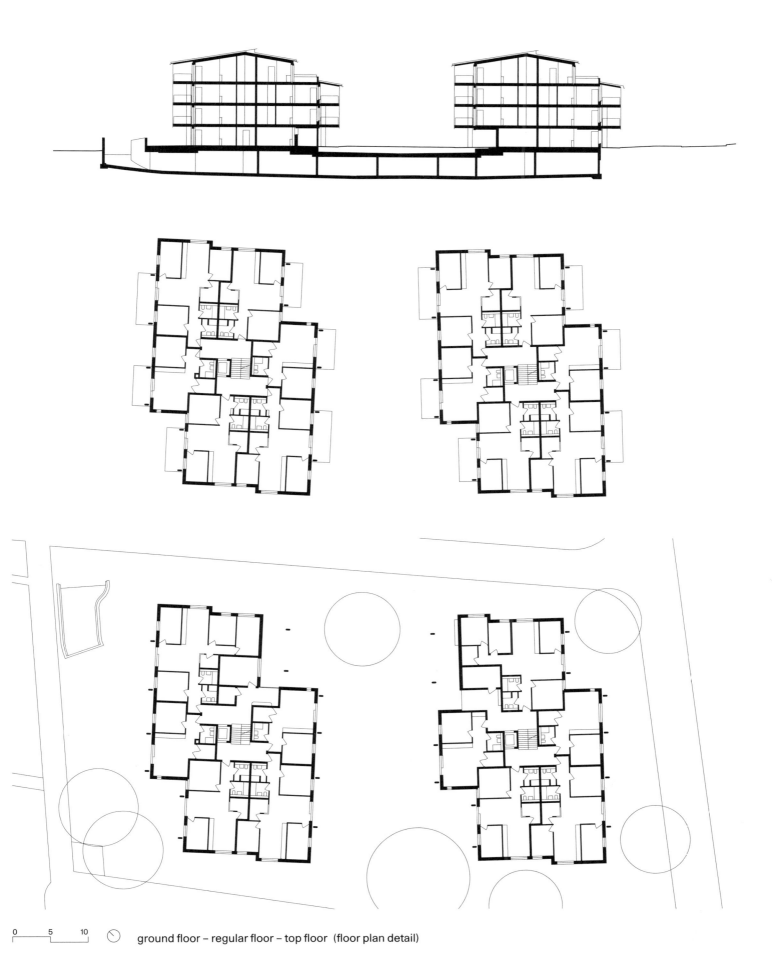

ground floor – regular floor – top floor (floor plan detail)

United Forces

2.5.2 Dreispitz Site Development

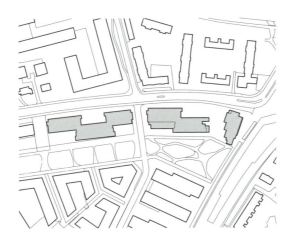

Schwamendingen is being ploughed up. The neighborhood, once home to loosely scattered linear and point blocks with abundant green spaces, is now being filled with large-scale buildings as part of the trend towards increased density, creating a new urban arrangement. Mounted between Wallisellenstrasse and the inchoate Dreispitz neighborhood park, three building plots are shaping the site by adding two longitudinal buildings and a high-rise. Displaced sections create a lengthwise shearing effect in the building volumes that works parallel to the street. This creates forecourts that encompass the entrances to the buildings, bundling them together with the publicly available space on the ground floor and creating a distinctive entryway that animates the street space. Deep covered walkways serve as opulent access decks that face the bustling street: a lively facade in place of nondescript stairwells.

Thanks to the staggered spatial layering inherent in the honeycombed floor plans, various spatial aspects merge seamlessly. A kaleidoscopically diverse living environment unfolds in the building interiors. The high-rise has its particular character defined by the ground floor, which is publicly accessible and related to the parking deck higher up in the building as well as the fanned-out plan structure of the residential levels. All apartments face the sunny side and are thus shielded from noise. The roof belongs to everyone, and it houses what may be the most beautiful laundry room in the city!

Address
Wallisellenstrasse, Zurich-Schwamendingen

Architecture
Steib Gmür Geschwentner Kyburz Partner (SGGK)

Landscape architecture
Atelier Loidl

Type of commission: Study commission 2020
Planning and execution: not carried out
Schedule of accommodation: 257 apartments, restaurants, offices
Client: ASIG Housing Cooperative

Apartment plans
→ 3.10.16
→ 3.10.17

ground floor – regular floor (floor plan detail)

United Forces

2.5.3 Lüdin Site Development

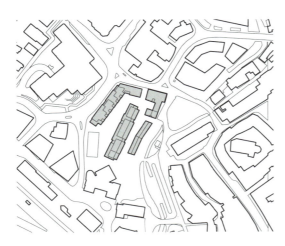

The design idea for this site takes its cues from its rich history as an industrial area. The bland, featureless anonymity which is becoming increasingly popular in suburban areas is here countered by an architectural concept that values the site's special characteristics. New and yet also familiar, the architecture immerses itself in the urban fabric.

Each of the three buildings has its own architectural character, which is determined by their location in the wider urban context and the individual typology of the apartments. A two-story studio building skirts the alley, crouching under its gently sloping pitched roof and providing a view of the neighboring building's main facade. A carefully structured building ascends at the center of the site.

With its emphatic architectural language, tiered gable roofs, and robust sheet metal cladding, the building harks back to the location's industrial past.

The western perimeter of the site is enclosed by a cubically staggered volume with brick panel cladding, giving it an urban look. It shields the courtyard from traffic noise and has a public ground floor. As is often the case, the location on a busy street requires a special floor plan solution. In this case, the section provides that solution: a height offset in the area of the enclosed walkway makes it possible to resolve the privacy question for the central apartment while also allowing the volume to adequately adapt to the sloping terrain along the street.

Address
Bahnhof-, Schützen-, Rheinstrasse, Liestal

Architecture
Steib Gmür Geschwentner Kyburz Partner (SGGK)

Landscape architecture
Nipkow Landschaftsarchitektur

Type of commission: Competition 2020
Planning and execution: 2021–2025
Schedule of accommodation: 135 apartments, commercial
Client: SIAT Immobilien AG represented by first Site Invest AG

Apartment plans
→ 3.10.18

ground floor – regular floor

2.5.4 Webergut Conversion

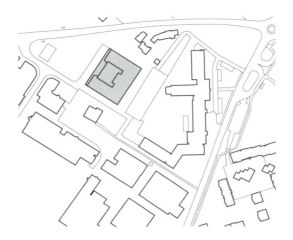

The task is urgent and highly topical: converting a bulky office building into a residential building requires shedding the self-referential appearance of the existing building and transforming it into an attractive living environment for special forms of housing with integrated workspaces. The recycling of building components, resource-efficient, low-CO_2 construction methods, and the strict budget are just as important as the question of how the building can undergo a visual makeover.

The answer sounds simple, but was hard to work out in practice. The existing facade was removed on the sunny sides, creating space for a balcony layer that wraps all around the building. The new, recessed facade functions like a membrane enabling the accommodation of a variety of different apartments independently of the existing column grid—everything from capsule apartments to the large shared apartment are in the mix. This creates a suitable environment for the diverse residents.

The rest of the existing building has been preserved and made ready for the future: a new staircase in the center of the structure serves all floors and frames the path through the building. The arid parking lot in front of the building has been turned into a garden available for the cultivation of fruit and vegetables. A bridge connects the building with the garden and defines the apartment building's front. A lively and unconventional working environment emerges on the ground floor, which—thanks to the initiative of its future users—exudes the pioneering spirit of the project.

Address
Weberstrasse 5, Zollikofen

Architecture
Steib Gmür Geschwentner Kyburz Partner (SGGK)

Landscape architecture
Nipkow Landschaftsarchitektur

Type of commission: Study commission 2020
Planning and execution: 2021–2026
Schedule of accommodation: 82 apartments, commercial spaces, co-working, restaurants
Client: Stiftung Abendrot, Basel

Apartment plans
→ 3.5.12
→ 3.6.7
→ 3.6.8
→ 3.8.2
→ 3.8.3
→ 3.12.14
→ 3.12.15

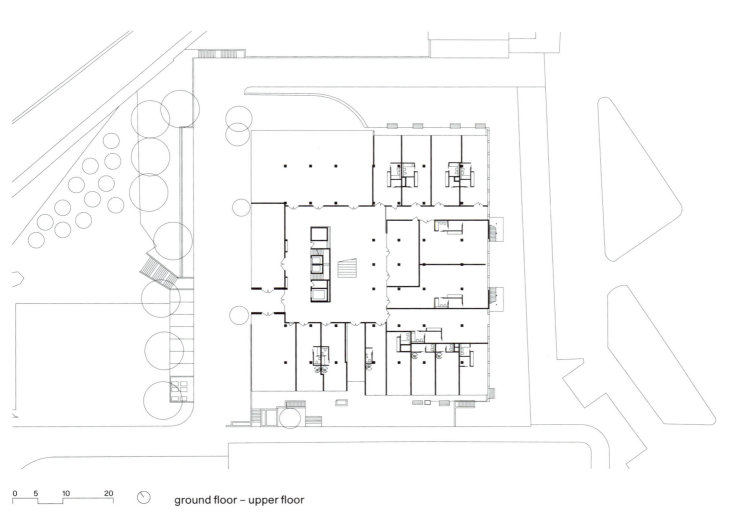

ground floor – upper floor

United Forces

2.5.5 Langgrüthof Apartment Block

In a brief span of time, Zurich's Albisrieden district has transformed from a quiet neighborhood with a disproportionate number of elderly people on the outskirts of the city center into a vibrant residential area for all age groups. The commercial sector, which was once overrepresented in the area, has increasingly been displaced in the course of this development. This makes it all the more significant that one of the private developer's main endeavors at this location is to combine residential and commercial space into a vibrant element of the neighborhood.

With two precisely placed buildings, the site of the Albisrieden window factory is reorganized and integrated into the neighborhood. The existing building, still used for production today, will be upgraded with a new hall and additional office space. The new residential building runs along Langgrütstrasse and creates a quiet, green courtyard from which all seventy apartments benefit. With only two staircases and elevators, these apartments are extremely easy to access.

The project offers a rich variety of different plan types for its mixed population. Among this eclectic mix, the compactly organized small apartments stand out. Thanks to the sophisticated built-in furniture, they function as temporary residences. A multipurpose room and a co-working space top off the spatial program and connect the small apartments to a lively community space.

Address
Langgrütstrasse 118, Zurich-Albisrieden

Architecture
Steib Gmür Geschwentner Kyburz Partner (SGGK)

Landscape architecture
Manoa Landschaftsarchitekten

Type of commission: Direct commission
Planning and execution: 2020–2024
Schedule of accommodation: 70 apartments, co-working space, community room
Client: Immo Albisrieden AG

Apartment plans
→ 3.9.13
→ 3.11.21
→ 3.12.16
→ 3.12.17

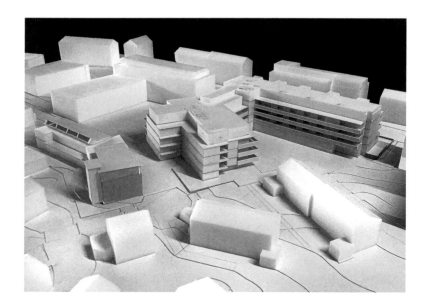

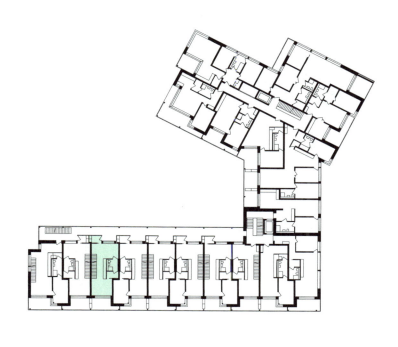

ground floor – third floor

United Forces 141

2.5.6 Spiserstrasse Apartment Block

A sturdy volume complements the fragmented perimeter of the block and does not shy away from the large scale that is inscribed in the site's urban DNA. The room towers of the deep building probe the full extent of the building regulations in order to elaborate on the location's usual design with a compact building figure and impart a heightened spaciousness to the courtyard.

The interior celebrates open hall living that alludes to the motifs present in the stately urban Art Nouveau houses. The deliberate omission of an additional floor and the commitment to an extraordinary building depth allow for an above-average room height that does justice to the hall spaces. All apartments have striking views on two sides, benefiting from ample sunlight on Spiserstrasse as well as the quiet atmosphere of the courtyard. Wide corridors and ceiling-high interior doors connect the living space with the courtyard in the smaller units. The interplay of bright and shady zones creates a sense of spatial intimacy and offers sanctuaries in the apartments' protective interiors. Generously sized balconies reinforce the urban character of the architecture and create a strong connection to the surroundings. The green facade answers to the demand for urban locations that stay cool during the summer. The maisonettes on the second floor are directly connected to the underground garage via internal stairs, making them a house within a house.

Address
Spiserstrasse, Zürich-Albisrieden

Architecture
Steib Gmür Geschwentner Kyburz Partner (SGGK)

Landscape architecture
Nipkow Landschaftsarchitektur

Type of commission: Study commission 2020
Planning and execution: not executed
Schedule of accommodation: 107 apartments, 6 residential studios
Client: Allreal Generalunternehmung AG, Stiftung Veronika Leutwyler, Zurich

Apartment plans
→ 3.6.9

ground floor – first floor – second floor

2.5.7 Lerchenweg Development

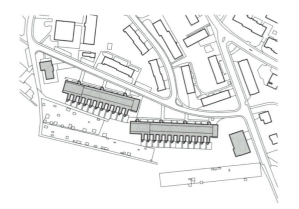

Located on the outskirts of the Kloten agglomeration near Zurich's airport, the property offers perfect conditions for living close to nature, since the forest is literally on the doorstep. The design proposal takes its cues from this idea, with two large buildings that give each of the apartments an unobstructed view of the forest. The design breaks the mold of the small-scale residential structure typical of the neighborhood, since the special location allows a shift in scale that is distinct from the congenial jumble of the existing developments. In this way, the proposed development provides a quietly striking gateway to the open landscape.

Outdoor corridors and wide balconies draw the life of the apartments outside and loosen up the appearance of the large facades. Shed roofs crown the apartments and indicate that the attic floor accommodates a special form of living: starting from a staircase, six small apartments bore through the building. They have elongated internal walkways, which are flanked by various niches, pass through kitchens and alongside bathrooms, and lead into studio-like spaces that receive light from above.

On the regular floors, access balconies combine the units into a single, common zone. All kitchens are oriented towards the circulation system, fulfilling the promise of a communal space. On the ground floor, the apartments extend into the open space with single-story extensions and form atriums that provide the backdrop for cozy garden living.

Address
Lerchenweg 10–40, Wallisellerstrasse 8/10, Kloten

Architecture
Steib Gmür Geschwentner Kyburz Partner (SGGK)

Landscape architecture
Nipkow Landschaftsarchitektur

Type of commission: Study commission 2021
Planning and execution: not executed
Schedule of accommodation: 249 apartments
Client: Pensionskasse Schaffhausen

Apartment plans
→ 3.6.10

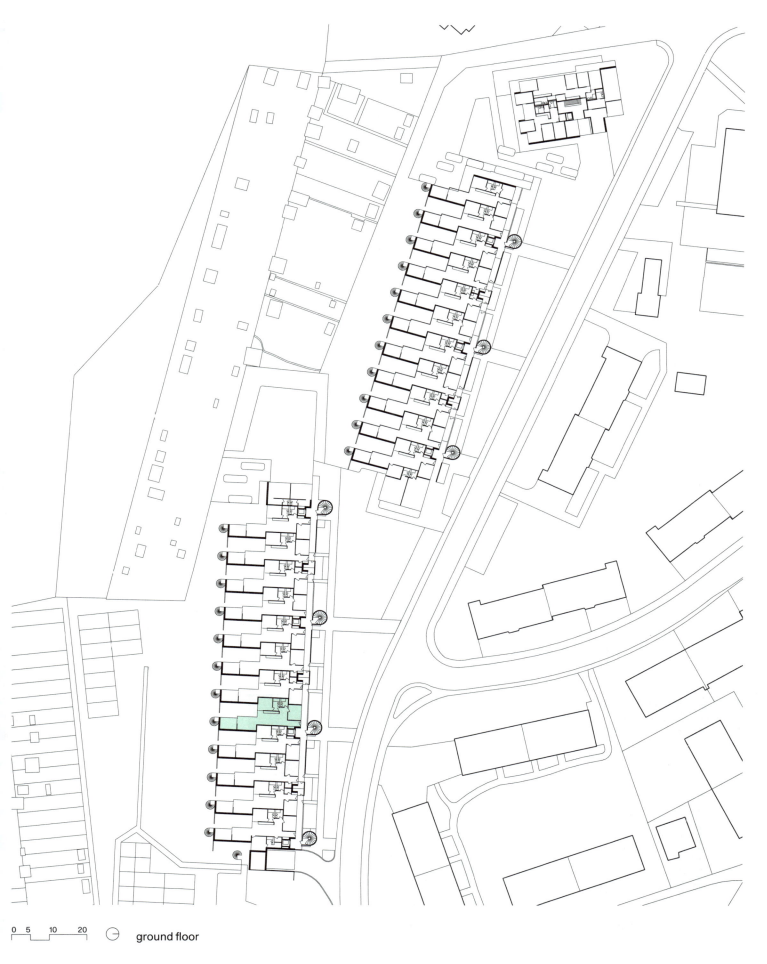
ground floor

2.5.8 Roswiesen-/Winterthurerstr. Developmen[t]

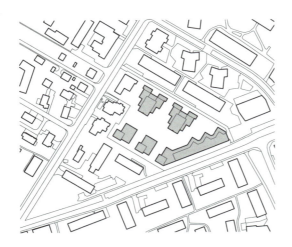

Even neighborhoods in Zurich with peripheral locations between rural and urban areas are not immune to the push towards denser built environments. In a residential city with so much luscious greenery, there is the risk that the balance between developed and open spaces could be lost. Schwamendingen is a typical example of a neighborhood confronted with this issue. It was originally built—rapidly but also carefully—as an assemblage of housing developments and green spaces. These qualities ought to be preserved even as Schwamendingen's density increases.

Compact point blocks, each of them several apartments across, gather around a central square that forms a social and spatial hub. Thanks to an incremental gradation in the height of these houses, they maintain a strong connection to the neighborhood. The typical permeability that characterizes the housing in the area is maintained, interweaving the new buildings with their immediate surroundings and with the city at large. The pronounced circulation concept, which required a high level of design dexterity in organizing the plans, also ensures an optimal relationship between building and open space.

Along busy Winterthurerstrasse, an extended row of buildings shields the housing area from noise. The main inroad into the city center is incorporated into the plan for the area and its spatial features are embellished. Despite the fact that the row is incredibly compact, all apartments contain open space that is shielded from noise. The protruding roofscapes that lend the houses a metropolitan grandeur are an architectural trademark of the development.

Address
Roswiesen-/Winterthurerstrasse, Zurich-Schwamendingen

Architecture
Steib Gmür Geschwentner Kyburz Partner (SGGK)

Landscape architecture
Atelier Loidl

Type of commission: Study commission 2021
Planning and execution: 2022–2025
Schedule of accommodation: 222 apartments, community space, commercial space
Client: BVK Personalvorsorge des Kantons Zürich

Apartment plans
→ 3.2.16
→ 3.2.17
→ 3.2.18
→ 3.9.14
→ 3.10.19
→ 3.10.20

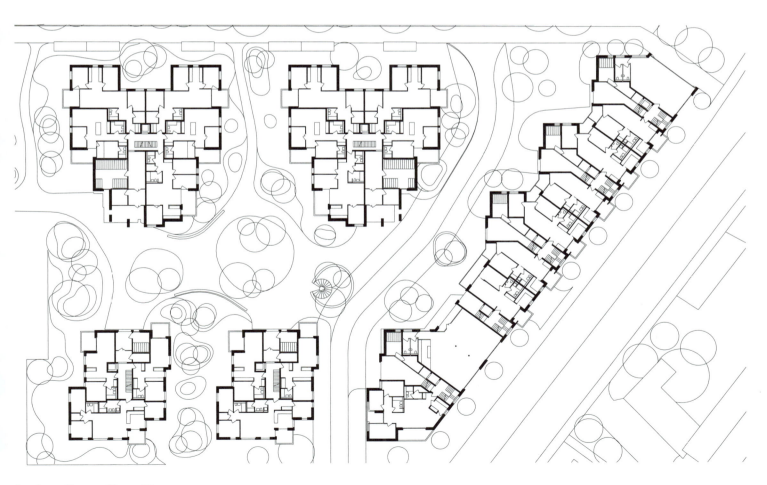

0 5 10 20   ground floor – fist floor

United Forces   147

2.5.9 Sennhof Development

Building row houses is no easy task! This type of building, which has historically taken on many different forms, has a tough time shaking the stigma of conventionality. This becomes especially difficult when the row houses consist of a crude repetition of residential units with bland architecture. There are several factors which add to the complications: the requirement that the houses have pitched roofs whose ridge is pointed in a specific direction, noise from the adjacent street, topographical challenges, the pressure to build at low cost, and the desire of investors to give each residential unit an individual entrance. To cut this Gordian knot, several units are combined under one roof to form large houses that reveal their richness in section. A cascading staircase that extends throughout the entire depth of the house not only connects the floors but also uses an array of spatial tricks to combine them into something which is clearly one single unit. A remarkable two-story space, hardly visible in the plan, unfolds beneath the stairs, endowing the apartments with almost monumental dimensions. In order to preserve space, two point-symmetrical units are dovetailed. The interlocking connects the apartments and creates entrances on both sides of the house. There is no front or back. The open space is integrated into all sides, making it a common aspect of all the apartments.

Address
Zollikerberg

Architecture
Steib Gmür Geschwentner Kyburz Partner (SGGK)

Type of commission: Feasibility study 2021
Planning and execution: not executed
Schedule of accommodation: 17 row houses
Client: UTO Real Estate Management AG

Apartment plans
→ 3.5.14

ground floor – first floor

United Forces 149

2.5.10 BRIAG Site Development (Building sites C, D)

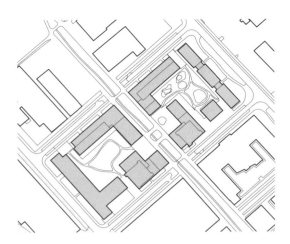

Regensdorf is undergoing a transformation: the rural small town on the outskirts of Zurich is experiencing tremendous growth. The development area north of the train station offers space for 5500 new residents—a staggering figure that will impose a rapid increase in density on the community.

In this context, the question arises of how to give the new precinct a distinctive identity that is also valuable to the public. There is an opportunity to plan two sites simultaneously, which together will span an exceptionally large open space perpendicular to the public park strip. The edges of the site are framed by ribbon developments and are left open to the east to accommodate two high-rise buildings that interact with the pair of high-rises on the neighboring site. At the urban level, scattered pavilion buildings organize the open space into a variegated fabric that initiates a lively relationship with the high-rise buildings.

The abundant palette of housing options is hard to beat in terms of diversity, and it is well known that diversity is a key ingredient to a thriving neighborhood. The culmination point is a tailor-made proposal for living in high-rise buildings: cross-stacked apartments form large two-story balconies in the corners of the buildings, which protrude from one apartment and are cut out of the volume of the other. The "hanging gardens of Regensdorf" translate a distinctive mode of dwelling into a unique architectural language.

Address
Althart-, Wehntalerstrasse, Regensdorf

Architecture
Steib Gmür Geschwentner Kyburz Partner (SGGK)

Landscape architecture
Atelier Loidl

Type of commission: Study commission 2021
Planning and execution: not executed
Schedule of accommodation: 448 apartments
Client: Brütsch/Rüegger Immobilien AG,
HRS Real Estate AG

Apartment plans
→ 3.7.15
→ 3.7.16

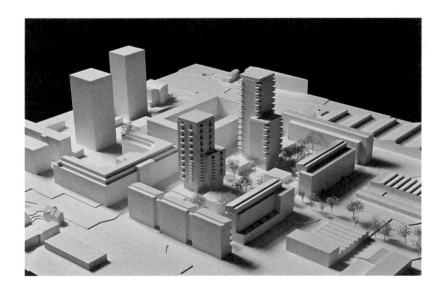

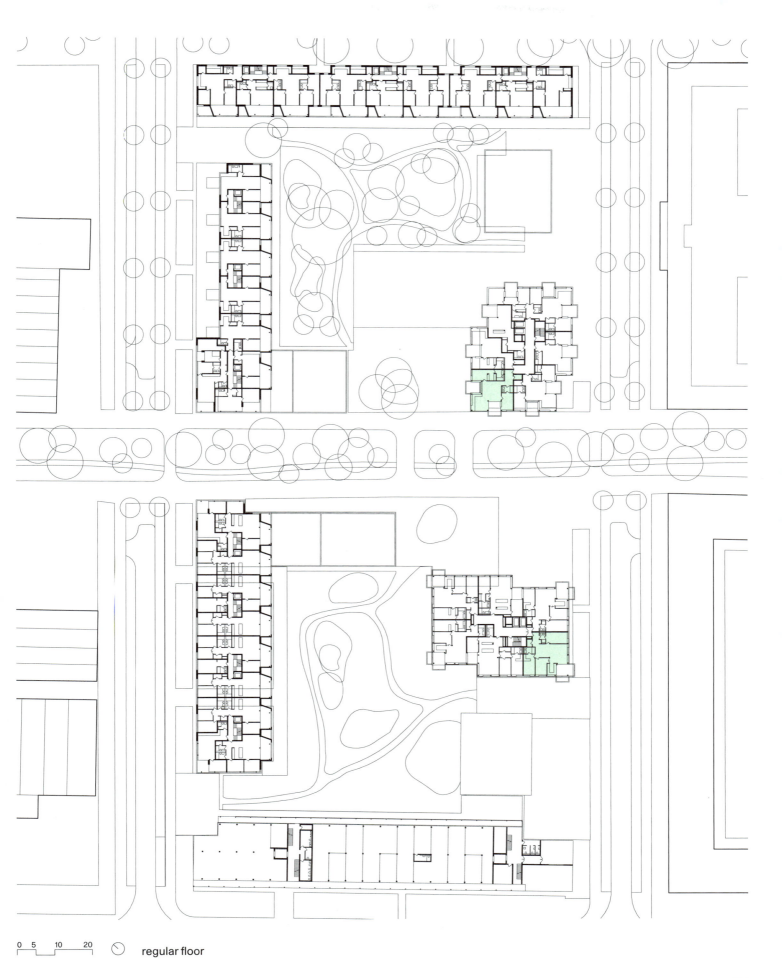

0 5 10 20   regular floor

United Forces 151

2.5.11 Scheuchzerstrasse Apartment Block

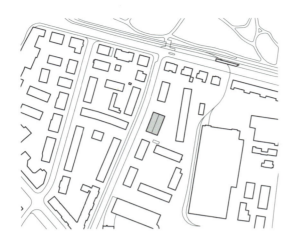

"Unconventionally well-adjusted" is the motto of the new replacement construction on Scheuchzerstrasse. The first four floors form the compact main volume which are characteristic of the neighborhood. With differently projecting balconies at the corners of the building and an asymmetrical window arrangement, the facades appear lively and varied despite the repetitive stacking of the floors.

Although the apartments are compact, they include everything one might desire in a contemporary city apartment. Practical built-in furniture and strategically placed mirrors make the rooms comfortable and rich despite their tight dimensions. The dining area and the living nook with its indispensable, well-furnished cozy corner are arranged in a diagonal relationship that embraces the balcony. The kitchen is located in the shaded center and functions as a linking element.

The crowning achievement is on the top floor, where two spacious, three-and-a-half-room apartments are located. The rooms gain a spatial advantage from the height of the roof and showcase it with a gallery. The setting evokes glamorous Californian country houses. The shape of the roof is based on the gable and hipped roofs of the surrounding area while at the same time reinterpreting them. The roof was designed to appear to float, as if it were very light. This is achieved by recessing the load-bearing facade, creating a protected outdoor space under the cantilevered roof that can be used as a walkway all around. Or, to use an analogy: the relationship between an inner tent and a fly is here translated into architecture.

Address
Scheuchzerstrasse 202, Zurich-Milchbuck

Architecture
Steib Gmür Geschwentner Kyburz Partner (SGGK)

Type of commission: Direct commission
Planning and execution: 2021–2025
Schedule of accommodation: 17 apartments
Client: private

Apartment plans
→ 3.4.11

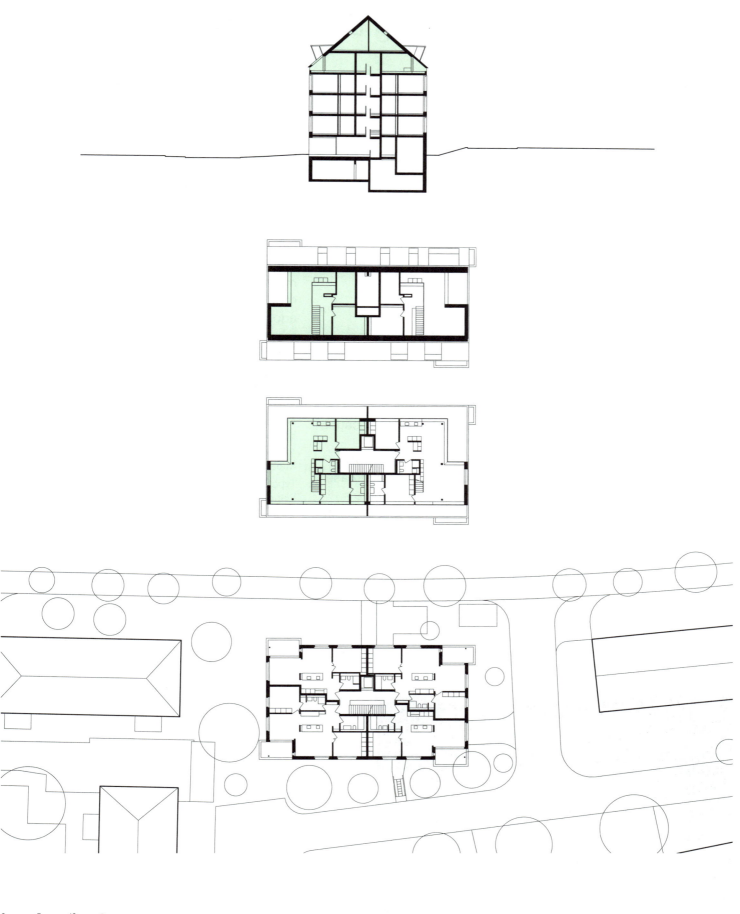

regular floor – top floor – gallery floor

United Forces 153

2.5.12 Berghaldenweg Development

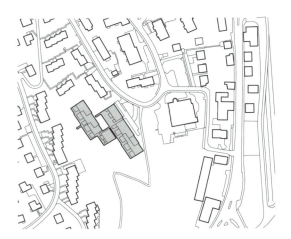

Building affordably on an extremely steep slope which is oriented in the "wrong" direction and only has one access point to the road is almost like squaring the circle. The story of this design idea was the story an exhaustive search across the terrain for the ideal location for the building.

The first draft envisioned three groups of houses, each accessed via an open staircase that does not count towards the building's cubic index. The arrangement of these groups is based on the principles which inform ski lift access. A wheelchair-accessible path follows the topography and connects the three staircases, which, paired with elevators, overcome the differences in elevation. The prominent pitched roofs, which mirror the sloping terrain, are also a response to the need to make the most of the possibilities of the section given the constraints imposed by the building code. The drawback of this solution lies in the underground garage, which had to take on considerable proportions due to official requirements.

Budgetary constraints led to a second draft that responds to the topography with a simple ribbon design that drastically reduces the need for excavation. An inclined elevator provides access to the linear blocks, which, thanks to the interlocking maisonette apartments accessible from two sides, do not require additional staircases. Solar panels adorn the roofs and meet the requirements of the 2000-watt society. The project was not abandoned due to a lack of ideas, but rather due to the municipality's rigid parking regulations.

Address
Berghaldenweg, Langnau am Albis

Architecture
Steib Gmür Geschwentner Kyburz Partner (SGGK)

Type of commission: Direct commission
Planning and execution: not executed
Schedule of accommodation: 32 apartments, studios
Client: Zurlinden Housing Cooperative

Apartment plans
→ 3.5.13

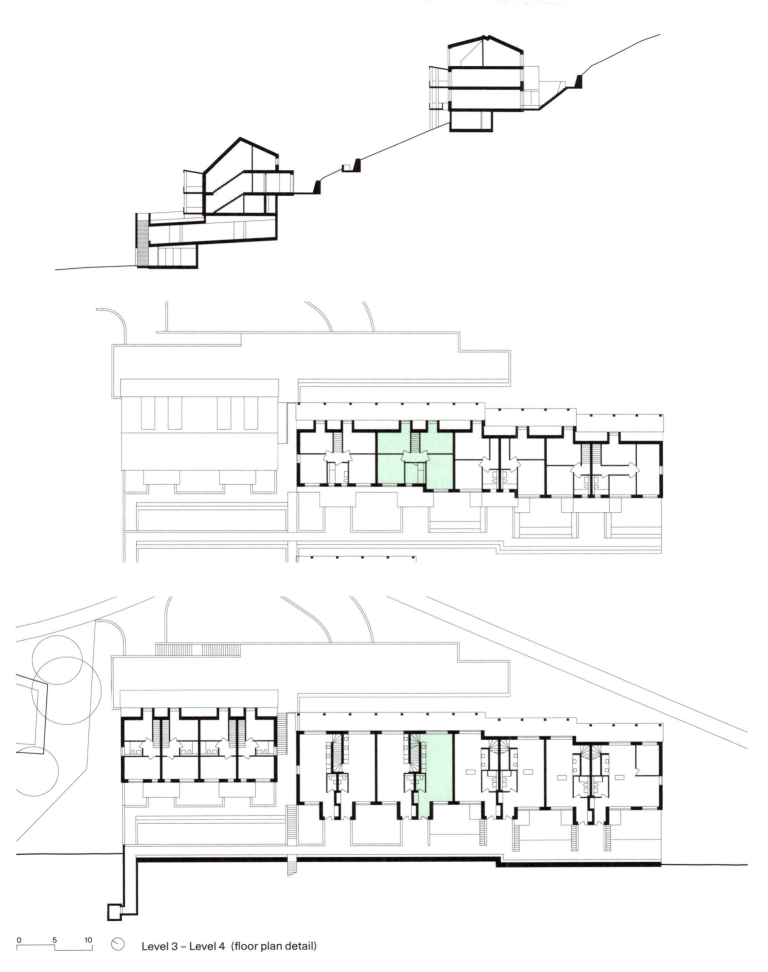

Level 3 – Level 4 (floor plan detail)

United Forces

2.5.13 Schärenmoosstrasse Conversion

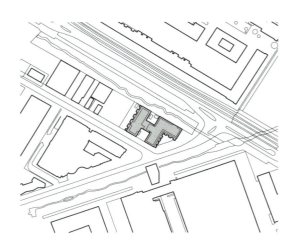

At the interface to Glattpark in Zurich's north, an abandoned office building awaits a new purpose. A lively residential building with commercial space and community facilities will soon be built at this location where Swiss television shows were once produced. How to recycle the building components is as much a focus as the careful handling of the building materials. Nevertheless, the transformation of the bulky functional building will not be child's play, since the building needs a facelift that will express its new function.

A spatial layer suspended from the roof masks the main facades and creates two-story balconies, because even progressive tenants feel the need for a private outdoor space.

The internal spatial organization and circulation must be rethought to make the building suitable for living and working. A group of trees transforms the forecourt into a homely living environment. The ground floor of the building hosts commercial space as well. An internal pathway leads to the entrance hall, which forms the entrance to the apartments at the functional center of the building.

The roof is accessible to everyone and connects the two parts of the building with community facilities. While the larger apartment's plans allow them to accommodate different layouts, the studios are designed like camping wagons. They are equipped only with the essentials and enter into a symbiotic relationship with the community facilities.

Address
Schärenmoosstrasse 115–117, Zurich-Oerlikon

Architecture
Steib Gmür Geschwentner Kyburz Partner (SGGK)

Landscape architecture
Andreas Geser Landschaftsarchitekt

Type of commission: Project competition 2022
Planning and execution: not executed
Schedule of accommodation: 97 apartments, commercial
Client: PWG Foundation, Zurich

Apartment plans
→ 3.8.4
→ 3.8.5

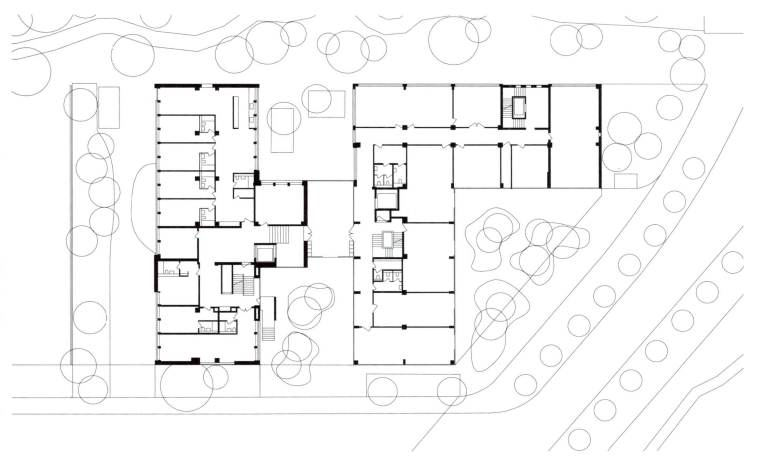

0 5 10   ground floor – regular floor

Food for Architects
Volume 2: Suddenly This Overview

Published by: Steib Gmür Geschwentner Kyburz Partner
General introduction and chapter introductions: Christoph Wieser
Project descriptions: Michael Geschwentner
Editor: Christoph Wieser
Translation: Hunter Bolin, Anna Dinwoodie, and Marc Hiatt for
Gegensatz Translation Collective
Proofreading: Marc Hiatt, Gegensatz Translation Collective
Design and layout: Sibylle Kanalz, Jürg Schönenberger, Nora Spaniol
Floor plan processing: Giuseppe Allegri
Image processing: Karin Prasser
Photo credits: Steib Gmür Geschwentner Kyburz, except for those by 360 360̸ p. 136; Georg Aerni p. 24, 26, 28, 38, 40, 74, 78, 84; Architron GmbH p. 126; Atelier Brunecky p. 86, 88, 92, 98, 106; Berrel Krautler Architekten GmbH p. 72, 124; Pit Brunner p. 60, 70; Roger Frei p. 30, 34, 44, 48, 50, 52, 80, 89, 118, 165; Zeljko Gataric p. 96, 108, 162; Edi Hueber p. 16; indievisual AG p. 148; maaars architektur p. 122, 146; Johannes Marburg p. 164; Naas & Bisig p. 22; Onur Ozmann GmbH p. 116, 152; Rita Palanikumar p. 132; Antje Quiram p. 42; Rafael Schmid p. 76, 104; Beat Schweizer p. 9 b.r., 62, 64, 82; Niklaus Spoerri p. 18; Studio Blomen p. 138, 156, 112; Seraina Wirz p. 56, 163; Zuend p. 134
Printing and binding: DZA Druckerei zu Altenburg GmbH, Thuringia

© 2023 Steib Gmür Geschwentner Kyburz Partner and Park Books AG, Zurich
© for the texts: the authors

Park Books
Niederdorfstrasse 54
8001 Zurich
Switzerland
www.park-books.com

Park Books has received support from the Federal Office of Culture with a general subsidy for the years 2021–2024.

All rights reserved; no part of this publication may be reproduced, stored in a retrieval system or transmitted in any form or by any means, electronic, mechanical, photocopying, recording, or otherwise, without the prior written consent of the publisher.

ISBN 978-3-03860-360-3

This book is volume 2 of Food for Architects, a set of five volumes in a slipcase which are not available separately.

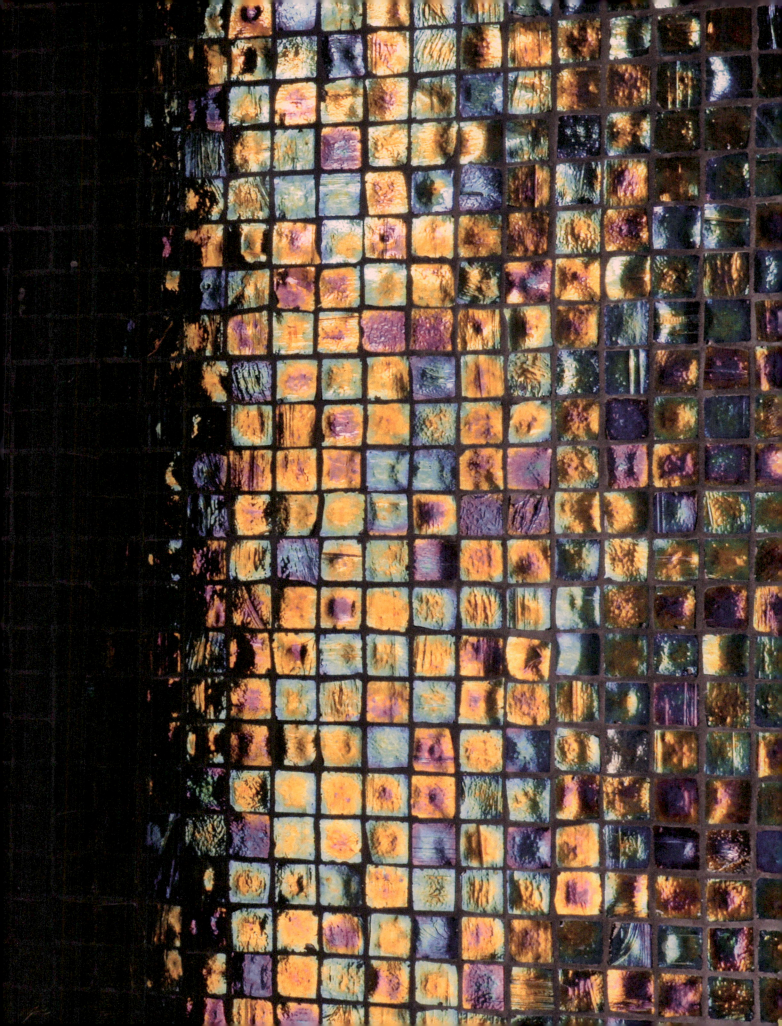

A Journey Through the World of Our Floor Plans

First Build the City, Then the Apartments
This volume exclusively showcases floor plans. Naturally, though, it also goes beyond that. "Everything is interconnected," as Alexander von Humboldt once wrote—an insight that also applies to the planning of an apartment. An apartment consists of various rooms, and is used as a place of retreat. Depending on its size, it serves one or more people. Despite the various forms of dwelling it enables—from one-person pads to multi-generational households—an apartment is always at once both a home and a habitat. When carefully set in relation to each other, entryways, bedrooms, bathrooms, toilets, living rooms, kitchens, and balconies provide a setting for private coexistence and the intimate needs of everyday life. "From small things big things one day come", sings Bruce Springsteen in his song of the same name. This simple insight, too, applies to designing an apartment.

Together, multiple apartments form a building. In addition to their individual rooms, buildings also include shared spaces like stairwells, entry halls, basements, attics, elevators, bicycle and laundry rooms, parking garages, and storage spaces for baby carriages. Also together, the residents of the building form a community. Even if their contact is limited, they know about one another. Ideally, they help each other out, lend everyday items, or make small talk in the laundry room. A functioning community is a privilege, but living together can also be maddening.

Alongside neighboring residences, a building forms part of an estate, a development, or a row. Exterior spaces are used by everyone. Maybe there's a playground or a community space on the ground floor. A shared stairwell can create a close-knit neighborhood. You might be able to identify the other residents of the development by sight. You make casual conversation at the bakery, at the estate's annual

Living together can also be maddening.

We're fascinated by the world of floor plans, but we understand that when we design these buildings, we're explicitly engaging in urban development.

get-together, or walking home from the bus stop. In the process, over the years, a lively and meaningful neighborhood develops.

The block forms part of a quarter. In addition to its residential buildings, it features a school, recognizably public thanks to its open spaces. The gymnasium is used in the evenings, an important part of the quarter's social apparatus. There's a church as well, distinguished by its privileged location. Ideally, there's a square where people come together. A cafe or kiosk invites passersby to linger, while a small weekly growers' market offers delicacies and regional products. In the pedestrian-friendly, tree-lined streets, we find a grocery store and a hairdresser, maybe even a shoemaker or wine shop. The ground floors of the buildings boast high ceilings, useful for a variety of purposes, offering space to small businesses. It's possible to have your workplace just a stone's throw away from your home.

Different topographies give rise to different patterns of urban development. Where it's flat, dense perimeter-block developments create an orderly and clearly structured cityscape. Streets are public, whereas enclosed courtyards are semi-private. As the terrain becomes hillier, perimeter blocks begin to dissolve. Individual buildings, centrally located on their plots, define these leafy urban areas.

Multiple quarters form a district, and all the districts together form a city. The map of the city reveals a picture of its urban development and planning: At the center are the medieval structures of the historical city. Next comes the influence of *Gründerzeit* ideals, of modernism, the notion of the garden city, and the effects of post-1960s growth, with all the associated public infrastructure buildings. A city's evolution resembles the rings of a tree trunk.

The train station is surrounded by busy commercial districts. Industrial plants line the river, whose power has long been valued. Today, many industrial zones have been converted to other uses, characterized by parking lots, cemeteries, perhaps even lakes. Universities, hospitals, town halls, churches, museums, and stadiums are important public facilities, and together

with their fields and open spaces they define urban development. Cinemas, theaters, opera houses, concert venues, clubs, restaurants, bars, cafes, galleries, and a range of shopping options make urban life attractive. The city is there for everyone. It offers space to the most diverse milieus.

But above all, it is residential buildings, with their mass and volume, that shape and define a city. We're fascinated by the world of floor plans, but we understand that when we design these buildings, we're explicitly engaging in urban development. For this reason, we're interested in the precise placement of each individual building in its surrounding environment. Each part belongs to a greater whole.

Every day, we ask ourselves the question: What sort of city do we want? The answer is challenging yet simple. Our cities should be like apartments, and our apartments should be like cities. In a word, they should be livable! Cities and apartments are both, in equal respects, our home.

Losing Helps
There are various ways to begin a design. Maybe you have a spatial concept, or an idea about how

Our cities should be like apartments, and our apartments should be like cities.

people might live. What's critical, though, is how you adapt, add on to, or correct an existing situation. "Urban planning first" is our motto.

Analyzing and understanding the location are indispensable. It's essential, therefore, to visit the construction site. Seeing it at night can help you identify overarching spatial characteristics and other features. Alongside the rough preliminary area and volume studies, we begin with simple working models. With a hot wire, we shape Styrofoam blocks. We search, test, and discuss. Sometimes chance helps too. We strive to achieve a holistic, balanced solution for an urban situation.

A Journey Through the World of Our Floor Plans

Only when we're satisfied with the urban planning model do we begin designing apartments. Usually, two partners take on this arduous work. The other two are incorporated into the process through weekly discussion sessions. A design needs to sit well with all of us. Having four partners is an advantage in this respect. One of us is always critical of the chosen solution and suggests a significant last-minute change which, even if it's a little frustrating, is always an improvement.

There are other questions that drive us: How do we design best? When are we at our most creative? We learn the most when we're eliminated early from a competition. At first, of course, we're disappointed, because the amount of work involved in a competition is im-

They just didn't recognize the brilliance of our ideas! But the real reason is simple: the designs that won the prizes were just better.

mense. We see participating in competitions as our daily training. Like in sports, losing is the key to improvement. We could very well choose to blame the jury for eliminating us—they just didn't recognize the brilliance of our ideas! But generally speaking, the real reason is simpler: the designs that won the prizes were just better.

As soon as a competition is over, the next one begins. We analyze our submissions and gather the documentation. We believe that Switzerland's comprehensive competition reports are a central factor in the fact that Zurich's apartments have such sophisticated floor plans. Judges' reports always form the foundations for our subsequent submissions. Alongside our own work on judging panels and ongoing personal development as architects, this helps keep us focused on contemporary issues in residential construction.

A Kitchen with a Space to Nap
Using reference floor plans is always a quick and easy way to start a design. Unfortunately, such allusions to architectural history never quite fit within the given parameters, the urban situation, or the resulting structural volume. So they need to be adapted. Working with plans from predecessors also poses another danger, since only two outcomes are possible: either your project is better or worse. Usually, it's the latter. We often measure ourselves, for example, against Wells Coates's Kensington High Street apartment block in London. We're fascinated by

his one-and-a-half-story residential halls. But to this day, we've never managed to implement the spatial concept. Nevertheless, architectural history is an important source for us. We seek out examples, study typologies, and take inspiration from the work of our colleagues.

Sometimes we set ourselves design tasks: How big does a balcony need to be to serve multiple functions? →2.2.1 To serve, even, as a living room →2.2.6 ? We separate a plan into its constituent parts and reassemble them. This kind of "deconstruction" can lead to new questions and new solutions. A kitchen, for example, could also serve as a connective space. Carefully positioned doors can give rise to surprising circulation possibilities →4.6 . Why not imagine a kitchen with a shower, a light-filled bathroom with a study corner or reading nook, or even a kitchenette with a space for napping?

While doing so, we always have to follow building code. Over the years, codes have become our friends, since they help us arrive at solutions. Regulations about extra length and height, for example, have produced interesting building volumes →2.4.3 . Such volumes, in turn, affect the floor plans. Basements aren't factored into floor-space calculations. If a basement is situated inside an apartment as a storage room, furnishing it with a window or with French doors can help it to augment a modestly sized apartment and even give it extra functionality →2.5.1 .

We're also unbothered by noise abatement regulations. Quite the opposite. Interpreting and implementing them, we find, often leads to innovative design approaches →2.3.18 . Among these are our "elephant trunk rooms." Sometimes, surprising proposals like this result merely from luck and coincidence. What's important is remaining open, so you can recognize an unlikely solution.

Sustainable building is another design challenge that intrigues and inspires us. It opens a broad new field for us architects. Solar panels can turn a building into a power plant (Heuwinkel, Allschwil). A defining parameter for our multifamily building in Wettswil was doing away with a parking garage, which translated to reduced excavation needs. Structural principles or the arrangement of cable shafts are other aspects that offer interesting potential.

Thinking with Your Hand
We enjoy talking about architecture. Anything is possible when you're talking. The most important and challenging work, however, involves translating thoughts and ideas to paper, and later to the screen. With the aid of a pencil's soft gray lead, with colored pencils, ballpoint pens, felt-tip pens, and (very important!) rulers, we begin the work we actually love the most—sketching. We start with clean transparent paper. We proceed line by line. Another layer follows; we draw line by line once again. We position the staircases beside the elevators, we measure with the ruler to ensure our dimensions are approximately correct, we search for an ideal floor plan. Suddenly, the pencil begins to guide us. We're thinking with our hand.

Designing means tearing things up and starting over. Working slowly, over and over again, testing out similar patterns yet arriving somewhere slightly different, we develop our apartments. The sketches blur; we use colors to clarify certain aspects; a pen line depicts potential circulation routes. Using quickly thrown-together spatial constructions, we test an idea until our hands and shirt sleeves are gray with graphite. For hours at a time, we search and study. We're never satisfied, because experience has taught us that a plan only gets better through tireless effort, in tiny little steps. Eventually, after countless rolls of drafting paper, the plan reaches the desired form and layout. Then we begin furnishing our imagined rooms. Where's the table? What do I see when I'm sitting right there? Where do the bed, cupboard, and television go? We need to carefully monitor the size of rooms, which is why a proper scale ruler, rather than one of those abominable set squares, is absolutely indispensable. But what if the apartment is too big? Then we have to start over from scratch. Where can we optimize in a logical way? Apartment designers need patience.

We draw a floor plan at least fifty times, usually more, working until it's perfect. We see the wisdom in the phrase "trial and error." Often, even determined labor at the work desk, repeated rounds of discussion, and hours of sketching fail to yield a harmonious result. Experience has taught us that obstinate searching doesn't necessarily lead to the goal. It can be more productive to nourish our subconscious and simply let go. We need to know and trust that on our way home, on a hike or a jog, while we're ironing, shopping, cooking, traveling, or watching a movie, inspiration will arrive. We believe in the sixth sense. Unexpectedly, out of the blue, every now and then, a bolt of "creative lightning" strikes. But it can't happen unless you're tirelessly working with your hands.

The Raw and the Cooked
When plans are drawn with soft graphite pencils, everything fits together perfectly. Repeated sketching makes the walls black, thick, and imprecise. But appearances can be deceptive. Now the real work begins; our colleagues take these blurry sketches and plug them into the computer. Our ancestors discovered that fire and heat alter food, which was crucial for the development of humankind. In a similar way, we view our sketches as raw ingredients—only on the monitor are they cooked up. Plans are developed, adapted, corrected, supplemented, and rejected so as ultimately to conform with build-

Sometimes, surprising proposals like this result merely from luck and coincidence. What's important is remaining open, so you can recognize an unlikely solution.

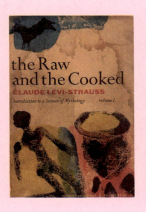

ing code regulations, accessibility demands, noise abatement rules, clients' desires, input from colleagues, and critique from our partners. When you cook, there are various ways to transform raw ingredients. Hand drawings are cooked in the computer in the same way—they're steamed, boiled, braised, and sometimes grilled. If we don't find a solution, we put them aside and preserve them for a few days. We pickle and marinate the plans in our heads. They're fermented and reshaped by all these processes and new conditions, until they've met the demands posed by the various construction phases.

As designs are reworked, they also become denser. Plans grow ever more precise, containing ever more information. Shafts are situated and filled with technical services, power outlets are placed, door openings and their frames are filled in, floor surfaces are decided upon, windows are fastened into their proper position within the spatial program. Everything is measured twice; the elevations are double-checked. A dense task list, coordinated with the relevant specialists, emerges.

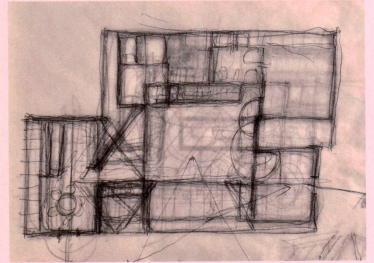

A floor plan only gets better through tireless effort, in tiny little steps.

A Journey Through the World of Our Floor Plans   13

Only when the floor plan is implemented at the construction site does it become safe from our last-minute tweaks. If it doesn't get built, it goes into our pantry, in the hope it will prove useful down the road. Like specimens in a medical museum, we store all our designed and discarded floor plans. Preserved in formaldehyde, they sit there waiting for us to pull them out, to start sketching again, to cook them up on the computer.

Diversity as Motivation
Our competition entry for the BRIAG site in Regensdorf, near Zurich, is an example of how we take pleasure in developing the widest possible variety of apartments, utilizing a range of housing typologies. The brief called for floor plans that would diminish noise pollution, facilitate living and working in a single space, and be adapted to the specific conditions of high-rises. We recommended maisonettes and apartments with two-story balconies. Our design embodies the experience we four partners have accumulated over the course of our careers. Unfortunately, it was a design that we had to consign to the category of "broken dreams."

Spaghetti and Floor Plans
Beyond designing apartments, we're all passionate about cooking. We also happen to share a favorite food. For over thirty years—parallel to our search for a flawless floor plan—we've sought the perfect plate of spaghetti.

All four of us partners have our strengths and weaknesses. Understanding these, in both architecture and cooking, simplifies our collaboration. At the same time, we trust the old adage that too many cooks spoil the broth. This is especially true for our joint projects. That's why we put faith in the partners responsible for the project, valuing their different ideas and opinions, and granting them the final say. We build using the power of arguments. In our weekly discussions, we all bring our specific strengths to the table, with the goal of improving a project, phase by phase. Planning and building is a lengthy and complex process. We've learned

We've learned that we function best when we all contribute and combine our different gifts.

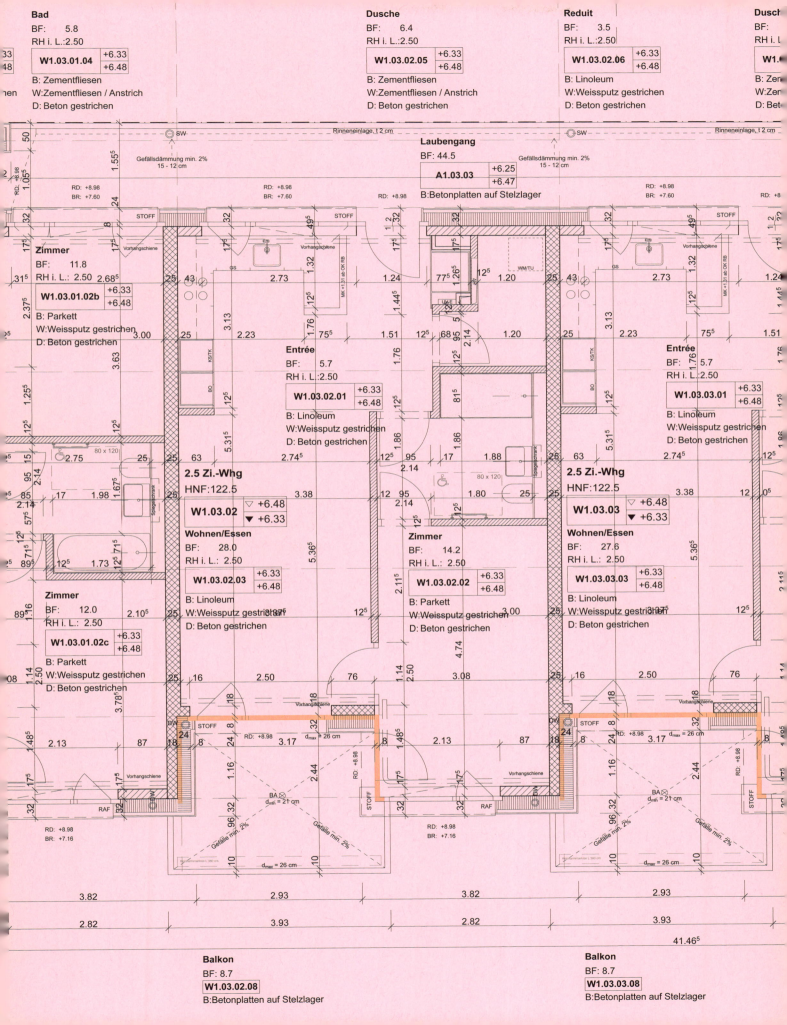

that we function best when we all contribute and combine our different gifts.

Fortunately, we're also different when it comes to cooking. For many years, Matthias Kyburz has applied himself to making the perfect meat sauce. This is because he has two favorite dishes—flawless lasagna and a classic spaghetti bolognese. We're well aware that homemade tagliatelle fits the latter dish better than spaghetti. But considering that this book also features our twelve "all-time favorite spaghetti dishes," we're willing to fudge a little. At the moment, Matthias is trying to identify which variety of milk is ideal for adding to the carefully mixed ground meat before dry white wine is added to the tomato sauce and boiled down.

Michael Geschwentner is working on mastering *cacio e pepe*. Since visiting Rome with his family, where he tried this variation of spaghetti every day, he's been testing out the ultimate

Only when the plan is implemented at the construction site does it become safe from our last-minute tweaks.

preparation method. What are the ideal varieties of pepper and pecorino? Should the pepper be roasted in the pan first, to make it more flavorful and aromatic when ground in a mortar and pestle? How much salted water from the cooked spaghetti is necessary to create the perfect creamy pecorino consistency, mixed in with the *al dente* spaghetti?

While in his work Patrick Gmür is fascinated by complexity and tries to make architecture that's as diverse and surprising as possible, when cooking, he prefers the simplest tomato sauce possible. You can find a peerlessly simple *sugo di pomodoro* in Marcella Hazan's superlative *The Classic Italian Cookbook*, consisting of only one can of pelati (i.e., peeled tomatoes), half an onion, and at least a hundred grams of butter. It may look simple, but it requires perfect preparation. Which butter, which kind of onion, and most importantly which brand of *pelati* create the most harmonious mix? How long should it stay on the heat? When is the spaghetti perfectly al dente? What's the best parmesan to add, and how long does it need to be aged to top off the dish?

Jakob Steib, on the other hand, loves pasta sauces that require as much simmering as possible, like a *sugo di melanzane* or a *sugo di pancetta e prezzemolo*. Preparing, carefully chopping, then repeatedly stirring and tasting, while in the meantime pondering a floor plan—that's Steib's preferred way of making a pasta.

For each of us, living without architecture is tough to imagine. Living without cooking pasta and eating it? Simply inconceivable. It's safe to say that, for us four partners, pasta is the staple item in our diet. On a near daily basis—certainly every Sunday evening—we stand in our kitchens and cook our pasta and the sauces that go along with them. It's a tradition that unites us, since we know that while making our favorite dish, we can process the foregoing week and prep for the week to come. We also know how our brains work: the best ideas hit in precisely these moments of well-deserved relaxation. We're bound together by our search for the perfect pasta, just as much as the ideal floor plan.

Joyful, Meaningful Work
Today, tenants have essentially no choice. When they finally manage to find an apartment after a long and aggravating search, they have to rent it at an inflated price, given the extremely low vacancy rates in most cities. For us architects, this imposes an important obligation: to never design, plan, and build terrible apartments! The residents will thank us for it.

Building housing is the most important task facing our profession for other reasons as well. The right to privacy is one of humankind's fundamental rights. And the prerequisite for this is a safe and secure home. We spend most of our lives in our homes. For this reason alone, planners like us bear responsibility. When it comes to an architecturally unsuccessful museum, we have the option to simply not visit. A bad apartment, however, will be occupied for years, even decades. This circumstance is a major motivation for us.

In the over thirty years we've been running our offices, we have designed almost exclusively apartment buildings. We're grateful that we've been able to see a whole host of them through to completion. Although we wrestle with similar tasks on a daily basis, under more or less identical conditions, sometimes—especially after losing a competition—we need to take a step back and thoroughly reexamine our approach. We look for ways to disrupt ossified routines that have crept in. To change our habits, we need to understand how we work together, and what factors shape our architectural designs.

An unfortunate condition of our profession is that the daily grind throws things in our way that limit the amount of time we can devote to our core business, constructive design. Because of this, lecture requests are always an interesting opportunity to take a timeout, to reflect on our oeuvre and present it to a receptive audience. We took one recent lecture invitation as a chance to comb through our earlier designs and buildings looking for generative floor-plan

> We spend most of our lives in our homes. For this reason, planners like us bear responsibility.

An unfortunate condition of our profession is that the daily grind throws things in our way that limit the amount of time we can devote to our core business, constructive design.

ideas. Visiting the archive, we were astonished by the richness and diversity of approaches. It felt like an expedition into the past, and ultimately into our very selves. We identified twelve themes that have defined our designs and the ways we organize apartment plans. Laying them out like this in 2019 led to the idea of writing a corresponding essay, and publishing a book. The volume before you is the result of this exploration. Peppered throughout the whole project, adding flavor, are accompanying spaghetti recipes.

Our selection is somewhat arbitrary and incomplete. We're aware that multiple themes are present in each of the floor plans presented. Even so, we've assigned each plan to a specific chapter. While there are similarities in the demands and challenges posed by each assignment, the slow simmering of our ideas always leads to different apartments. The same goes for our search for the perfect spaghetti. We hope you enjoy journeying through the world of our floor plans.

Patrick Gmür

A Journey Through the World of Our Floor Plans

Contents

3.1	Circulation	p.22
3.2	Central Room	p.36
3.3	Two-Story Balcony	p.58
3.4	Two-Story Interior	p.74
3.5	Multi-Story Apartment	p.94
3.6	Deep Floor Plans	p.114
3.7	High-Rise Living	p.136
3.8	Converting/Expanding	p.158
3.9	Outdoor Spaces	p.168
3.10	Form Follows Law	p.190
3.11	Compact and Affordable	p.214
3.12	Bespoke Apartments	p.238

3.1 Circulation

One of the more figurative and precise terms in the English language is "dead-end." As is well-known, a dead-end is a street accessible only from one end or, in housing, a room that has only one door. Concretely, it means that we have to exit the same way we entered.

Our primal instincts tend to react strongly to this: they tell us that we are safer when there is more than one way in and out of a particular space. Consider how much more spacious an apartment feels when we can walk from room to room. Now consider how this effect is amplified when there are various ways to get between the bedrooms. The arrangement of adjoining rooms also plays an important role. For example, the kitchen can also serve as a passageway from one room to the next, which makes it a central place for everyday life. When we sit down to design apartments, we always consider the paths through it to be an essential feature.

3.1.1 "This Must Be the Place"

1993
3.5-rooms
73 m²
Hinterfeld Apartment Block
→ 2.1.1

Here, the kitchen is the hub and, like a ship's galley, is located in a separate room. It regulates movement throughout the apartment, serves as a center of gravity for the plan and emphasizes its importance as a functional and social node. And it keeps smoke from the kitchen from trickling into other rooms of the apartment.

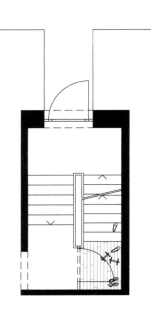

3.1.2 "Sweet Dreams (Are Made of This)"

2001
3.5-rooms
101 m²

James Development
→ 2.2.2

The fact that the building code requires the attic floor to be recessed is turned into a spatial feature: the staircase-and-elevator combo sit in the middle of the apartment, and all the rooms are arranged around it. The rooms in the apartment alternate between spatial relationships to the inside and outside. The path through the bathroom ensures that personal hygiene is convenient and puts the "wet room" on a par with the others.

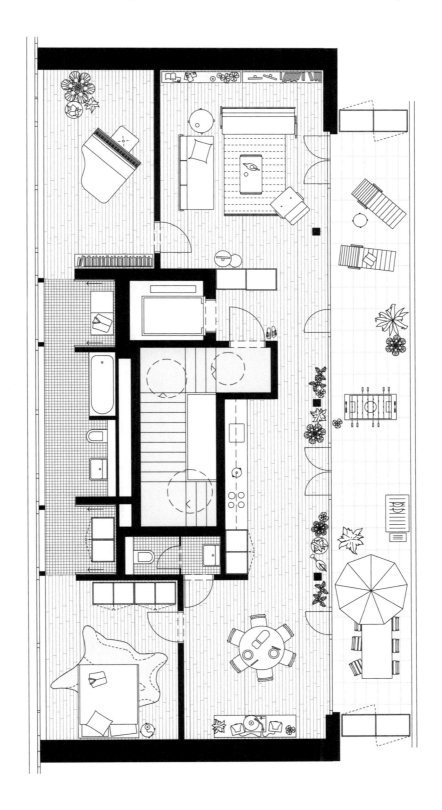

Circulation

3.1.3 "The Cabinet of Dr. Caligari"

2001
4.5-rooms
137 m²

James Development
→ 2.2.2

One spatial compartment leads to the next, until suddenly a cascade forms and rushes through the apartment, creating a rich blend of different spatial experiences. Like a spatial hall of mirrors, the alternation between the moods that light and space evoke creates an intimate sense of well-being in an expansively laid out interior world.

 What Does Chronic Sinusitis Have to Do with Living Space?

Gabriela and Richi have traveled a lot in their time. A considerable collection of souvenirs from all over the world bears witness to their travels. A boar's head from Scotland adorning the wall in the entryway is a favorite piece of Richi's; he is fascinated by Celtic culture.

At the moment, one room is still occupied by a grown-up son from a second marriage. Junior's nighttime escapades are starting to get on the couple's nerves, however, and as soon as he moves out, that room will be used as a snoring room, since Gabriela suffers from chronic sinusitis.

They will continue to share the large bathroom, which opens onto the terrace. The dining room, furnished specially for the purpose, regularly serves as a venue for large-scale culinary events. On these evenings, the kitchen is a flurry of chaotic activity, so it's lucky that the spacious kitchen is separated off.

Through the window, Richi—who does most of the cooking in this relationship—sees the arriving guests, who are first offered an aperitif in the living area. Pretty formal, but that's how Gabriela likes it; her upbringing in a Catholic boarding school comes out in situations like these!

Circulation 27

3.1.4 "Around the World"

2002
5.5-rooms
154 m²
Roost Development
→ 2.2.3

This classic circuitous layout loops around the bathroom unit, which occupies the center of the apartment and divides the plan into an individual and a common area. Each of the rooms forms an integral link in the sequence of rooms. No dead end halts the flow of space: the route traverses the entire plan without coming to an end, leaving the visitor with an impression of maximum spaciousness.

28

3.1.5 "You Spin Me Round (Like a Record)"

2011
4.5-rooms
101 m²
Claridenstrasse
Development
→ 2.3.8

Once again, the bathroom is located at the central axis of this circular plan. This time, however, there are no corridors, which frees up space for movement while maintaining a vast, spacious feel. The classic enfilade is given a new twist by being routed around the spatial center along the facades leading from one room to the next.

Circulation

3.1.6 Claridenstrasse Development – 2011 – 3.5-rooms – 83 m²
→ 2.3.8

3.1.7 Claridenstrasse Development – 2011 – 3.5-rooms – 84 m²
→ 2.3.8

3.1.8 "Light at the End of the Tunnel"

2014
3.5-rooms
89 m²

Am Rietpark
Apartment Block

→ 2.3.19

From front to back and back again, the path extends from one room through the bathroom units into the second room, then through the living room back to the starting point. The sight-line through this "car wash" makes this plan appear larger without handing any of the valuable area of this compact apartment over to access.

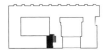

Circulation

3.1.9 "Living Next Door to Alice"

2019
3.5-rooms
70 m²

Alte Landstrasse
Development
→ 2.4.10

The staircase is only the teaser to the path through the apartment, which merges seamlessly with the apartment's larger access concept and extends the spatial cascade of the . The internal pathway makes the apartment appear larger than it is. Hidden niches, surprising spatial connections, and protean possibilities for traversing the space combine the individual rooms into a large whole.

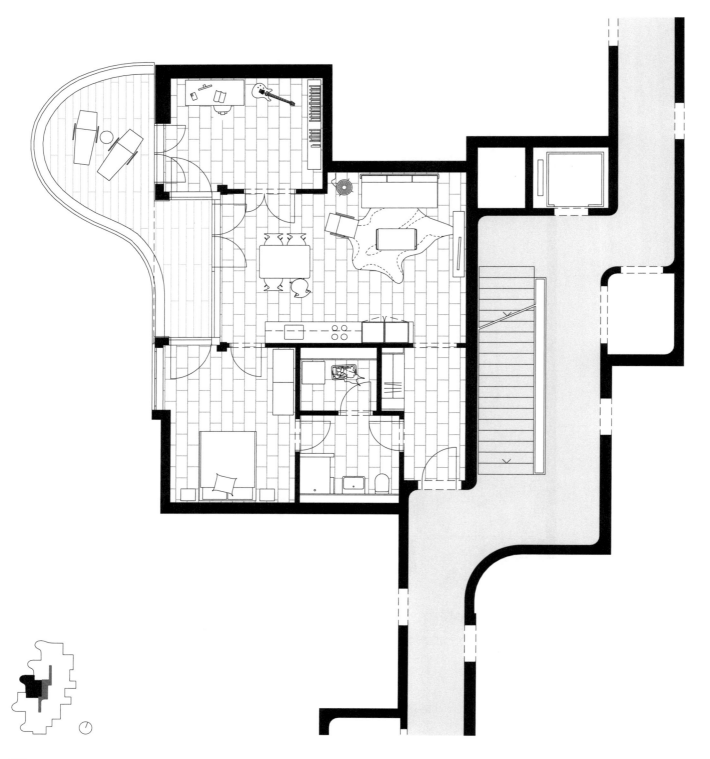

32

There are two activities that form part of our everyday routines: designing floor plans and cooking spaghetti! What they have in common is that they are always similar and yet always different. Housing is our passion. Pasta, or rather more accurately carbohydrates, make us happy. Below is one of our favorite summer dishes.

Spaghetti with Marinated Tomateos

Recipe taken from: Rose Gray and Ruth Rogers, The Cafe Cook Book: Italian Recipes from London's River Cafe, New York 1998

Serves four

Ingredients
600 g fresh cherry tomatoes
3 tablespoons plucked basil leaves
6 tablespoons good olive oil
2 tablespoons red wine vinegar
1 tablespoon of balsamic vinegar
Salt and freshly ground pepper
400 g spaghetti

Method
1. Cut the ripe cherry tomatoes in half and squeeze out the juice and seeds.
2. Mix six tablespoons of olive oil with the vinegars and season with salt and pepper.
3. Add the tomato halves and mix well. The tomatoes should soak up the flavors of the marinade.
4. Add the plucked basil leaves, cover, and let marinate for one hour.
5. Cook the spaghetti in a pot of boiling water until it is al dente, drain, and return to the pot.
6. Over high heat, stir in the tomatoes with the marinade.
7. Drizzle with olive oil and serve.

3.2 Central Room

The idea of creating a single room that can be used to access all the others in the apartment is certainly intriguing. This central distribution room structures the plan clearly and concisely. The foyer has the most communal character of all the rooms in the apartment. It is even suitable as a dining room, for example.

When opened, the double-doors or floor-to-ceiling doors (depending on the use of the adjoining rooms) link the space with the kitchen, the living room, the library, or the private sleeping area. For its residents, every apartment is a place of special significance. Supplied with a central room like this one, it very concretely turns into the center of their world!

3.2.1 "Duele el corazón"

1999
5.5-rooms
127 m²

Kurfirstenstrasse
Apartment Block
→ 2.1.4

This is a plan with a big heart! With rooms stretching three meters high, the living room is not only the center of the apartment, but also the hub of family life. The rigid and clean configuration of different spatial layers is deceptive, since spatial diversity abounds within the building. The section reveals the secret of the large living hall, which is created by the staggered arrangement of the building volume.

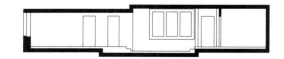

3.2.2 Just Around the Corner

2001
4.5-rooms
130 m²

James Development
→ 2.2.2

The spacious entryway promises upscale living. This is the place where people enter, take off their shoes, hang their coats in the wardrobe, welcome their guests, and later bid them farewell. A centrifugal spatial structure unfolds from this center, with interconnected rooms that serve as long internal walkways. Diagonal relationships create an impressive visual expanse.

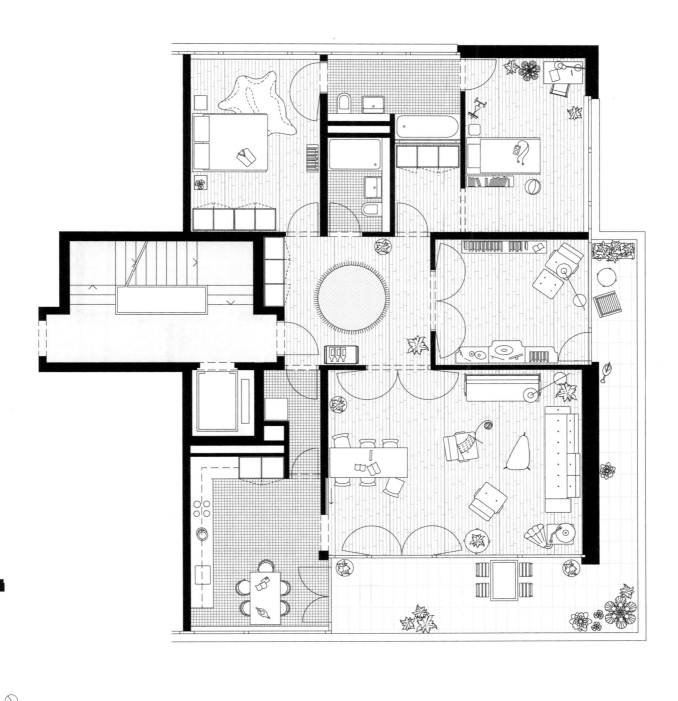

Central Room

3.2.3   "Enter Sandman"

2001
4-rooms
106 m²
James Development
→ 2.2.2

When the entryway grows to the size of an entire room, it becomes more than a point of arrival and departure. With such grand proportions, it takes on a decisive role in the plan, and functions as an extension of the living spaces. Double-doors accentuate the abundant spatial relationships, conjuring up a sense of openness in the plan even when space is at a premium.

3.2.4 "One from the Heart"

2001
4.5-rooms
120 m²

James Development
→ 2.2.2

The central living hall is by no means a modern invention, it's a spatial concept deeply rooted in the history of housing. We've only forgotten how to make use of it. Here, it is combined with the eat-in kitchen and the sunroom. With glazed double doors, the distinction between inside and outside is blurred. When the doors open, a grandiose living situation emerges, combining plants, tables, wing chairs, and a sofa in a single space.

Central Room

3.2.5 "Stretch Out and Wait"

2002
2.5-rooms
75 m²

Roost Development
→ 2.2.3

The living room is slightly displaced from the center of the plan while also being extended and stretched, allowing it to span the periphery of the apartment and connect the rooms. Corridors are no longer necessary and the spatial dimensions maximize the spacious feel of the apartment. The entryway cannot be dispensed with, since it provides privacy to the living area. Cozy niches provide an optimal stage for furniture.

3.2.6 "Surfin' USA"

2011
4.5-rooms
102 m²
Brüderhofweg
Development
→ 2.3.6

Thinking outside the box, the designers have transmuted the central living space into a jack-of-all-trades. The kitchen island divides the entrance area without impinging upon the broad spatial dimensions. Two wings extend the living area to meet the facade. They form easy-to-furnish alcoves that stabilize the living space. A deftly placed sliding door broadens the spatial perspective and extends the living space further.

Central Room 43

3.2.7 "Bend Ya Back"

2011
2.5-rooms
70 m²

Brüderhofweg
Development
→ 2.3.9

From compact to large—but only thanks to a trick that plays with the geometry of the space, "folding" the plan at a ninety-degree angle just past the central room, making it so the apartment bores through the building volume. Once one reaches the bedroom, and with it the end of the path, the main room is no longer visible. The spatial microcosm contains all kinds of unforeseen features. The kitchen island partitions the living space without detracting from its size.

3.2.8 "Miller's Crossing"

2013
4.5-rooms
109 m²

Kleeweidstrasse
Development
Study commission
→ 2.3.16

Tucked neatly into the belly of the apartment, the living room forms the center of a star-shaped plan. Sloped walls facilitate a lithe spatial flow and route the path diagonally from the entryway into the living room. The bedrooms are arranged as satellites. Their doors are located at the edge of the amphora-shaped living area, and are protected by the tapering of the balcony on the eastern side. A double door makes the third room an extension of the living area, and the fireplace is embedded in the opposite wall.

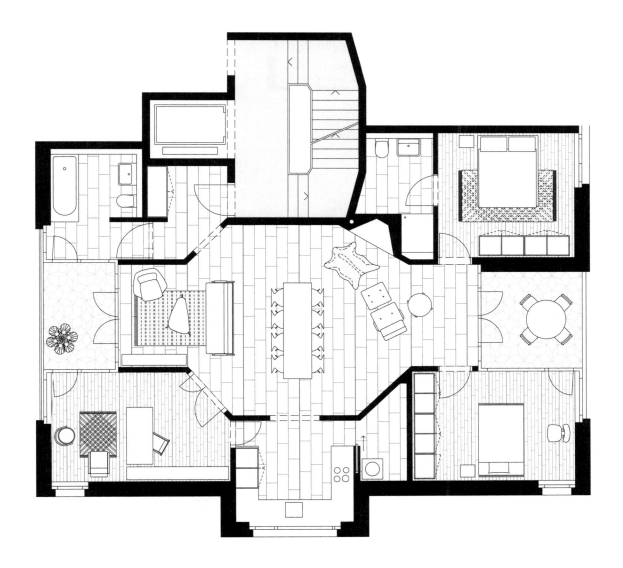

Central Room

3.2.9 Kleeweidstrasse Development – Study commission – 2013 – 3.5-rooms – 91 m²
→ 2.3.16

3.2.10 Kleeweidstrasse Development – Study commission – 2013 – 4.5-rooms – 109 m²
→ 2.3.16

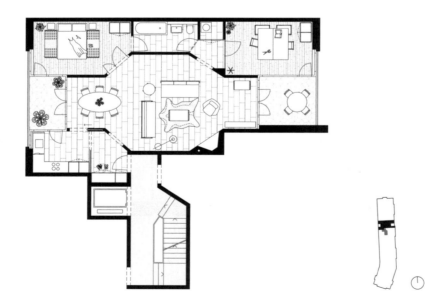

3.2.11 The Apartment without a Past

2016
4.5-rooms
95 m²

Developments 5–7,
Waidmatt

→ 2.4.1

Once frowned upon as a means of access in social housing, the outside corridor has experienced periodic revivals. This plan solves the problem of limited privacy with a sunroom in the front, which can serve as an entrance, a private outdoor space, or even an orangery. It provides cover, shielding the central living area from prying eyes while adding an exterior annex to the apartment.

Central Room

3.2.12 "Bad Reputation"

2016
4.5-rooms
96.5 m²

Developments 5–7,
Waidmatt

→ 2.4.1

This plan is defined by the conservatory, which acts as a buffer to the outside corridor and an extension of the living area. The double doors accentuate the transverse axis of the apartment, which creates a sequence of rooms and connects the interior of the apartment with the arcade without sacrificing the need for privacy. The bathroom doors are tucked away in niches. This simple trick supplies privacy to the more intimate spaces of the apartment.

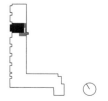

48

3.2.13 "Wie Flasche leer"

2019
4.5-rooms
112 m²
Sonne Development
→ 2.4.11

The polygonal shape of the building produces a change of direction in the central living space. This dilates the spatial perspective and produces two different zones which are spatially connected yet can serve separate functions. At the inner corner of the building, two rooms flank the living room. The spatial figure fans out, offering a spacious and versatile habitat despite the small size of the facade.

Central Room

3.2.14 "Mama Mia"

2019
4.5-rooms
98 m²
Sonne Development
→ 2.4.11

Coming from the entrance, one walks into the central living room at a diagonal. This, in addition to the sloping walls, makes the room appear larger and offers a direct view to the outside. Placing the rooms at the corners of the plan reduces the area taken up by thoroughfares. This has the added bonus of making the apartment feel dynamic despite the simple layout. It also creates two spatial niches in the living room which, with the simple addition of some furniture, will make for perfect quiet zones.

3.2.15 "Dancing Queen"

2019
3.5-rooms
83 m²
Sonne Development
→ 2.4.11

Apartments with only a one-sided orientation tend to exude a monotonous spatial feel. To avoid this, the walls in this apartment are staggered back towards the interior. Viewed from the kitchen, which sits at the helm of the plan like a DJ booth, the living area extends visually across the entire width of the apartment. This effect is achieved by the open doors. Thanks to the balcony, the two rooms are provided with corner windows which—like bay windows—once again broaden the panorama at the narrowest point of the living area.

Central Room

3.2.16 "Lights in the Dusk"

2021
4.5-rooms
113.5 m²

Roswiesen-/
Winterthurerstrasse
Development

→ 2.5.8

When deep volumes have several apartments per stairwell, the distance from the apartment door to a facade that admits light is sometimes substantial. To lessen this effect, the transverse living area is drawn out: it absorbs sunlight at the front via a carefully placed window, is indirectly lit in the middle by the kitchen (located in a side arm), and tumbles out at the end over a balcony into the view.
A diagonal sequence of two small rooms connect to form the entryway. It makes for a ceremonial arrival and connects the entrance to the living area like an umbilical cord.

52

3.2.17 "Chef's Table"

2021
4.5-rooms
108.5 m²

Roswiesen-/
Winterthurerstrasse
Development
→ 2.5.8

Two chambers at the entrance produce a sidestep and merge into the living area, which widens to serve as a strong backbone for the sofa area. The shaded central area of the room signals comfort and security while simultaneously drawing the gaze towards the light and the view. The double doors of the adjacent room offer an additional view to the outdoors and make the living room larger to the eye. Situated in the corner is the main feature: the kitchen. Anyone using it inhabits a threshold between inside and outside the apartment.

Central Room 53

3.2.18 A Friend of Mine

2021
4.5-rooms
119.5 m²
Roswiesen-/
Winterthurerstrasse
Development
→ 2.5.8

The living area sprouts arms that lead to the bedrooms and wrap around the kitchen. The kitchen could accommodate a table, which in everyday life would serve as a meeting place, a workplace for homework, or a place for reading the newspaper. The bedrooms are situated at both ends of the space, lending them an added sense of privacy. They extend the plan lengthwise and a stroll through the living room, passing behind the table and sofa, reveals a panoply of spatial features. In this way, the apartment once again appears larger than it is.

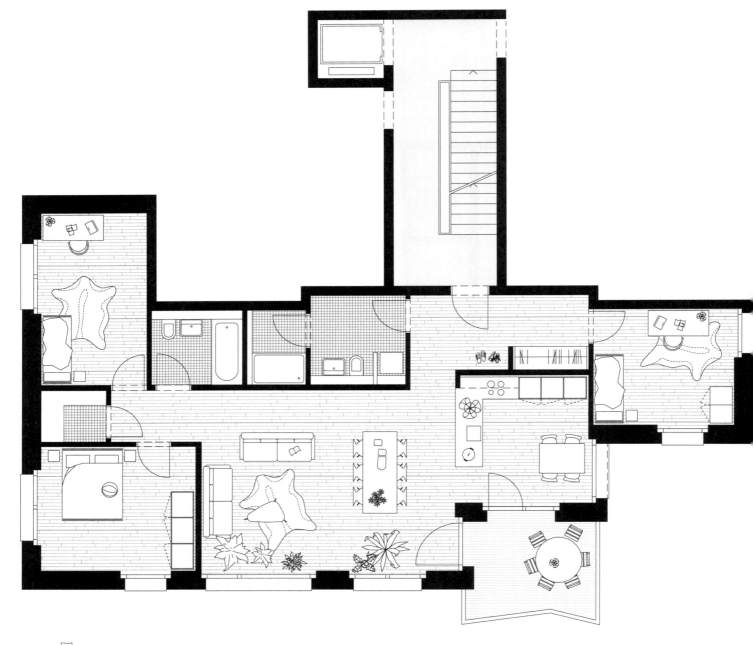

We love summer the best. The pleasantly mild evening temperatures encourage us to spend time outdoors. Unfortunately, now and then the rush to get a competition entry submitted restricts us, preventing us from enjoying this season properly. Below we present a spaghetti recipe that can be made quickly after coming home late in the evening. The lemon and thyme give it the flavor of vacations in the south.

Spaghetti with Lemon and Thyme

Serves two

Ingredients
2–3 tablespoons thyme leaves, finely chopped
Zest of an organic lemon, grated
Juice of the organic lemon
6 tablespoons good olive oil
Salt and lemon pepper
400 g spaghetti
Parmesan

Method
1. Remove thyme leaves from their sprigs, chop finely, and place in a bowl.
2. Finely grate the lemon peel and add to the thyme leaves.
3. Squeeze the lemon and add the juice to the bowl.
4. Add six tablespoons of olive oil and mix well.
5. Meanwhile, cook the spaghetti in boiling water until al dente, drain, and return to the pot.
6. Mix the spaghetti with the sauce well, adding a little water from the pasta pot.
7. Serve.

3.3 Two-Story Balcony

In recent decades, several key factors have changed the role balconies play in apartment buildings. The introduction of daylight saving time, social transformations, people having to work less, the demand for facades with green space, or simply the desire for more "quality time" require that the outdoor spaces on our apartments expand continuously to be amenable to new uses.

We think a lot about what balcony size is functional. How much privacy is desirable, how much light and shade the rooms surrounding the balcony require, and a familiarity with inspiring examples make us return time and again to the two-story balcony.

3.3.1 Stag Hunt

2000
4.5-rooms
120 m²

Paul-Clairmont-
Strasse Apartment
Block

→ 2.2.1

How does innovation find its way into housing construction? It's simple: take an aspect that has been neglected and reinvent it. Here, the balcony is transformed into a hanging garden, a two-story outdoor living room with ample space for potted trees and a quick spin on the tricycle. A double door leads the way from the balcony through the apartment and seamlessly intertwines an open floor plan with clear spatial partitioning.

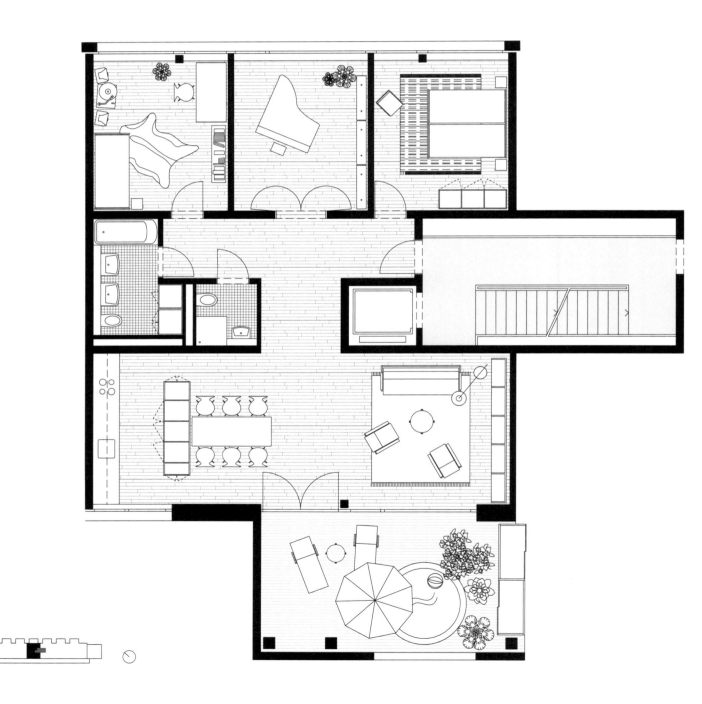

3.3.2 Waidmannsheil

2000
5.5-rooms
140 m²

Paul-Clairmont-
Strasse Apartment
Block
→ 2.2.1

With just a simple trick, a four-and-a-half room apartment becomes a five-and-a-half-room apartment. With the living and dining room fixed in place, the kitchen changes location as one moves through the floors. A tower with two additional rooms is annexed at the rear. As a result, the two other rooms both contain a corner suitable for furniture, with a window inspired by the Berlin-style living room; it looks out from behind the tower. Thanks to the floor-to-ceiling twin doors, the spectacular depth of the building can be fully appreciated.

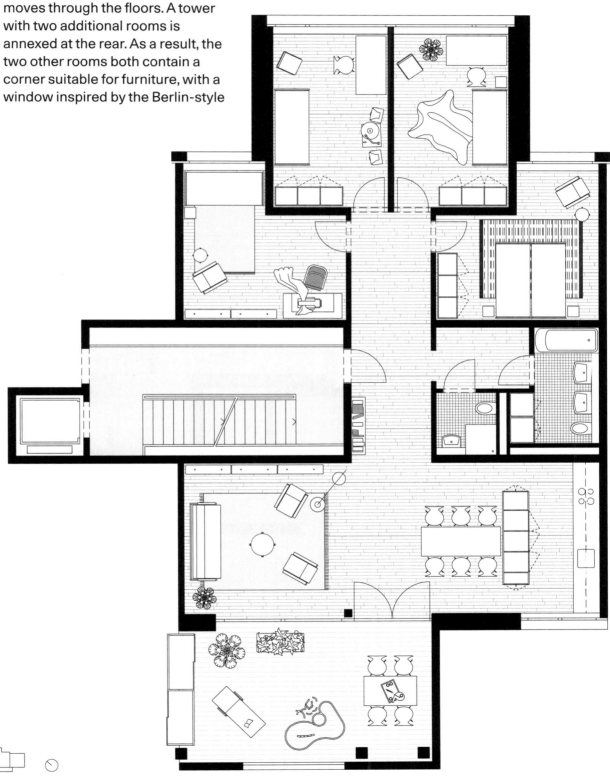

Two-Story Balcony

3.3.3 "Drifting Clouds"

2001
3-rooms
73 m²

James Development
→ 2.2.2

A configuration based on three rooms—all slightly larger than usual yet equal to one another in size—where the kitchen and balcony swap sides each level, are enough to create a two-story outdoor space. Thanks to its size and the surrounding walls, it feels like a patio. The exceptional depth of the balcony only works thanks to the two-story structure, which offers a view of the sky above while also maintaining privacy.

3.3.4 "Reduce to the Max"

2001
4-rooms
85 m²

James Development
→ 2.2.2

This type of apartment is a jack-of-all-trades. By dividing up the living space, the three-room apartment becomes a four-room apartment that can be shared or become home to families with several children. Diagonal room layouts and floor-to-ceiling twin doors ensure a spacious character. The entrance acts as the apartment's hub and the spacious additional storage space is upgraded to a utility room. The two-story balcony on this apartment is a significant amenity.

Two-Story Balcony

3.3.5 "Double Trouble"

2001
5.5-rooms
155 m²

James Development
→ 2.2.2

Learning from Paul-Clairmont-Strasse: the two-story balcony appears here as part of a maisonette apartment whose offset floor levels are revealed in the section. This creates a generous diagonal space, which makes the apartment appear larger. The view from the corner room extends over the balcony into the kitchen, which is large enough to accommodate a family dining table. The bedroom level benefits from the stairwell and landing, which adds flexible extra room for work or to play.

Two-Story Balcony   65

3.3.6 James Development – 2001 – 4.5-rooms – 130 m²
→ 2.2.2

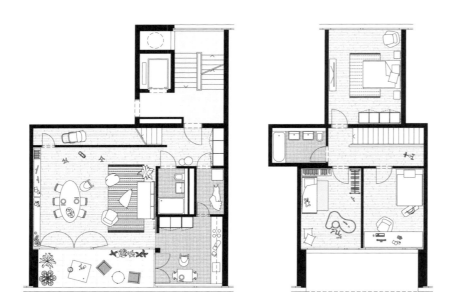

3.3.7 James Development – 2001 – 4.5-rooms – 135 m²
→ 2.2.2

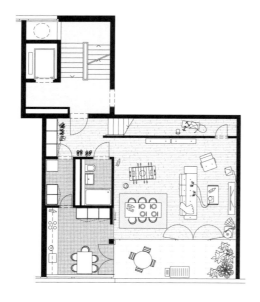

3.3.8 "Let the Sunshine In"

2012
3.5-rooms
86 m²

Schweighof
Development
→ 2.3.11

The two-story balcony-in-miniature allows more light to suffuse the living space, augmenting the spatial ambiance of this relatively small apartment. In this case the balcony's recess extends up into the attic level, making it possible to do without an alternating arrangement. The room adjoining the balcony can function either as an extension to the living room or a children's room at a comfortable remove from the parents' area.

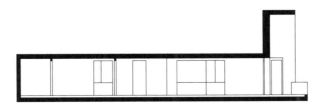

Two-Story Balcony 67

3.3.9 "Irgendwie, irgendwo, irgendwann"

2012
5.5-rooms
157 m²

Hard Turm Park
Apartments
and Offices
→ 2.3.13

This is where it all comes together: setting the plan at an angle enhances sunlight, gives the rooms an orientation point on all four sides, and opens up a diagonal line that produces an immense spatial depth and a line of sight running the length of the apartment. The two-story balcony is triangle-shaped, measuring four meters at its deepest point. It offers both sheltered one-story and massive two-story areas with enough space for tall, potted trees.

Dear Max, the Model Railroad Has to Go!

Finally enough room for the patchwork Lässer and Spirig family! Most importantly, the apartment has three balconies, the largest of which has trees growing literally to the heavens; with nearly six meters to the overhang above, it's roomier than normal! A hanging garden, according to Max Lässer's daughter—no, not Max Lässer the musician—who is currently learning in school about the Seven Wonders of the World.

The room with the double doors has been converted into a home office by Nicola Spirig—again, no, not the triathlete—while Max's model railroad has been relegated to the basement—something he submitted to only under vehement protest.

With its open kitchen, the large living area is the family's gathering place, and frequently serves as a home theater as well. Bojan, Nicola's son, prefers to watch his favorite series on the big screen, usually binge-watching a whole season in a single night, until he finally crawls into bed with bloodshot eyes the next morning.

Luckily, the bedrooms are tucked away in the rear part of the apartment; this way, there is a quiet area available for the other family members to withdraw to.

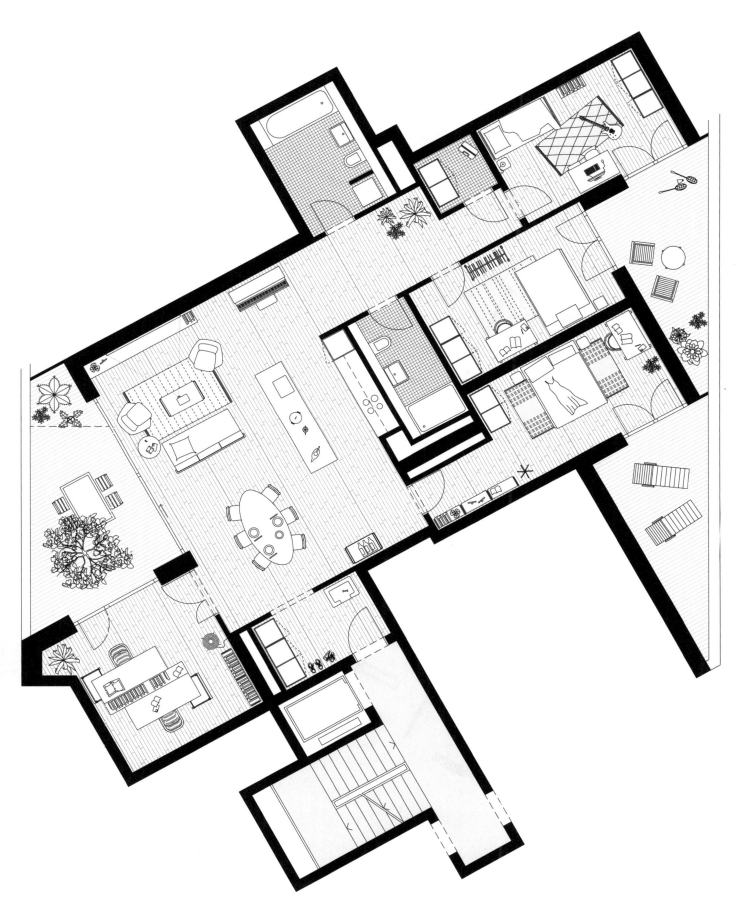

Two-Story Balcony 69

3.3.10 Hard Turm Park Apartments and Offices – 2012 – 4.5-rooms – 130 m²
→ 2.3.13

3.3.11 Hard Turm Park Apartments and Offices – 2012 – 2.5-rooms – 71 m²
→ 2.3.13

70

The two-story balcony has been a part of our work for quite some time. We have learned that this preoccupation with a spatial idea always follows the same rules, even if the results are different. The privacy screen placed opposite the lower balcony, for example, necessarily changes the positioning of the kitchen. Just as with the well-known *spaghetti alla carbonara*: the ingredients are always the same, but the result is always different.

Spaghetti alla carbonara

Recipe taken from: Rose Gray and Ruth Rogers, The Cafe Cook Book: Italian Recipes from London's River Cafe, New York 1998

Serves four

Ingredients
150 g pancetta slices (3 mm thick), cut into strips
1 tablespoon good olive oil
1 red onion, peeled and finely chopped
400 g spaghetti
3 tablespoons chopped parsley
30 g soft butter
50 g freshly grated Pecorino Romano
50 g freshly grated Parmesan
9 large egg yolks

Method
1. Heat the olive oil in a thick-bottomed saucepan and sauté the onion for about fifteen minutes until very soft and translucent, but do not let it brown.
2. Turn the heat down to low and add the pancetta strips. Sauté for around ten minutes, until browned but not crispy.
3. Meanwhile, cook the spaghetti in boiling water until al dente, drain, and let dry.
4. Also on a low heat, add the parsley and butter to the pancetta.
5. When the butter has melted and the pot is hot, add the spaghetti and mix well.
6. Add the Pecorino and half of the Parmesan, followed immediately by the egg yolk. Again, mix well, being careful not to let the pot get too hot. The egg should not set but cover the pasta as a creamy sauce.
7. Sprinkle with the remaining Parmesan and serve immediately.

3.4 Two-Story Interior

Our goal is to create apartments with captivating spatial designs. With the addition of extra-high ceilings, a multi-floor apartment building takes on a distinctive identity of its own. For example, a two-story room breaks the mold with respect to the conventional approach to three-dimensionality in individual apartments. Of course, this type of design requires more space, but the benefit is that it allows light deep into the apartment, opening up the option of an interior kitchen, for example.

Given how many people inhabit these comparatively massive building volumes, this kind of spatial opulence becomes a fascinating approach. The two-story windows naturally create facades with different proportions and dimensions. While the two-story hall certainly presents many challenges from a design perspective, it guarantees an absolutely singular living environment in return.

3.4.1 For Princesses and Princes

2007
5.5-rooms
202 m²

Alte Landstrasse
Apartment Blocks
→ 2.2.12

The spatial secret is revealed in the section: the building is constructed in terraces down a steep, sloping terrain, thereby incorporating several different living levels. The living room has an extra-high ceiling, and sits in the belly of the apartment. On one side, it opens in an upward direction toward the kitchen, and on the other it overlooks the outdoor space below. Gently inclined stairs ensure a fluid transition between the different levels. The bedrooms adjoin bathrooms, and are placed in front of the living room. The living room and kitchen receive soft light from overhead.

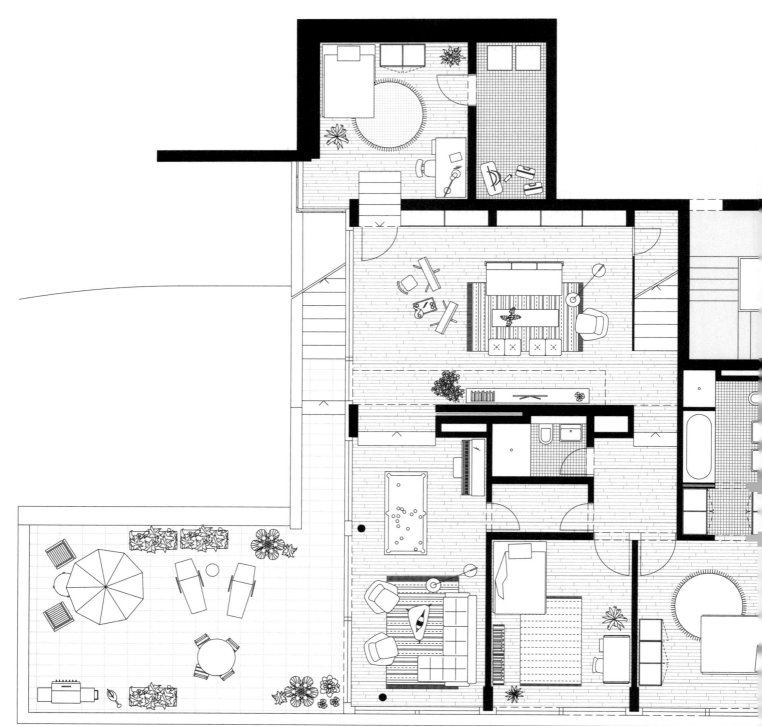

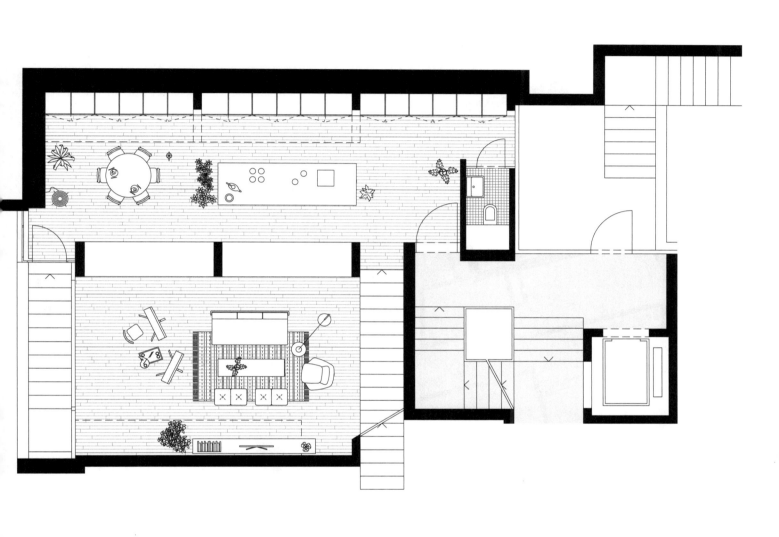
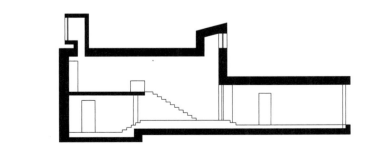

Two-Story Interior

3.4.2 The Misunderstood, Part 1

2008
3.5-rooms
113 m²

Neufrankengasse
Apartment Block
→ 2.2.14

Like windshield wipers, the walls change position from floor to floor. The living room protrudes through the building volume at an acute angle, creating triangular, two-story spaces inside and on the balcony. This feature produces a glorious spatial richness that provides more light to the deep floor plans and creates unforeseen prospects. The kitchen, which contains a large utility area, is placed in a "side pocket." A circular pathway connects the rooms to the living room.

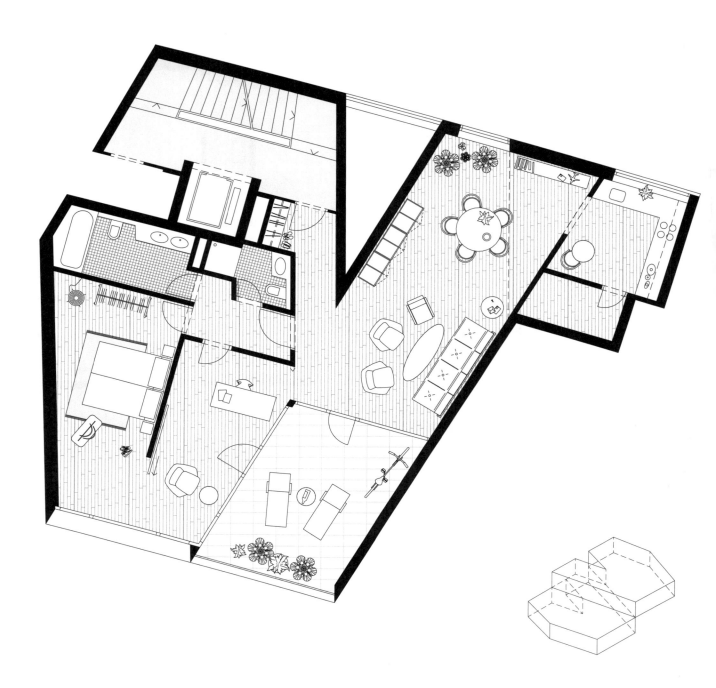

78

3.4.3   The Misunderstood, Part 2

2008
3.5-rooms
85 m²

Neufrankengasse
Apartment Block
→ 2.2.14

The spatial concept for this building was inspired by Frank Lloyd Wright's Price Tower. The triangular two-story rooms are more efficient than their rectangular counterparts, and the tapered geometry lures the gaze. Aside from these special features, the plan checks all the boxes of conventional housing: the kitchen is in a central location, the bedrooms are adjacent to bathrooms and located at a remove from the living space, and the compact entryway defines the path in to the apartment.

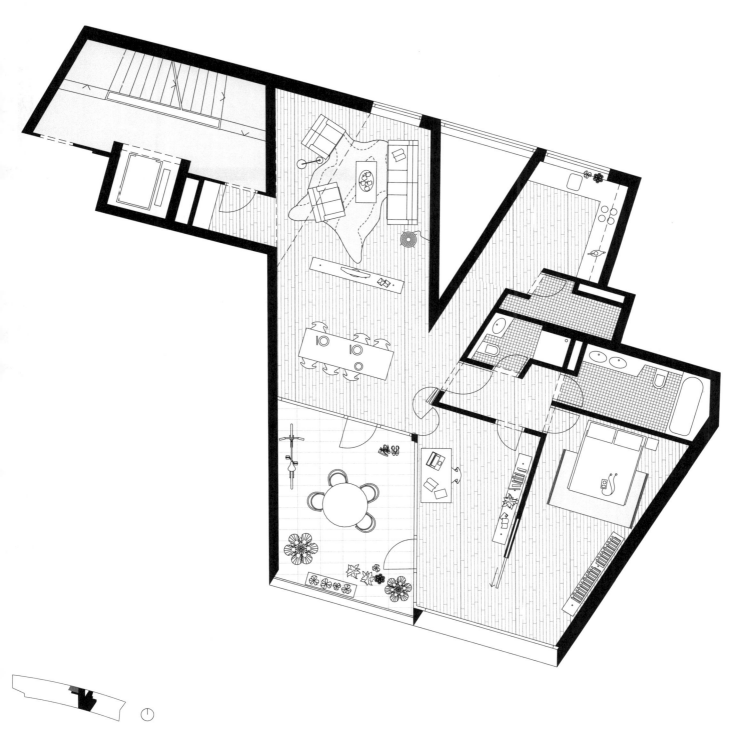

Two-Story Interior

3.4.4 "How Deep Is Your Love"

2007
3.5-rooms
167 m²

Hard Turm Park
High-Rise
→ 2.2.9

With a thirty-meter-deep building volume, the scene is set. In this building, it's not the facade that is two-stories high, but a hall extending five-and-a-half meters up in the center of the plan. The walls shift, partition the space, and thus take the hard edge off the view through the lengthy living room. The cockpit kitchen forms the tip of the inlaid space, and the cozy seating area its tail. Behind the scenes of the hall, the bathroom—organized as an enfilade—provides a hidden path to the bedroom.

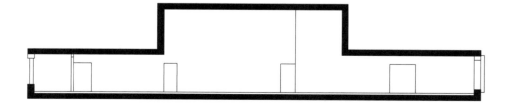

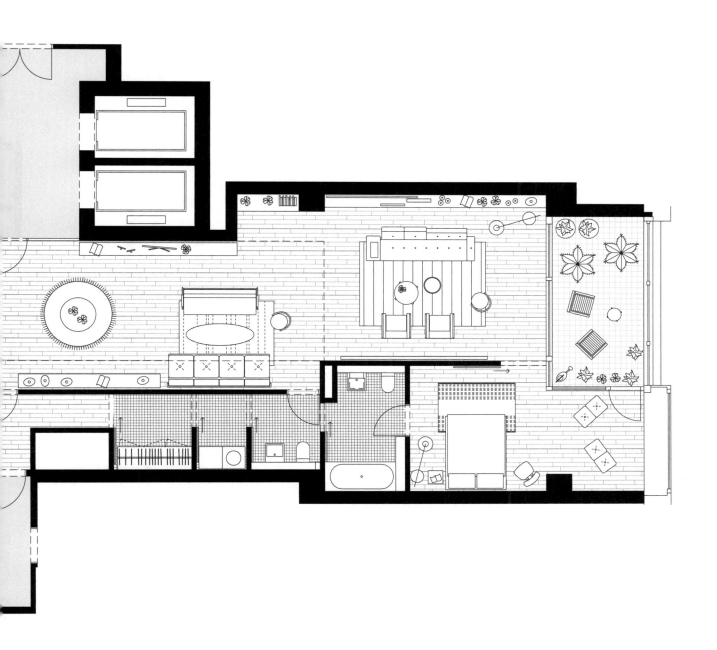

Two-Story Interior

3.4.5 "Lucy in the Sky with Diamonds"

2010
3.5-rooms
118 m²

Fellenbergstrasse
Development
→ 2.3.5

On the roof of the terraced volume, the top floor apartment has two living levels. From the entrance to the apartment, the view sweeps over the dining area down to the extra-high living room, finally reaching the terrace before petering out into the distance. The kitchen sits screened off in a side wing which contains a long window that makes this plan appear longer. There is also a niche carved out of the 3.2-meter-high living room for a favorite chair or desk.

My South German Opa's Bons Mots

For now, Tita and Jürg still savor their top-floor apartment with its huge sprawling terrace; the impending arrival of a latecomer to the family has confronted the couple with the question of whether they really do need one more separate room. The apartment is probably big enough, with its two-part living area and the alcove where Jürg's piano currently stands—in his youth, Jürg dreamed of a career as a professional musician.

Their Number One Daughter anticipates this decision with growing skepticism; she definitely doesn't want to leave! She loves sitting at the dining table, enjoying Tita's cooking creations while getting lost in the view down the stairs, through the living area, and out into the distance.

She's more of a stay-at-home type, it's true, and doesn't think much of her friends' nighttime forays through Zurich's party scene, but hey, to each her own, as her South German Opa used to say!

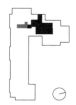

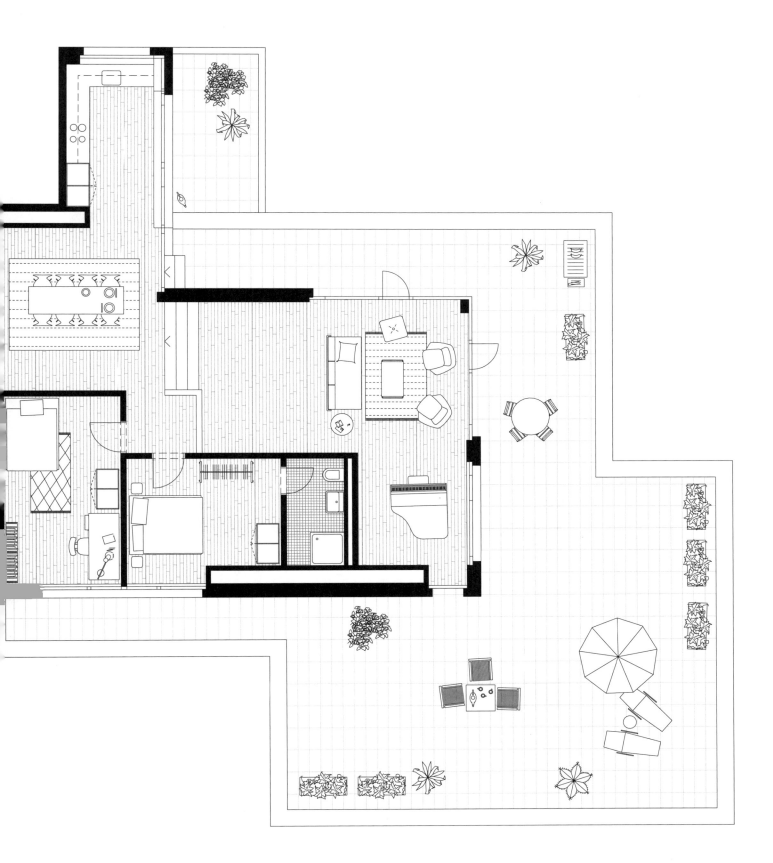

Two-Story Interior 83

3.4.6 The Day Before You Came

2012
2.5-rooms
70 m²

Schweighof
Development
→ 2.3.11

The two building sections sit at different heights: one lower and one higher. This effect is most noticeable on the top floor, where there is a narrow interstitial space with an extra-high ceiling. The way in which the volumes meet turns out to be a stroke of luck for the apartment. The living room and kitchen have a long overhead strip that operates like a periscope, capturing daylight from above and to the side. The compact plan gains space and the lighting gives it a special ambiance. The wall receives plenty of daylight, which makes it ideal for hanging large pictures or reading the newspaper in the far corner.

3.4.7 "I Have a Dream"

2012
4.5-rooms
114 m²

Schweighof
Development
→ 2.3.11

The floor beneath the attic lends itself particularly well to innovations in the sectional design, because instead of having oversized terraces, the apartments can take on more height. The ceiling of the continuous living room is raised one story at each end, so that the dining table is located in a feudal two-story space. On the other hand, thanks to its extra-high ceilings, the balcony space funnels plenty of light into the living space. The subtle offset in the flanks partitions and diffuses the usual "tunnel" of the through rooms.

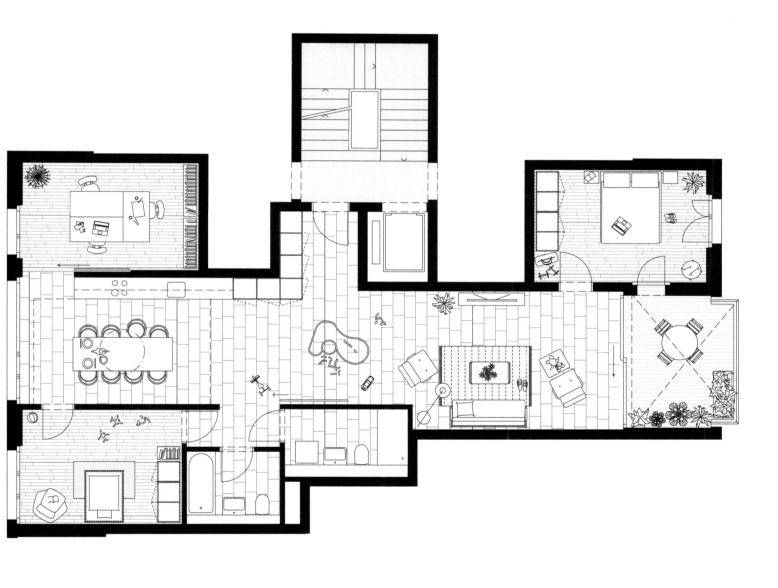

Two-Story Interior

3.4.8 "Alles nur geklaut"

2012
4.5-rooms
116 m²

Schweighof Development
→ 2.3.11

The outside corridor is an efficient passageway for accessing the housing row. In turn, the adjoining living space needs spatial protection to truly embody its potential as a cozy corner that lends a sense of comfort to the apartment. A large skylight provides a striking spatial feature and plenty of daylight. The balcony is also two-stories high and channels daylight into the depths of the apartment. The bedrooms are located on a separate floor level, which facilitates a retreat from the common living space.

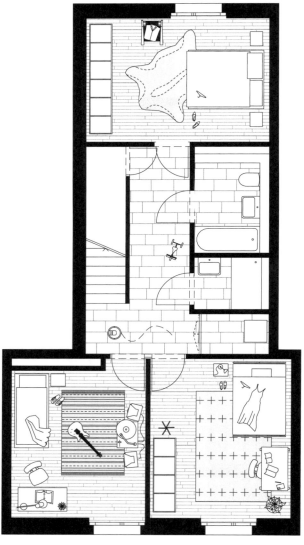

86

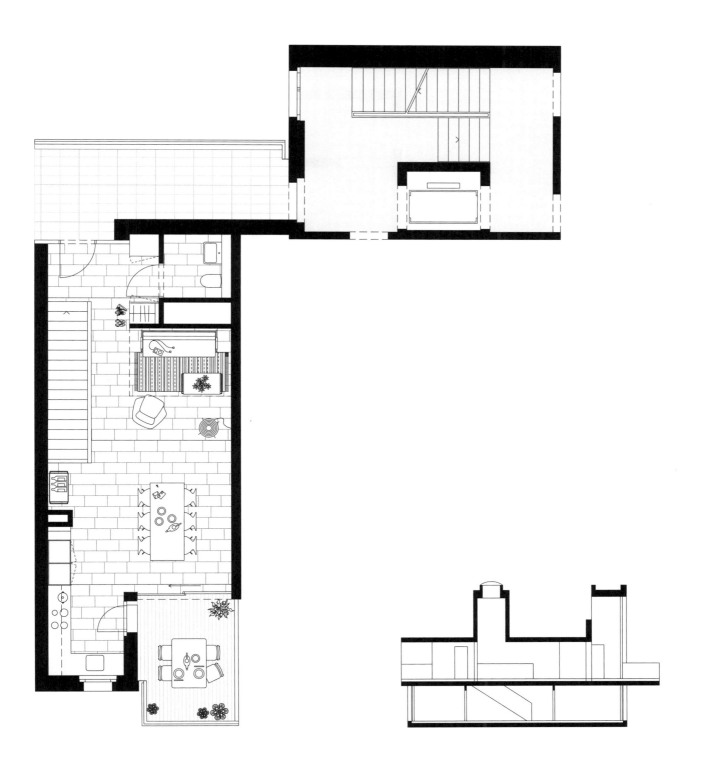

Two-Story Interior 87

3.4.9 "Was erlauben Strunz?"

2014
4.5-rooms
85 m²

Am Rietpark
Apartment Block
→ 2.3.19

The apartment is located at an intersection overlooking the courtyard, stretched over two different wings of the building. The two-story interior compensates for the drawbacks of the location and creates a special quality with enhanced lighting and a pleasantly introverted mood. This is achieved with a solution that has proven effective many times over: changing the layout of the plan on every level, and so freeing up the overhead spaces.

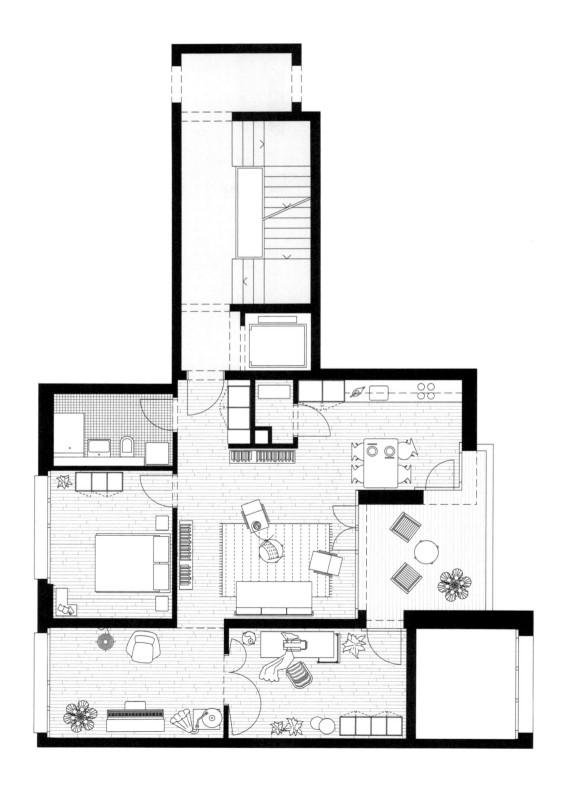

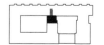

3.4.10 "Let there be Light"

2014
3.5-rooms
77 m²

Am Rietpark
Apartment Block
→ 2.3.19

Advanced Tetris: The airspace of the apartment below pierces the plan of the unit above, leading to a variation in the floor plan idea. One room disappears, while the living room extends into an L-shape, to embrace the loggia. At the facade a two-story spatial section rises up; it has a tall window that lets plenty of light fall deep into the apartment, giving the compact layout a studio-like character.

Two-Story Interior 89

3.4.11 "Forever Young"

2021
4.5-rooms
116 m²
Scheuchzerstrasse
Apartment Block
→ 2.5.11

The roof of the compact house is stretched over the glass-encased living areas like the fly of a tent and appears to hover above the volume. The dormer windows are punched into the roofing like peepholes with a direct view of the sky. An impressive two-story living space is created under the pitched roof, rising dramatically towards the apex and housing a gallery with a staircase that directs the view to the street as if from an observation platform.

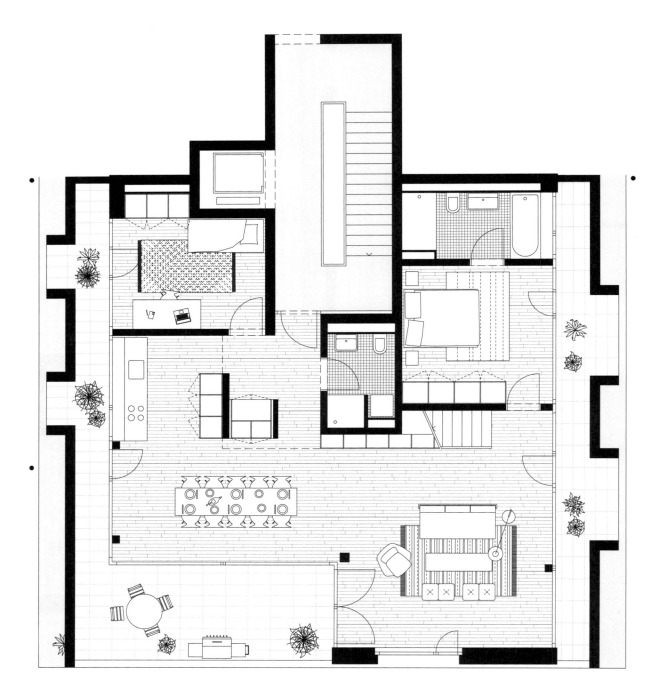

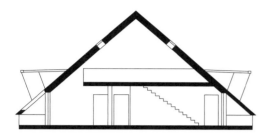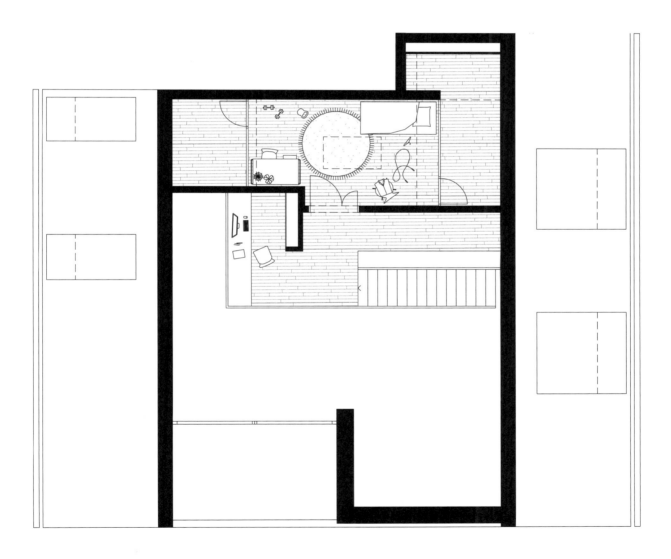

Two-Story Interior

When we eat out in Zurich, we eat at our regular haunt, the Restaurant Italia. By now we know each other. The procedure is always the same. I ask for the menu, study it in detail, and when it is time for my order to be taken, I say: "Today I'm in the mood for *spaghetti all'amatriciana*." Even after 575 iterations of my longitudinal study, it continues to always be perfectly prepared. With huge thanks!

Spaghetti all'amatriciana

Recipe taken from: Ristorante Italia, Zurich

The recipe was posted by Anna Pearson via the Instagram account @editiongut. Pearson received permission to publish the recipe from chef Mischa Käser, whom we admire.

Serves four

Ingredients
80 g frying bacon, cut into strips
One large onion, finely chopped
1 tin pelati, crushed by hand
1 chili, without seeds, finely chopped or some chili powder
15 g butter
Salt and pepper
400 g spaghetti
100 g pecorino

Method
1. Heat a large saucepan, put in the bacon and sauté until it takes on some color.
2. Reduce the heat, add the onions and sauté for about fifteen minutes until soft but without changing color.
3. Add the hand-crushed pelati and season with the chili to taste.
4. Lightly salt, cover the pot, and let it simmer for thirty minutes on a low heat.
5. Remove the lid and cook for a further fifteen minutes.
6. Add butter and mix finely with a hand blender.
7. Add salt to taste.
8. Meanwhile cook the spaghetti in a pot of boiling water until al dente, drain, and add to the pot.
9. Mix the spaghetti well with the sauce.
10. Add finely grated pecorino and a little hot pasta water.
11. Serve.

3.5 Multi-Story Apartment

We always endeavor to break out of the narrow constraints that define contemporary housing construction. From our perspective, multi-story living is one way to do the trick. Despite the fact that they require quite a bit of space and therefore might be considered uneconomical, these typologies are extremely attractive from a spatial point of view.

The multi-story apartment is ideal for implementing Le Corbusier's principle of the *promenade architecurale* or modeling a spatial plan in the tradition of Adolf Loos: living environments can be enhanced with staircases and areas with extra-high ceilings, views and spatial relationships that alternate with low, narrow corridors. Besides these things, it makes sense to place individual and common areas on different floors.

3.5.1 "If You Don't Know Me by Now"

1990
6-rooms
140 m²

Weizacker
Apartment Block
→ 2.1.1

Typically, the spaces in multi-story apartments are separated according to function. For example, here the living rooms are downstairs, while the private bedrooms are upstairs. In this apartment, the kitchen adjoins an enclosed entrance courtyard, which becomes an extension of the apartment. The generous upstairs hall extends the bedrooms, and the naturally lit bathroom is designed as an enfilade.

3.5.2 "Come Rain or Come Shine"

1990
5.5-rooms
130 m²

Weizacker
Apartment Block
→ 2.1.1

The slope which the building sits on lends it a terraced structure, which affords the rooftop apartments three levels with different room heights. The living, kitchen, and dining areas are staggered half a story and connected by a gently inclined staircase, while on the floor below, the compact bedrooms merge with the spacious hallway to create a private zone.

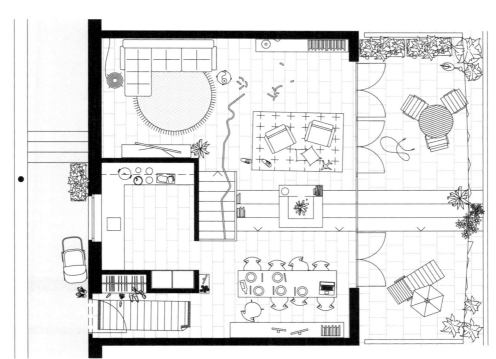

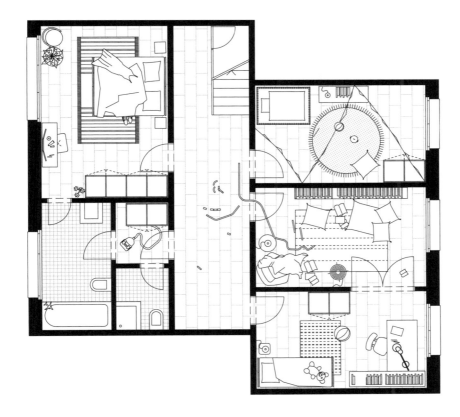

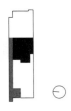

Multi-Story Apartment

3.5.3 "Schuld war nur der Bossa Nova"

1998
3.5-rooms
114 m²

Heimeli
Apartment Blocks
→ 2.1.3

Before the stricter regulations on barrier-free construction discontinued the maisonette apartment style, individual apartments spread across several floors was a sure way to create versatile worlds for living in. This apartment spans three floors, starting from the garden and culminating in the attic. The apartment appears as a multi-story spatial continuum thanks to a criss-crossing Venetian staircase.

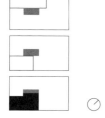

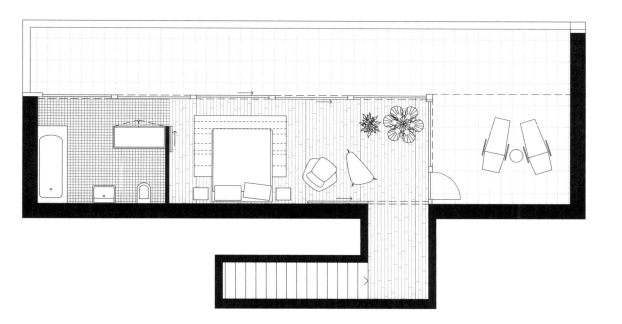
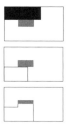

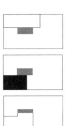

Multi-Story Apartment

3.5.4   "Does Your Mother Know"

2002
4.5-rooms
117 m²
Roost Development
→ 2.2.3

It is quite challenging to build ground-floor apartments on sloped terrain. Due to the slope that lies behind them, they are usually oriented to only one side. To make up for this, the maisonette punches through the structure with a staircase and captures light from the opposite side on the upper level. The separate entrance turns the sleeping level into a true secondary unit. The kids love this, because it gives them a hidden path to slip past their parents' watchful gaze.

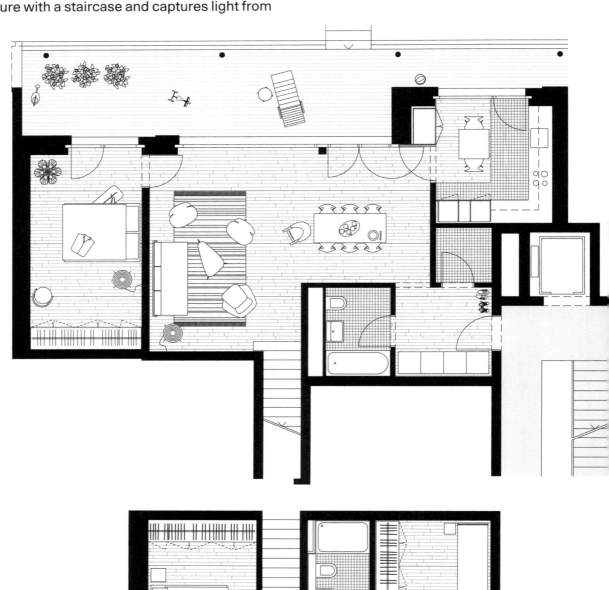

3.5.5 "Come as You Are"

2007
5.5-rooms
168 m²
Altwiesen
Development
→ 2.2.10

The potential of a multi-story apartment is found in its section—so we had best make use of it! Here, a two-story atrium activates the center of the apartment and connects the two floors spatially and acoustically. The apartment becomes a house within a house. Large utility units mutate into household rooms, and one's first encounter upon entering the apartment is with the kitchen. From a comfortable seat at the kitchen table, you can observe the hustle and bustle outside the door.

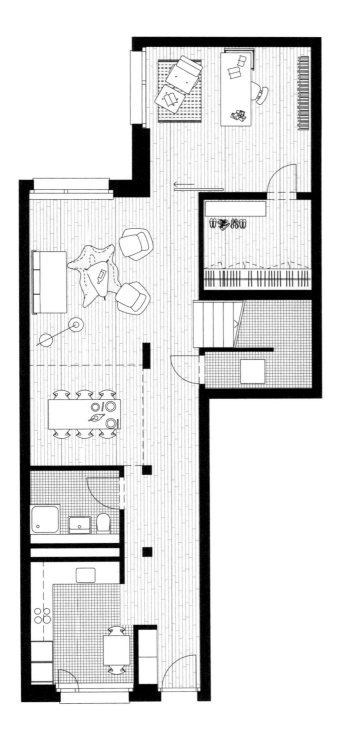
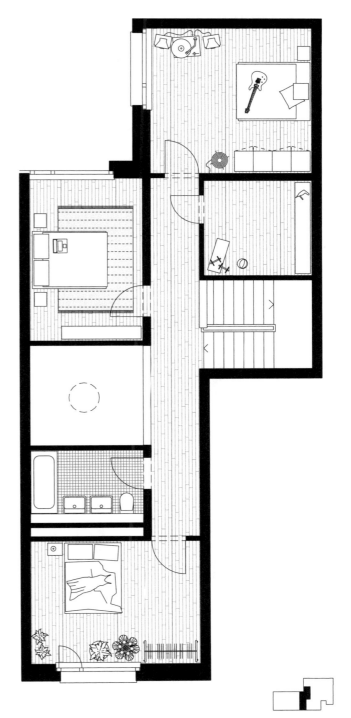

Multi-Story Apartment 101

3.5.6 "New Kid in Town"

2007
4.5-rooms
120 m²
Altwiesen
Development
→ 2.2.10

The fact that the floor containing the bedrooms and the floor containing the living area are separated gives the apartment a more direct relationship to the semi-public outdoor space. The kitchen functions as an interface between the community life of the housing development and the private interior world, while the spatially sheltered living area promises comfort and security. Everyone is familiar with the images of terraced housing estates, which promote intimate social bonds and foster strong identities. This is the way people like to grow up.

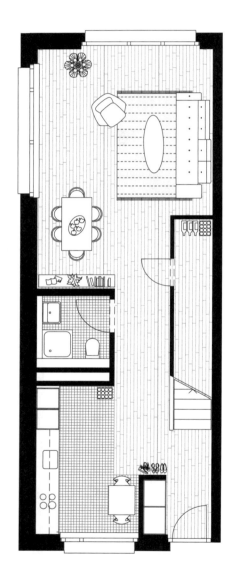
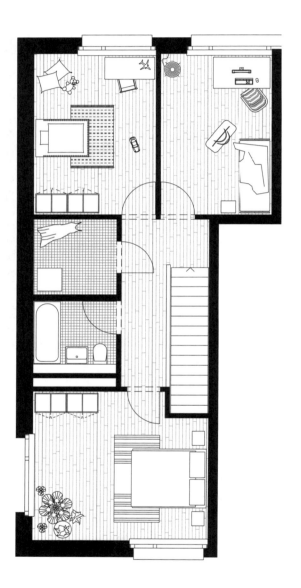

3.5.7 It's About Space

2007
5.5-rooms
152 m²
Altwiesen
Development
→ 2.2.10

This apartment is another example of how multi-story apartments create new possibilities for everyday living. Here, the kitchen is located at the back of the apartment, creating a versatile studio facing an entrance that can open up to the outdoors independently of the private areas. A room with overhead lighting in the center of the apartment illuminates all three floors and connects the multipurpose floors in different ways to create a diverse living environment.

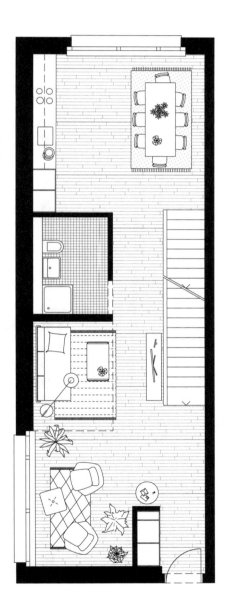
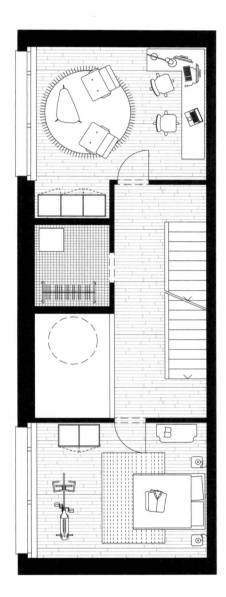
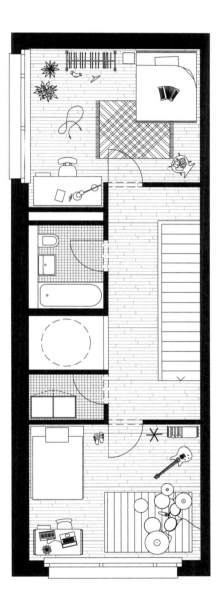

Multi-Story Apartment

3.5.8 "Rear Window"

2010
4.5-rooms
121 m²

Bombach
Development
→ 2.3.3

This is how a maisonette solves the noise problem: the two-story overhead space becomes a ventilation snorkel for the living area, which avoids having to open itself to a noisy environment by drawing air from the bedroom level via the corridor. Complicated?

Ingenious is more like it! Even simply sitting at the dining table becomes a spatial experience, and the compactly shaped apartment unfolds an unimagined spatial grandeur. The kitchen is again located in the epicenter of the plan and acts as the kernel of the apartment.

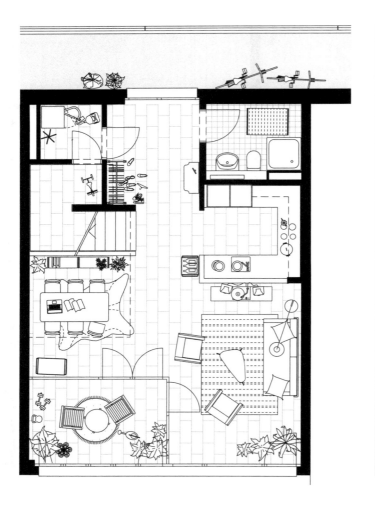
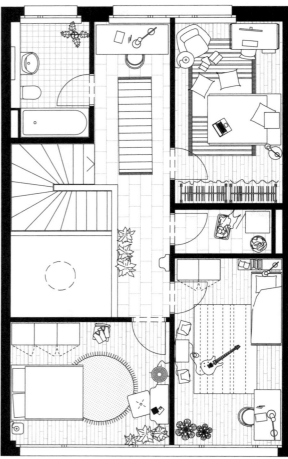

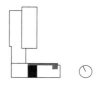

3.5.9 "Should I Stay or Should I Go"

2010
5-rooms
170 m²

Brünnen Development (Building site 12)
→ 2.3.4

The row house arranged in the shape of a vest pocket forms part of a large residential building: those who live on the bottom floor can drive directly up to the front door by (electric) car. The staircase leads to the kitchen and dining area, which provides views across the lower one-and-a-half-story living room and out into the garden. Up above are the bedrooms and a naturally lit hallway. The circular route through the dressing room and bathroom lends the compact apartment a touch of high-end spaciousness.

Multi-Story Apartment

3.5.10 "Love Is in the Air"

2012
4.5-rooms
99 m²

Schweighof Development
→ 2.3.11

A rental apartment with a garden, integrated into a large residential development is something only a maisonette-type construction can pull off. That's because it solves the question of the privacy of the upstairs bedrooms. The staircase creates a narrow two-story space that is lit by a window. The entrance leads to the stairs and provides direct access to the bedrooms. This setup is ideal for teenagers, because it gives them more privacy.

3.5.11 "Pump It Up"

2012
5.5-rooms
147 m²

Hard Turm Park Apartments and Offices
→ 2.3.13

The sleeping quarters in the top floor were the inspiration for a floor plan that turns the maisonette into a multi-story apartment with a little attic floor. The two-story design can be observed on the balcony, visible from the upper room. After taking a shower in the morning, you walk down the stairs and enter the kitchen. The nook behind the kitchen is reminiscent of old Engadine houses, whose master bedrooms were located above the kitchen, where they benefited from the excess heat generated by the stove.

Multi-Story Apartment

3.5.12 "Walk on the Wild Side"

2020
2.5-rooms
78 m²

Webergut
Conversion
→ 2.5.4

The mere fact that this building was converted from an office block creates the opportunity for special kinds of living. Only three elements—the stairs, kitchen, and bathroom—have a pre-determined location; the rest of the apartment can be customized according to individual needs. A studio that looks directly out from the first floor to the public outdoor space can be used for work, while the upper level has a private retreat with its own separate entrance via the outside corridor.

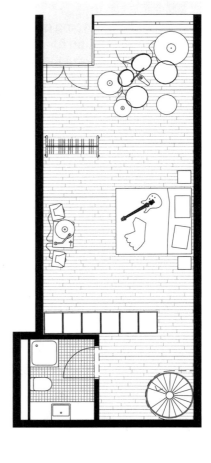

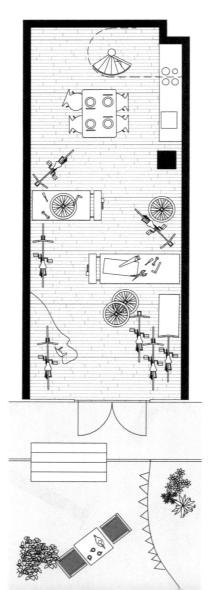

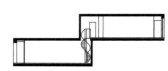

3.5.13 "The Other Side of Hope"

2022
5.5-rooms
107 m²

Berghaldenweg
Development
→ 2.5.12

The steep terrain makes it possible to access the maisonettes directly from the outside on the slope. This eliminates the need for staircases and elevators, which in turn reduces the amount of space the building occupies. Superimposed, partially spiral staircases con‑ nect the floors in the diagonal. Once again, the narrowness of the parallel walls is overcome. The stacking ensures that the build is compact and efficient, while the diagonal spatial relationship guarantees spaciousness.

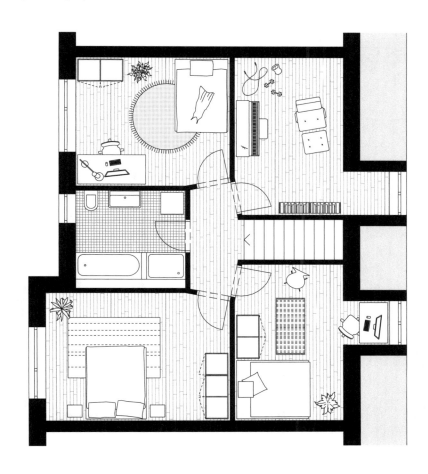

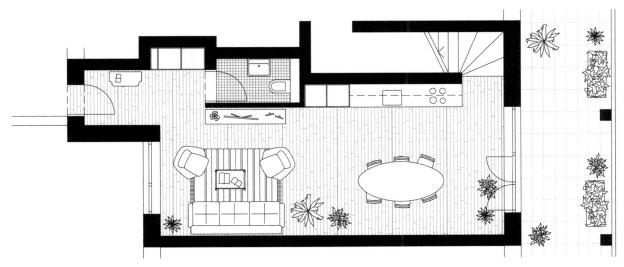

Multi-Story Apartment 109

3.5.14 "Gone with the Wind"

2021
5.5-rooms
112 m²

Sennhof
Development
→ 2.5.9

Yin and yang for terraced houses: on the first floor, the living rooms of two units are located between parallel dividers, while the upper floors utilize the entire width of the two spatial fields diagonally. This maximizes the space allotted to the horizontal axis of the building. This system makes room for cascading staircases. Beneath them, a spectacular two-story area is created in the living room, wresting an unimagined spatial opulence from the compact apartments in the section.

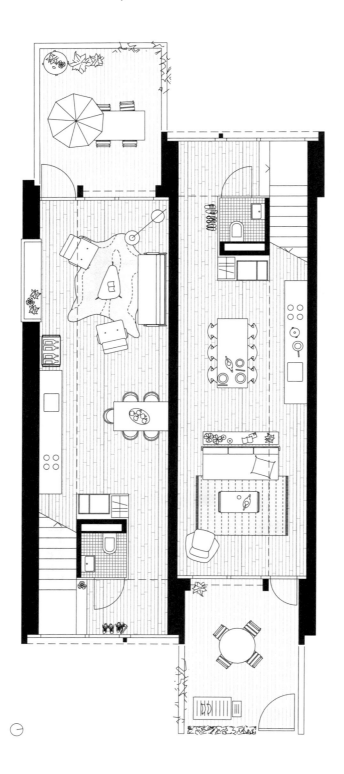
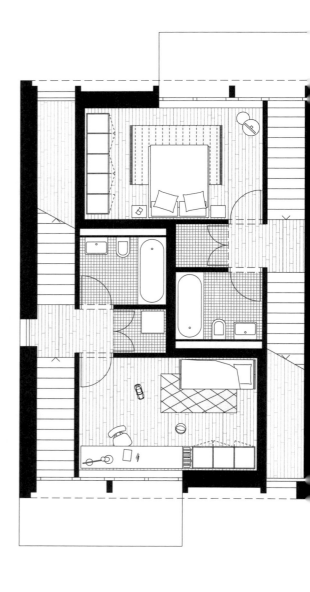

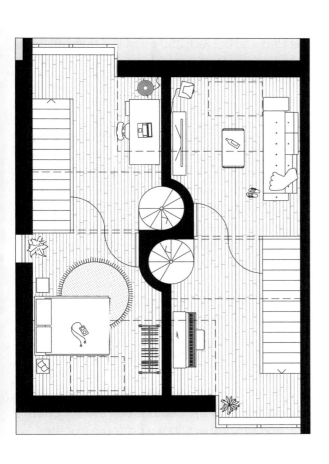
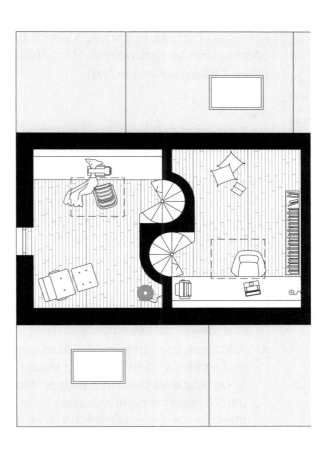

Multi-Story Apartment 111

In multi-story living, a wide variety of room sequences can be tried out. The decisive issue is which sequence the individual and common rooms will be arranged in in relation to the entrance. It is also possible to pursue different architectural ideas. The multi-story room, the extra-high balcony, or the internal apartment staircase are possible themes. Recipes can also be combined when cooking spaghetti.

Spaghetti with Two Kinds of Artichoke

A combination of two recipes: Marianne Kaltenbach, Aus Italiens Küchen, Basel 2011 and Rose Gray and Ruth Rogers, The Cafe Cook Book: Italian Recipes from London's River Cafe, New York 1998

Ingredients for Marianne Kaltenbach's dish (serves four): 6 Italian artichokes with the stem, (2 for the artichoke bottoms), 1 1 lemon, 6 tablespoons olive oil, Salt, pepper, 1 large garlic clove, 2 tablespoons parsley

Method
1. First prepare the artichokes: remove the top third and the hard outer leaves. Cut off the stem and peel except for the white core.
2. Prepare two artichoke bottoms and set aside. Cut the others in half, remove the leaf tips and the fuzzy choke. Immediately soak the artichokes in light lemon water to prevent the cut surfaces from discoloring.
3. Take them out of the water one by one, and cut them lengthwise into slices 1 cm thick. Cut the stems into strips 3 cm long.
4. Add them to a pot with oil, 100 ml water, and a little salt and cover and steam over a good heat until the water evaporates (about seven or eight minutes). Check from time to time. Once there is no more liquid, the artichoke slices should be cooked. The artichokes should soften but not become overcooked.
5. Three to five minutes before the cooking time is up, add the pressed garlic and the finely chopped parsley.

Ingredients for the artichoke pesto: 6 small artichokes, 100 g pine nuts, 2 garlic cloves, peeled and halved, 250 ml milk, 1 handful parsley leaves, 150 ml olive oil, 50 g butter, 400 g spaghetti

Method
6. Prepare the artichokes, first by breaking off the dark green outer leaves until only the tender, light leaves remain. Cut off the hard tips of the hearts and peel the stems. Cut the artichokes in half lengthwise and scrape out the choke with a spoon.
7. Place the artichokes, pine nuts and garlic cloves in a blender. Process to a coarse puree.
8. Add milk, parsley, and Parmesan and blend again briefly. Slowly pour the olive oil into the mixture to make a creamy paste. Season with salt and pepper.
9. Take a ladle of pasta water and stir the butter into the mixture.
10. Slowly heat the pesto. Cook the spaghetti and the two artichoke bottoms in salted water until al dente, drain, and mix with the artichokes and the artichoke pesto. Sprinkle with Parmesan.

3.6 Deep Floor Plans

Our architecture is increasingly determined by economic pressures to make the most out of a plot of land and, on the other hand, the demand to build as compactly as possible for the sake of the environment.

"How Deep Is Your Love?"—this schmaltzy song by the Bee Gees encourages us to keep coming back to explore the potential of plans with maximum possible depth. The contemporary demands for light, air, and sun still retain their relevance. The height of the rooms is a simple way to meet these demands: the higher the rooms, the deeper the daylight is able to penetrate into the apartment.

3.6.1 "The Belly of an Architect"

2004
3.5-rooms
131 m²

Imbisbühlstrasse
Apartment Block
→ 2.2.6

High rooms are ideal for deep floor plans, creating a quality of living that harks back to late 19th century apartments. In addition, the enhanced lighting allows the balconies to be larger than usual. Living takes place in the "belly" of the plan—an area that is at once secluded, cozy, and easy to furnish. A wide hallway opens up the full depth of the apartment via a sliding door that unveils the adjoining room. The kitchen has been shifted forward, making it into an appealing cooking station complete with panoramic view.

Deep Floor Plans

3.6.2 "Tunnel of Love"

2004
3.5-rooms
131 m²

Imbisbühlstrasse
Apartment Block
→ 2.2.6

Thirty meters: it's hard to imagine anything deeper! But this apartment pulls it off thanks to three-meter-high ceilings and a courtyard carved out of the side of the building, which provides Mediterranean lighting. This hollow also creates an interesting spatial arrangement that allows the dining table to occupy a prominent position in the plan. The pair of rooms link up with a bathroom unit to form a private retreat, while the extended living room with its hefty balcony accentuates the extraordinary depth of space.

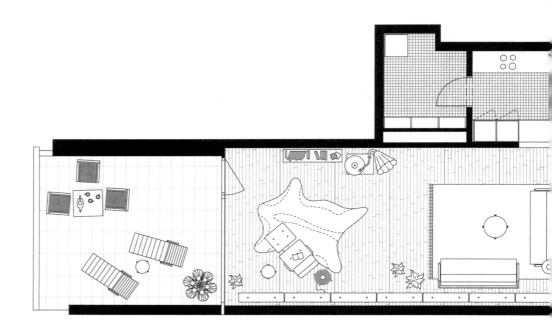

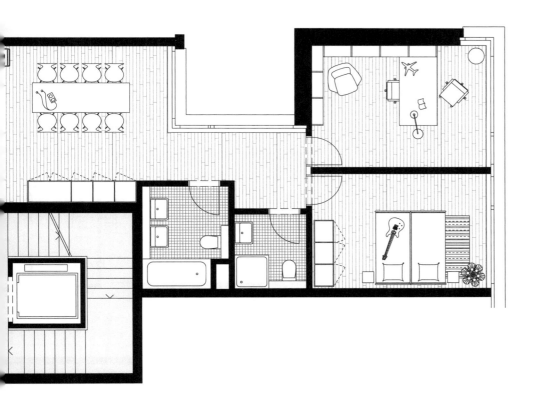

Deep Floor Plans 119

3.6.3 "Yellow Submarine"

2005
3.5-rooms
95 m²

Büelen
Apartment Blocks
→ 2.2.7

A skylight juts through the floor above and bathes the kitchen—located in the center of the apartment—in a magically muted daylight. From here, the plan unfolds southward towards the living area with its balcony and northward towards the bedrooms, which form a private cluster of spaces.
It's not only the kitchen that benefits from the overhead light: the back of the living room is also engulfed in a pleasantly lit atmosphere which radiates a comforting, cozy ambience.

The U-Boat Kitchen Is the Cat's Pajamas

A U-boat kitchen, the guests exclaim once they've stepped into the apartment and been led past the skylit kitchen alcove into the living area. This remark makes Magdalena happy every time; it proves her partner Mildred's theory that a lovely apartment is the only place where individual style can still develop.

Sure, it's a bit of an exaggeration, but it's true: everyone walks around in the same clothes, rides an e-bike, and listens to the same insipid music!

Magdalena's personal touch carries over onto the large balcony, where she cultivates a rare type of flower that demands an excep- *tional amount of attention. Mildred, on the other hand, doesn't think much of plants, especially if you can't smoke them, as she likes to say. For her part, she's made one of the rooms into a study/music room, where she improvises scores by Karlheinz Stockhausen on her old Moog synthesizer—even though the old fool's 9/11 comment was absolutely outrageous!*

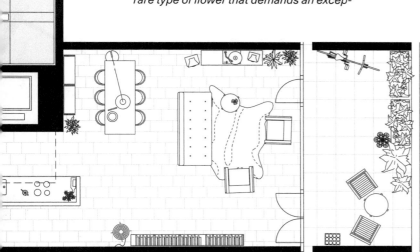

Deep Floor Plans

3.6.4 "Stranger than Paradise"

2012
5.5-rooms
179 m²

Hard Turm Park Apartments and Offices
→ 2.3.13

Various factors contributed to the decision to rotate the plan: on the one hand, the orientation to the south enhances the sunlight. On top of that, a four-sided orientation is created, which creates surprising sight-lines to the outdoor space. A diagonal spatial figure is inserted into the structure, which extends the interior spatial perspectives considerably and produces a branching floor plan. The triangular balcony is two stories high and allows ample light into the apartment.

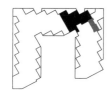

122

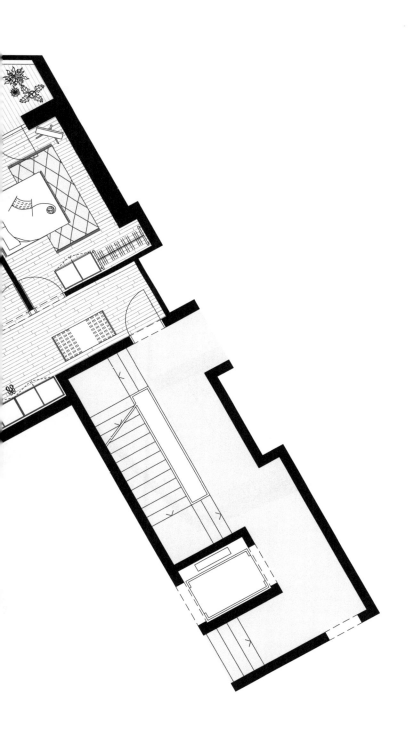

Deep Floor Plans

3.6.5 "Welcome to the Jungle"

2013
4.5-rooms
137 m²

Zollstrasse Ost
Development
→ 2.3.17

Dispensing with a standard level allows a room height of 3.4 meters, which provides leeway to reinterpret conventional room layouts. The bathroom becomes a cavernous compartment system, the kitchen emerges gradually from out of the wardrobe furniture, and the living room juts through the deep structure with a fluctuating room width. A bend in the area surrounding the entrance provides zoning and different lighting moods. The rooms attached to the side of the living room widen the appearance of the space.

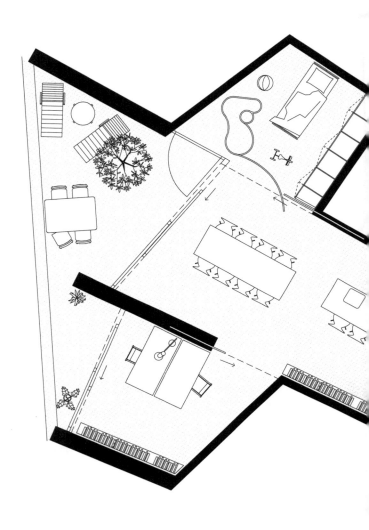

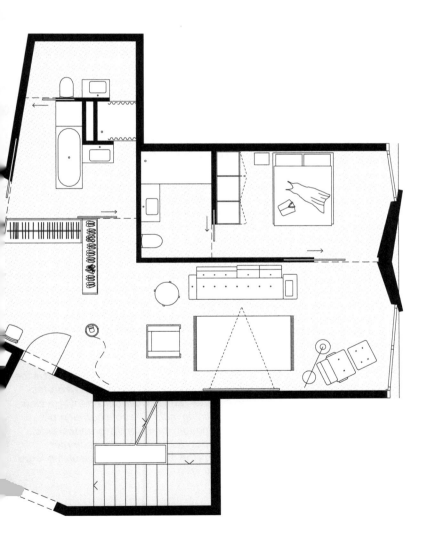

Deep Floor Plans 125

3.6.6 "We Are Family"

2017
5.5-rooms
139 m²

Langgrütstrasse
Apartment Block
→ 2.4.3

The generous width really does the trick: a corridor becomes the spatial backbone of the apartment, which reclaims the lost virtues of the traditional hallway. It becomes an extension of the rooms and turns everyday living into a strut down the runway. Of course, the hallway also swallows all kinds of furniture and becomes a remarkable entrance that flows into the living area, which in turn spreads out to the side and leads out onto the balcony, which forms the end point of the path through the apartment.

The Extended Family Is Still a Thing

The extended Endres family has finally found a decent—and still affordable—apartment in a beautiful, kid-friendly neighborhood. It was hard enough; not all city dwellers want to live in a big experimental cave of an apartment, or in a post-hippie commune!

Ordinary as they are, this apartment satisfies their requirements perfectly. Each child has their own bedroom where they can enjoy some seclusion, shut themselves away and let off steam. That cuts down massively on the potential for arguments!

The large hallway is priceless, serving as bedroom extension, playroom, walk-in closet, and simply as a parking spot for the mountain of shoes that pile up in the alcove next to the front door. It even has a convenient storage closet—although Ricardo Endres misuses it as a wine cellar.

All the way at the front of the apartment is the spacious kitchen, which provides a protective corner recess while still enabling a view of the dining table. The sofa corner provides enough space for the grandparents' massive couch, and on balmy summer evenings the family eats outside on the large balcony.

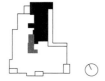

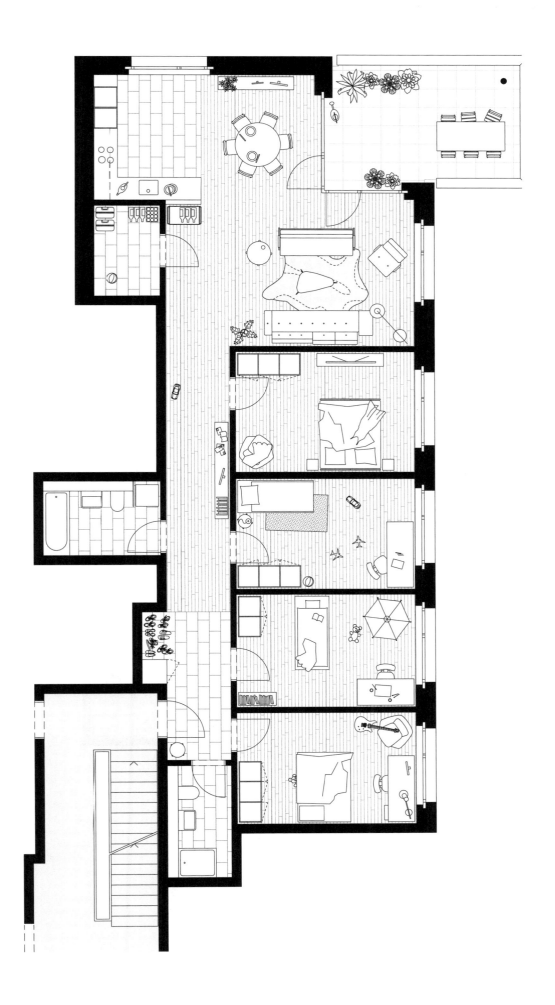

Deep Floor Plans

3.6.7 "Coffee and Cigarettes"

2020
2.5-rooms
82 m²

Webergut
Conversion
→ 2.5.4

Because these apartments were converted from a bulky office building, their plans are unusual, with what is a generous room height for residential buildings and a dynamic building depth. Suddenly, alcoves in the shady interior of the apartment become remarkable: a guest bed is tucked behind a curtain or the home office gets its own private corner. The entrance area is wider than usual and allows the living hall, which receives light from two sides, to flow through the structure.

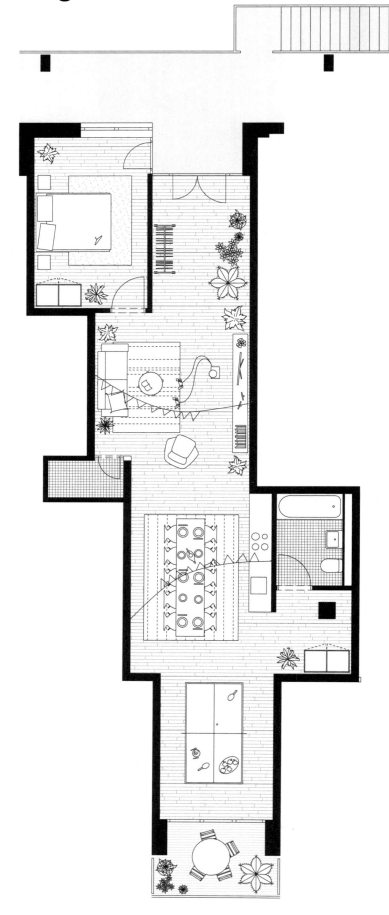

3.6.8 "Birth of the Cool"

2020
4.5-rooms
126 m²

**Webergut
Conversion**
→ 2.5.4

Loft-style living in a former office building: two sturdy columns divide the exuberant living hall, mimicking the feel of a studio. The ends on the facades taper to give the rooms space on the sides. This, in turn, widens the center and creates space for individual living arrangements. Perhaps there is a snooker table or a long table. An e-bike leans casually against the wall, second-hand furniture adds a popular vintage look, and the bathroom is cleverly hidden behind an alcove.

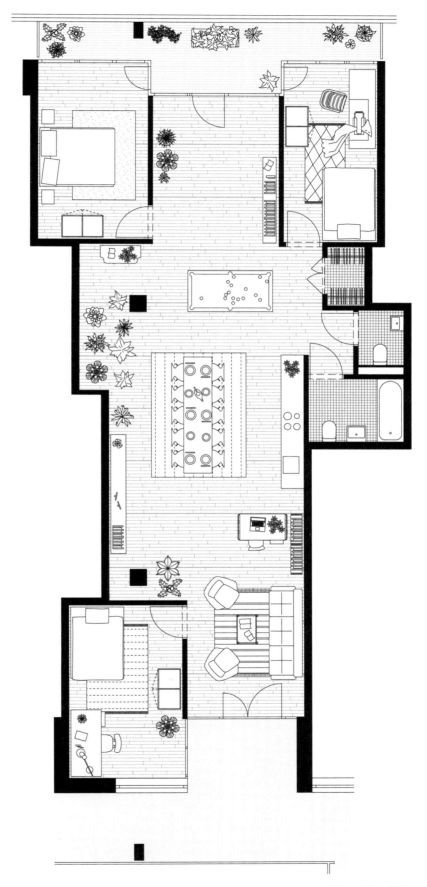

Deep Floor Plans 129

3.6.9 "La vie en rose"

2020
4.5-rooms
116 m²

Spiserstrasse
Apartment Block
→ 2.5.6

This opulent living hall is a child of the fin de siècle; it contains the kinds of spatial motifs that bring a touch of magic to a floor plan. A bedroom located next to the living room extends the view through a double door. Next to it, a window casts daylight onto the wall. In the center, a cozy twilight atmosphere prevails, which brightens up again by the time it reaches the dining room table in the kitchen. The room at the side widens the end of the living hall and provides a circular pathway to the entrance.

Of Catholics, Ex-Bankers, and a Longing for New York

Actually, Domenico has always wanted to live in a loft. The ex-banker lived in New York for many years, and that city has left its mark on him. Zurich is definitely not New York, but still, the new apartment gives off a similar atmosphere—just not with quite the same coolness factor as the Big Apple.

The three-meter-high living hall, lit from two sides, with floor-to-ceiling double doors and a half-open industrial-style kitchen, does, in fact, evoke the feeling of living in a loft.

So it's fitting that Domenico has recently launched a new career; he now builds stage sets for the theater. His wife Livia—since she comes from an extremely strict Catholic family, a church wedding was a must—is a high-school teacher; she appreciates the perfect layout of the rooms, as the two kids have been able to create a separate realm at a sufficient distance from their parents' bedroom. The kids even have their own bathroom—although fights over who gets precedence in the mornings have already gotten heated, and led to multiple hastily convened emergency meetings at the big family table.

Deep Floor Plans

3.6.10 "Backyard Boy"

2020
4.5-rooms
102 m²
Lerchenweg
Development
→ 2.5.7

The private courtyard turns the first-floor apartment into a real atrium apartment. The living space stretches outward through the kitchen, brushes by a window at a corner of the courtyard, forms a cozy corner, and ends in a bedroom that gently puts the brakes on the forward spatial momentum. This kind of intimate garden courtyard centers the living environment and protects it from the public open space. The interweaving of inside and outside invites the seasons into the apartment and creates a special atmosphere.

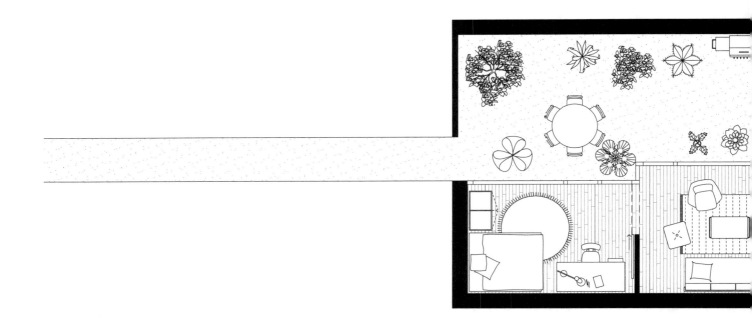

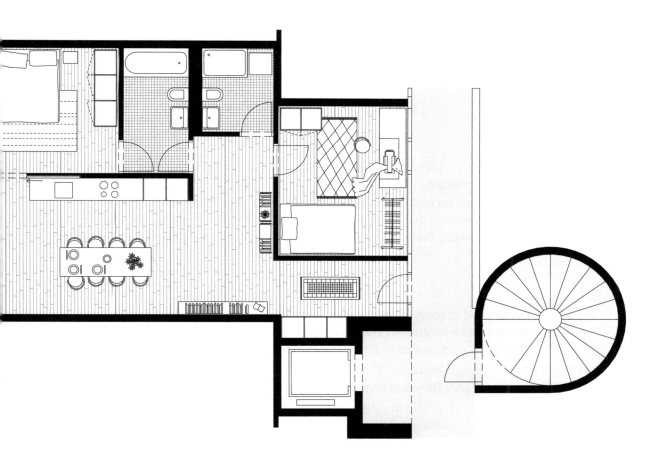

Deep Floor Plans 133

Of course, we know that spaghetti with this sauce does not exist in Bologna. This *ragù* is best with home-made tagliatelle or in a lasagna. Tortellini as well as dry packet pasta like penne, rigatoni, or fusilli also go wonderfully. Since we're only listing spaghetti recipes in our book, we'll make an exception here. It's like with our apartment buildings. We're flexible with these as well.

Spaghetti with Bolognese Meat Sauce

Recipe taken from: Marcella Hazan, The Classic Italian Cook Book, New York City 1973

Serves six

Ingredients
1 tablespoon vegetable oil; 50 g butter; 85 g chopped onions; 3 celery stalks, chopped; 4 mid-sized potatoes, chopped; 800 g chopped minced beef; Salt; Freshly ground black pepper; 250 ml full-fat milk; Freshly ground nutmeg; 25 ml dry white wine; 500 g Italian canned tomatoes with the juice, finely chopped; 600 g spaghetti; Generous knob of butter for the pasta; Parsley, chopped; Freshly grated Parmigiano Reggiano

Method
1. Place oil, butter, and onions in a large saucepan and turn heat to medium. Sauté onions, stirring, until translucent, then add the chopped celery and carrots. Cook for about two minutes so that the vegetables are well coated with fat.
2. Add the minced beef, a large pinch of salt and a little pepper. Crumble the meat with a fork, stirring carefully and until it no longer looks raw and red.
3. Add the milk and simmer, stirring frequently, until it has evaporated completely. Grate a tiny pinch of nutmeg—about 1/8 teaspoon—into the pot and stir.
4. Pour in the wine and let it evaporate slowly, then add the tomatoes and stir all the ingredients thoroughly. When the tomatoes begin to bubble, reduce the heat so that the sauce cooks very gently. Only a bubble should rise to the surface here and there. Simmer for at least three hours, stirring occasionally. If the sauce becomes too dry, add a little water. At the end, however, there should be no liquid left and the fat should separate from the sauce.
5. Cook the spaghetti in a pot of boiling water until al dente, drain, mix with the sauce, add the butter, sprinkle with the chopped parsley, and serve.

3.7 High-Rise Living

Three conditions distinguish the floor plan of a residential high-rise from a traditional multi-story building. Since the view is not restricted by neighboring buildings or trees, lighting the space poses no problem. And yet, at a certain height, one no longer wishes to linger directly against the facade. The view down into the depths is uncomfortable, contradicting the need for safety and a sense of domestic wellbeing. This perception leads to the positioning of primary functions—such as living and sleeping areas—in the "second row."

"Servant spaces" like the kitchen or bathrooms, by contrast, can be arranged along the facade. This privileged location requires that ancillary rooms be conceptualized differently. The outdoor space must also be designed anew: due to extreme exposure to wind, the classic balcony is not possible; alternatives are needed.

3.7.1 "Where Eagles Dare"

2007
2.5-rooms
123 m²

Hard Turm Park
High-Rise

→ 2.2.9

On both sides of the entryway, the plan spreads its wings at once over a total of thirty meters, permitting the tower's panoramic view to come dramatically into its own. The staggered back walls provide contour to the extended space. The living space with its bench seat along the facade shapes the space to a close on one end, while the bath at the other corner of the building, the smallest and most intimate room, obtains spectacular positioning—baths with a view and a glass of whiskey in hand!

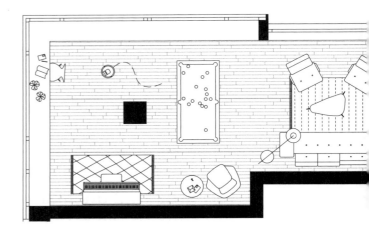

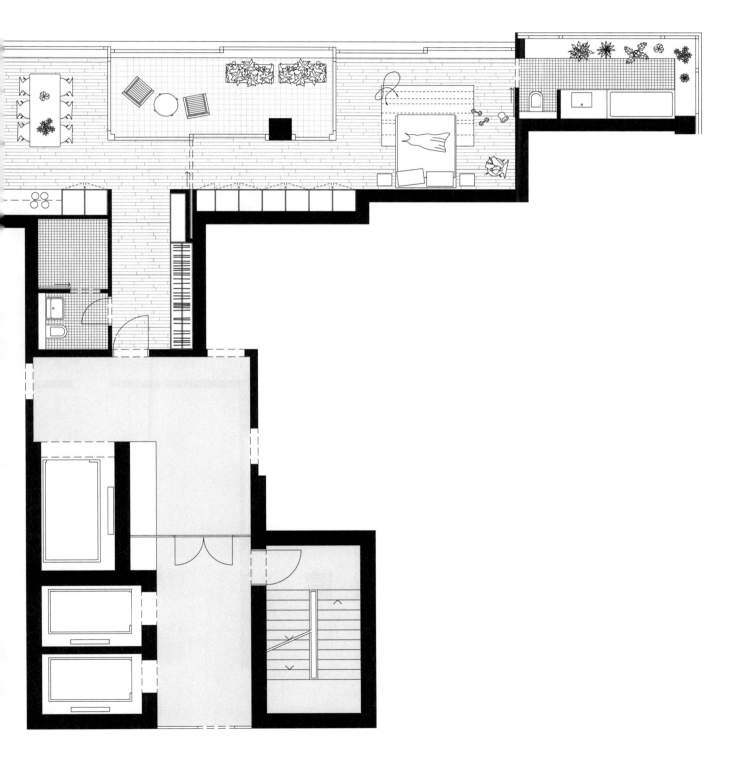

High-Rise Living 139

3.7.2 "Night on Earth"

2007
2.5-rooms
102 m²

Hard Turm Park
High-Rise
→ 2.2.9

Even with all possible enthusiasm for the view, the exposed quality of living in a high-rise awakens a strong inclination to draw back. This allows us to reconsider the customary spatial organization. The living space withdraws into the protected second row, while the bath and kitchen come up against the facade. This produces a specific feeling of domestic contentment: cooking and care for the body with a view. The balcony becomes a sunroom, and the corner niche offers a panoramic view from the desk.

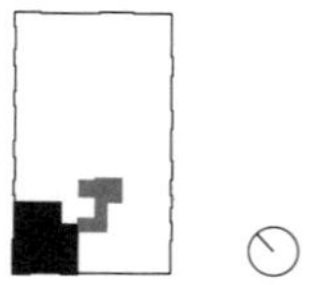

140

3.7.3 "Funky Friday"

2007
2.5-rooms
123 m²

Hard Turm Park
High-Rise
→ 2.2.9

The high-rise liberates residents from curious neighborly gazes. The most intimate spaces can be shifted to the corner of the building, where a spectacular panorama beckons. Thus the bath becomes a panoramic space, marking the culmination of the interior pathway that binds the various spaces together into one large spatial entity. Entering the apartment, the eye roams from the ample entryway, over the living space stretching out at a diagonal, and into the distance.

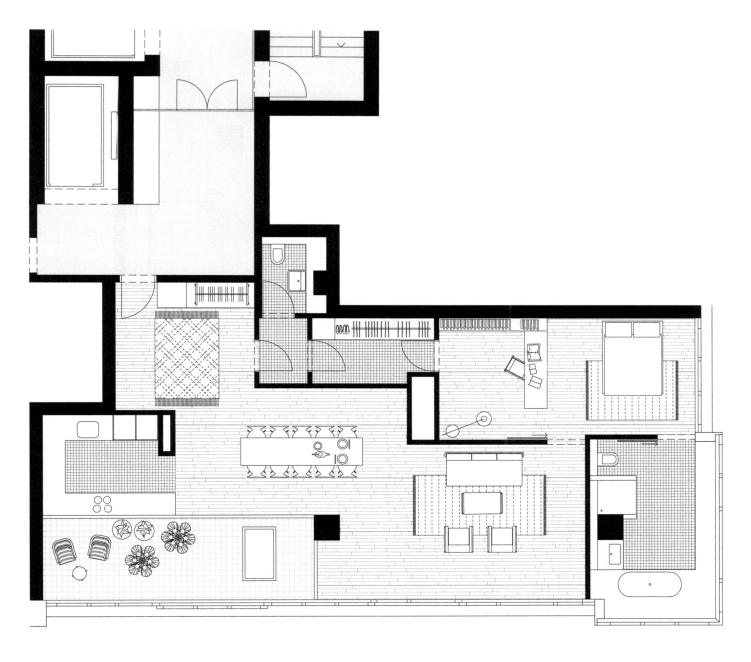

High-Rise Living

3.7.4 "Gimme Shelter"

2007
2.5-rooms
89 m²

Hard Turm Park
High-Rise
→ 2.2.9

The abundance of daylight in a high-rise feeds logically into a new living concept: the kitchen becomes the cockpit, the bath an extended arm of the bedroom with an outlook. The living space lies snugly in the second row, behind the leafy sunroom. The innermost spatial row accommodates the entryway complete with wardrobe, and ensures discreet access to the guest bathroom, which provides an opening to the hidden path through dressing room and shower to the bedroom.

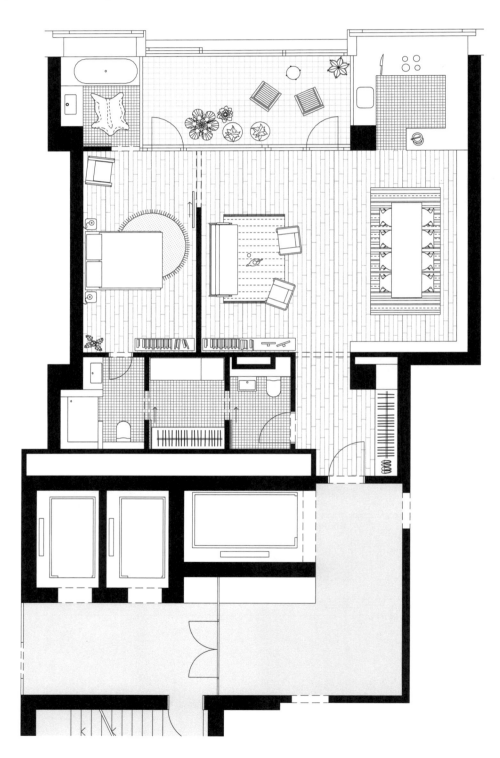

3.7.5 "Help Me Make It Through the Night"

2007
2.5-rooms
112 m²

Hard Turm Park High-Rise
→ 2.2.9

To enhance the effect of the panoramic view from a high-rise even further, we create a two-story space: a stage for the dining table with a spectacular view from gallery level of the city below. A spatial continuum winds across the plan. Precisely designed furnished zones create a pleasurable coziness. This time, the kitchen is in the second row, yet receives lots of natural light due to the two-story space. In the sleeping gallery, one can bathe next to the bed while enjoying the sunset.

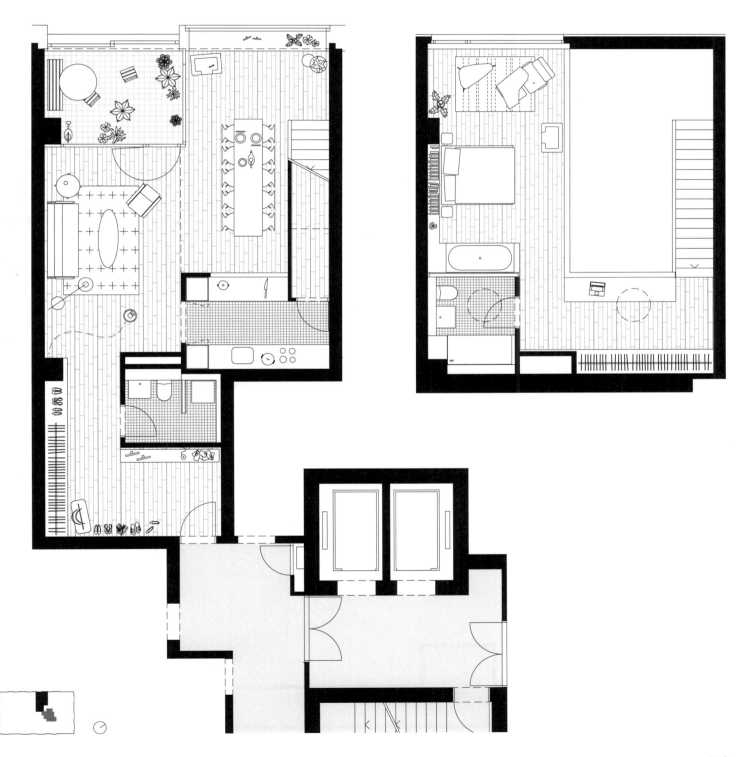

High-Rise Living

3.7.6 "Paint It Black"

2009
2.5-rooms
135 m²

Am Rietpark High-Rise
→ 2.3.1

The building's orientation to the north delivers the decisive argument for an apartment that stretches spectacularly across the entire length of the building, its spatial form determined by the dynamism of the rear side.

The pathway through the apartment leads along the facade, past the kitchen to the corner room, which is limited by the height of the apartment below. The living hall has a two-story area that gives the space its center.

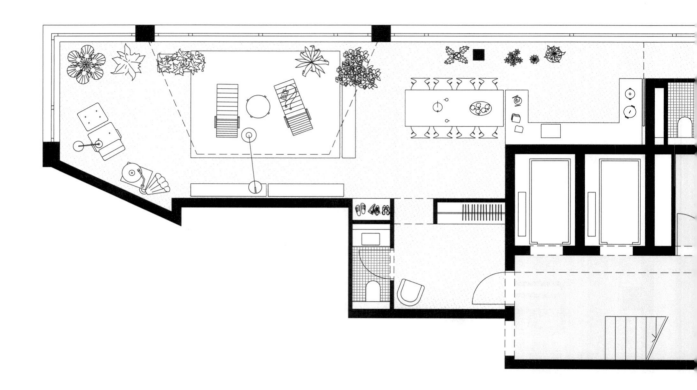

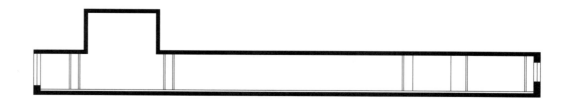

144

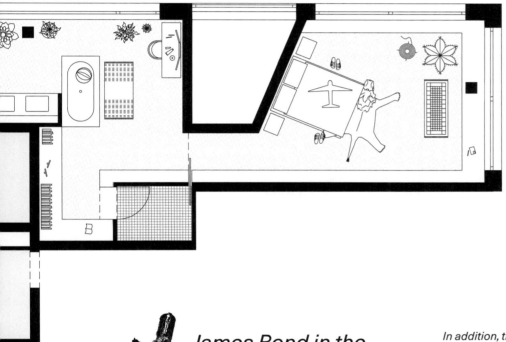

James Bond in the Bathtub

Viktoria works as an architect; she knows all about apartment design. That's why she was absolutely dying to live in this apartment; it completely breaks with the familiar mold!

Her partner Matthias works in the same field; he is more concerned with hospital buildings, however, and so values finally getting to live in a great apartment all the more! It isn't even really an apartment in the traditional sense, but rather one large space that stretches out endlessly along the facade, forming alcoves that can be put to use.

There's an open bathtub here, a kitchen niche with a view there; and then the bedroom is hidden away behind a wall—of course Viktoria immediately noticed that this encompasses airspace belonging to the apartment below.

In addition, the living area is endowed with a two-story section that captures the light; this is the couple's pride and joy. Viktoria's mother, on the other hand, finds it all a bit decadent—but that doesn't bother Viktoria much; she enjoys the panoramic view from the bathtub, imagining herself in a James Bond movie.

High-Rise Living

3.7.7 "Knowing Me, Knowing You"

2009
1.5-rooms
62 m²
Am Rietpark High-Rise
→ 2.3.1

The apartment as a large open space that the section articulates into multiple zones: A wedge-shaped, two-story-tall airspace illuminates the kitchen and offers the dining table a privileged location. On the opposite side, the airspace belonging to the apartment below pushes the floor up, creating a heightened stage for the bed, from which the panorama can be enjoyed while reclining. This is reminiscent of design concepts from the "Swinging Sixties," which celebrated audacious spatial landscapes for decadent dream homes.

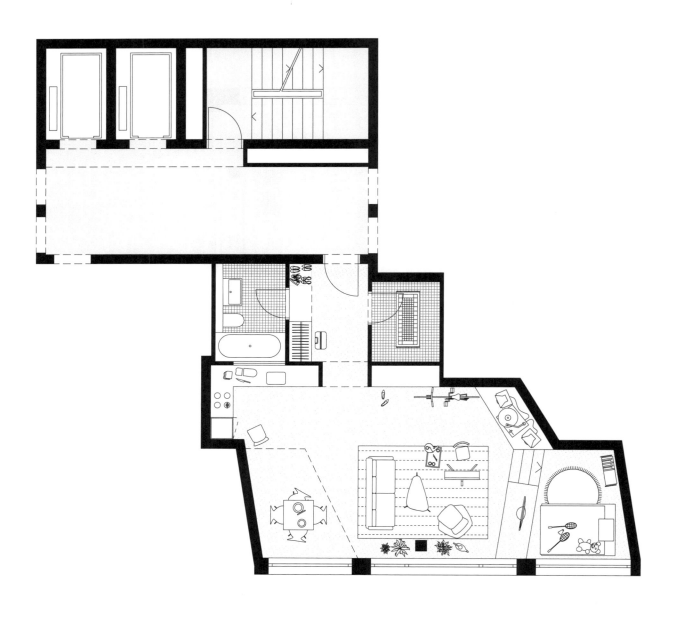

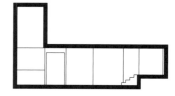

146

3.7.8 "A Year in the Kitchen"

2013
2.5-rooms
79.4 m²

Steinach High-Rise,
Saurer WerkZwei
→ 2.3.15

Mies van der Rohe showed the way with the Lake Shore Drive Apartments: living untethered from the earth, structured by a loose spatial arrangement with built-in furniture, glass double doors, and sliding walls, and afforded by the apartment's flowing transitional spaces and an intensive relationship to the panorama revealed by the ribbon windows. The kitchen has command of the floor plan. It lies in the center of the apartment and offers the chef views in all directions.

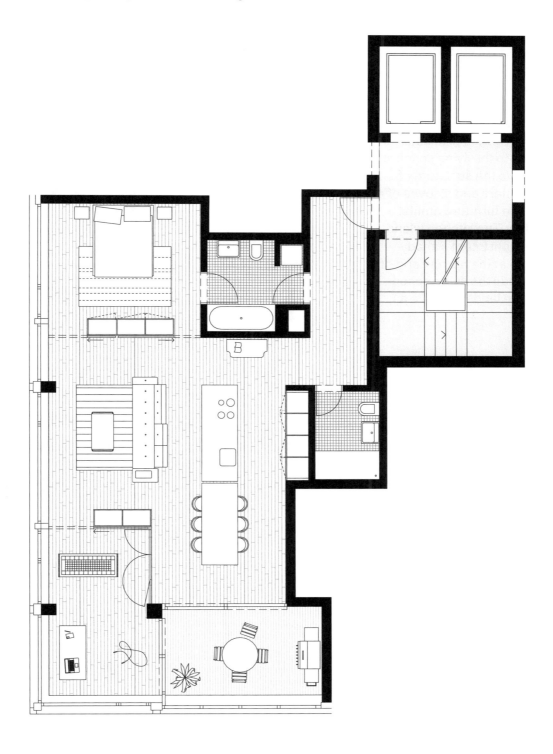

High-Rise Living 147

3.7.9 "Will the Circle Be Unbroken?"

2009
4.5-rooms
103 m²

Steinach High-Rise,
Saurer WerkZwei
→ 2.3.15

The apartment takes the form of a tunnel through the depth of the building, creating expansions of the space to the south that capture the light and the view. Sliding walls along the room edges give additional expanse to the living space and visually dissolve the structure of the space. Corners and alcoves offer footholds to the furniture amidst the spatial flow. The kitchen island activates the apartment's shady center. A room at the narrow end of the plan expands the living space directly into the landscape like a telescope.

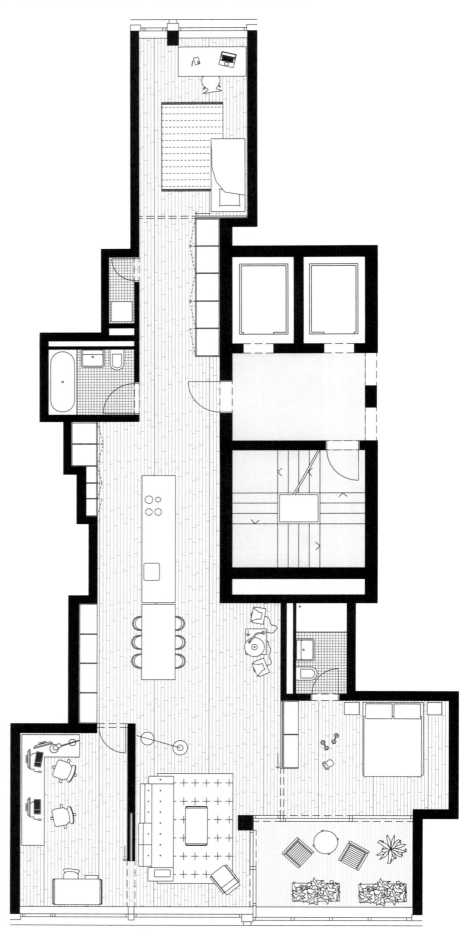

148

3.7.10 "Come In, Stranger"

2018
4.5-rooms
127 m²

Uetlibergstrasse High-Rise
→ 2.4.5

On the tower's top floor, the deck lies protected in the building's corner and offers a panoramic view. The plan itself is constructed like a Russian doll: shielded from the more public and imposing living area, a private realm lies in the second row, with the dressing room as opening note, a bathing niche, and a bedroom. The intimate retreat, secluded from guests, is reminiscent of the living worlds created by Carlo Mollino, who introduced a dandyish theatricality.

High-Rise Living

3.7.11 "Kitchen Fit for the Gods"

2018
2.5-rooms
72 m²
Uetlibergstrasse High-Rise
→ 2.4.5

The space takes shape around the kitchen at the center of the plan, forming niches adjacent to the entryway and reaching its apogee in the living area by the bay window. From here, a door leads into the bedroom and further into the bath, which in turn possesses a connection to the entrance area and thus also serves as a guest bathroom. Despite its compact layout, the apartment feels varied given its circular traffic pattern. The panorama can be experienced in a variety of ways.

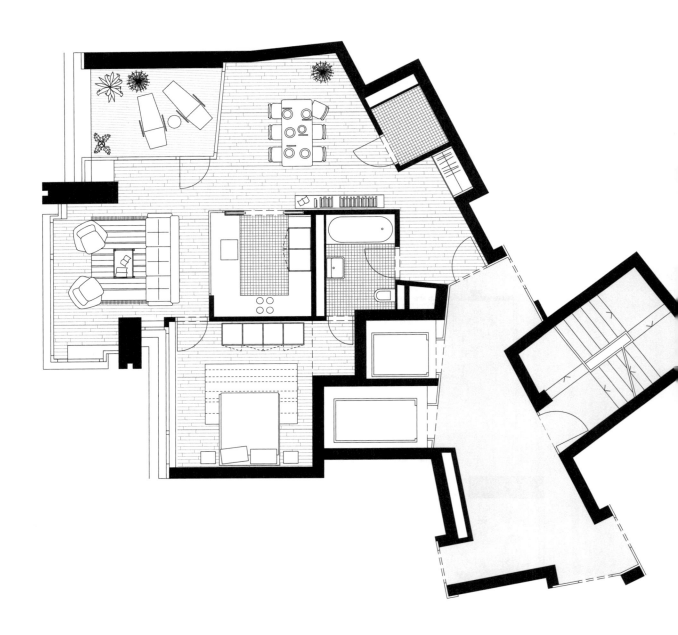

3.7.12 "You'll Never Walk Alone"

2013
3.5-rooms
94 m²

Uetlibergstrasse
High-Rise
→ 2.4.5

The dining area is shifted back to the second row, while the kitchen receives prominent placement along the facade. The living space lies within the glazed oriel, which communicates with the space of the city. A hidden path along the inside of the facade connects the living space with the kitchen and the room that, in this constellation, can be used communally. In the center of the apartment, the dining room nestles up against the back of the kitchen, lit via the deeply retracted balcony.

High-Rise Living 151

3.7.13 "Gone Fishin'"

2019
4-rooms
87 m²

Zwhatt Site High-Rise
→ 2.4.9

Glass double doors illuminate the living space, which forms the communal center of the diagonal array stretching from the entryway to the dining room. Only the profusion of daylight in a high-rise makes this unusual organization possible, fostered additionally by the two-story-tall enclosed patio. The living space could occupy the corner area equally well, shifting the dining table in the center, as reminiscent of the eating halls in worker housing of the Neues Bauen era.

3.7.14 "Blinded by the Light"

2019
3.5-rooms
85 m²
Zwhatt Site
High-Rise
→ 2.4.9

This flexibility of this apartment type is astounding. This time, the central space becomes an eating hall with kitchen, obtaining light from glass double doors. The pathway to the living area leads into the light, which reaches into the apartment through precisely placed windows and discreetly configures the shape of the space. The depth of the building's shell allows for atmospheres that feel fresh and yet familiar, as they borrow from a culture of dwelling that is accustomed to valuing soft, twilit lighting conditions.

High-Rise Living 153

3.7.15 "Come Together"

2021
3.5-rooms
115 m²
BRIAG Site
Development
(Building sites C, D)
→ 2.5.10

The corner of the building is used to assign a varying position to the balcony on alternating floors. The usability of the two-story outdoor space is protected by high siding. The kitchen with its dining table in the corner of the building has the quality of a bay window. The focal point is the living area, with the rooms lying along the perimeter; this gives rise to a sense of expansive spaciousness.

3.7.16 For Urbonauts

2021
4.5-rooms
131 m²

BRIAG Site
Development
(Building sites C, D)
→ 2.5.10

Balconies crisscrossed atop one another offer a private outdoor space that, due to its position at the corner of the building, attains the magnitude of a room. The kitchen is placed next to the balcony, extending an invitation to al fresco summer dining. Emanating out from the entryway, which grants a direct glimpse of the view, the living area stretches out toward the facade. The dining table lies in the center, with the sitting area before it. Staggered openings onto the bedrooms offer privacy despite their direct access to the living area.

High-Rise Living 155

An apartment floor plan in a high-rise building is dependent on many conditions. Statics are affected by wind or earthquakes. Fire safety regulations have an effect on escape routes and the choice of materials. The building depth is influenced by economics. The shaft concept is of great importance. It's like cooking: we know that too many cooks spoil the broth. This recipe fits the bill. Woe betide if the clams do not open …

Spaghetti with Clams

Recipe taken from: Rose Gray and Ruth Rogers, The Cafe Cook Book: Italian Recipes from London's River Cafe, New York 1998

Serves four

Ingredients
3 kg clams, cleaned and washed
100 ml olive oil
150 ml white wine
3 garlic cloves, cut into slices
3 small, dried chilies, crumbled (without seeds)
320 g spaghetti
3 tablespoons chopped parsley
Salt and freshly ground black pepper

Method
1. Heat one third of the olive oil in a large pot with a lid.
2. Add half of the wine, one clove of garlic and one crushed chili pepper.
3. Add half of the clams to the pot, cover with a lid, and cook over high heat until the mussels open, shaking the pot.
4. Place the opened clams and the broth in a large bowl and repeat this step with the remaining mussels.
5. Once all the clams are cooked, chop the remaining garlic and fry it with the chili in the remaining oil until it is lightly brown.
6. Add the clams and the broth and immediately remove from the heat.
7. Cook the spaghetti in plenty of salted water until al dente, drain, and dry well, then add to the clams.
8. Mix everything well to combine the pasta with the broth.
9. Stir in the chopped parsley and black pepper and serve immediately.

3.8 Converting/Expanding

The present moment calls on us to treat existing structures more attentively, preserving and converting these whenever possible. Anxieties around climate change, our consumption of energy, and the desire for resource-conserving construction all lead to new building criteria. That goes for residential buildings as well.

Aging office buildings, say, are refitted as apartments. Pre-existing bearing structures, extant building cores, above-average ceiling heights, extreme building depths, and a lack of outdoor spaces necessitate new forms of housing and therefore a different concept for apartment floor plans. A newfound feast!

3.8.1 "Nightshift"

2007
3.5-rooms
98 m²

Steinhofweg
Apartment Block
→ 4.10

The simple yet sensibly laid out residential building, featuring three apartments, obtains additional living areas and a large deck with the renovation. The cell-like layout of the original plan is enriched by contemporary spatial ideas. The circular traffic pattern through the kitchen and dining room around the bathroom at the core of the design ensures an abundant experience of space. The connection between bedroom and bathroom can be regulated by opening and closing the room-width double doors.

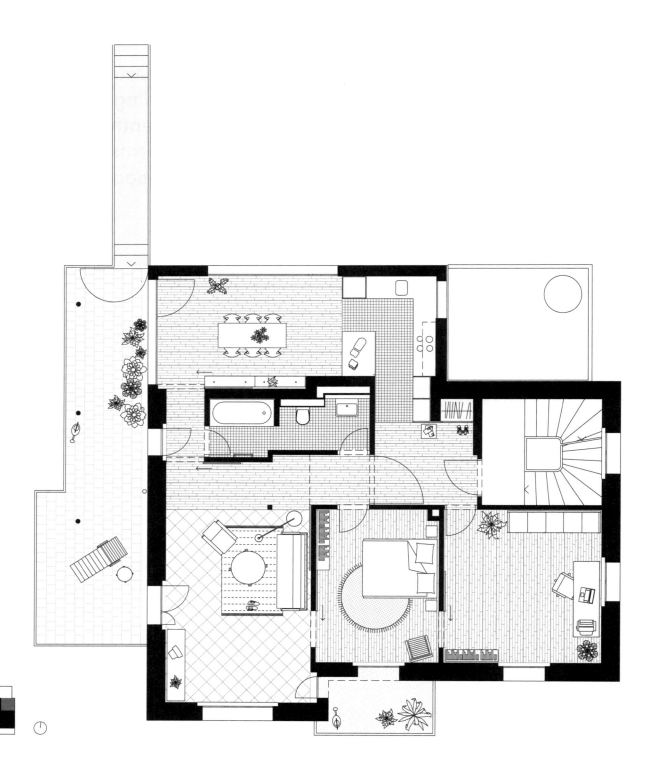

3.8.2 "Chli stinke muess es"

2020
2.5-rooms
88 m²

Webergut
Conversion
→ 2.5.4

Building within an existing structure shakes up stagnant housing concepts—especially when an office block mutates into a residential building. The center of the twenty-meter-deep apartment becomes suddenly interesting, obtaining a hall-like character thanks to the three-meter-high ceiling. The living area narrows toward the facade to make way for the neighboring apartment and the bedroom. Thus the living hall becomes an atelier, study, home gym, or venue for a large company of friends chatting long into the afternoon or late into the night.

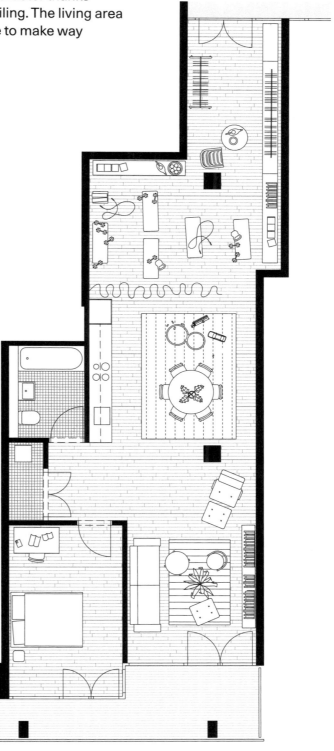

Converting/Expanding

3.8.3 "London Calling"

2020
2.5-rooms
63 m²

Webergut
Conversion
→ 2.5.4

The top-floor apartment makes do without separated rooms. The focal point of the plan has a sleeping alcove, which can be closed off with a curtain. Who needs light for sleeping anyway? Oriented toward the stairwell is a vestibule that can be opened up or separated off with glass double doors. With the door opened during the day, the atelier becomes a semi-public workspace.

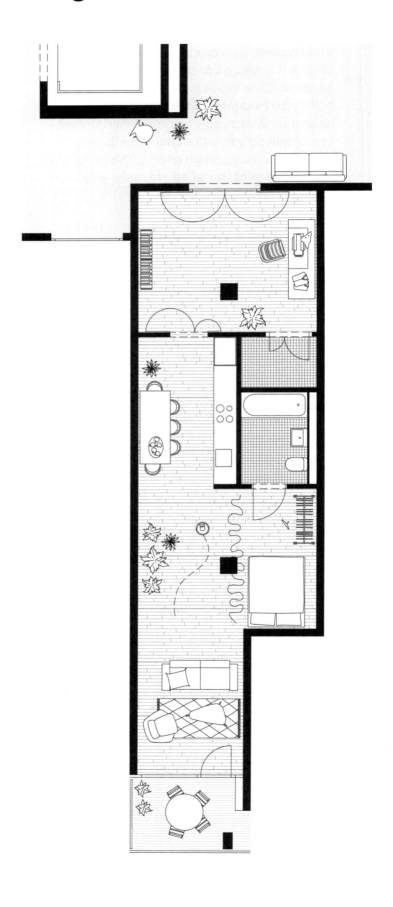

162

3.8.4 "Even Cowgirls Get the Blues"

2022
2.5-rooms
49 m²
Schärenmoos-
strasse Conversion
→ 2.5.13

Little pads, little problems? Forget it; working within an existing building continues to pose challenges! Pre-existing earthquake-proof walls prevent the facade from being opened up completely. The offset partition separating the rooms therefore brings twin advantages: more light penetrates the living area through the open corner, and the line of sight that leads outside is expanded. Furthermore, the bedroom door is shielded by the wall. Even when the door stands open, the bed is afforded privacy within its nestled niche.

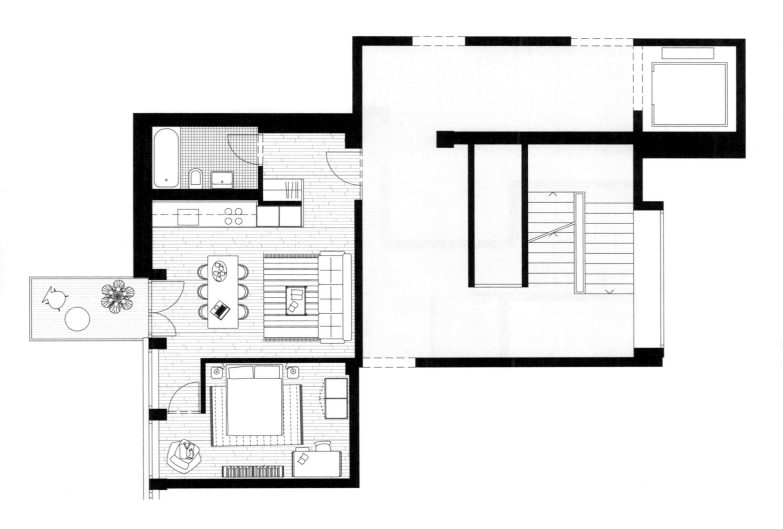

Converting/Expanding

3.8.5 "Alone and Forsaken"

2022
4.5-rooms
89 m²
Schärenmoos-
strasse Conversion
→ 2.5.13

Efficient conversion of a cumbersome office building requires a cunning approach. The apartment uses the geometric advantage of the long flat stretch of its facade, grouping two rooms together with the open kitchen in the inner corner. This makes for an exciting spatial situation, part of which is an elongated hallway that brings light inward through another room. Moreover, £a remarkable spatial perspective emerges, wresting a surprising spaciousness from this compact plan.

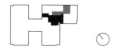

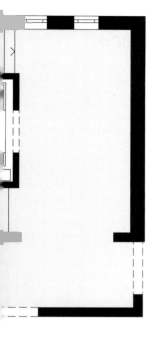

Three in the Labyrinth of Life

The avant-garde of housing design has recently been drawn toward Zurich's north. An office building in this district belonging to the broadcasting company Schweizer Fernsehen was recently converted into an apartment building. Cheap rent and a lively neighborhood that encourages unconventional living arrangements—that's what Daniela, Petra, and Aleksandra were looking for, and they found it.

Even so, one wants the comfort and coziness of home, and it's a relief to close the door from time to time, when the building's vitality starts to become tiring. The big balcony and the open kitchen convinced them, as did the unconventional expansiveness of the apartment, with its labyrinthine corridors. Reminds me of The Shining, Daniela said on the first day. The corridors also provide a generous private sphere, with the rooms well separated.

Petra snapped up the room at the remote end of the apartment; her current love life calls for, shall we say, a bit more privacy.

All they have to share is the bathroom, which has already led to some dicey situations; luckily, the three friends have handled these magnanimously.

In housing construction, we learn a lot from our colleagues. We study every jury report carefully. It's similar with cooking. Our friends' recipes are the best. This one comes from Ursula Müller and Andreas Billeter—who brought it back from Salinas, a Lipari island, as a souvenir. The flavor conveys a lovely idea of that place. Like in a competition. We're pleased when we can incorporate fine, unfamiliar solutions.

Spaghetti with Capers and White Onions

Recipe from Ursula Müller and Andreas Billeter

Serves four

Ingredients
3 tablespoons capers (ideally from Salinas), drained
3 tablespoons white onions, finely chopped
Juice of one lemon
3 tablespoons olive oil
3 tablespoons Parmesan, grated
1 tablespoon sweet dessert wine
400 g spaghetti

Methods
1. Set the water for the spaghetti to boil.
2. Rinse three tablespoons of capers, drain well, chop finely and put in a bowl with the spaghetti together with the onions, also finely chopped.
3. Add the lemon juice, olive oil and Parmesan. Mix everything well.
4. Cook the spaghetti until it is al dente, add to the bowl, and mix well.
5. Add a little hot pasta water.
6. Serve.

3.9 Outdoor Spaces

Aside from a harmonious floor-plan layout, an apartment's connection to its immediate outdoor surroundings is one of the most exciting design requirements. Every room with direct access to the outdoors benefits from this additional value. Thus, whenever the location or the brief allows, we try to have as many apartments as possible share in a garden area or rooftop garden that is as large as possible.

Small apartments with compact layouts, in particular, benefit enormously. Don't we all dream of a dwelling with its own secluded terrace or shady garden?

3.9.1 "Home Sweet Home"

2001
4.5-rooms
135 m²

James Development
→ 2.2.2

The maisonette benefits from its location on the top floor. There, the rooftop terrace unfurls on a diagonal, offering lots of space—accessed directly by the stairway—for gardeners to indulge in their passion at a lofty elevation and with a view of Uetliberg mountain. On the entrance level, a two-story-tall loggia amplifies the lavish offering of outdoor space, making the maisonette a "Tiny Home" with rooftop garden.

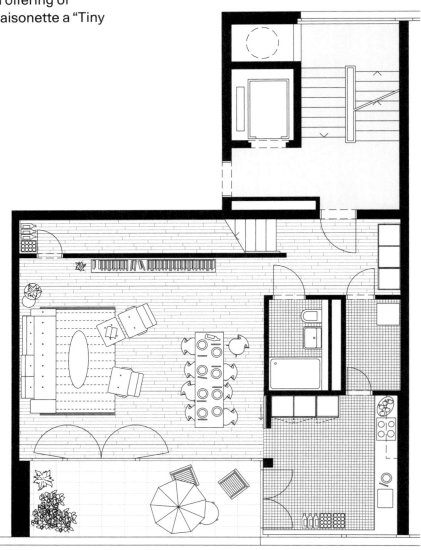

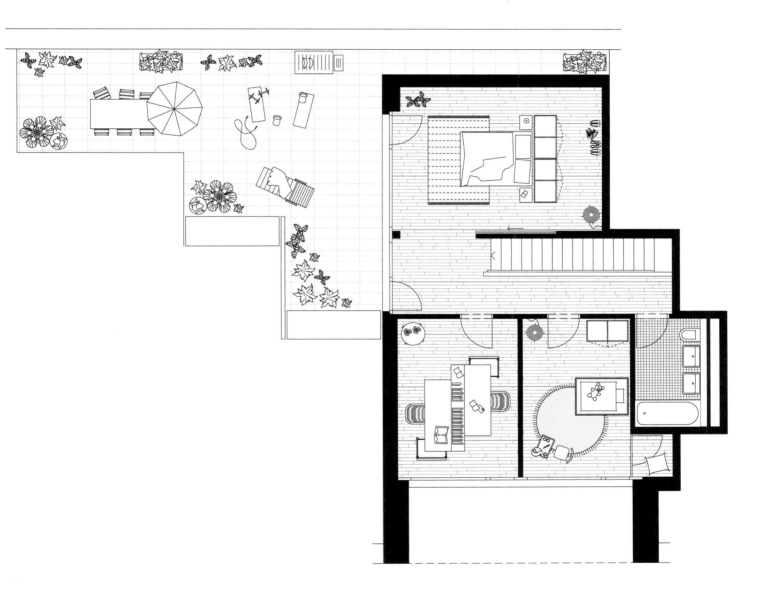

Outdoor Spaces

3.9.2 Morning Dew

2005
5.5-rooms
190 m²

Kurlistrasse
Apartment Block
→ 2.2.8

The apartment sprawls across three stories. Concealed by terraces lying at mezzanine-level, it exudes the atmosphere of an atrium in a Mediterranean home. This trick of the layout permits the graduated terrace landscape with pergola to be accessed from every level of the dwelling via an outdoor staircase.

Wide tiered bench seating faces the apartment, underscoring the intimate character of the rooftop courtyard. Covered with vines and tendrils, the pergola frames the spectacular view and defines the spatial limits of the terrace.

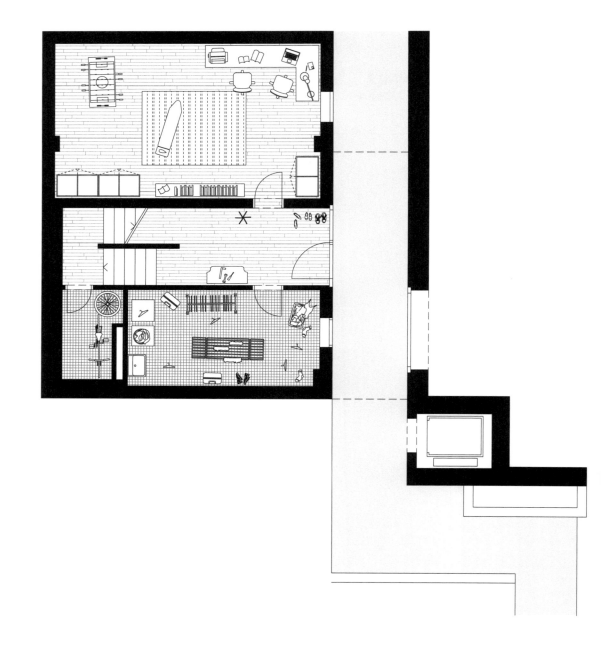

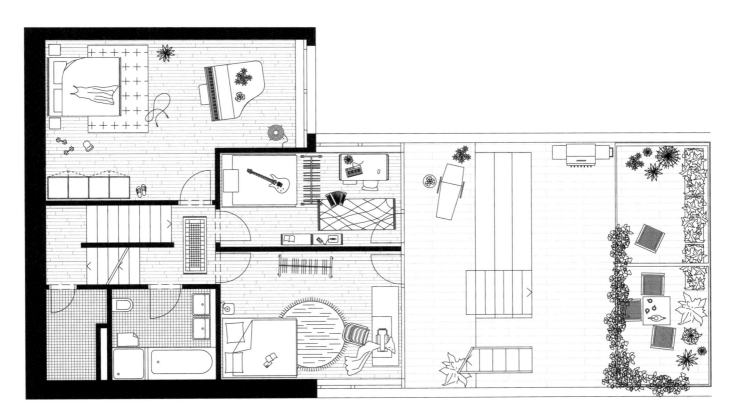

Outdoor Spaces

3.9.3 "Once Upon a Time"

2005
4.5-rooms
126 m²

Kurlistrasse
Apartment Block
→ 2.2.8

Its complement is a classic maisonette with rooftop terrace overlooked by a balcony. The apartment is accessed from the alley via an entryway set at mezzanine level. From here, the eye is drawn down to the bedroom level and up to the living space—the spatial surplus of a split-level construction. The cozy corner in the living space offers a protectively defined space for furnishings. From the sofa, the eye roams across the balcony, through the corner window, and off into the landscape.

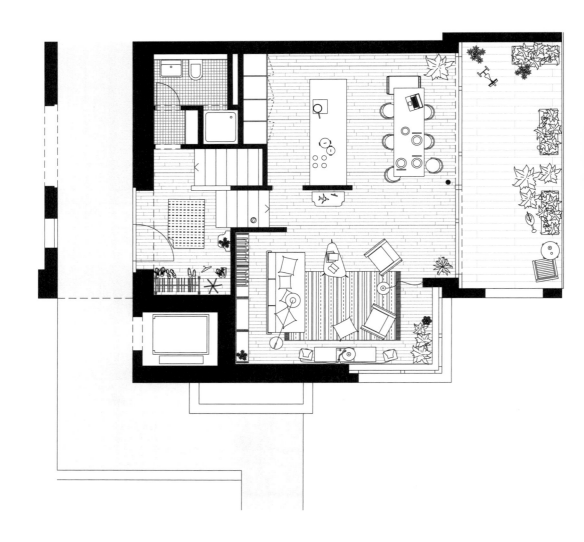

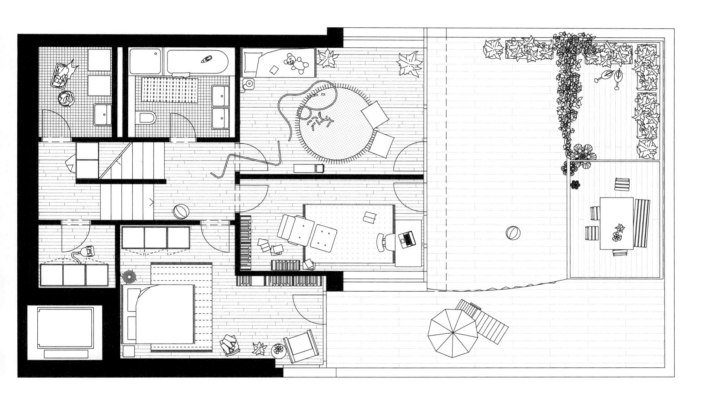

Outdoor Spaces   175

3.9.4 "Early Sunday Morning"

2007
4.5-rooms
137 m²

Rütihof
Apartment Blocks
→ 2.2.13

The idea was to create a stage for the view out onto Lake Zurich by way of a long, straight line of sight from the entrance all the way to the balcony. This creates a pull toward the panorama, marked by narrow segments that flare out. The concave wall of the adjoining rooms alleviates the narrow feeling of the corridor and amplifies the perspectival effect. Looking out from the living space, the double doors create a transverse spatial relationship between the bedroom, hearth, and picture window.

176

3.9.5 Quiet Afternoon

2009
4.5-rooms
121 m²

Park Residence
→ 2.3.2

The southern-facing apartment is embraced by two triangular loggias. The triangular form allows for a balcony depth of more than three meters and efficient illumination of the living space, with muted light filtering in from both sides. The atmosphere is reminiscent of Eduard Neuenschwander's cavernous ateliers. The entire length of the second loggia is used for lighting, as the living area's window facade can be expanded into the bedroom via a sliding door. The same contrivance increases the amount of light falling into the kitchen.

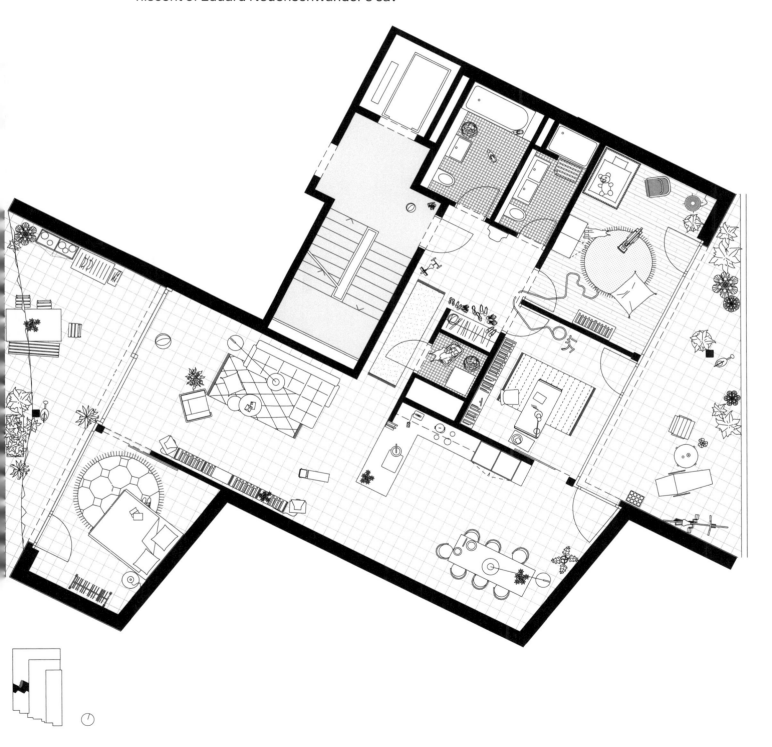

Outdoor Spaces

3.9.6 "Rock the Casbah"

2010
5.5-rooms
198 m²

Bombach
Development
→ 2.3.3

The constricting corset of zoning law often impinges on the layout of the top floor. Not in this case. Massive buildings have the advantage of producing lots of space at the penthouse level. The arrangement of the rooms allows for a diversity of spatial relations: from intimate spots of retreat to bedroom as extended living space, one has everything that makes for an abundant floor plan. To all this is added two terraces, one of a lavish, communal character, the other more private.

Outdoor Spaces

3.9.7 "1000 and 1 Nights"

2007
4.5-rooms
146 m²

Scheffelstrasse
Apartment Block
→ 2.3.6

The offset shell of the building lends a particular quality to the penthouse apartment, with its multiple levels and outdoor spaces. From the bedroom level with its spacious entryway, the eye travels over the dining area to the living space, and through the picture window into the distance. The gently sloping ceiling ties the levels together and accentuates the angle that draws the eye to the outward view. Particularly delightful is the bathroom with windows set at an angle to the tub; shielded from eyes peering inward, it transforms personal care into a special experience.

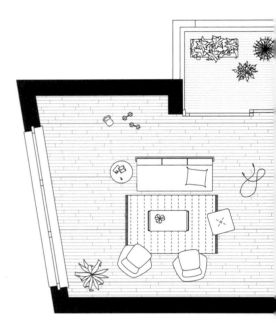

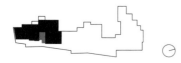

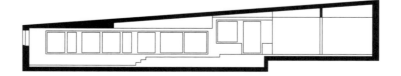

Outdoor Spaces

3.9.8 "Make Some Noise"

2012
2.5-rooms
57 m²

Apartment Block in the Aeschbach Quarter
→ 2.3.12

More than a walkway: the four-meter depth of the outdoor corridor transforms the profane entrance area into a communal terrace around which small apartments are convened. The kitchen functions as a buffer to shield the bedroom, which is turned away from the arcade in order to maintain the privacy it needs. One imagines Mediterranean climes, where the outdoor entry area becomes a semi-public space that encourages neighborly connections. Forgot to get eggs? The neighbors are happy to help.

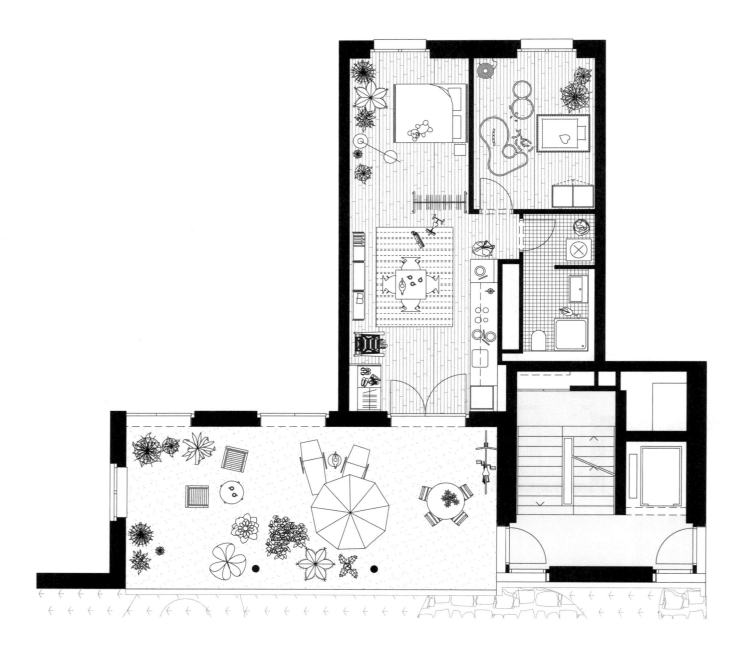

3.9.9 Apartment Block in the Aeschbach Quarter – 2012 – Studio – 33 m²
→ 2.3.12

3.9.10 Apartment Block in the Aeschbach Quarter – 2012 – 3.5-rooms – 77 m²
→ 2.3.12

Outdoor Spaces   183

3.9.11 Flower Power

2017
4.5-rooms
121 m²

Langgrütweg
Apartment Block
→ 2.4.4

The privileged location of this residence compels a careful incorporation of spatial capacity on the top floor—at times occasioning the willing sacrifice of indoor living space. But the terraces are all the more spacious for it, creating distinct spaces oriented toward all directions, and giving the top floor the look of a true penthouse apartment. The plan makes use of the apartment's multi-sidedness, dispensing bedrooms in all directions. The living area takes center stage, while the kitchen is placed in a side pocket.

3.9.12 "I Still Miss Someone"

2018
4.5-rooms
95 m²

Sandacker
Apartment Blocks
→ 2.4.8

Building regulations affecting the top floor can bring forth rare fruits: the small spatial extension at the end of the living area obtains indirect light from the side and serves as a reading corner or work cubby. At the axis of the drawn-out living room, a window extends the impact of the space's perspective into the outdoors. The two long, narrow terraces pick up on the theme of cross-connections breaking through the linearity of the space.

Outdoor Spaces 185

3.9.13 The Journey Is Its Own Reward

2020
3.5-rooms
97 m²

Langgrütghof
Apartment Block
→ 2.5.5

The balcony lies like a ring around the apartment, reiterating the theme of the internal circuits. From the entryway, the path leads into the bedroom, through the bathroom, on into the music room and into the living area, through the half-open kitchen and storage room, back to the starting point. Why so many doors? Loosely adapted from Luigi Caccia Dominioni's idea, the intention is to combine efficient spatial connections with paths that allow for a cozy meandering through the dwelling. It also makes a compact plan feel spacious.

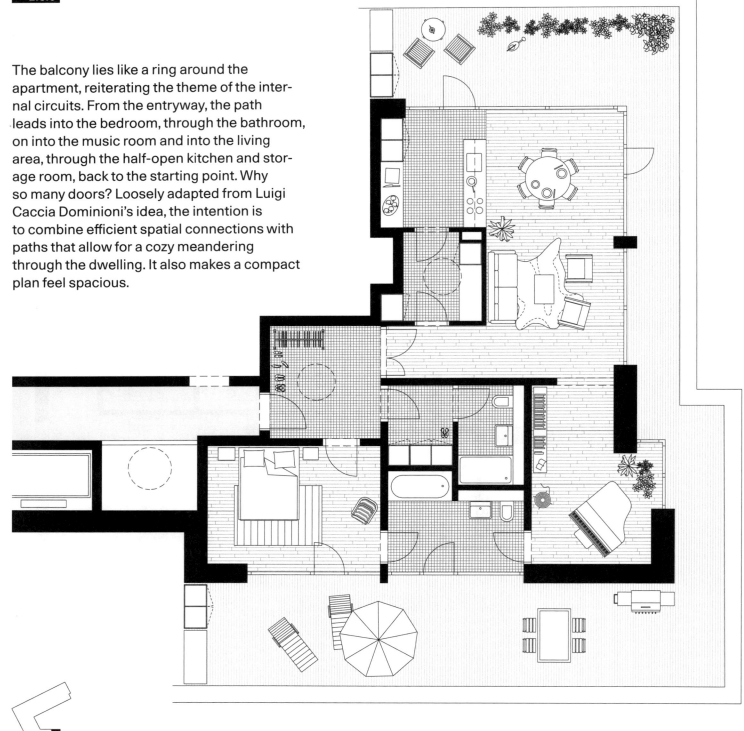

3.9.14 "Tage wie diese"

2021
4.5-rooms
104 m²

Roswiesen-/
Winterthurerstrasse
Development

→ 2.5.8

Noise protection laws can be addressed with recesses into the building, bestowing an abundant offering of outdoor spaces. Every room receives access to an outdoor space. Likewise the living area, the kitchen, and the entryway, which captures daylight and opens up the kitchen with its dining table from two sides. In the living area, skillfully placed bedroom doors free up a cozy corner to be well furnished, providing a back for the sofa and directing the eye diagonally out of doors.

Outdoor Spaces 187

Of course, we cook seasonally. A few years ago, friar's beard was largely unknown in our country. Housing is not subject to seasonal supply, but to the zeitgeist. At the turn of the millennium, it was a time for spacious family apartments, today it's small apartments for singles or seniors. Legal stipulations also have an influence. Accessibility or noise requirements no longer permit certain apartments. That's why we're pleased whenever we can discover another loophole.

Spaghetti with Agretti and Tomatoes

Recipe taken from Elisabeth Bronfen, Besessen, Basel 2016

Serves four

Ingredients
1 bunch agretti
2–3 tablespoons olive oil
1 garlic clove
2 sardine fillets
1 small, red chili
1 tablespoon capers
1 dozen Datterini tomatoes
1 tablespoon lemon juice
15 g butter
Parmesan

Method
1. Rinse and then drain the capers.
2. Wash the barbe di frate and cut off the roots generously.
3. Finely chop garlic and chili pepper.
4. Pour olive oil in a pan that will later hold the spaghetti. Add garlic, capers, tomatoes, and chili and sauté on low heat for ten minutes.
5. Cook spaghetti in boiling salted water until al dente.
6. Three minutes before the cooking time is up, add the agretti to the spaghetti and stir well.
7. Drain the spaghetti and add to the pan with the garlic, capers, tomatoes, and chili. Stir well, add an additional two or three tablespoons of salted pasta water and the lemon juice.
8. Season with salt and pepper, add butter.
9. Serve.

3.10 Form Follows Law

There's no point in moaning or complaining about it: laws are made to be followed. So we always grab the bull by the horns and take rules and regulations as engines for generating design ideas. In response to the increased minimum distances to the plot boundaries for stories above a certain height or buildings over a certain length, we design specific volumes, which in turn form the basis for unique apartment floor plans.

To comply with noise abatement regulations, we devise new room types such as an "elephant's trunk" room, or position jutties resembling the ear of an African elephant along the street facade in order to protect all the rooms behind from outdoor noise. These kinds of architectural tricks mean all rooms can be fitted with windows that can be opened while ticking all the regulatory boxes.

3.10.1 "Herzilein"

2005
4.5-rooms
108 m²

Büelen
Apartment Blocks
→ 2.2.7

A penthouse-level setback enforced by building regulations is used to create a four-sided terrace, which, thanks to a recess on the side facade, partially turns into a wind-protected patio, with a large table where food can be served directly from the kitchen. The living space spans the entire length of the terrace, capturing the panorama. On the other side, the bedrooms and bathroom form the private area of the apartment, which, befitting its elevated status, is entered through a spacious entrance area.

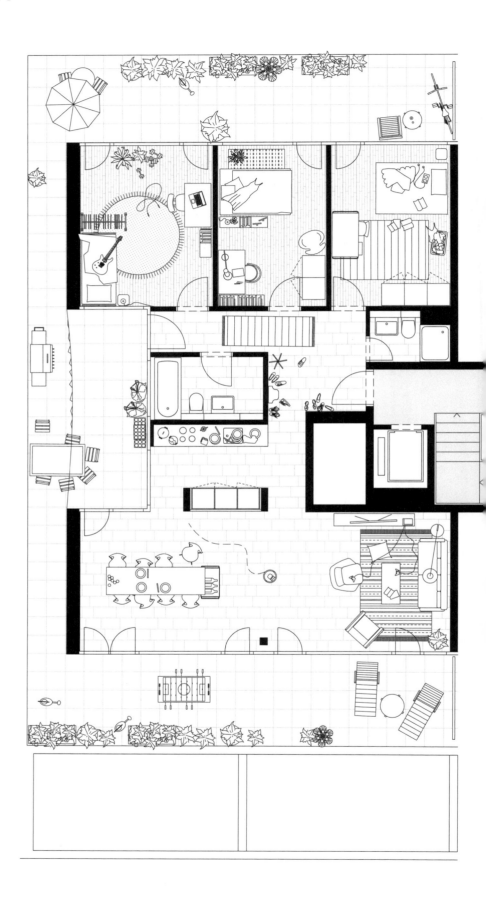

Even a Notorious Bachelor Needs a Home

A day/night floor plan is what Jörg calls it— and as a real estate professional, he knows all about these things. He doesn't mean it disparagingly; on the contrary, he and his roommates, Michel and Marc, appreciate the clear division between the private bedrooms and the large living area that, along with the kitchen, forms the center of this apartment shared by the three older gents.

The three men know each other from earlier periods of their lives, and after a long night spent drinking together at the famous Kronenhalle restaurant, made a spur-of-the-moment decision to move in together. All three are notorious bachelors, not ready for long-term relationship stress, be it with women or men.

So the shared apartment is a godsend! They love to cook, so the kitchen is coveted ground; they have a large group of friends who are always being invited over. Then they're off, and old stories are dished up after the meal, taking on epic proportions under the influence of abundant Tuscan red.

Michel is the only one who often retires early, going to strum a few last chords on his Fender Jaguar, which he bought at online auction and which supposedly once belonged to Kurt Cobain.

3.10.2 "Marmor, Stein und Eisen bricht"

2010
4.5-rooms
121 m²

Bombach
Development
→ 2.3.3

For this development, the only solution for noise abatement was including a patio, which ventilates the living area and simultaneously provides outdoor space that reduces noise in accordance with legal requirements. The solution to this problem becomes a feature: outside, there's bustling traffic, inside there's a sheltered and cozy atmosphere. The dining table fits snugly in a nook, with the kitchen connected to the living room.
A third bedroom with private bathroom on the entrance level forms a separate unit.

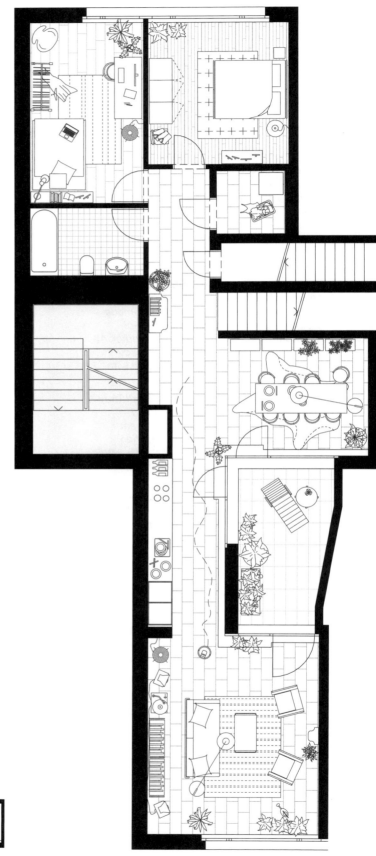

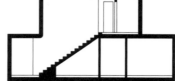

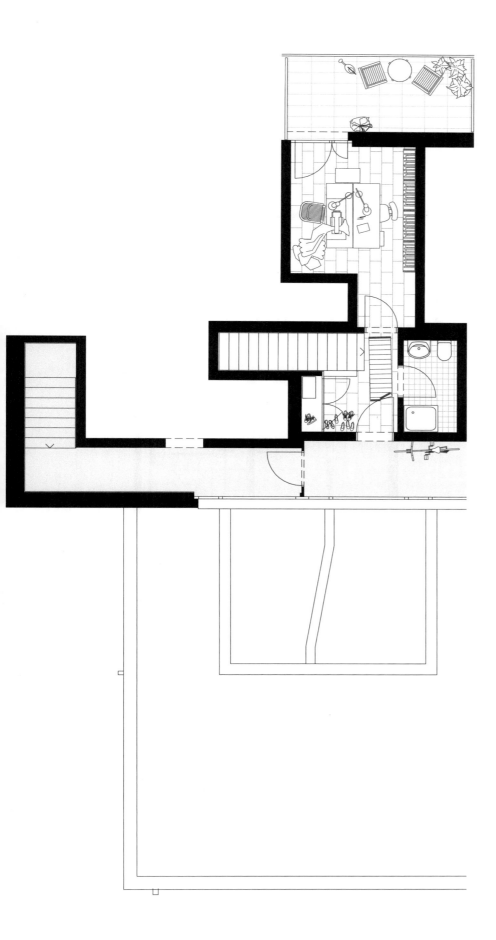

Form Follows Law

3.10.3 "Enjoy the Silence"

2010
3.5-rooms
88 m²
Fellenbergstrasse
Development
→ 2.3.5

Noise abatement regulations strike again: the hallway serves as a "snorkel" for the kitchen and living room, providing air through a glass door onto a quiet balcony at the end of the corridor on the side of the building furthest from the noisy street. The generous corridor width is due to building code regulations. This connective element thus forms a spacious area, providing enough room for a desk. The bedrooms are located on the interior corner of the building, using the line of the facade in a strategic fashion.

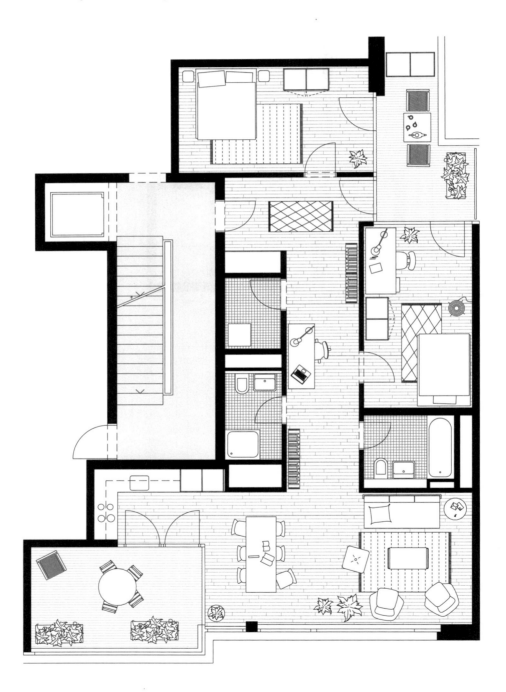

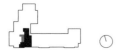

3.10.4 "Livin' la Vida Loca"

2010
4.5-rooms
107 m²
Fellenbergstrasse
Development
→ 2.3.5

Here, the kitchen becomes the "cockpit" of the apartment, with its view of the Uetliberg mountain and flanked by a dining table in a cozy corner. The living area is on the other side, connected to the kitchen and dining area via the apartment entrance, where once again, fresh air can be provided via the building side furthest from noise. The circular flow of the design around the apartment's core connects the private area of the bedrooms and ensures people can access the spacious bathroom unnoticed. This means that they don't have to walk through the dining area—in the worst-case scenario, parading past their guests in their pajamas.

Form Follows Law 197

3.10.5 "Working on a Dream"

2012
3.5-rooms
95 m²

Holunderhof Development
→ 2.3.10

When the north facade is exposed to noise, it provides an opportunity for an unusual entrance situation: the floor plan widens out towards the north and tapers off towards the south. As a result, the entrance receives a lot of daylight, and the kitchen, which is located in a little pocket along the facade, benefits from the extra space. A bedroom slots into the corner, snatching light via the enclosed balcony. This nested plan offers maximum connection points with the south side, which is furthest from the noise.

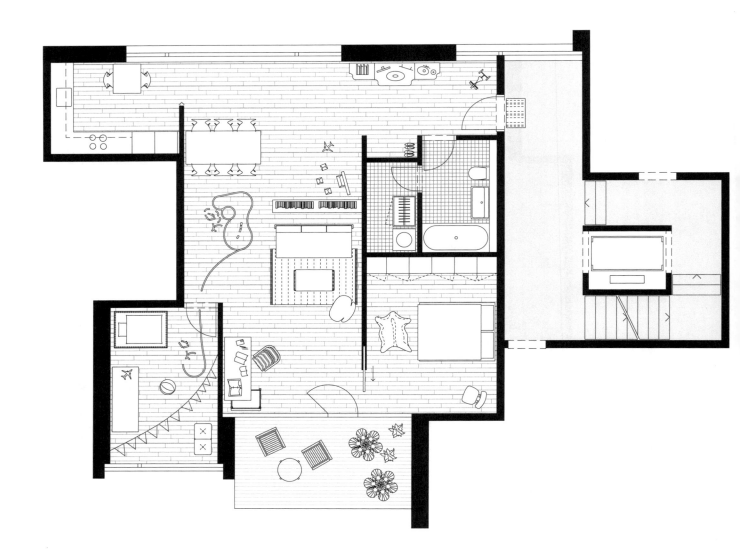

3.10.6 "Wake Me up before You Go-Go"

2012
4.5-rooms
103 m²

Holunderhof
Development
→ 2.3.10

Again the question arises of how the floor plan can derive maximum benefit from the facade on the building's quiet side. In this case, the answer lies in staggering the depth. The rooms are layered one behind the other and offset from each another. In this way the living room, which is positioned behind another room plus the kitchen, is nonetheless able to take in air and light via the loggia. The double folding doors extend the axis running through the corridor, expanding the space and strengthening the living area's relationship with the outside.

Form Follows Law 199

3.10.7 "Jenseits von Eden"

2014
4.5-rooms
107 m²
Reitmen Development
→ 2.3.18

Solid parapets block out traffic noise for the apartments behind them. In accordance with regulations, these are unusually high, limiting the views of the outside. The plan responds by placing the kitchen in the center of the apartment, inverting the typical layout. This cuts the living room in two, creating two room zones along the facade. Higher-than-average rooms and glossy painted ceilings compensate for the limited sunlight. The route through the split bathroom and the kitchen breaks up the length of the apartment.

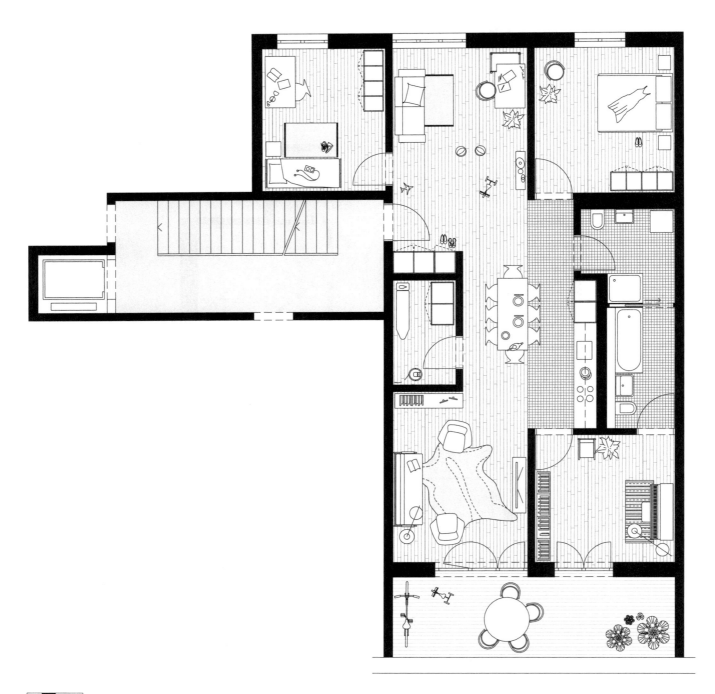

3.10.8 "A dr Ysebahn"

2014
4.5-rooms
102 m²

Reitmen
Development
→ 2.3.18

This was the birth of the snorkel room! Our aspirations to maximize the available floorspace made it necessary to position a bedroom next to the source of noise. An appendage to the room that is narrow, but still easily furnished, is ventilated via the side furthest from the noise and creates a connection to the other room. The circulation design is varied, resulting in an eclectic plan that also eliminates unnecessary circulation space. The clipped corners of the rooms emphasize the diagonal relationship between the living and dining areas.

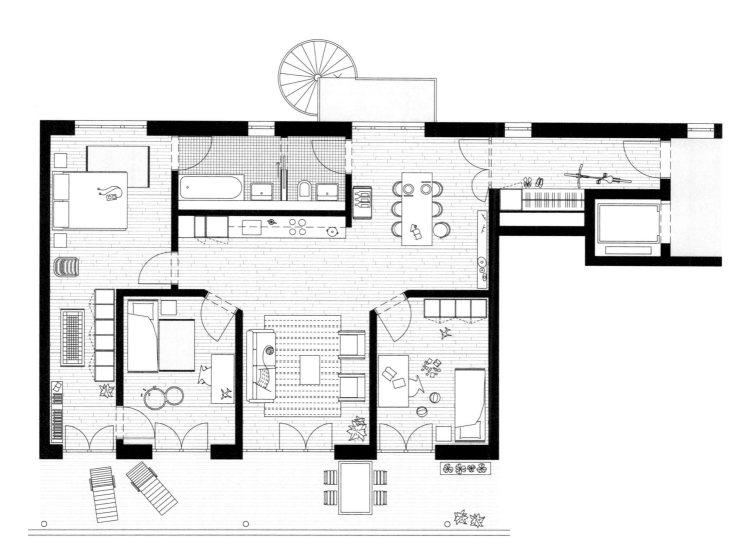

Form Follows Law

3.10.9   Reussbühl Ost Development – 2017 – 2.5-rooms – 65 m²
→ 2.4.2

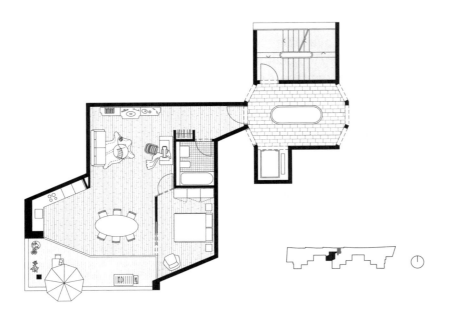

3.10.10   Reussbühl Ost Development – 2017 – 2.5-rooms – 68 m²
→ 2.4.2

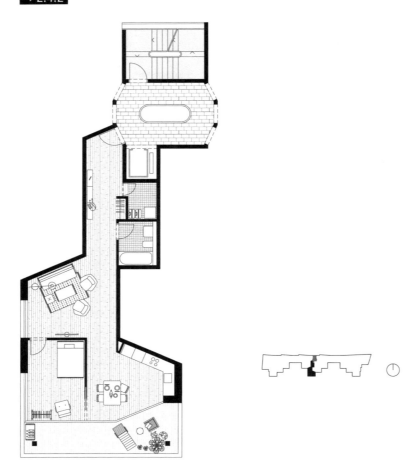

3.10.11   Reussbühl Ost Development – 2017 – 4.5-rooms – 118 m²
→ 2.4.2

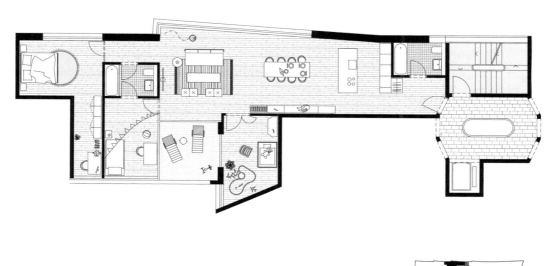

3.10.12   Reussbühl Ost Development – 2017 – 2.5-rooms – 65 m²
→ 2.4.2

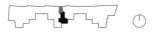

Form Follows Law 203

3.10.13 "Mit 17 hat man noch Träume"

2019
4.5-rooms
98 m²

Chirchbüel Apartment Blocks
→ 2.4.12

Notwithstanding the strict noise abatement requirements, you couldn't get a more compact space. From the entrance area, which even affordable apartments need, you reach the living room, which gets natural light from two sides and is divided by a corner kitchen. A protruding bedroom visually extends the space, creating a four-and-a-half room apartment, despite the limited width of the footprint. The design flows past the bathroom and through the snorkel-shaped room and a third bedroom to complete a circular traffic pattern through the apartment.

3.10.14 "Keep the Fire Burning"

2019
5.5-rooms
108 m²

Stelzen
Apartment Blocks
→ 2.4.13

Escape routes are measured from the furthest corner of the apartment to the stairwell via the outdoor walkway. But what if the permitted distance is—only just—exceeded? The solution is a "satellite" room with its own bathroom located on the first floor, with a direct exit (in other words, an escape route) that is connected to the rest of the apartment via an internal stairway. This workaround offers a solution to the fire safety issue, and a separate room for an older relative. Additionally, the room contains a jutty for a table or sofa.

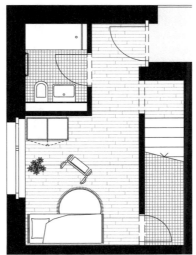

Form Follows Law 205

3.10.15 "Home of the Brave"

2020
4.5-rooms
109 m²
Eich-/Birken-/
Lagerstrasse
Development
→ 2.5.1

More than just a cellar: the building code requires that every apartment contain a reasonably sized storage space. Here, this is located in the center of the floor plan and is glass-paneled to draw daylight into the small space. There is space for a guest bed or a desk with a view into the kitchen, which occupies the other half of the apartment's core and frees up two clearly defined spaces along the facade, where furniture can be easily placed. The bedroom by the apartment entrance offers a refuge for residents, for example teenagers coming home late at night.

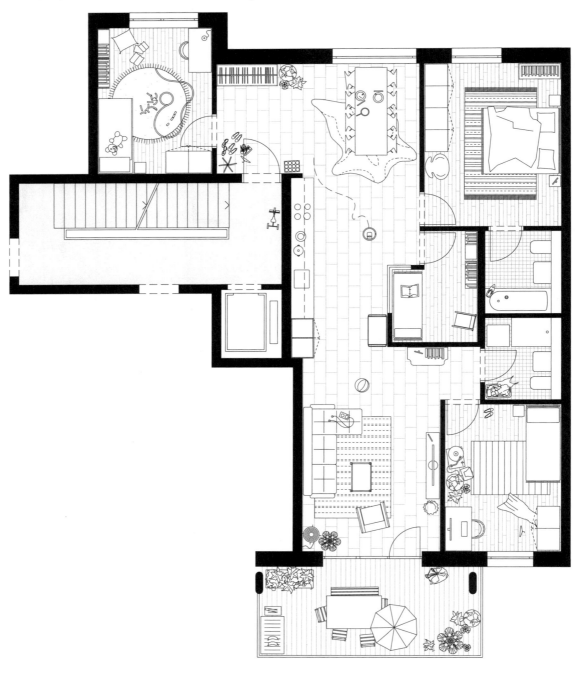

3.10.16 "Knock on Wood"

2020
4.5-rooms
106 m²
Dreispitz Site
Development
→ 2.5.2

The floor plan meanders through the building, grabbing rooms on the left and the right that can be ventilated from the quiet side of the building. The same applies to the living space, which stretches from one side of the apartment to the other and is extended by the kitchen. Which offers enough space for a small dining table—the most popular location in everyday apartment life, and one that epitomizes comfort. A corner window offers sweeping views of the city and the outdoor passageway, which acts as a connective patio area.

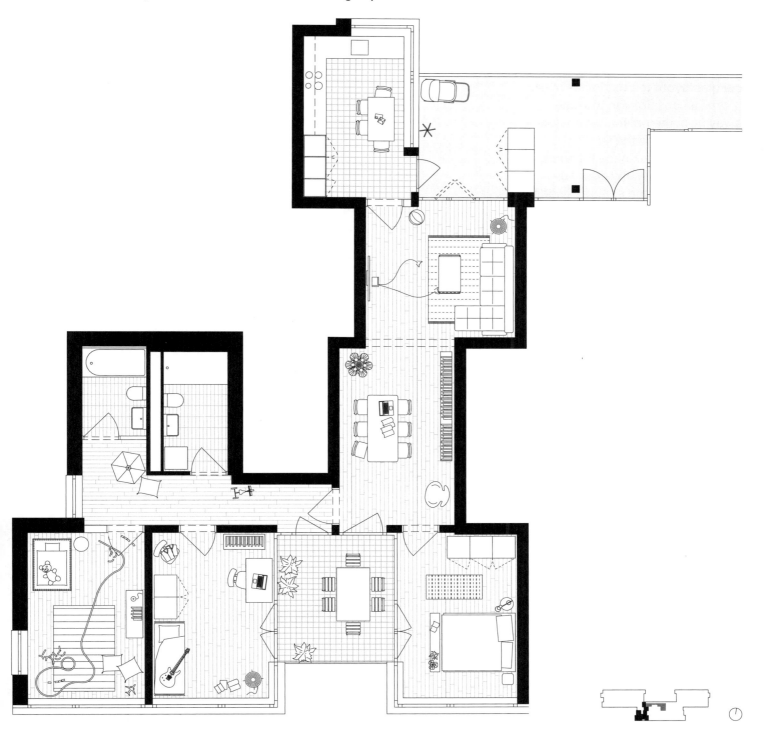

Form Follows Law 207

3.10.17 "Holz isch heimelig"

2020
4.5-rooms
114 m²

Dreispitz Site
Development
→ 2.5.2

At the building's hinge, the floor plan winds its way through the volume, taking advantage of the cellular layout to position as many rooms as possible on the side away from the noise. The enclosed balcony extends the line of the facade to create space for two bedrooms and a balcony door adjacent to the living space. Divided into various zones, this area extends to the kitchen entrance. The dining table is located here, while a sectional in the middle of the space exudes coziness.

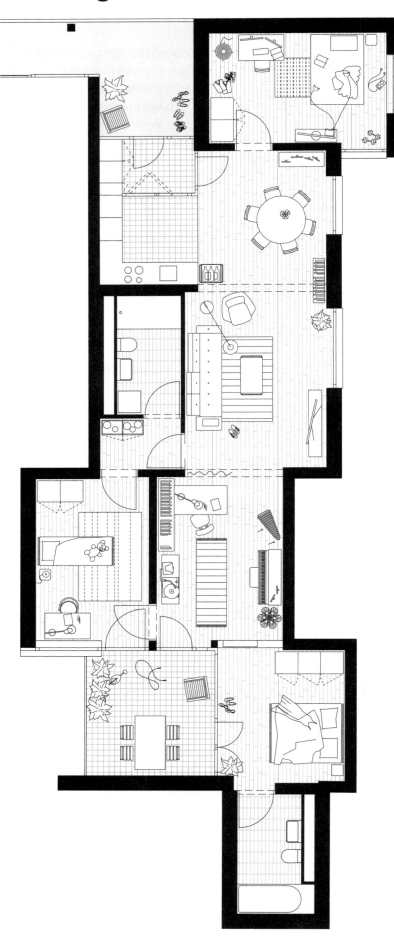

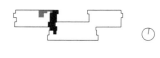

3.10.18 "Fred vom Jupiter"

2020
2.5-rooms
61 m²

Lüdin Site Development
→ 2.5.3

A split-level connective design solves the issue of limited privacy that usually comes from outside corridors. Passing by the neighboring apartment located on a higher level, you arrive at a naturally lit entrance that leads into a living and dining room divided into two areas. The kitchen faces the street, while the living area benefits from the protection and tranquility offered by the loggia. Guests can directly access the bathroom, which is also connected to the bedroom.

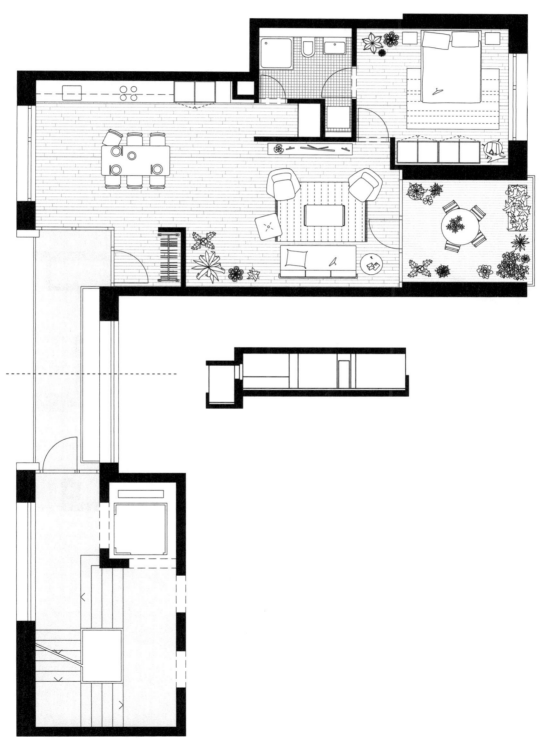

Form Follows Law

3.10.19 "Smells Like Teen Spirit"

2021
3.5-rooms
89 m²
Roswiesen-/
Winterthurerstrasse
Development
→ 2.5.8

A spacious entrance area provides storage space for shoes and coats. But it also represents an upscale style of living, and functions as an area from which people can easily move around the apartment. From here, you can reach a kitchen with cockpit-like qualities, which also offers a solution to noise issues. The recessed bedroom lies on the quiet side of the building and is directly connected to the bathroom, as is another room that adjoins the balcony. The large dining table sits snugly in a corner of the living room.

3.10.20 "Because the Night"

2021
3.5-rooms
91 m²

Roswiesen-/
Winterthurerstrasse
Development
→ 2.5.8

This design is highly compact while also complying with strict building codes. All rooms that should be kept quieter have windows that open on the side furthest from noise. At the same time, the street side has a befitting facade, with kitchens and enclosed balconies bringing everyday life into the public space. The bend at the end of the living area creates space for the bedrooms, which cluster around the quiet balcony. The hall distributes between the different rooms, while also minimizing circulation space. Despite its compact layout, the apartment exudes comfort and personality.

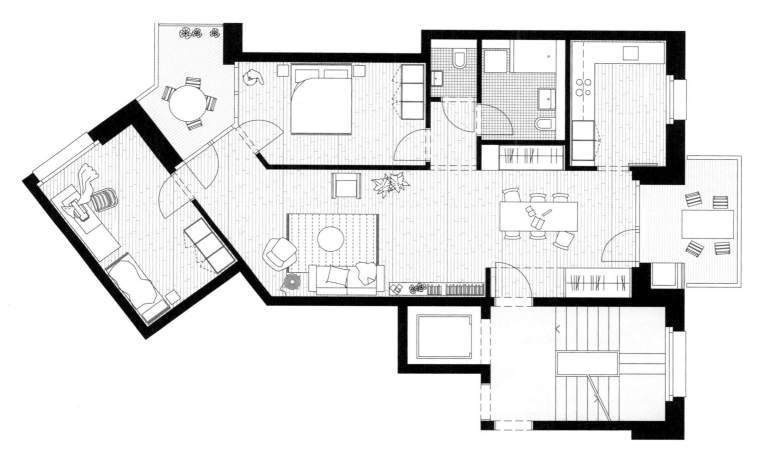

Form Follows Law

Building regulations belong in our designs, projects, and buildings just as the indispensable basics belong in cooking. Similar to the way we cook spaghetti al dente for all our pasta dishes, we study the building codes and work with their conditions, always with the intention of applying the set requirements in ways that optimize the floor plan. Getting pesto sauce right also depends on the small preparatory details.

Spaghetti with Pesto

Recipe taken from Marcella Hazan, The Classic Italian Cook Book, New York City 1973

Serves six

Ingerients
100 g fresh basil leaves
8 tablespoons good olive oil
45 g butter, room temperature
2 tablespoons pine nuts
2 garlic cloves
Coarse sea salt
50 g freshly grated Parmigiano Reggiano
2 tablespoons freshly grated Pecorino Romano
600 g spaghetti

Method
1. Lightly crush the garlic with a knife so that it bursts and the peel comes off. Remove the peel.
2. Briefly immerse the basil in cold water. Then wash and pat dry carefully and thoroughly with paper towel.
3. Place the basil leaves, olive oil, pine nuts, garlic, and a large pinch of sea salt in a large mortar. Crush the ingredients into a paste.
4. Stir in the grated cheeses by hand.
5. Pour in the olive oil in a very thin stream and stir it into the mixture with a wooden spoon.
6. When all the olive oil has been used, add the butter with a wooden spoon and spread evenly.
7. Cook the spaghetti in a pot of boiling water until al dente, drain, mix with the pesto, and dilute with one or two tablespoons of the hot pasta water.
8. Stir well and serve.

3.11 Compact and Affordable

Our apartments have to be compact, sustainable, and above all, affordable. These are our three basic conditions for every contract. We work to achieve these goals and search for solutions that have a positive impact on the environment, the economy, and ultimately, on rents.

With every design, on every construction site, we continue to learn. Strategic, design-based decisions, such as omitting certain functions, reducing spaces, or optimizing connections to stairwells and elevators, are the most successful. A clear structural plan with optimal spans and a direct transference of forces, positioning bathrooms on top of each other, and a straightforward concept for service conduits help to reduce costs. Repetition and prefabrication are further methods for cutting building costs.

3.11.1 Is This Where You Live?

2010
4.5-rooms
95 m²

Bombach Development
→ 2.3.3

This apartment thrives on the reduction of means. Starting in the entrance area, the floor plan develops a spatial shape that extends to the combined kitchen and living area and the balcony, laying a varied path through the apartment. Every corner, every wall can be furnished, and the doors are cleverly positioned. Even though every inch of floorspace has been used, there is a feeling of spaciousness, and the diagonal arrangement of the rooms provides an additional visual flourish.

3.11.2 Through the Center and Away

2011
4.5-rooms
109 m²
Brüderhofweg
Development
→ 2.3.9

Between the entrance and the bedrooms, the living space stretches through the building to the kitchen, which, together with the dining area, embraces the balcony. The visual extension of the living room through the kitchen beyond it belies the compact nature of the floor plan. Furniture can be added to any area, which contributes to the feeling of spaciousness. In addition, the corner window in the living room is carefully positioned in relation to the seating area, providing a diagonal view of the outside.

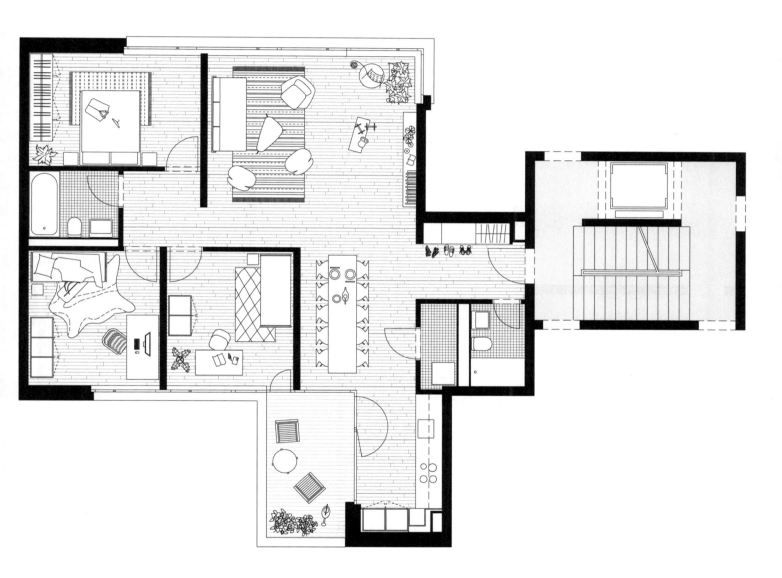

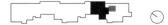

Compact and Affordable 217

3.11.3 "French Kiss"

2011
4.5-rooms
124 m²

Brüderhofweg
Development
→ 2.3.9

Proof that a living space can be interesting even when little space is available. A lateral offset divides the living area, creating a diagonal space that runs from the corner window to the outdoor corridor. The corner kitchen lets the gaze roam freely while keeping the kitchen space separate. Bedrooms are distributed throughout the plan, spanning two private poles. At the entrance is the parents' room with private bathroom, while children can reign supreme in their rooms at the other end of the apartment.

3.11.4 "Rock Around the Clock"

2012
3.5-rooms
92 m²

Schweighof
Development
→ 2.3.11

Here, the rooms are arranged in an enfilade around a central core. The living area and eat-in kitchen with loggia form a right angle. In this way, they define two distinct areas, ensure orientation on both sides, and allow daylight to penetrate through the apartment. Why place the bedrooms in the corners? To save space! This reduces circulation areas to the absolute minimum; only the entrance is separate, the rest is living space.

Compact and Affordable

3.11.5 "The Sorrows of Young Werther"

2012
Studio
24 m²

Binz 111
Apartment Blocks
→ 2.3.14

The staircase is protagonist here; since the living area is so compact, the connective elements have to compensate for the lack of space. Multiplying this spatial unit creates a building with a continuous gridded structure, which is what makes it possible for the "Goethe staircase" to pierce diagonally through the building in the first place. This high degree of repetition in turn enables components to be prefabricated and reduces costs, making it cheaper for students to live comfortably in the expensive city of Zurich.

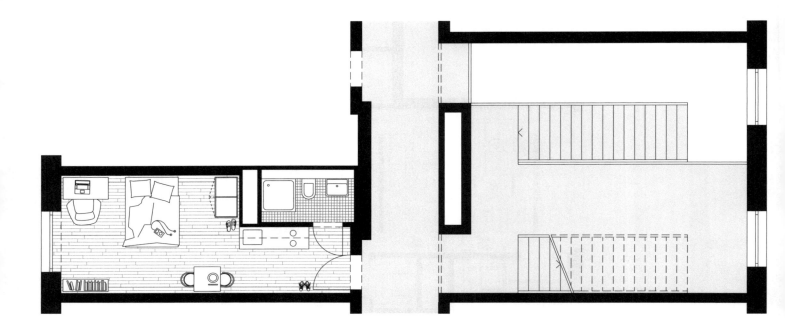

3.11.6 My First Apartment

2012
Studio
26 m²

Binz 111
Apartment Blocks
→ 2.3.14

The studios line up along the covered walkway, forming a vibrant neighborhood along its margin. The walkway itself provides the kitchens with light and encourages encounters between the residents. Hidden from prying eyes, the sleeping alcove lies behind the bathroom that forms the apartment's core. If you've had enough community, simply draw the curtain across the kitchen window. If need be, lone wolves can hang a poster of their favorite band against the panes. I wonder who lives behind the photo of Iggy Pop?

 ## Fake Hippies and Other Idle Contemporaries

Emil isn't one to deny himself life's pleasures. After completing high school and qualifying for university, he spent—or wasted, according to one's point of view—most of his time partying and traveling the world.

Until his despairing parents gave him the choice: either back to school or it's game over—in other words, his allowance will be completely cut off.

So now he sits in his small—but still quite decent—studio, with his own kitchen alcove and bathroom, ruminating on life. His mechanical engineering courses at ETH Zurich are just a pretense to buy him some time; he's really more interested in the fine arts, but his old man is always getting on his case, giving him an earful about "starving artists" and "all that's for hippies and other losers."

So it's just fine by Emil that his neighbors, from all over the world, often come to visit and share his sorrows. His little kitchen table has already seen some raucous evenings bingeing Japanese rice wine or Greek mastika liqueur!

Compact and Affordable 221

3.11.7 "Happy Together"

2012
7.5-rooms
172 m²

**Binz 111
Apartment Blocks**
→ 2.3.14

A shared apartment spanning two floors offers an advantage in that communal spaces are separate to the bedrooms. After all, who wants to stumble through their roommate's party in their pajamas to get to the bathroom? Still, one bedroom is located on the entrance level to ensure the apartment is wheelchair accessible. The living area is also located in the corner and is separate from the kitchen, so that parallel activities are possible.

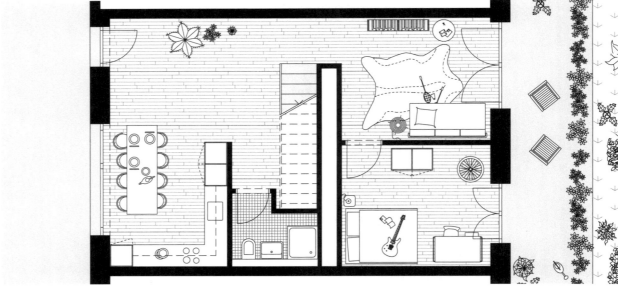

222

3.11.8 "Bend It Like Beckham"

2013
3.5-rooms
82 m²

Kleeweidstrasse Development
→ 2.3.16

Being economical with circulation areas enables an apartment to be compact, and a direct traffic pattern from room to room reduces unnecessary corridor areas. Here, a diagonal helps out once again, visually enlarging narrow floor plans in a Euclidian manner. Right angles usually offer the most efficient solution to spatial problems. So the sloping walls here are a means to an end rather than simply formalist: they open up the L-shaped living space from one facade to another, making it seem larger.

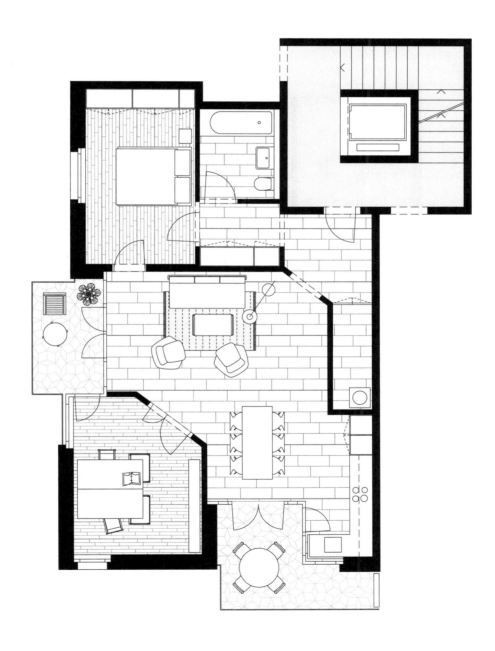

Compact and Affordable   223

3.11.9 "So weit die Füsse tragen"

2014
5.5-rooms
113 m²

Am Rietpark Apartment Block
→ 2.3.19

A quite rare example of a hallway apartment that is able to wrangle unique qualities out of a demanding concept. The corridor begins in the bay of the apartment entrance, leads past the bedrooms towards the daylight, flows into the living room, and finally ends in a room that functions as an extension of the living room. The kitchen joins in with this cellular system, extending the living space to the far side via a floor-to-ceiling double door.

224

3.11.10 "Pump up the Volume"

2015
5.5-rooms
101 m²
Lauriedhofweg
Development
→ 2.3.20

Low-cost apartments with pre-specified dimensions were requested for this development. The key was to radically reduce the number of connective elements while increasing the number of rooms for the same floor space. Doing so allowed us to turn a three-and-a-half room apartment into a four-and-a-half room apartment. The kitchen and living area is just big enough to accommodate all the essentials. The bathroom docks directly onto the living room via a hallway, as do the bedrooms, with their doors precisely positioned to offer enough privacy.

Compact and Affordable   225

3.11.11 "Dream Baby Dream"

2015
2.5-rooms
55 m²
Lauriedhofweg
Development
→ 2.3.20

Ultra-compact, yet spacious: the conservatory, kitchen and living area, and balcony are arranged in a row, conveying a surprising degree of spaciousness without actually taking up too much of the living space. The winter garden creates a buffer, offering space to design the transition area between the apartment and the covered walkway. With abundant greenery, the inhabitant lives in a forest behind a veil of green that controls the view. The bedroom is well hidden and can be accessed through a small anteroom.

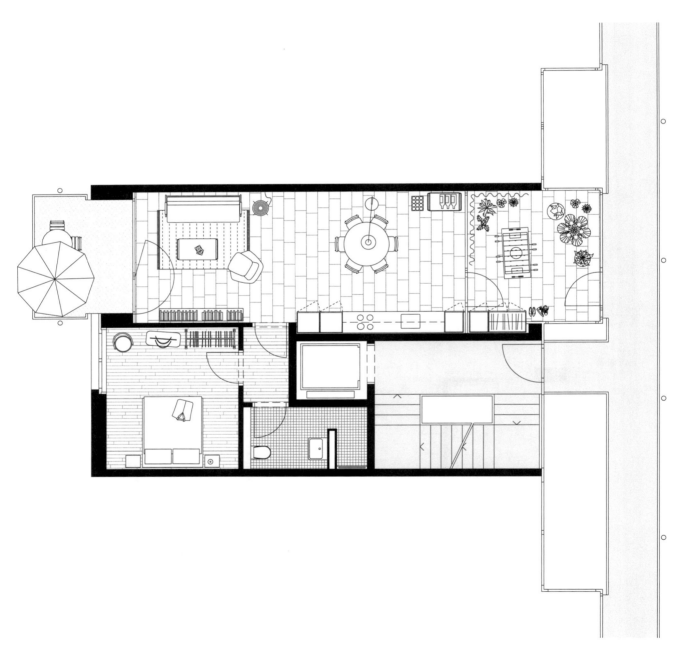

3.11.12 "Walk the Line"

2015
4.5-rooms
101 m²

Parkside
Apartment Block,
Saurer WerkZwei
→ 2.3.21

Buildings where elements are connected efficiently offer an ideal basis for cost-effective residential construction. The challenge lies in the interior areas of the building, those areas between the stairwell and the light-giving facade that the floor plan has to negotiate. Here, one's view moves from the entrance over the entire apartment length to the outside. Curved around the corner room, the living and dining area shortens the distance and adds to the living space. The corner room can also serve as an extension of the living room, or an additional bedroom.

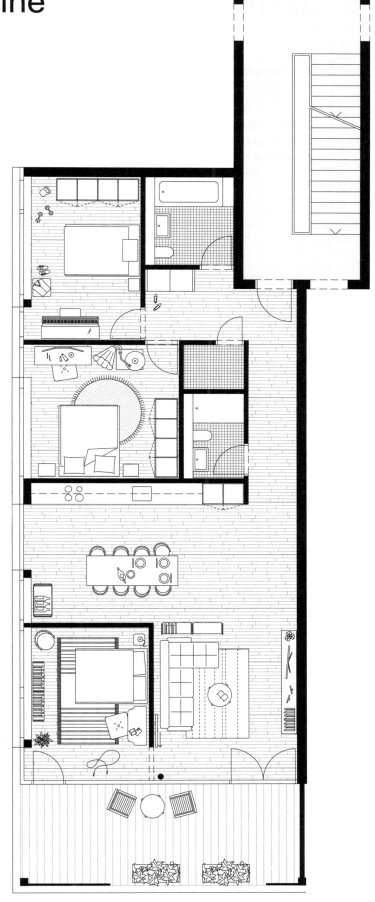

Compact and Affordable 227

3.11.13 Trim and Terrific

2018
4.5-rooms
87 m²

**Hirtenweg
Development**
→ 2.4.7

The incredible simplicity and snappy efficiency of this floor plan arose from radically streamlining the body of the building. Connective elements and balconies are attached as satellites, enabling a compact arrangement of the space: while the centrally located kitchen and living area also functions as a divider. The bathroom, guest bath, and storage closet form an entity together with the entrance. The bedroom doors are arranged to provide sufficient privacy and ensure that there is space to add furniture to the living room.

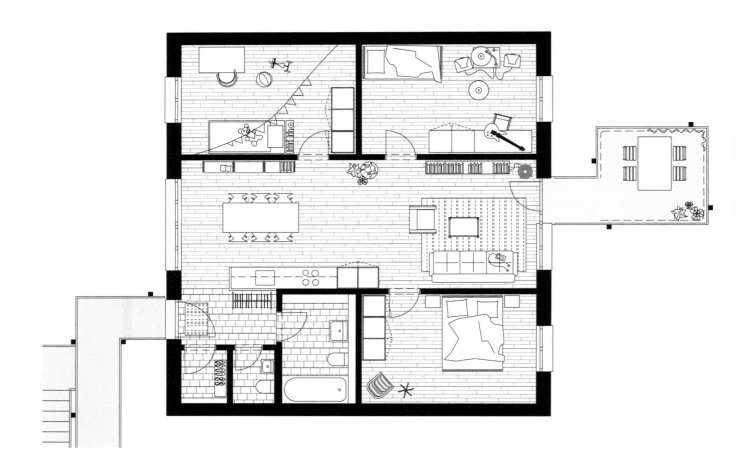

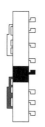

3.11.14　　Hirtenweg Development – 2018 – 4.5-rooms – 87 m²
→ 2.4.7

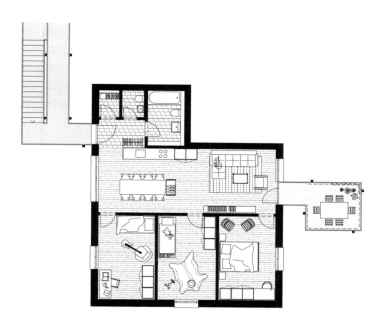

3.11.15　　Hirtenweg Development – 2018 – 2.5-rooms – 55 m²
→ 2.4.7

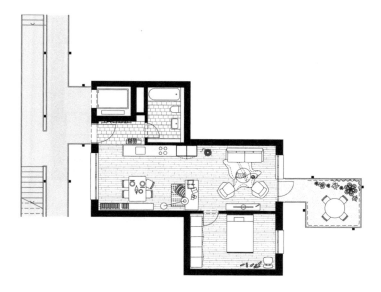

Compact and Affordable　　229

3.11.16 Blood Red Shoes

2018
3.5-rooms
76 m²

Sandacker
Apartment Blocks
→ 2.4.8

Even though the plan maximizes space, this apartment features all the hallmarks of sophisticated residential construction. The spacious entrance with storage closet offers plenty of room for people to take off their shoes. Moving out from here, the living area is split into two zones to accommodate the dining table and a sectional sofa. The kitchen is situated in the corner and has access to both zones. A door leads directly from the kitchen to the loggia—a little, yet luxurious extra touch.

230

3.11.17 "Tom's Diner"

2018
4.5-rooms
101 m²
Sandacker Apartment Blocks
→ 2.4.8

A corridor-based plan with a circular design. The entrance offers lots of space for putting down your things when you get in the door. A floor-to-ceiling twin door draws daylight into the entrance area, casually conjuring up a dignified sense of luxury within a compact floor plan. The short corridor leads to the living room, which unfurls out on two sides and is dominated by an open, L-shaped kitchen. From here, the viewer's gaze moves through the living area and out to the balcony.

Compact and Affordable

3.11.18 "Space Is the Place"

2019
2.5-rooms
63 m²

Alte Landstrasse
Development
→ 2.4.10

This building with multiple apartments on each floor is a space machine streamlined for performance: requiring just one elevator for well over thirty residences. One impressive side effect is the exciting way in which areas are connected. Although space in the apartment has been maximized, a stairwell with light-flooded areas and curved sets of steps ushers in an opulent living atmosphere. Within the apartment itself, the idea of circular flow and diagonal views holds sway. The latter particularly benefits the dining table in its position in the jutty-like transition between the building corner and balcony.

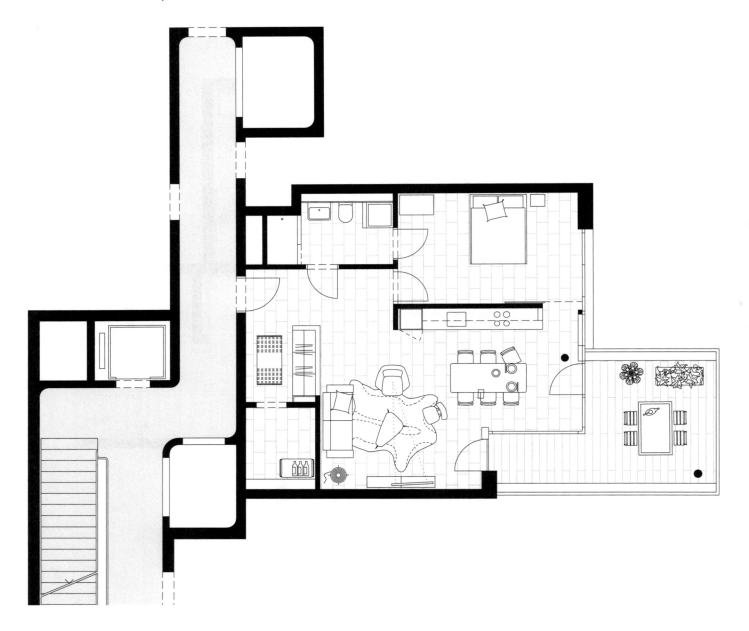

3.11.19 "Schmidtchen Schleicher"

2019
4.5-rooms
98 m²
Alte Landstrasse
Development
→ 2.4.10

The bathroom functions as a passageway, giving guests discreet access to the toilet from the entrance area, with more direct access available from the bedrooms on the other side. This efficient use of space and the skillful design of the living room brings spaciousness to the compact plan without the need for additional floor space. The curved balcony extends the kitchen outside, and a snug corner provides room for a couch.

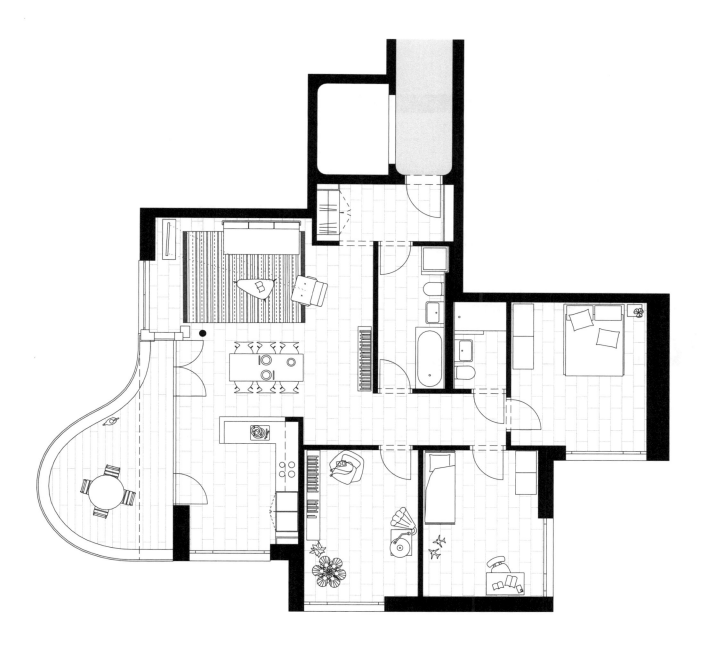

Compact and Affordable 233

3.11.20 Hell's Kitchen

2019
3.5-rooms
67 m²
Stelzen
Apartment Blocks
→ 2.4.13

A complex position in the corner of the building provides the plan with its own separate focus, using the tight space available to its advantage. The kitchen, dining area, and living space are divided into a cellular layout, which cascade diagonally toward the stairwell along with the bedroom with private bathroom. The second bedroom occupies the corner, which does away with the need for additional connective areas.

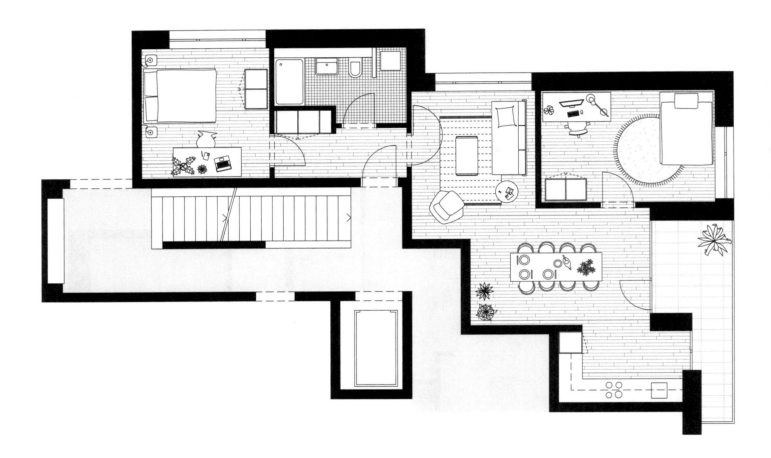

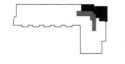

3.11.21   Langgrüthof Apartment Block – 2020 – 4.5-rooms – 105 m²
→ 2.5.5

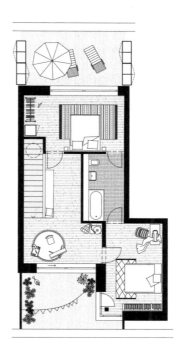
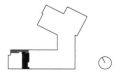

Compact and Affordable   235

On a trip to Rome, Michael ate this classic of Roman cuisine every day—sometimes twice a day. Since then, he has been perfecting this simple dish and its preparation. Is the pepper briefly heated in olive oil before being crushed? When is the cheese mixture added and how much pasta water is needed to make a creamy sauce that evenly coats all the spaghetti? Careful craftsmanship is also important when designing homes!

Spaghetti Cacio e Pepe

Recipe taken from Richard Kägi, Kägi kocht, Baden 2020

Serves four to six

Ingredients
2–3 tablespoons black pepper, coarsely crushed in a mortar
400 g spaghetti
4 tablespoons olive oil
160 g freshly grated Pecorino Romano

Method
1. Cook the spaghetti in boiling water until al dente.
2. Coarsely grind the peppercorns
3. Heat the olive oil in a large saucepan (where the spaghetti can also fit), add the ground pepper, and stir in the oil for about thirty seconds until the scent of the pepper comes out of the saucepan.
4. Add about 150 ml of pasta water and bring to a simmer. Stir well. Turn off the heat.
5. Stir in the pre-cooked spaghetti and three quarters of the grated cheese, stirring until the cheese melts and a creamy sauce is formed.
6. Add a little more pasta water (about 60 ml), add the remaining Pecorino and season with plenty of black pepper.
7. Serve immediately.

3.12 Bespoke Apartments

We take advantage of the requirements set for the optimal design and development of a site to create specific apartments—by which we mean ones that offer something unique. Particularly for housing developments with similar floor plans, such apartments constitute the cherry on the Black Forest cake.

Housing construction is like figure skating: compulsory figures are one thing, freestyle's another. It gives us great pleasure to design dwellings, large or small, deep and narrow or with extra-high ceilings, that capitalize on their particular location or distinctive function.

3.12.1 "Eat the Rich"

2001
3.5-rooms
101 m²
James Development
→ 2.2.2

What kind of life do urban nomads look for in a high-rise? One answer is openness, making the view come alive everywhere and consolidating the plan into a single flowing space. The kitchen is placed prominently in the center, a show kitchen with an extra-large work area. A sliding wall and two floor-to-ceiling doors to the bedroom allow for a maximally open configuration. Even the bathroom is a continuation of the space, facilitating a direct flow from entryway to study.

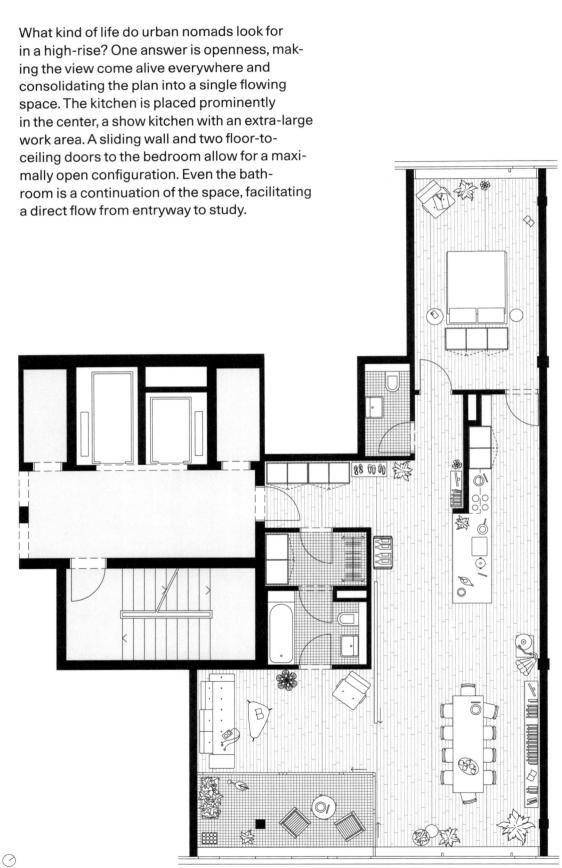

3.12.2 "La Cage aux Folles"

2001
6.5-rooms
187 m²

James Development
→ 2.2.2

An apartment shared among roommates places particular demands on a plan. Areas of private retreat are just as important as spaces for communal activities. The large kitchen, with a long table from the secondhand shop, can be shut off from the living area by a sliding door. The shared workspace is similarly separated from the living area by a floor-to-ceiling double door. When work is over, opening this door creates a spatial connection that brings light into the apartment from both sides.

Bespoke Apartments

3.12.3 "Jetzt musst du springen"

2004
4.5-rooms
109 m²

Birnbäumen
Apartment Blocks
(Building site 1)
→ 2.2.4

One cannot but savor this unique hillside location with its view of the valley floor. The living areas shoot out of the building like fingers, offering a sublime extended window facade facing the northern view. Direct sunlight from the south graces the living area, which culminates in the large balcony. The spacious entry hall underscores the tasteful comfort of this sophisticated residence.

All That Matters Is the Wife and Kids Are Happy

"A springboard to sunlight" is what Mara calls her new apartment, with its sweeping living room projecting outward and its fantastic balcony, which faces three directions, opening up a magnificent view of the landscape.

Her husband Julian is less impassioned; he contents himself with a "Well, not too bad," as befits his British reserve. Privately, he appreciates the comfort and convenience of the apartment, with its beautiful big entry hall, two bathrooms, and open kitchen, where you can enjoy the spectacular view and watch the sun go down while chopping the vegetables.

He was originally inclined to be rather skeptical; he'd grown quite fond of the apartment they'd been forced to leave in a beautiful old building. Of course, it helps that their daughter is "insanely stoked" with the new "joint," since she finally has space in her room for her grandmother's sewing machine, which she can spend hours working at.

Their youngest, for his part, is still gloating over his big coup. He got the room with the nicest view, by making such an awful fuss when it came to assigning the bedrooms, until it was too much for his parents and they relocated to the back.

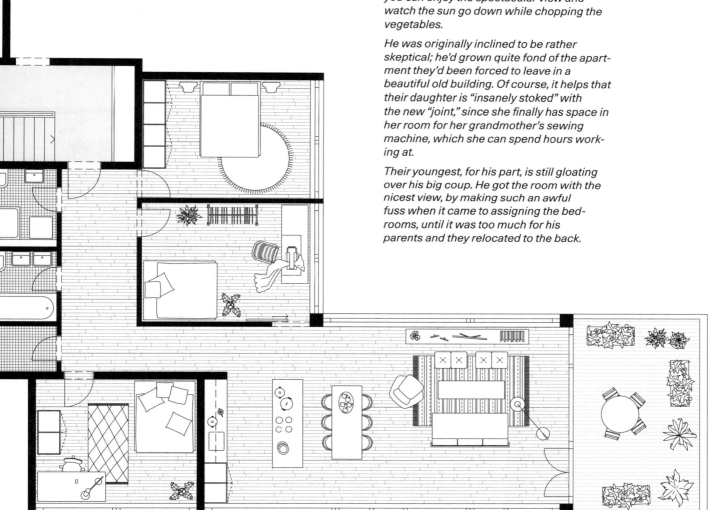

Bespoke Apartments

3.12.4 "Noblesse oblige"

2004
5-rooms
165 m²

Im Forster
Apartment Blocks
→ 2.2.5

Residential pier, version two: Once again, the goal is to encapsulate the advantages of the hillside location in a unique floor plan idea. The opulent foyer, flanked by floor-to-ceiling double doors, stages the path to the living area where, through the panorama window, the eye roams into the distance. At the end of the living area is a satellite bedroom with dressing room and bath. The balcony obtains the generous dimensions of a rooftop terrace, offering enough space for a large company of illustrious guests.

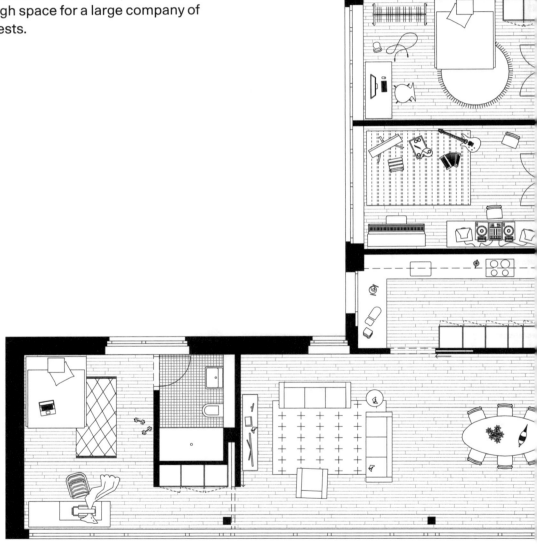

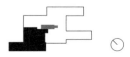

244

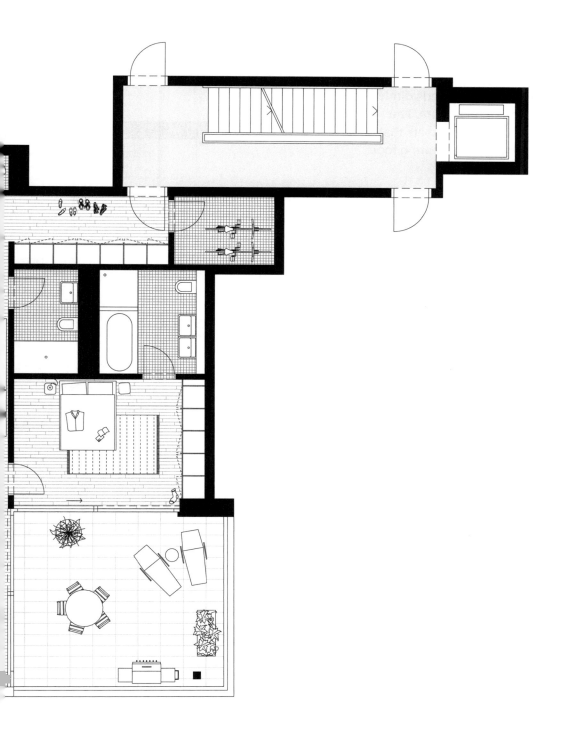

Bespoke Apartments 245

3.12.5 "A River Runs Through It"

2004
3.5-rooms
120 m²

Im Forster
Apartment Blocks
→ 2.2.5

Entry into the apartment is spread over a number of stages. The first occurs between the stairway and an alcove used for arrival and the shedding of shoes and jackets. Following this is a spacious hallway, used primarily to express the individuality of the inhabitants. A precious Japanese vase stands dimly lit; next to it hangs a tasteful picture. The prestigious open kitchen suggests that cooking here is more than just preparing food.

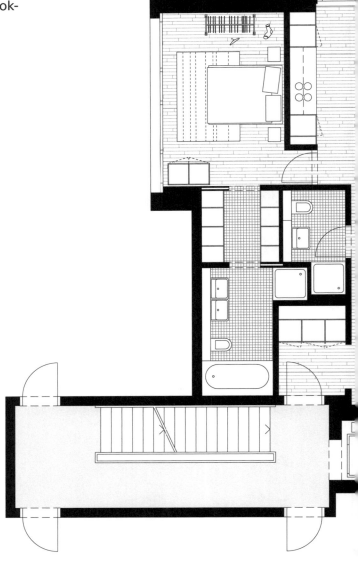

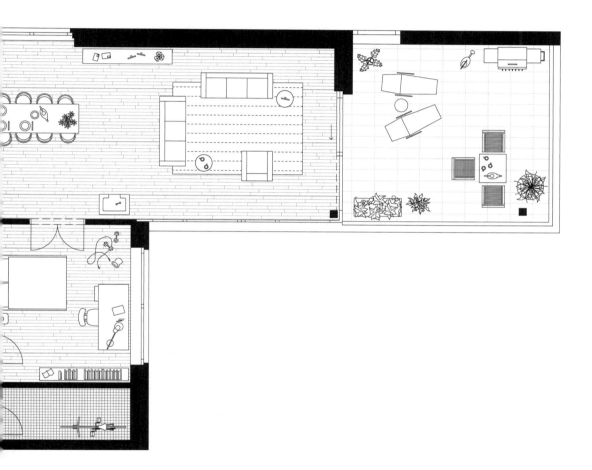

Bespoke Apartments 247

3.12.6 "Am Anfang war das Feuer"

2004
6-rooms
192 m²

Imbisbühlstrasse
Apartment Block
Study commission
→ 2.2.6

An unconventional layout gives this apartment life: The three-and-a-half-meter-high living hall moves into the center, while the connection to outdoor space unfolds indirectly via an elevated balcony that directs the eye toward the heavens. The surrounding rooms can be utilized as extensions of the space. The kitchen, situated in a narrow branching side space, joins with the facade and brings light into the hall. The design concept breaks a taboo, challenging established floor plan models and introducing new perspectives on apartment design.

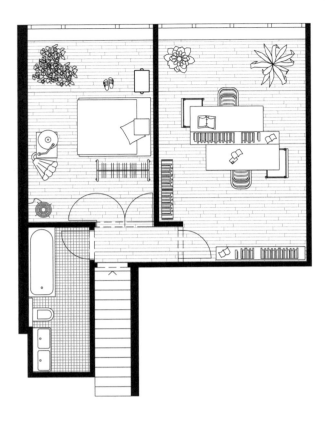

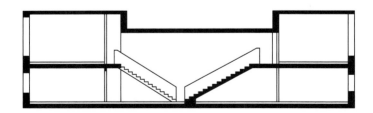

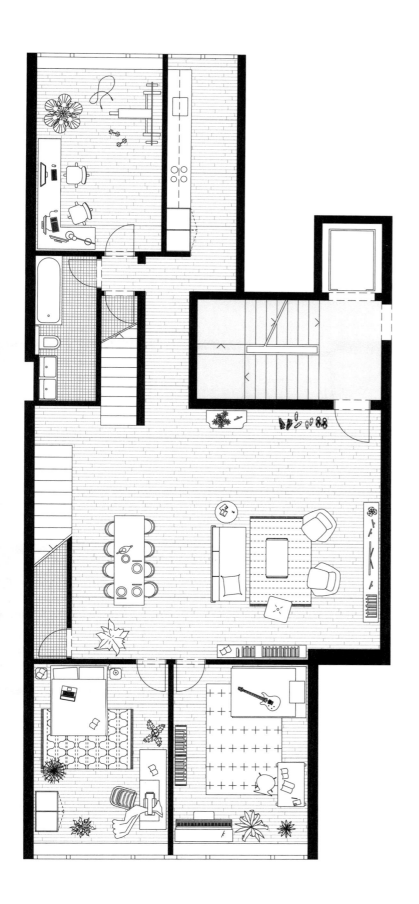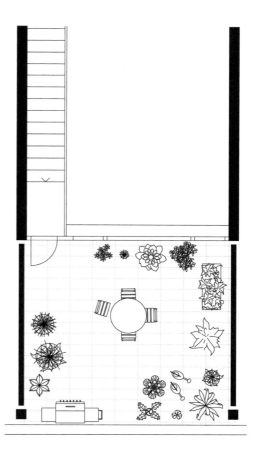

Bespoke Apartments 249

3.12.7 "It's a Long Way to the Top"

2004
5.5-rooms
187 m²
Imbisbühlstrasse
Apartment Block
Study commission
→ 2.2.6

A blueprint for an indirectly lit living hall, taken to the extreme. No wonder the built project is rather less bold than this preliminary sketch. The explosive power of the space lies in its layout: The living hall is placed between a balcony that has been shifted aloft and a bedroom tower with bath permeated by muted side lighting. The kitchen lies hidden in a spatial extension. The audacious design draws on precedents proving that precisely directed light can evoke a protective, almost devotional atmosphere. In a chiaroscuro-like approach, light adds shading to the space, enhancing its vivid quality.

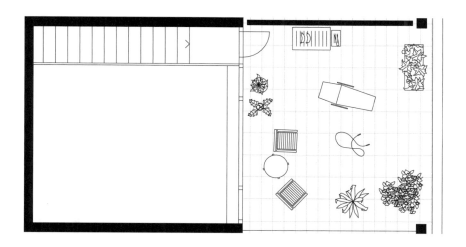
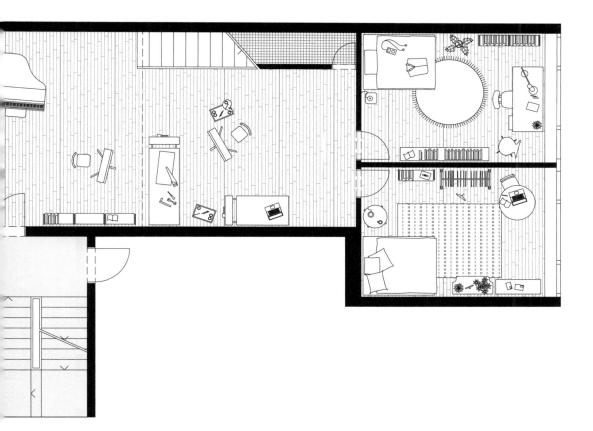

Bespoke Apartments 251

3.12.8 Greenland

2007
5.5-rooms
130 m²

Brünnen
Development
(Building site 11)
→ 2.2.11

The living area projects out like a diving platform into open space, further lengthened by the expansive balcony. The kitchen and dining area benefit from the expressive shape of the space, which can be seen in the curtained glass facade. In contrast, the row of bedrooms on the quiet side of the building is sheltered by a connecting room. The spacious entryway centers the plan. A shared room, accessible directly from the stairwell, can be put to many possible uses.

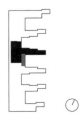

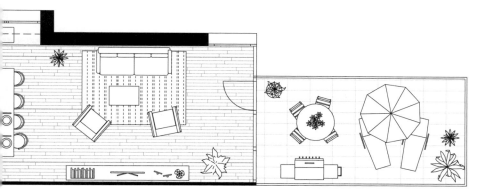

Bespoke Apartments

3.12.9 "Zehn kleine Jägermeister"

2011
2.5-rooms
115 m²

Meisenrain Studios
→ 2.3.7

Studio apartments are widespread in Gockhausen and make a big contribution to the vibrant mood in this small suburban community. This cluster of studio apartments, spanning the space between two shear walls and allowing individualized modifications, follow this tradition. The quality is in the design: different levels staggered at half- and full-story heights open up a unique atmosphere, enhanced by the stepped ceiling shape and skylights. Each unit can be accessed through a patio that makes the setting for each of the apartments in this collective development feel intimate.

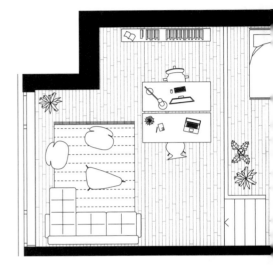

Separate Rooms Are for Squares!

Natalie is thrilled with her new home, composed of a single large space partitioned only by an elevated area for the living room suite and double desks. The bed is secluded in an alcove behind the bathroom block, the only place in the apartment closed off by doors.

Hold on, that's not completely true, Natalie would interject here; there's a staircase leading into the den in the basement, which is lit by a shaft and serves as a secret hideaway. This is where her life partner paints to his heart's content while listening to his favorite album, "London Calling" by The Clash, on full volume in an endless loop. Luckily, no one else knows!

The couple finds the little walled-in inner courtyard particularly charming; serving both as a garden and an extension of the living area, it is also the way to enter the apartment, walking past the billowing tide of plants!

254

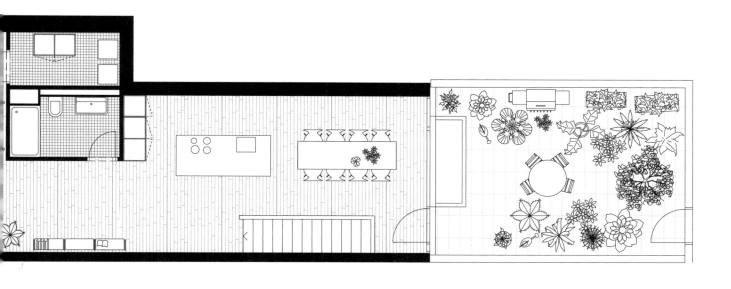
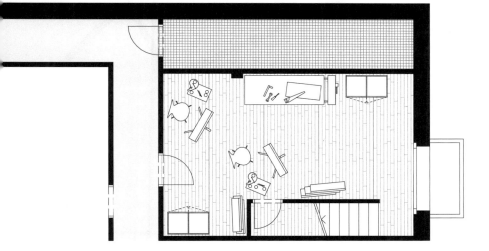

Bespoke Apartments 255

3.12.10 Don't Open the Door to Strangers

2013
3.5-rooms
136 m²

Zollstrasse Ost
Development
→ 2.3.17

The combination of residential and work spaces is a time-tested recipe for ground floors in the city. Widespread in London and New York, yet mostly unknown in our latitudes, the activated basement level shows its potential as atelier space. The apartment lies on the raised ground floor; a staircase leads into the sunken atelier, which receives daylight thanks to high windows. Passersby are greeted with a multifaceted view: from street level, the eye is directed both upwards and down.

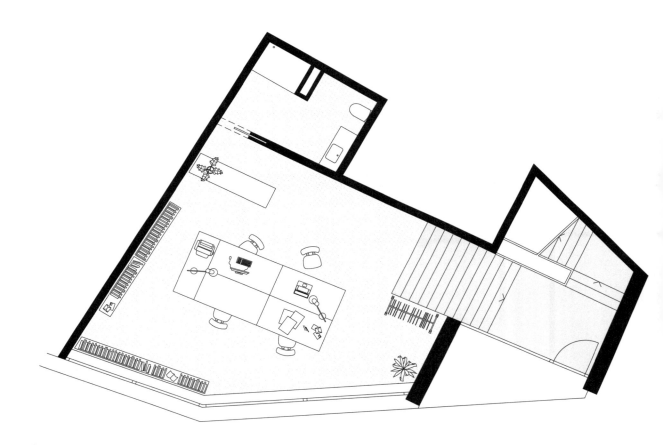

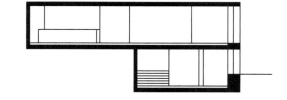

256

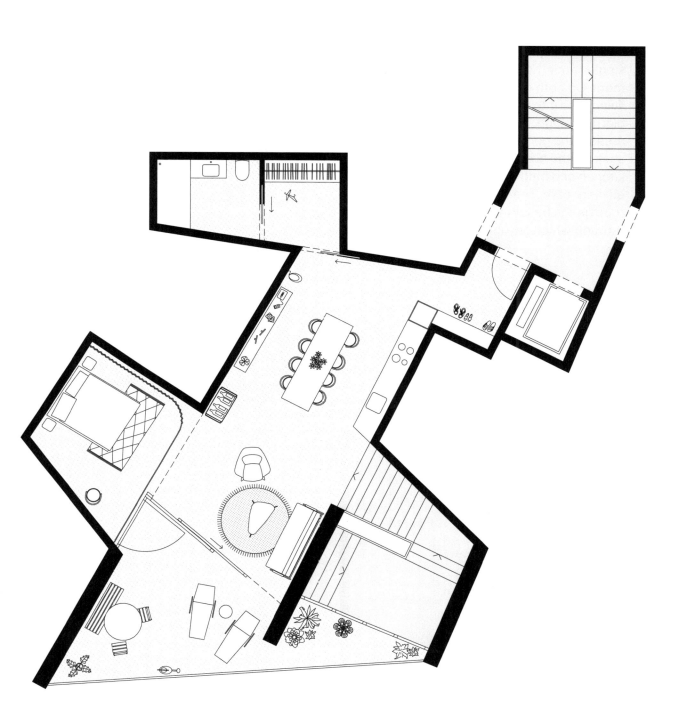

Bespoke Apartments 257

3.12.11 "Coming Home for Christmas"

2018
2.5-rooms
53 m²

Tiny Homes
Forchstrasse
→ 2.4.6

The name says it all: the advantages of a single-family house fit into a compact apartment. On both ends, patios expand the living area into the outdoors and extend the plan's footage. The larger of the outdoor areas is the garden substitute; the smaller shelters the bedroom. In the center, the kitchen and bathroom together constitute an efficient core. There is even a recreation room in the basement, accessed by a staircase through which daylight enters.

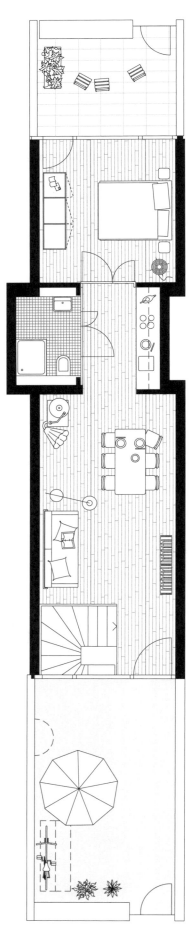

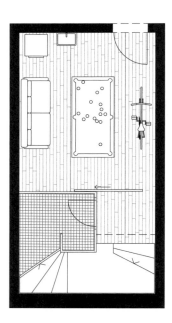

3.12.12 "Subterranean Homesick Blues"

2019
3.5-rooms
64.1 m²
Stelzen
Apartment Blocks
→ 2.4.13

Commercial spaces in peripheral areas can be hard to rent out. That's why the public floor at street level is linked to the apartment above. This way, the footage can be used as commercial or atelier space and the public area enlivened. The spiral staircase is situated so that daylight falls into the back of the atelier from above. The entrance into the apartment leads through a small patio, which brings light into the center and creates a snug atmosphere.

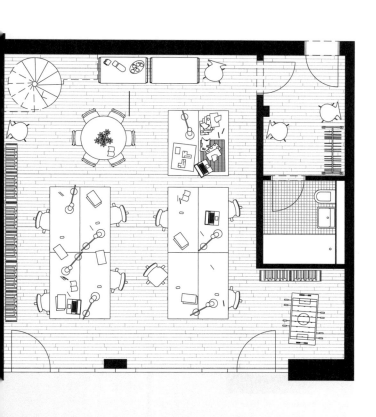
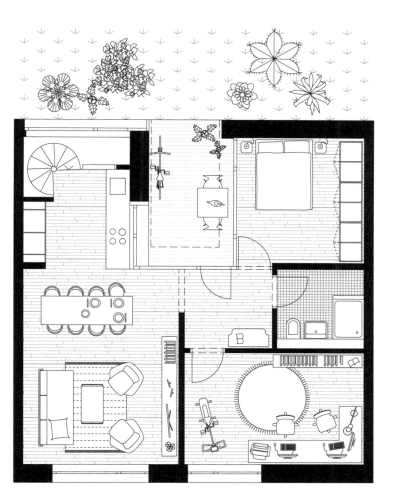
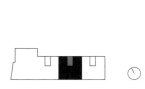
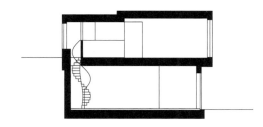

Bespoke Apartments 259

3.12.13 "Don't Look Back in Anger"

2019
2.5-rooms
47 m²

Stelzen Apartment Blocks
→ 2.4.13

Facing south toward the view, a covered walkway connects a row of small apartments on the top floor. This unusual starting position determines the floor plan, which interprets the outdoor space as entrance patio and private sitting area all at once. The recess shields the apartment from the walkway and orients the space inward. The kitchen serves as social condenser, enabling interface as needed between the communal space and the apartment.

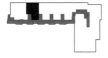

3.12.14 "Get the Party Started"

2020
6.5-rooms
178 m²
Webergut Conversion
→ 2.5.4

The plan of this shared apartment offers a simple yet effective solution to the need for both community and the option to withdraw. A row of bathrooms divides the apartment into two areas, shielding the bedrooms from the living area. A discreet shortcut permits quick access from the entryway to the bedrooms—a welcome way to avoid a noisy party without falling into the clutches of tipsy guests.

Bespoke Apartments 261

3.12.15 "The Lives of Others"

2020
7.5-rooms
213 m²

Webergut Conversion
→ 2.5.4

Two friendly couples, each with many kids, wish to share an apartment with a large living hall and communal kitchen. Nevertheless—or perhaps just for that reason—possibilities for withdrawing into privacy are extremely important for the inhabitants' mental state and social climate. Thus was born a sort of Russian-doll design, with two autonomous units within a single large apartment. A locker-room concept, with partitioned shower stalls and toilets, solves the problem of the morning bathroom rush hour.

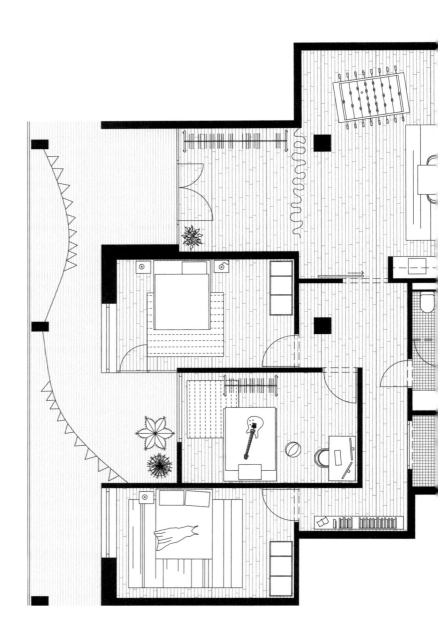

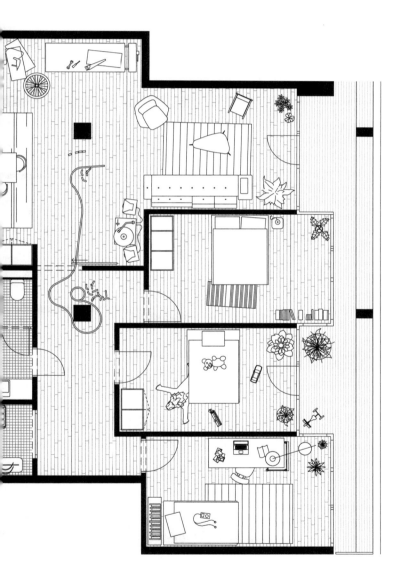

 Just Wait till the Kids Get Older!

The Gonzalez and Pantelic families, each with two children, met through the participatory apartment allocation process and came to like each other. They even had a say in the floor plan for this conversion project, shaping the communal apartment largely according to their wishes.

The idea of an apartment inside an apartment is particularly ingenious. Both families have a private area with their own separate entrance to the bathroom, which is outfitted with stalls like a gym locker room. This system stands the tests of the morning rush hour, when the place sees a lot of action. The door between the bathroom areas is open for now, "but just wait till the two girls are older and want their privacy in the bathroom," as Frau Pantelic is apt to warn whoever's around.

Okay, well then we'll just renovate, is the response of both men. In any case, the clincher is the huge living hall with its long dining table and motley assortment of furniture from secondhand stores in the neighborhood. A party atmosphere prevails here on weekends, since both families like to invite friends and neighbors over to share in the abundant free-spiritedness of their newfound lifestyle.

Bespoke Apartments 263

3.12.16 Jamie Oliver Kitchen

2020
4.5-rooms
221 m²

Langgrüthof
Apartment Block
→ 2.5.5

Cooking is the owner's passion, and on a grand scale! The direct entrance from the stairway testifies to lavish catered dinner parties. The dining hall is located on the lower level, with a ceiling height of over three meters. In contrast to the spacious opulence of the living areas, the bedrooms are grouped closely together and connected through serpentine hidden pathways. Behind the curtain of the impressive public spaces, a compartmentalized, private realm of life lies hidden.

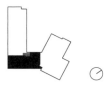

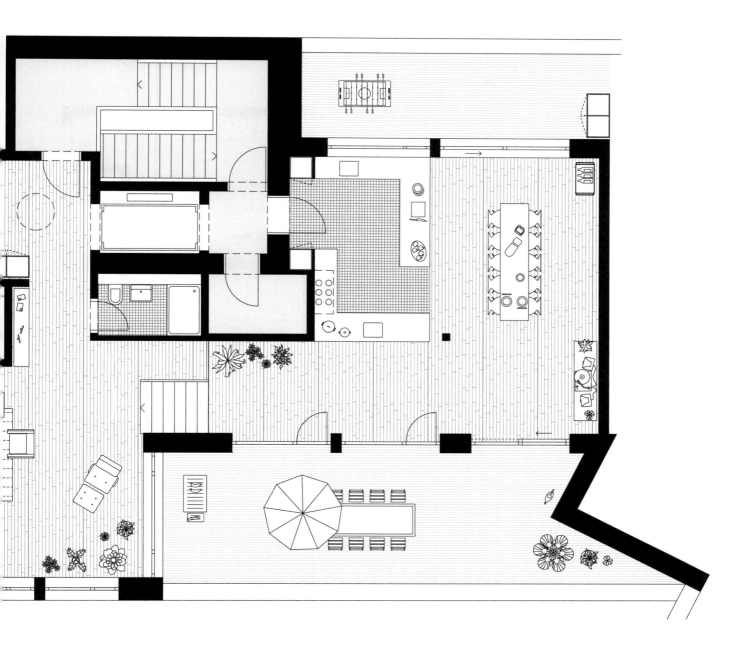

3.12.17 "Motorcycle Emptiness"

2020
4.5-rooms
226 m²

Langgrüthof
Apartment Block
→ 2.5.5

The building's underworld as a spacious recreation room with direct access to the underground garage: so you can roll calmly onto the studio floor on a vintage motorcycle. The basement level is attached to the apartment and accessible via an internal staircase that lets in daylight. The apartment plan is developed around the staircase with a circular traffic pattern that leads past all the bedrooms and traverses the living area with open kitchen. Alcoves provide a multifaceted spatial contour.

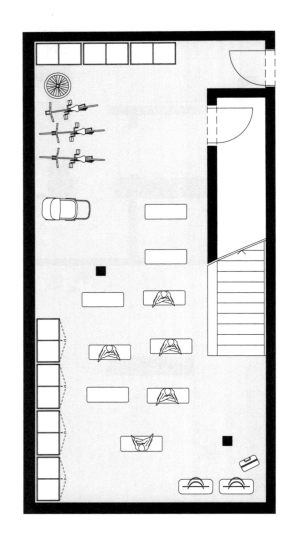

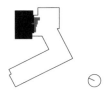

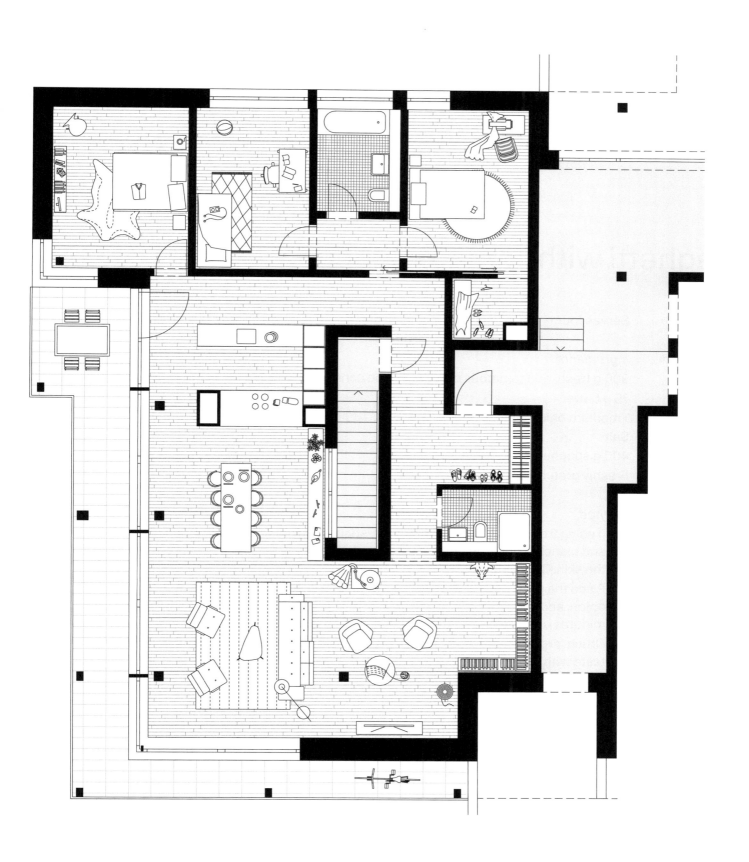

Bespoke Apartments 267

Just like in the movies, the best spaghetti recipe comes at the end. A plate of this dish inevitably recalls all past trips to Italy. Childhood memories come to mind with every bite. No sauce tastes as pure and irresistible as this one. As in real life, the simplest is often the most effective—the same is true for bespoke floor plans!

Spaghetti with Tomato Sauce

Recipe taken from Marcella Hazan, The Classic Italian Cook Book, New York City 1973

Serves four

Ingredients
900 g fresh, ripe tomatoes or 500 g Italian canned tomatoes, finely chopped, with juice
75 g butter
1 medium onion, peeled and halved
Salt
400 g spaghetti
Freshly grated Parmesan

Method
1. If using fresh tomatoes, make a cross-shaped incision at the stem-end of each one and blanch them all in boiling water for thirty to sixty seconds. Remove and peel off the skin. Chop into small pieces.
2. Place the prepared fresh or canned tomatoes in a heavy saucepan. Add butter, onion, and salt and simmer very gently but steadily in an open pot for forty-five minutes until the fat separates from the tomatoes. Stir occasionally.
3. Crush larger tomato pieces in the pot with the back of a wooden spoon. Season to taste with salt. Remove the onion and toss the spaghetti in the sauce. Serve immediately with sprinkled Parmesan.

Food for Architects
Volume 3: Always the Same, Only Different

Published by: Steib Gmür Geschwentner Kyburz Partner
General introduction, chapter introductions, and recipes: Patrick Gmür
Floor plan descriptions and family stories: Michael Geschwentner
Sautéing and simmering: Patrick Gmür
Spaghetti photography: Annette Helle
Editor: Christoph Wieser
Translation: Hunter Bolin, Anna Dinwoodie, Hanna Grześkiewicz, Marc Hiatt, Rob Madole, Joel Scott, and Gráinne Toomey for Gegensatz Translation Collective
Proofreading: Marc Hiatt and Joel Scott for, Gegensatz Translation Collective
Design and layout: Sibylle Kanalz, Jürg Schönenberger, Nora Spaniol
Floor plan processing: Giuseppe Allegri, Lukas Felleisen, Lyle Stemper, Cristina Alén Mendes, Hilke Horsthemke, Paloma Romero, Anna Caviezel, Isidor Escobar
Image processing: Karin Prasser
Photo credits: Steib Gmür Geschwentner Kyburz, except for those by Georg Aerni P. 214; Roger Frei P. 22, 58, 74, 94, 114, 236; Sven Fricker P. 136; Zeljko Gataric P. 7; Juliette Haller, AfS P. 9; Annette Helle P. 35, 57, 73, 93, 113, 135, 157, 167, 189, 213, 237, 269; Rita Palanikumar P. 2, 3, 4 , 5, 6, 168
Printing and binding: DZA Druckerei zu Altenburg GmbH, Thuringia

© 2023 Steib Gmür Geschwentner Kyburz Partner and Park Books AG, Zurich
© for the texts: the authors

Park Books
Niederdorfstrasse 54
8001 Zurich
Switzerland
www.park-books.com

Park Books has received support from the Federal Office of Culture with a general subsidy for the years 2021–2024.

All rights reserved; no part of this publication may be reproduced, stored in a retrieval system or transmitted in any form or by any means, electronic, mechanical, photocopying, recording, or otherwise, without the prior written consent of the publisher.

ISBN 978-3-03860-360-3

This book is volume 3 of Food for Architects, a set of five volumes in a slipcase which are not available separately

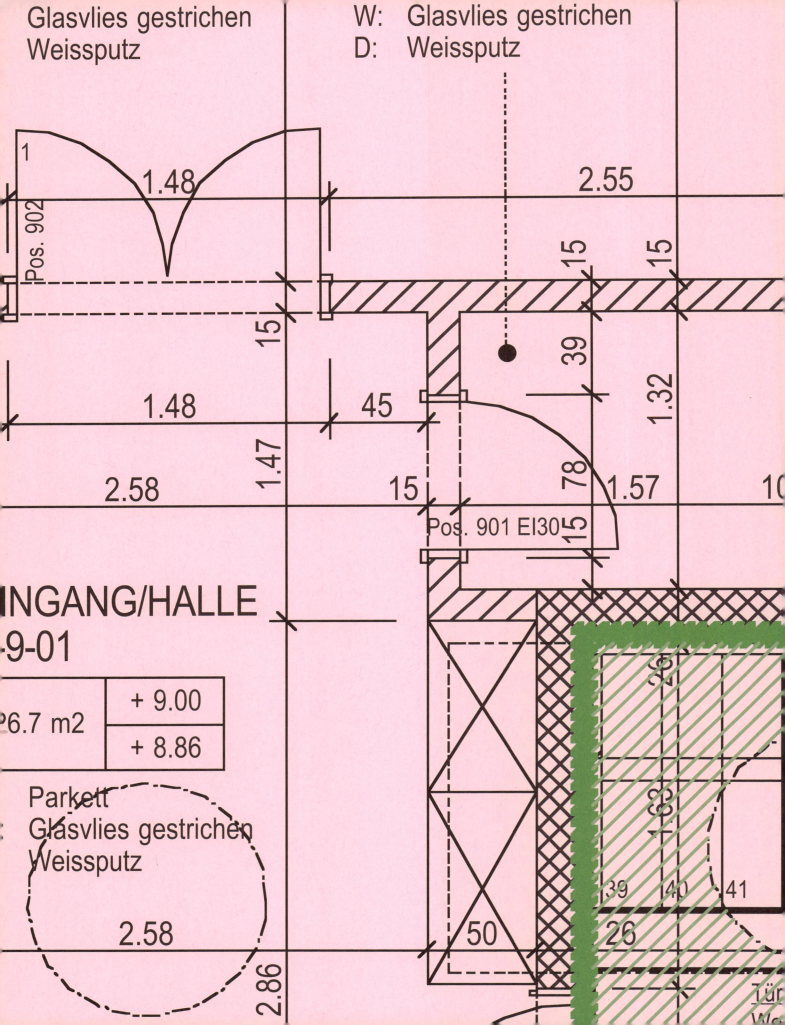

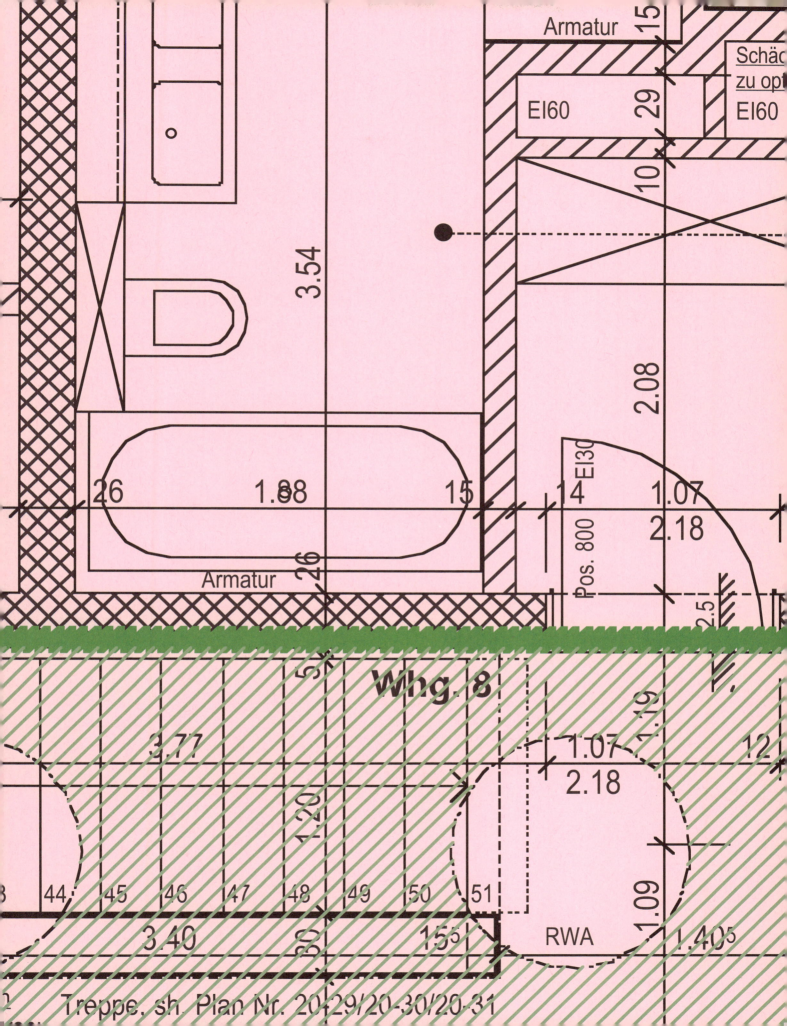

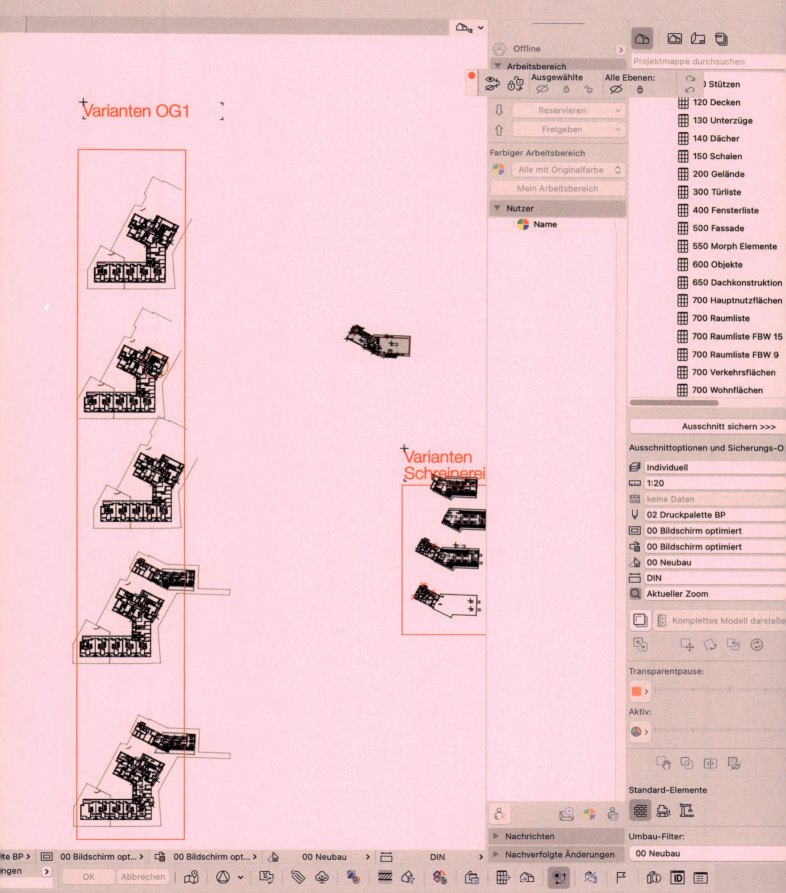

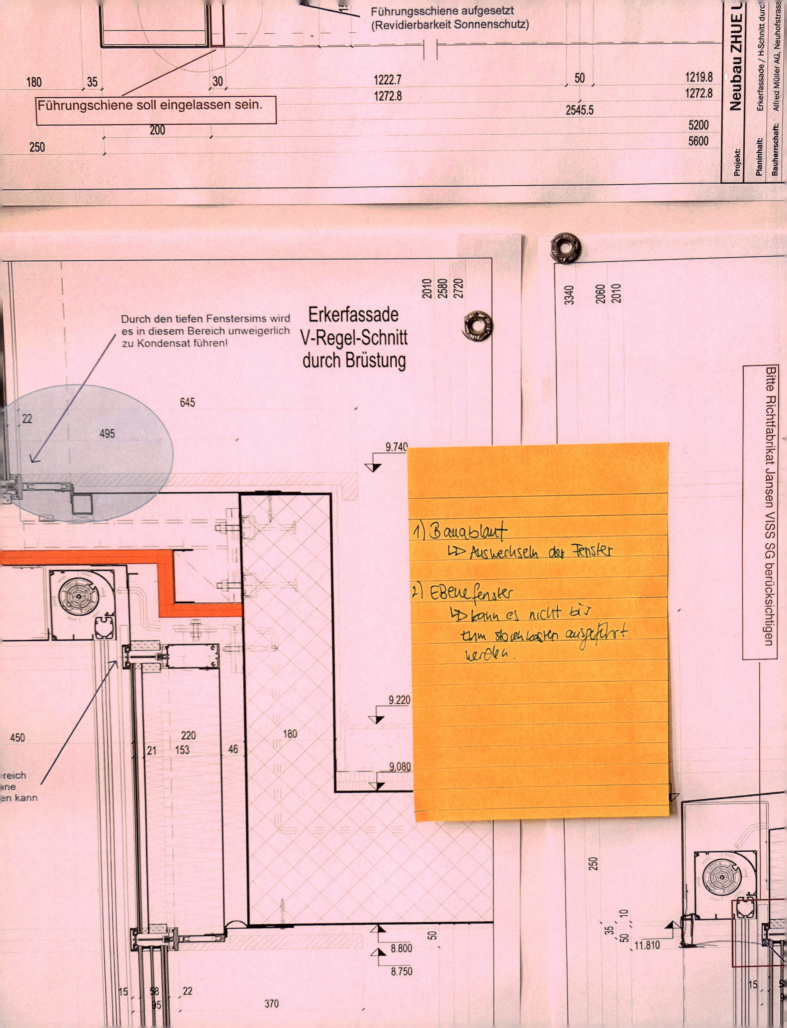

The Lives and Homes of Others

Drawing up architectural designs requires us to imagine the lives of others. We imagine tear-jerking Hollywood romances and tales of trials and tribulations like in an arthouse film. We draw inspiration from life in all its diversity and complexity. Joy, happiness, and love are just as much a part of it as sadness, disappointments, and loneliness. We imagine a peaceful afternoon as well as loud family gatherings. In the process, we imagine people preparing meals, and the sounds and smells that waft from the kitchen. We imagine children at play and young adults returning to their former childhood bedroom only to realize that they have outgrown it.

now and then, we feel the urge to translate these very same moods into a floor plan design.

We invent life stories—some more straightforward than others. We envision traces of memories, but also the scars of everyday life. There is more to architecture than being able to decide on the optimal arrangement of apartment floor plans, finding the best possible configuration of the various functions of the rooms, and adhering to the economic requirements—you also need to be able to create specific moods. Being an architect is like being a scriptwriter. We aspire for our sketches, plans, and models to evoke images, sequences, and

Quiet Sunday mornings are just as integral to the atmospheres we dream up as balmy summer nights. In our minds, we conjure up both the hazy glow of winter and the searing summer sunlight. We reminisce about the antique stone floors or hand-laid tiles in a cozy hotel. Every

scenes from films. The capacity to imagine particular life circumstances informs our design choices. The everyday lives of our fellow human beings pique our interest just as much as our own lives. We avoid anything that we would find personally bothersome. When designing, planning, and building, our ideas slowly become reality, step by step.

Time to Say Goodbye
When someone moves into one of our apartments, we have to bid farewell to it forever. For those of us who design apartments, this event marks the end of a long and labor-intensive process, which began with the first clumsy sketches.

What interests us is the everyday use of a home, where our architecture recedes into the background.

These sketches then undergo a series of revisions and refinements, from which a working floor plan emerges. During the final visit before handover, we get to stroll through the empty rooms one last time and check whether they correspond to our architectural ideas. A photographer documents the pristine, yet empty apartment for us. No matter how good the pictures may be, they are always somewhat sterile, because they lack the key ingredient: life.

In the past, we followed the tradition of presenting the completed buildings to our fellow architects at an open house. But we don't design for our colleagues, we build for future residents.

Above all, the uninhabited apartments signify that while our work may be finished, their raison d'être as living spaces is only just beginning. From now on, the apartment belongs to the new owners or tenants. Only now will our ideas and visions be put to the test to see if they can withstand the test of everyday life—or whether our daydreams were mere fantasies. Usually, we don't get the chance to verify this, for the front doors remain forever shut to us. Only rarely do we find out what it is actually like to live in the apartments we have designed and how our spaces are filled with furniture and memories. Without feedback, it is hard to conduct quality control.

Ten Years Later
A defining feature of our day and age is that people are mainly interested in the new. That is why most architectural journals only publish buildings that have been completed very recently. More than twenty years ago, we worked together with the architect and lecturer Michael Alder—who unfortunately passed away much too soon—to launch an architecture magazine that focuses solely on buildings that are at least ten years old. After all, only time and daily use can attest to the viability of a floor plan.

The present volume deals with all of this as well. It collects portraits of tenants living in the apartments we designed, providing a glimpse into the past of our work. At the same time, it offers the opportunity to interview and photograph residents as they go about their everyday life in their homes. Of course, to ensure that we received honest answers, we were not present at these conversations and photo sessions. Interviews and photographs are inseparable: they are most effective when placed side-by-side.

Wo ist Zuhause, Mama?
We have no interest in "clean" living environments with pristine interior design. What interests us is the everyday use of a home, where our architecture recedes into the back-

We learn that on the one hand, there is still room for improvements to our floor plans, but on the other, that we are all settled nomads.

The Lives and Homes of Others 9

We imagine a peaceful afternoon as well as loud family gatherings.

feel their apartment is unique and tailored to their particular lifestyle. In the 1960s, one of Johnny Cash's more poignant song lyrics was "Wo ist Zuhause, Mama" (Where is home, Mama?). We used this line to title our first publication about a large selection of our buildings. Even though the publication has long been out of print, the phrase has lost none of its relevance.

ground. This volume shows what it's like to live in our apartments. When these rooms and spaces are inhabited, they are endowed with a soul. And it is only the assorted furniture, the colors of the rugs or curtains, the art on the walls, the family heirlooms, the children's toys scattered all around, the little odds and ends, the various chairs and sofas, the messy dining room table, the vacation snaps, a colorful bouquet of flowers, plates, the unkempt bed, the unanswered letters, the cluttered bookshelf, the shoes piled up at the front door, the clothes, or the chaos in the kitchen that reveal the everyday life specific to an individual apartment. These glimpses into people's homes demonstrate that our designs accommodate many different ways of living and are subject to constant change.

Knowing this brings us a great deal of satisfaction, especially because today, the economic pressures on apartment design prevent any exceptional features from being added to buildings, meaning that windows, kitchens, and bathrooms are often built according to set formulae. It is crucial that residents

Sedentary Nomads

We would like to thank all those involved who have opened their doors to us and readily provided information about their everyday lives in the apartments we have designed. Their feedback, paired with the photographs, are extremely valuable to us. These intimate glimpses into familiar yet unknown homes show how different lifestyles interact with our designs. The evocative pictures captured by photographer Rita Palanikumar teach us that on the one hand, there is still room for improvement when it comes to our floor plans, but on the other hand, that we are all sedentary nomads. One resident even remarked: "I never want to have to move!" Which as architects is about the most touching complement we could imagine receiving.

Patrick Gmür

It is only the assorted furniture, the colors of the rugs or curtains, the art on the walls, the family heirlooms, the children's toys scattered all around that reveal the everyday life specific to an individual apartment.

Contents

4.1 Brüderhofweg top floor p.14
Esther Hodel, Pascal Müller

4.2 Paul-Clairmont-Strasse first floor p.28
Daniela Saxer, Martin Thürlemann

4.3 Hard Turm Park fifth floor p.44
Stephanie Kasper-Kräutler, Raphael Kräutler

4.4 James Long Building maisonette p.56
Franziska Manetsch, Andrzej Egli

4.5 James Long Building first floor p.72
Marianne Baumgartner, Luca Camponovo

4.6 Hinterbergstrasse top floor p.90
Rosmarie Baumann-Ott, Max Baumann

4.7 Scheffelstrasse second floor p.106
Monika Walther, Klas Johansson

4.8 James High-Rise tenth floor p.118
Christoph Schuepp

4.9 James High-Rise sixth floor p.132
Karin Briefer-Diezi, Marc Briefer-Diezi

4.10 Steinhofweg first floor p.146
Jeannette Murer, André Murer

4.11 Haus Hirschi maisonette p.160
Daniela Anderhub, Maurizio D. Sacchet

4.1　Brüderhofweg top floor

Fondue Night on the Terrace with a 360-Degree View

Esther Hodel and Pascal Müller,
both architects,
with Anouk und Eloïse

4.5 rooms
120 m²
Move-in date 2019
→ 2.3.9

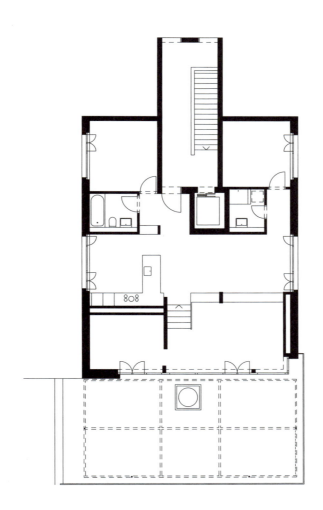
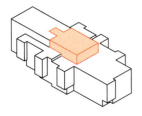

Reducing connective areas adds spatial abundance to the apartment.

The bedrooms are arranged in three corners of the apartment, ensuring privacy. The central area is for communal life.

The diagonal line of sight transforms the apartment into a house.

"Everyday life happens at the kitchen table or the table on the terrace."

Esther Hodel, Pascal Müller

How did you find this apartment?
[EH] I was working at SGGK when the firm won the competition for this project. [PM] And I knew the Frohheim building cooperative, the developers, because our firm (Müller Sigrist) had already worked with them. So we knew when the apartments were being advertised and we applied. We wanted one of these top-floor apartments.

Why do you live here?
[PM] We really liked the high ceilings in the living spaces adjoining the terrace right away. And the surrounding neighborhood, with its soccer fields, the school, and the Allenmoos pool, is also great for our kids. [EH] Yeah, that's true. But you found it hard early on to leave the vibrant, inner-city life of District 5 in the center of Zurich. We were living in an apartment there in an old, privately owned building. So we didn't know how much longer we would be able to stay there. That's another reason we moved.

How was moving here for your kids?
[PM] Changing schools wasn't easy for our older daughter Anouk. So she only changed with the new school year. But she started playing soccer at the local club down the road, so she already knew some of the kids by the time she started. [EH] Eloïse was just starting preschool, so the move was no problem for her.

What do you like about the apartment?
[PM] The rooms with their high ceilings, and the 360-degree views. That's really beautiful. The terrace, too. There are a lot of things about this apartment that we like. [EH] The rooms are also well distributed: every part of it has a nook where you can get out of the way if you want to. Everyone has their niche, even though the apartment is 120 square meters, so it's not huge. [PM] Right, the apartment seems a lot bigger than it actually is. [EH] I also like the different door heights ... [PM] ... and the shelving by the entrance. Or the low parapet in the living room with the balustrade on top. That way you can look outside even while you are sitting down. [EH] You can sense the architects' signature in all the beautiful details.

What don't you like so much?
[PM] There's no storeroom. [EH] Yes, it would be handy to have more storage space. [PM] And the downlights. We put tape over some of them. We have a real landing strip on our ceiling.

What was it like to furnish this apartment? How did you approach it?
[EH] We drew up a plan for our furniture, but it still wasn't all that simple. [PM] Yeah, the extra-long dining area, for example. We ended up extending the table and putting in an additional light. [EH] We had a lot of built-in cabinets in our old place. For the new apartment, we had to buy cabinets, even though we didn't actually like them.

Why didn't you install the cabinets you needed yourselves?
[EH] Because we know we're not going to live here forever. There's something permanent about built-in cabinets. We're not crazy about that. [PM] We did make changes, of course. The kids didn't have any closets in the beginning. Those came later.

What is your favorite spot, your cozy corner?
[PM] My favorite spot is the built-in desk in the dining area. I have a beautiful view from there, and I can follow a soccer game while I'm working. [EH] Anouk also likes to do her

homework at that desk. It's like a cockpit. I like to hang out on the stairs a lot. That's my spot. I find them comfortable. Or down on the bench in the living room. When we have guests, the table is the center. I like that *tavolata*.

What room is the heart of the apartment?
[EH] This intersection between the kitchen and the dining area. That's the key spot in the apartment.

Do you sit at the kitchen table much?
[EH] Whenever all four of us are together, actually. Everyday life happens at the kitchen table or the table on the terrace. We mostly use the dining area with guests or on Sunday evenings, when we've cooked something special.

"I like to hang out on the stairs a lot. That's my spot. I find them comfortable."

What does the bedroom mean to you?
[EH] A lot, because I like to read in bed. I like that room, how colorful it is, and the high ceiling. And the view, particularly in the morning. [PM] The direct access to the terrace is also great.

What do you think of the bathroom?
[EH] It's functional. Not a room I'm particularly fond of being in. [PM] The same goes for me.

How do you use the terrace?
[PM] It's a big additional room outside. In the winter, we also did a fondue night on the terrace one time.

What's your routine when you come home?
[PM] I hang up my jacket in the entryway, then I go into the kitchen, because we put our shoes on the shelf from this side. The kids have their space on the side of the entryway.

And then?
[EH] Then we're in the kitchen or the dining area. It takes a long time before one of us goes downstairs to the living room. We prefer to be there in the evening, unless we go onto the terrace during the day.

Does the floor plan influence how you live?
[PM] Yes, because the bedrooms are set up like satellites. When Anouk comes home, for instance, she can disappear right into her room. To get to our room, on the other hand, we have to cross the entire apartment.

Does the kitchen foster your love of cooking?
[EH] It's wonderful that the workspace is in the middle of the apartment. I also like that the kitchen isn't isolated, especially when we have guests over. We had a gas stove in our old apartment. Here, we have an induction stove, so we couldn't use the copper cookware anymore and we put it on the shelf near the entrance. I think that's a lovely place for it. A lot of it comes from Paris. Every pan has a story.

Do you have a favorite piece of furniture? What's its story?
[PM] Mine are the two Prouvé lamps. I think they're particularly beautiful and functional at the same time. [EH] For me, it's the sideboard by Jean Prouvé. We've had it for a long time, and it has a special meaning for us, because it was a wedding present. At the time, the furniture was sold out—so I called a lot of furniture stores to see if they might still have the sideboard. Ultimately, Vitra got wind of that—and they then did a reissue of five units.

[PM] That's how we got a custom-made version of an industrially produced piece of furniture.

"We like the rooms with their high ceilings and the 360-degree views. That's really beautiful."

Do you feel at home here? And if so, why?
[PM] Yes, because of the apartment. Otherwise, I'd miss the bustling life of the inner city, the streets, the trams, the shops on the ground floor. There's none of that here. [EH] I like the apartment a lot too. Also the views of the greenery on Zürichberg, Käferberg, and Uetliberg.

With respect to shops on the ground floor, isn't there a restaurant here?
Do you ever eat there?
[PM] Oh yeah, the food is very good. We were just there yesterday. [EH] Or we go there to eat with friends. Incidentally, the owners, Maria and Stefano, also live in the development.

4.2 Paul-Clairmont-Strasse first floor

The Balconies Are Really Great. That's Not Something You See Every Day.

Daniela Saxer with Martin Thürlemann,
architect and economist,
with Frederik and Oskar

5.5 rooms
first floor
137 m²
Move-in date 2008
→ 2.2.1

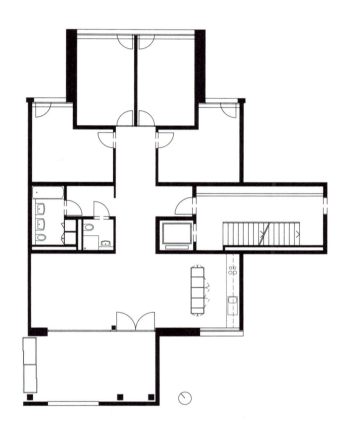
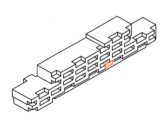

The desire to construct a residential building with readily usable, patio-like balconies was decisive for the design, from situating the building all the way to the choice of materials and color scheme. The direct connection between the communal kitchen, eating and living areas, and the spacious balcony is key.

The two private interior rooms took as their model the "Berlin room," which connects the street-facing front rooms with those in back facing the inner courtyard. The window alcoves measure 210 centimeters—perfect for a bed.

The ribbon windows let lots of daylight into the bedroom, with floor-to-ceiling doors conducting this light into the extra-wide hallway.

Paul-Clairmont-Strasse first floor

Extending more than twenty meters into the building's depths, the apartment is well lit thanks to large windows and bright, reflective stone floors.

Paul-Clairmont-Strasse first floor

To protect the two-story balcony from prying eyes, the kitchens are illuminated through window slits. The glass at counter-top level is covered with frosted window film.

Paul-Clairmont-Strasse first floor

"With the small amount of furniture that we had, it looked like a dollhouse at the start."

Daniela Saxer, Martin Thürlemann, Frederik, Oskar

Who are you?
[DS] My name is Daniela Saxer, I'm an architect, and I've been living in this building since 2008. [F] I'm Frederik, I'm in my second year of high school, and I like to play soccer. I was born here. [MT] My name is Martin Türlemann. I'm an economist, and I've been living here since 2008. [O] I'm Oskar. I'm twelve. Uh, yeah, and I play floorball.

How did you become aware of this apartment, or the building?
[DS] It was a coincidence. I was familiar with the building, but we were living in a three-room apartment in Wipkingen at the time. Frederik was on the way. I made an appointment with a colleague one day, and her sister was living in a shared apartment here. They were moving out and looking for a smaller apartment. Knowing that, we checked in with the co-op and got the apartment.

Did you know right away that you definitely wanted this apartment?
[MT] I thought it was really beautiful, but at the same time, it was a long way from downtown. I had to get used to the location at first. [DS] It was the same for me. It was the first time we had moved to the outskirts of the city. Fortunately, the neighborhood has changed a lot since then, with all the co-ops that have built projects here, and the traffic calming on Birmensdorferstrasse. Or what they've done with Triemliplatz. There used to be just an underground pedestrian walkway. You couldn't cross the street above ground. It's practical for the kids, too: the school is nearby, so is the the Heuried sports center. In the beginning, the generous dimensions of this five-and-a-half bedroom apartment also took some getting used to. With the small amount of furniture that we had, it looked like a dollhouse at the start. But of course, it was also wonderful to have so much space all of a sudden.

What do you still like about this apartment?
[O] I like the location. We live near the school, the hospital, and the tram stop. It's a beautiful apartment, and we look out onto trees. There's really nothing that bothers me.

Nothing, or almost nothing?
[O] Well, the children are really loud in the mornings. [DS] Our bedrooms are all facing the new Triemli 1 development. As a residential complex it's great for kids, but sometimes it feels like we're at an endless birthday party. What I especially like about this apartment is the balcony. We use it a lot, for lunch, an evening coffee, to hang the laundry, and so on. In all weather. It's covered and shaded. Yeah, it's fantastic! [MT] The balconies are really great. There's even a built-in cabinet out there with lots and lots of storage space. You don't see that every day. There are also little things that contribute to the quality of the environment. I think this apartment was very much designed on the basis of the needs of its residents. [F] I can't imagine where else we would live. It's also cool that I have four colleagues here. That makes it even better. There's just one thing that I don't really like: everyone can see in during the winter. I feel a little bit like I'm on display. [MT] We like the living room and the kitchen a lot. Especially in the summer, it's open and bright here. It's a bit dark in the winter. Sometimes I wonder if the wide hallway isn't too wide, and maybe that absorbs the light. And the Triemli hospital parking lot bothers me. Fortunately, we can't see it very well because

of the thick vegetation. [DS] Yeah, the Triemli hospital really isn't just a neighbor. [MT] I also think it's too bad that there are a lot of "dead" outdoor spaces in the area. It means that everything is concentrated in the center, which means in front of our building and our bedrooms. [DS] I think the building itself works very well. The bedrooms are on the one side, the balconies on the other. So people can be sleeping while others are entertaining guests and no-one gets disturbed. There is something that I don't like so much: the kitchen is a bit dim because of the small window and the frosted glass. But that's just an issue for us on the first floor. Fortunately, I don't like to cook and don't do it often. It also would have been nice if there were an electrical outlet in this wide hallway. But that's just a detail. [F] What I also like about this building is the big windows. I like them a lot. They let a lot of light in, and when I look out, I'm looking right at trees. [DS] It's also interesting that the apartments are reflected. It gives us a lot of privacy. Something else I like: the kitchen counter is very high, so when you're looking out from the living room, you are not looking into the kitchen, yet the kitchen is open. What fascinates me is how our neighbors have furnished their apartment. The extent of the variations is incredible. The floor plans are very flexible.

"I can't imagine a better total package than here."

What is your favorite spot in the apartment?
[O] Frederik's room [F] But you have a nice sofa bed. If I were you, I'd spend a lot of time in your bed. [DS] My favorite spot is the balcony. [F] Mine is the sofa in the living room, and my room. [MT] And no one says the bathroom? *(Everyone laughs)* I like being on the living room sofa best.

Where is the heart of the apartment? Where do you come together, when you come home?
[O] In the living room.

Not at the dinner table?
[DS] We rarely eat together in the evening during the week. Everyone has practice.
[MT] And there are always textbooks and notebooks on the dinner table anyway. Frederik and Oskar do their homework here.

What role does the bedroom play in your everyday lives?
[DS] For me, it's an important room that I can withdraw to. But it's also become a work space for me since the Covid pandemic. My home office. [F] For me, my room is also my retreat.
[MT] For me, the bedroom is also a place where I work and where I can be alone. I can concentrate well there, not as much in the common spaces.

Oskar and Frederik take their leave.

What does the bathroom mean to you?
[DS] We have one bathroom with a shower and a toilet, and one big one with a tub, a toilet, and a washing machine. To me, they are very functional places. That also has to do with the fact that the bathrooms don't have any windows.

What is your routine when you come home?
[DS] I go from the coat rack to my room. I put my bag down there, and then I go from room to room and see who's home. Depending on what's going on, I'll go into the kitchen and cook, sit on the sofa and relax, or retreat to the balcony. [MT] I take off my shoes and jacket, put my bag down in the middle of the wide hallway so that it's right in everybody's way *(everyone laughs)*, then I also look to see who's there and decide what I need to do.

"Everyone can see in during the winter. I feel a little bit like I'm on display."

Do you have a favorite piece of furniture? And if so, does it have a story?
[DS] My favorite piece of furniture is the sofa, because I designed it myself. [MT] I almost have to say the wing chair. I bought it in a secondhand shop and brought it home on the tram. [DS] Yeah, the wing chair is important. It's been with us for a very long time.

What makes you feel at home here?
[DS] For me, there are three things: the beautiful, ample apartment, the lovely neighborhood, and our furniture. I have a relationship to all the furniture, and the way the apartment is furnished is extremely important. And then, of course, there are my housemates, who aren't entirely irrelevant *(laughs)*. [MT] Our family feels really good here. I can't imagine a better total package than here. [DS] It's an apartment, but also a place where you can settle down and make yourself at home. There's a lot of space, it's well thought out, and it has everything that a family needs. In your last publication (Wo ist Zuhause, Mama?), you mentioned that these apartments are a kind of surrogate single-family home. I've never heard of a family here that is looking for a single-family house. Hardly anyone moves away from here.

In the sense of "I don't ever want to leave"? Daniela, that's something that you said to me once. And you're not the only one. We thought it was so nice that we chose it as the title for this book.
[DS] Oh, you really have to choose your words carefully *(laughs)*. I'm glad that's the title. Because it's true, I never want to leave here again!

Paul-Clairmont-Strasse first floor

4.3 Hard Turm Park fifth floor

A Feeling of Togetherness without Many Doors

Stefanie Kasper Kräutler and Raphael Kräutler,
art and cultural educator and architect,
with Liv and Rona

3.5 rooms
fifth floor
142 m²
Move-in date 2016
→ 2.3.13

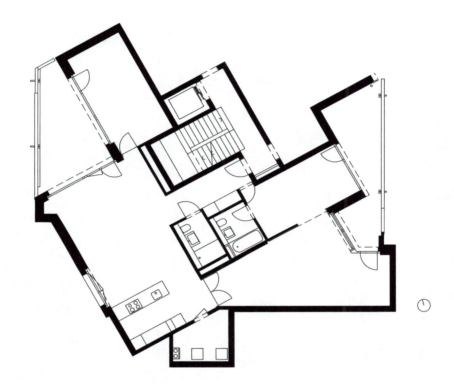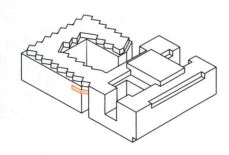

To the south, the office building shields the apartment block from the noisy highway access road. In order to retain optimal alignment nevertheless, the apartments are turned to the side. What appears complicated offers many advantages: the apartment profits from being oriented toward three directions.

The twisted apartment orientation occasions triangular balconies, whose shape reduces the costs of constructing the building facade.

Bright, spacious rooms distinguish the apartment. The bathrooms are compact. Our goal was to offer the inhabitants areas that are as large and as neutral as possible. A utility room also enhances the apartment's value.

Hard Turm Park fifth floor   51

"The dinner table. Whenever we all come together, it starts here."

Stefanie Kasper Kräutler,
Raphael Kräutler, Liv

Who are you?
[L] My name is Liv and I go to school in Pfingstweid. My little sister Rona goes to preschool at Hard Turm Park. [SK] I'm originally from eastern Switzerland, but I've been living in Zurich since college. It's also where we met. [RK] The first time I opened my own architecture firm, the offices were just around the corner, in the middle of the industrial precinct. I've always been fascinated by this "wild" environment, with its train tracks and vacant lots.

How did you find this apartment?
[RK] We liked the architecture of this building and its location, so we bought the apartment off the plan, and we've lived here since construction was completed. [SK] Raphael was always keeping an eye out for an apartment, and then we found this one. I was excited about it just based on the visualizations of the rooms. I also liked the area from the start: these industrial complexes that are being transformed, the proximity to the inner city, and more generally, the appeal of a neighborhood in transition.

What do you like about your apartment?
[L] There are hardly any doors. You can see everything. [SK] I like the openness too. It gives the apartment a lavish sense of space. At the same time, the apartment has a distinct structure. It's clear. [L] I think the shape of the apartment is beautiful. There's something very particular about it. I can't really describe it. [SK] I know what you mean. There are a lot of angles. It breaks away from the box design and makes various paths possible. The ceiling height is also great. [RK] Yeah, I particularly like the fluidity of the rooms. And the view. Having air and a view is a privilege in the city.

Does the open floor plan also work for you as a family?
[SK] Right now, we like that structure a lot. There are also doors that you can close. The apartment is big enough that you can retreat somewhere private. Obviously, it's different from a single-family house with multiple floors. The beauty of it is that you can see what the others are doing, which creates a feeling of togetherness.

What doesn't work so well in the apartment?
[RK] The stairwell is so minimal that it's better to use the elevator. But otherwise, everything is like we imagined it. [SK] It's true. I can only think of one thing I don't like: there's not much storage space, which is why we had built-in cupboards installed. Between the four of us, we accumulate a whole lot of stuff....

What was it like to furnish this apartment?
[RK] It was fun: we moved from a 75-square-meter apartment to a 140-square-meter apartment. We arranged all our furniture, but the apartment still felt empty. [SK] So we added new furniture little by little. But there was no concept to it. It happened step by step. For instance, the girls' bedroom has been rearranged a few times.

What is your favorite spot?
[L] It depends what I'm doing. But I basically feel good everywhere [SK] For me, it's the living room whenever friends are here or I'm reading a storybook with the girls. I prefer the back of the living room for watching movies. All of the rooms are very welcoming. I like the kitchen a lot. It has an overview of the apartment and a beautiful view out the window. [RK] I like to be in the kitchen too. I prefer the

back of the living room for relaxing, the front for more active pursuits.

Which spot is the heart of the apartment?
[RK] The dinner table. Whenever we all come together, it starts here.

What does the bedroom mean to you?
[RK] When I want some peace and quiet, I go to the bedroom. [SK] Me too: retreat, relaxation. Right now, it's also a room for the whole family. Sometimes the girls still come and sleep with us at night, if they have bad dreams.

What does the bathroom mean to you?
[SK] I love the bathtub. For me, that makes it another room for relaxing in. I especially like being there in the morning, when everyone else is still sleeping. [RK] For me, it's not so important. I also don't need a bathtub.

"I also liked the area from the start: the proximity to the inner city and the appeal of a neighborhood in transition."

The balconies?
[RK] Actually, they aren't really balconies, just exterior rooms. They're like little gardens. Being there is a real joy for us. We spend a lot of time outside. I think it's wonderful to be able to see and hear nature even on the fifth floor. [SK] A lot of interesting things are happening in the adjacent vacant lot right now. Just recently, there was a street food festival. The apartment has great sound insulation. You really don't hear anything. In the beginning, we had to adjust to the fact that we couldn't hear our neighbors at all. It's also practical, because there can be a lot going on in the vacant lot, but we don't hear any noise. The other balcony in the courtyard is completely different. I like to read there. It's pleasantly cool, and more private as well. [RK] Yeah, we tend to spend time on the balcony overlooking the inner courtyard during the day, and on the one by the vacant lot in the evenings, or when we have visitors. It's great that we have both options.

What's your routine when you come home? Is there a particular flow?
[RK] I usually hang up my jacket, take off my shoes, put down my phone, and then head to the kitchen. [SK] Yeah, into the apartment, then back into the light—meaning the living room—to the dinner table or the kitchen.

Do you use the different circulation options?
[SK] Yes, but usually without thinking about it. Sometimes I think that I could have taken a different, shorter route. [RK] When I go to the bathroom at night, I don't go around the bed. I go via the living room, just because that route has fewer curves. Our kids also really love the circular layout. There's something playful about it.

Does the kitchen foster your love of cooking?
[RK] I think the kitchen is great. When we have guests, we can cook and still be part of the conversation. That's quite a normal feature, but it is wonderful. It means you don't have to have all the cooking already done by the time the guests arrive. [SK] I had only ever had enclosed kitchens before. I've changed my mind since we moved here. I love open kitchens now too. It's a different kind of cooking. The flows are more spontaneous, simpler, and fit our current everyday lives better.

What is your favorite piece of furniture? And does it have a story?
[SK] For me, it's the Chinese wardrobe. I saw it in an antique shop when I was in college, and I fell in love with it immediately, but it was way

beyond my budget. So I worked all summer to be able to afford it. It's been with me ever since. DA The dinner table. I like its design a lot, but also the meaning it takes on in the apartment.

"The beauty of it is that you can see what the others are doing, which creates a feeling of togetherness."

Are you happy here?
RK Absolutely. It may sound like a cliché, but we often come home from vacation and wonder why we ever left. SK We never wanted a house in the country, and that still feels right. Here there are endless possibilities, including for our kids, especially with all the green spaces. We can go to the vacant lot, the river, the Werdinsel, the Josefswiese, or Pfingstweid Park. There's nothing that we lack.

What is the community like here in the neighborhood?
L We have very nice neighbors. SK I rave about our neighbors too. This hasn't been a residential neighborhood for very long. The people who moved here are very open. The mix is nice. People say hello on the street, sometimes do things together, but you can also retreat into your own private space—just a pleasant mix of closeness and distance.
RK A lot of us moved here at the same time. That creates a connection.

4.4   James long building   maisonette

Enough Space to Continuously Collect Furniture and Its Stories

Franziska Manetsch and Andrzej Egli,
both architects
with Lilith

4.5 rooms
fourth/fifth floor
135 m²
Move-in date 2007
→ 2.2.2

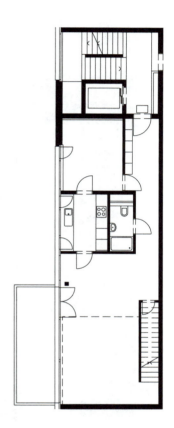
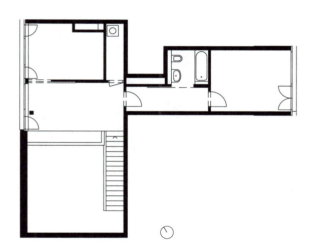
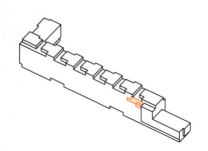

We posed the question, "How would we want to live?" and our answer was the design of this floor plan!

James long building maisonette

The two-story living room creates a spatial unity with the balcony.

A large sliding door allows the bathroom to connect to the dressing room. An unexpected spatial combination is the result.

62

A bedroom is always a
personal haven.

The apartment becomes a stage
for one's own life.

"I hope we never have to leave!"

Franziska Manetsch, Andrzej Egli, Lilith

Who are you?
[AE] My name is Andrzej Egli, I'm an architect. [FM] And I'm Franziska Manetsch, also an architect. We've lived here since the building was completed.

How did you find this apartment?
[FM] We were living in two separate apartments, but we wanted to move in together. As it happened, there was an article at the time in the magazine Hochparterre featuring the floor plans for all the apartments in the James development, which was under construction at the time. We kept studying the plans—and I fell in love with this type we're living in now. But Andrzej's response was: "there's no way I'm moving out there!" [AE] I wasn't able to imagine living so far from the inner city. No, never. [FM] Then we got the chance to visit the construction site, and we were totally taken with this apartment type. On the way back, Andrzej also felt that it wasn't all that far. After that, it was clear that we wanted this apartment.

What was it that finally convinced you to move here?
[FM] Above all, the architecture. The apartment isn't in our ideal neighborhood, but nowadays we have a strong connection with the place. Also because of our daughter Lilith, who goes to school here. Our apartment just makes up for everything. [AE] Yeah, it's a kind of apartment that you hardly ever see as a rental. And when you do, it's unreasonably expensive.

What do you particularly like about this apartment?
[FM] We were particularly fascinated by the high ceilings from the start. But also the constellation of rooms, like how the kitchen relates to the dining area. I think that's fantastic. When we have guests over and we're busy in the kitchen, you catch the conversation, but you're also a bit concealed. [AE] But we had to remove the kitchen door. It took up too much space and covered part of the window. Actually, there should be a sliding door here.

What else do you like?
[FM] The spaciousness of the enfilade that the length of the apartment creates, and then the same thing on top in the opposite direction. Also the perspective from facade to facade. I struggled with the black baseboards in the beginning. Now I see their architectural, spatial quality. I think they give the apartment a certain elegance and distinguish it from a standard apartment design. I also thought the handles in the kitchen were a bit clunky, but when you use them, they're really practical. The bathrooms are also mainly functional. [L] But the sink in the downstairs bathroom is too small. And so is my room. [AE] The bedrooms are very small, actually. Ours is the biggest and it's fourteen square meters. But since there's just a bed in there, it's okay. But our daughter's room is only twelve square meters, with two doors, a skylight, and the whole facade—its hard to furnish.

Apart from that, was it easy to furnish the apartment?
[FM] We knew from the start how we wanted to furnish the apartment: we moved in with just a few pieces and then bought furniture and lights little by little. Like the lights over the dinner table. That took forever. First we had a floor lamp, which meant indirect light. Then we bought these lights, and now we can't imagine being without them anymore.

What is your favorite spot? What is your cozy corner?
[FM] I like to be in the kitchen a lot. I like to cook, and I spend most of my time there. And then the dinner table. But really, I like it everywhere. [AE] The sofa. The library. The balcony. The thing about this apartment is that, because the bedrooms are relatively small, we actually have a lot of open space—the hallway, the kitchen, the living room, the dining room, the stairs. That's why there are a lot of different spots and corners where we like to spend our time.

Do you spend time in particular places in the apartment at certain times of day?
[FM] There isn't any direct sunlight in the living room during the winter months, but that's not a problem for me at all. It's very bright anyway.

Do you have curtains?
[AE] Yes, but not because people can see in so much as because of the atmosphere of the room. We know from our friends in the building across from us that people can see into our apartment very well. By contrast, we mostly see rooftops. We had no curtains for years.
[FM] You mentioned people seeing in. We recently celebrated my birthday here. Friends from across the way were there, and after they went home, they took a photo of the people who were still at the party from their apartment. It's incredible everything you can see in the photo, but also how beautiful the photo is. They should have taken a picture right at the start of the party! I like that the common spaces are so generous. it means that we can invite a lot of people.

Which room is the centerpiece of the apartment? Where do you spend the most time as a family?
[FM] The dinner table is very important for us. Lilith does all her homework here. In any case, I think it's the best table, because oval is the perfect shape. It doesn't matter if you're sitting at it with one other person or in a big group, you always feel good here.

What does the bedroom mean to you?
[FM] For me, it's an important haven. It's a quiet oasis. The atmosphere is also completely different in terms of the lighting, because it gets morning light there. [AE] And it's a special spot, with the fully glazed facade. There's something airy about that room. And no one can see into the bedroom from the opposite buildings. That's also nice.

"We kept studying the plans—and I fell in love with this type we're living in now."

What is the significance of the bathroom?
[FM] For me, the bathroom has to be functional. I go in there for five minutes, and then I'm out again. [AE] I really like to take baths in the winter, and then I'm often in the bathroom for an hour. We like that you can open the sliding door and expand the bathroom. The small skylight also lets the daylight in—it's amazing what that does.

The balcony?
[FM] We use the balcony a lot. In the summer, it's an additional room. Then we rarely use the kitchen, because we like to use the grill, especially on weekends. The balcony is a magnificent size—there's room for a dinner table, a deck chair, plants, and even our grill.

The storeroom?
[FM] That's the room we sometimes fight about. I stuff everything in there with no restraint, and that really annoys Andrzej. [AE] There are things in there that we really need to get rid of.

What is your routine when you come home?
[FM] I always go straight to the kitchen. That's because we always put the mail in the kitchen. But even when I haven't emptied the mailbox, I always end up in the kitchen first. During the week, I usually go up to sleep in the bedroom first. [AE] Me too. I always put my wallet and keys in the kitchen.

You like to cook. Does the kitchen foster that?
[FM] Yes. Even though it's pretty small, it is really good for cooking. Also, I like that I can see into the apartments across from us while I'm in there. It's like watching TV. Also, the extra deep countertops along the glass facade mean that I can plate up food for twenty people without any fuss.

"I wasn't able to imagine living so far from the inner city."

Do you have favorite pieces of furniture? If so, which ones? And are there stories behind them?
[FM] With us, almost every piece of furniture has a story. We have been continuously collecting, and we still are. I'm completely crazy about the Wegner armchair. Andrzej wanted it from the start, but I had reservations, because it reminded me of a birthing chair. Then we were in the factory in Denmark and we were able to pick out the hide. The longer we have it, the more I love that armchair.

Do you feel at home here?
[FM] Yes, we're very happy here. The moment we come home from vacation and walk in the door is a moment of happiness. I hope we never have to leave!

James long building maisonette

4.5 James long building first floor

An Apartment in Constant Motion and Change, Like Life Itself

Marianne Baumgartner and Luca Camponovo,
both architects
with Mai and Liv

4.5 rooms
first floor
114 m²
Move-in date 2021
→ 2.2.2

The determining design concept is the ample entryway—the heart of the floor plan, connecting the individual rooms. Light falls into the entry through the open doors.

Dining and living areas, with the intimate nook, entryway, and kitchen, can be used either individually or as a continuous spatial sequence.

James long building first floor   81

Children should feel at home in an apartment too. This is where they grow up and should get to develop freely. Too much architecture can get in the way.

James long building first floor   83

We won the competition for the James development in 2001, while still a young and inexperienced firm, implementing rules that determined our design for the 275 apartments. One of these was that every window should have a lintel. This was not for architectural reasons; rather, we inserted this provision as a covert backup measure—had we surpassed the stipulated costs, we could have done away with all the window lintels, amounting, at this construction volume, to significant savings.

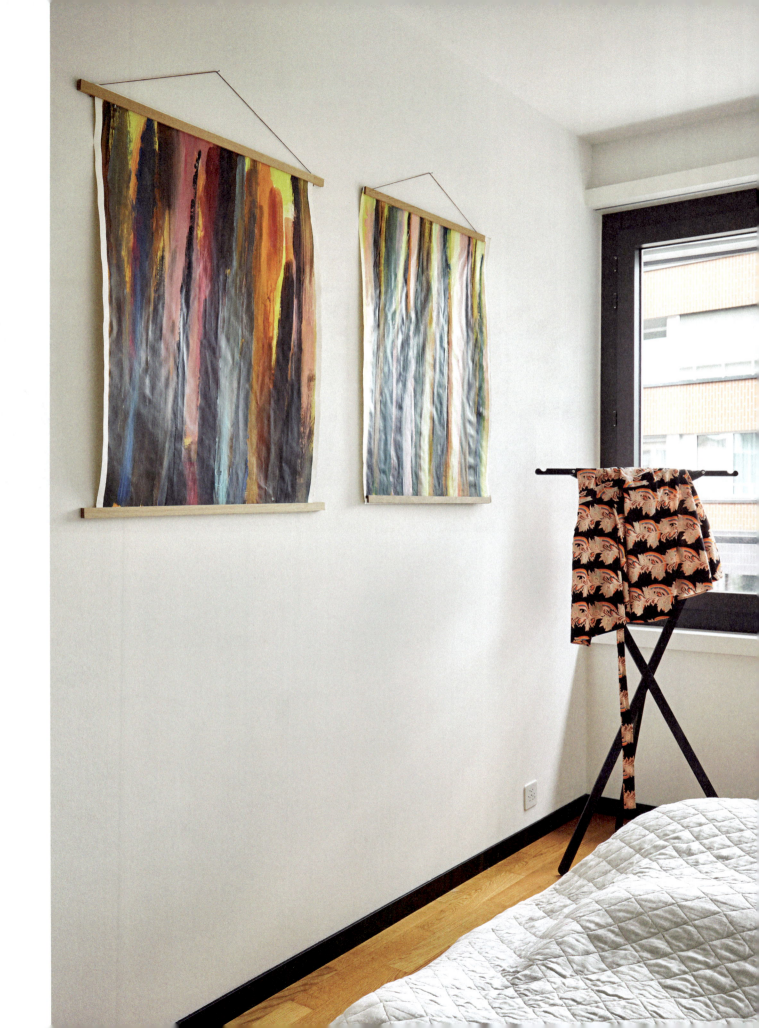

"We had a story about every neighbor. And now, people can also see into our bedroom."

Marianne Baumgartner, Luca Camponovo

Who are you?
[MB] We are Marianne and Luca, who became a family with Mai and Liv here at the James development. We're architects, and our children want to be farmers, but they're still in primary school and kindergarten right now.

How did you become aware of this apartment?
[MB] We knew about the project, and we heard through the grapevine that an apartment was being advertised, so we applied for it immediately. [LC] Do you mean the first or the second apartment? [MB] The first. That was 2010/2011. But then our family situation changed, and we definitely wanted more doors. When we heard that an apartment was available in the long building, we wrote to the management immediately. The next day, we got the acceptance notice without having seen the apartment.

What stood out to you about the first apartment? And what do you particularly like about the second one?
[LC] The apartments are completely different. The first fit our lifestyle during that phase well. It was open. It had a long hallway from one facade to the other, which made it like living in a loft. The kitchen was right in the middle. When we had visitors, you could cook and talk to them at the same time. The view was nice: the vastness of it, and the sunsets. [MB] When there were two and then three of us, the first apartment was great. With four, it became stressful—partly because of the lack of doors. After eight or nine years in the high-rise, we moved into this apartment. We wanted to have a view of the countryside. Here, the kids can go directly outside and back into the apartment. The floor plan is also more traditional, which fits better with this phase of our lives. [LC] What I really like about this apartment is the cellular layout. It's easy to withdraw, even in the kitchen or the living room. It's completely different from living out in the open.

What don't you like as much?
[LC] Details, like this lower window lintel, for instance. If it wasn't like that, you would have twenty more minutes of sun. But at the same time, there's something to be said for this withdrawn idea of living too. [MB] We still haven't gotten used to the fact that the bedroom faces the "alley." So the roller blinds are actually always down. When we lived in the high-rise, we were the ones who could see into every bedroom. We had a story about everyone. And now, people can also see into our bedroom.

What was it like to furnish the apartment? How did you approach it?
[LC] At first, we thought about it based on the floor plan, but then most of our decisions were ad hoc, and we changed them again later. [MB] For instance, we still don't have any lamps. That drove me crazy in the winter. The lamp that's in the entryway was also our table light. With us, the furniture is always moving around. I think it has to be like that. We also live differently depending on whether it's winter or summer. We thought for a long time about who would sleep where, because those allocations would have to remain in place for a while. Everything else could be changed. When there were still just two of us living in the high-rise, we kept changing how we used the rooms. Sometimes I feel like not everything has found its place yet. Like the dinner table. It was made by Super Studio, we bought it in a secondhand shop. I love that table, but it's impractical. It can only seat four.

When we have visitors, we have to add other tables.

What's your favorite spot in the apartment?
[LC] On the sofa bed or the hammock on the balcony. In the summer, we really mostly live outside. I also like to be in the living room.
[MB] I prefer the sofa. I like this corner of the apartment.

"This table. It supports everything: we do arts and crafts, paint, and eat here."

What's the centerpiece of the apartment?
[MB] The table. It supports everything: we do arts and crafts, paint, and eat there. [LC] And the entrance. Our parents often watch our kids. That's where the handoff happens. We exchange a few words—it's a lovely spot.

Where do you come together, when you come home?
[MB] Also in the entrance. The kids often bring their toys here when someone is cooking.

What does the bedroom mean to you?
[MB] That room is really just for sleeping.
[LC] That was another of our requirements: a bedroom for sleeping. I think it's great to have a room where nothing much happens besides sleeping, except maybe reading. A retreat.

How do you use the bathroom?
[LC] The bathroom is particular, because it's a passageway. It's part of the broader flow, which our kids love when they're chasing each other. For me, it's mostly functional. I'm not a guy who likes a wellness oasis. [MB] When you say it's "functional," I immediately think of a bathroom with white tiles and a washer and dryer. For me, that would be horrible. I like it when the bathroom is open. We don't close the doors. It's part of the whole thing, which I think is very harmonious.

How does the floor plan affect how you act?
[LC] I really like the differentiation in the plan. It makes it possible to inhabit the space in a variety of ways. For instance, I like to close the double-folding door when everyone is asleep. Then I have the living room all to myself, or for a one-on-one conversation.

Does the kitchen layout support your love of cooking?
[MB] No, more likely it inhibits it. I struggled with it at the beginning, partly because the kitchen in the first apartment was very big and a social meeting point. This kitchen is more like a workshop, which also has advantages.
[LC] You get the evening sun for a long time while cooking, or you can have some coffee in peace. It's less of a show kitchen than in the other apartment. [MB] What's also nice is the relationship to the stairwell. When one of the kids comes home, I see it. Like seeing the Mambo King at the window. [LC] Yes, the immediacy! It almost has the quality of a single-family home.

Do you have a favorite piece of furniture? And does it have a story?
[LC] For me, it's the Mickey Mouse chair. I got it at a design warehouse sale. It didn't have a cover, so my mother sewed one. Now it's a very special chair, a real joy. [MB] My sister was really infuriated by that chair. She never thought that we would buy such an ugly piece of furniture. My favorite piece of furniture is the table, even though it's too small. And the Bill stool, which my father was once so bonkers as to paint. Also, the Eiermann chairs, which we had restored for so much money that we could have bought new ones. And, of course, the shelves that we built ourselves. I started on them when I was living in a shared apartment in Lausanne. Then I added to them. Later on, we

were looking for a wardrobe for our kids, and suddenly we were using these shelves and put doors on them. The shelves have evolved with us. They're very important to us.

Do you feel at home here? And if so, why?
[MB] I definitely feel very at home here.
[LC] I feel at home here too. That also has to do with the neighborhood, the location, the people who work here, the fact that the swimming pool is nearby, as well as the school. It's like a rock that you throw in the water and create ripples. We've never had dreams of a single-family house.

But you work at the same architecture firm. Don't you want to build something for yourselves?
[MB] Yes, of course. Ideally, a five-family building. Nothing new, but a redevelopment. That would be fantastic. But whether it would be a good thing for us to build for ourselves is another question. In our projects, we often design everything down to the last lamp, but we still don't have any of our own! [LC] You're not free in a rented apartment. So we've thought about whether we should rent a shell construction nearby that we could convert ourselves. There was one proposal like that. That's something I'm interested in: renting, but designing for ourselves. I think the culture of rental management has to change in Switzerland. It's important to involve the tenants.

"My sister was really infuriated by that chair. She never thought that we would buy such an ugly piece of furniture."

4.6 Hinterbergstrasse top floor

Confirmed Renters Owing to New Perspectives and an Urban Environment

Rosmarie Baumann-Ott and Max Baumann,
artist and architect

4.5 rooms
third floor
135 m²
Move-in date 2008

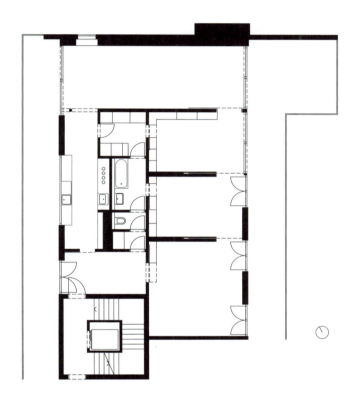
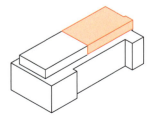

Leaving out the hallway decisively alters the plan of this top-level apartment. Each room receives additional doors, from the outdoor areas to the bedrooms to the vestibule. Various circulation patterns emerge and diverse spatial combinations become available. The kitchen and the ancillary rooms are thus enhanced, while the individual rooms become larger.

Hinterbergstrasse top floor

The terraces extending along both sides of the apartment also help with circulation. Each interior room is connected to an outdoor space.

The two outdoor areas are connected by the dining room strung between them.

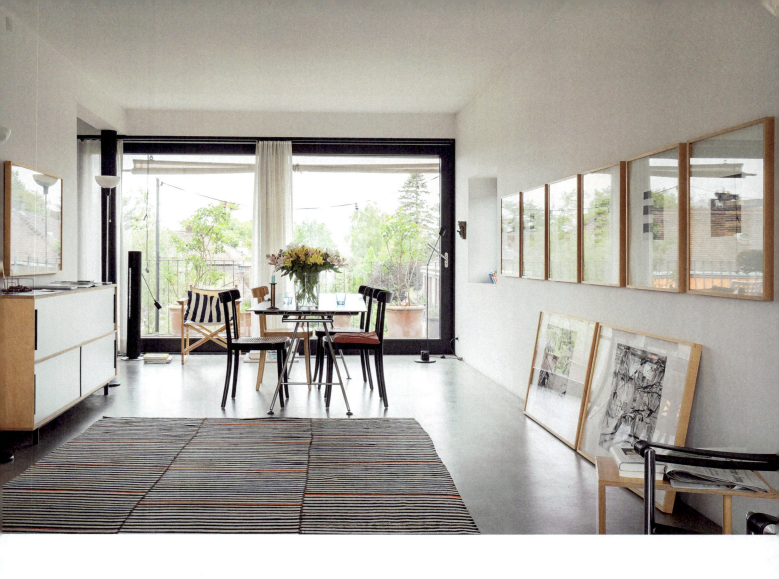

Hinterbergstrasse top floor

Hinterbergstrasse top floor 97

Large sliding doors convey the impression of living in a spacious one-room apartment, while still retaining the possibility of closed-off rooms.

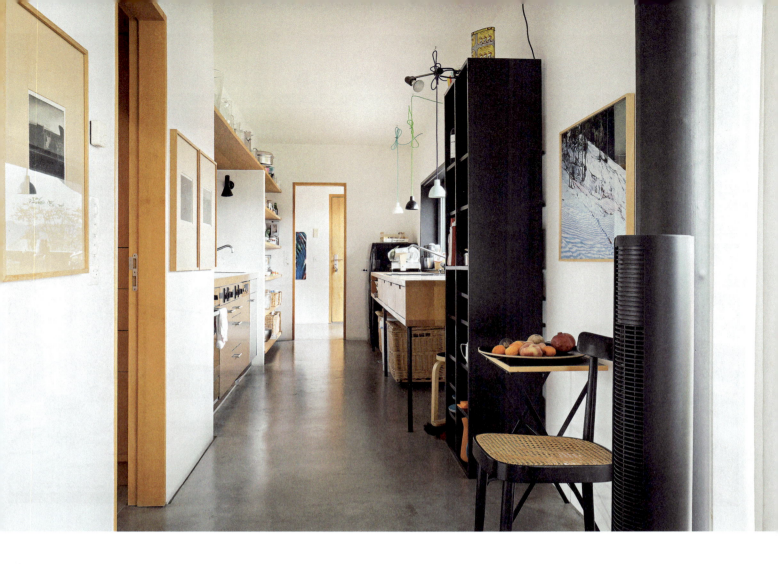

The many doors give rise to a wide variety of perspectives and lines of sight.

Because they form part of the thoroughfare, even ancillary rooms like the bathroom become part of everyday life.

"I come into this apartment to rest, read a lot, and paint."

Rosmarie Baumann-Ott, Max Baumann

Who are you?
[MB] I was an architect and I built a fair number of apartments. But not only that. [RB] I'm an artist.

How did you find this apartment?
[MB] Fifteen years ago, we built several homes in a place where we'd already been living for forty years. Of the two rural four-family houses, we kept one apartment for ourselves, and sold the others. While construction was underway, we needed a place for the interim, so we came here. When we were both still working, semi-rural living worked out well for us. But we ended up staying here. We like the urban environment, which gives our lives a new perspective. Now we're confirmed renters.

What do you like about this apartment?
[MB] It's not a typical apartment. There are various paths and rooms with distinct qualities. And because of the enfilade, you're never either just in the bedroom or not in the bedroom. You're always everywhere, somehow.
[RB] That's one difference between us. I'm not an architect, and I like that I have a room to myself that I can close off. I like the circulation, but I also like to be alone. I feel very good in this apartment, particularly since I've been able to hang my pictures in my room, so that there's a kind of counterweight to the furniture in the rest of the apartment.

What don't you like as much?
[MB] In my opinion, when things don't fit in at first glance, you have to find a solution for them. In housing construction, I think people have a lot of ingrained models and ideas, like what a kitchen is supposed to be like. But our kitchen isn't that kind of kitchen. You have to come to terms with it. For instance, we have baskets under the table so that everything isn't lying around. [RB] Or a toaster, for example. You don't see one because there's no room for one. That's why we don't have one.
[MB] Yeah, sometimes you have to economize a bit. If you don't, you'll soon be unhappy. I prefer not to have a toaster than to have one that I have to use every day. Or where do you put your clothes? That's a question that concerned me throughout my entire career. In my opinion, clothes don't belong in the bedrooms. We have a lot in the basement, and only the bare minimum up here. We've never had a traditional wardrobe, only built-in closets. They determined the space and that had to suffice. Living with the minimum is my *Wohnkultur.*

What was it like to furnish this apartment?
[MB] We knew how we wanted to furnish it very quickly. We don't have a big living room suite. It would only get in the way. When we have visitors, we sit at the dinner table. The table is the center. We already had the table. Otherwise, we would have chosen one a bit longer, because for us it isn't just a dinner table. It's also a shelf for books and things like that.
[RB] This elongated room that stretches from one facade to the other wasn't easy to furnish. But I'm very happy with how it looks now. The long wall helped, because we could hang our pictures there.

Where is the meeting point in the apartment?
[RB] The whole living area. But it changes depending on the time of day. In the morning it's incredibly beautiful on the sofa, the armchair, or the daybed. The whole living area. But it changes depending on the time of day. In the morning it's incredibly beautiful on the sofa, the armchair, or the daybed.

Do you have a favorite spot? A cozy corner?
[RB] My cozy corner is the little sofa. I feel really good there. [MB] It varies. It depends a lot on the light. I'd say the three armchairs. Each of them has a different perspective, and they're good at different times of day. For instance, from one of them, the sun on the oleander looks amazing in the morning.

What does the bathroom mean to you?
[MB] For us, the bathroom is purely functional. This bathroom doesn't bring up a lot of emotion. Except the colors, which I like. In the places we've lived in the past, we've never had a bathroom with a nice view or a large size that invites you to linger.

And the exterior room?
[MB] We spend a lot of time on the terrace. Particularly in the summer, of course. [RB] I also go out there a lot on the west side in the spring, when it's not too hot yet. I can read there and enjoy the sunset. We move around a lot in the apartment, and we often sit in different places.

"Because of the enfilade, you're never either just in the bedroom or not in the bedroom. You're always everywhere, somehow."

This apartment is just made for that.
[RB] Yeah, that's true. One person can walk behind the other without the one in front realizing it. And you can also get out of the way easily when you need quiet. With my own room, I live in a way that's opposite to the openness, flow, and circulation that the floor plan suggests. On the contrary, I need to be centered.

You already mentioned the particular nature of the kitchen.
[MB] Yes, usually kitchens are arranged in one of two ways: one is a separate room, and the other is open to the living or dining room. Ours is a third type: the kitchen is the hallway. Like in the old Italian houses, you go through the kitchen into the apartment. It's nice. The kitchen is integrated, but not dominant.

Do you have a favorite piece of furniture? Does it have a story?
[RB] For me, it's the sofa from Le Corbusier. I had to wait for it for decades, because there was no space for it in the old apartment. When I finally had the sofa and could curl up on it, it became like another retreat for me.
[MB] I don't have a favorite piece of furniture, but I enjoy the different views from the three armchairs that I mentioned.

What makes you feel at home here?
[MB] It's the rooms. It's nice to hang out in them and enjoy the things that are there, like the art objects. We live with them. That's home.
[RB] I come into this apartment to rest, read a lot, and paint. I also like it aesthetically. There are a lot of energy centers in this apartment. I really appreciate that. They make it my home.

4.7   Scheffelstrasse second floor

There from the Final Push, Now Nine Years at Home

Monika Walther and Klas Johansson,
architect and finance mathematics engineer
with Nils and Linnea

4.5 rooms
second floor
119 m²
Move-in date 2013
→ 2.3.6

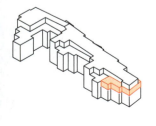

Living and dining room, kitchen, and entryway form a spatial unity that defines the plan. Large corner windows with wide sills create a direct connection between this communal area and the various neighborhoods the apartment looks out on.

Scheffelstrasse second floor

The architecture is toned down in the private rooms, which feel spacious thanks to large windows. Each room retains its own character.

Forming part of the entryway, the kitchen is the meeting place and focal point of the apartment.

"When you come home, you're actually already in the middle of the apartment. That encourages communication."

Monika Walther, Klas Johansson

Who are you?
[MW] Eleven years ago, I was working for Jakob Steib's firm. After about two years, I changed to the client side, and now I work at Pensimo Management AG as a developer's representative/project manager supervising major renovation and new construction projects. So I've always been very involved with building homes and I see how people live in them before the renovation and after, during the warranty inspection. It's exciting, but it's also important to get an idea of how residents furnish the apartments, what parts of a plan turn out to be practical, and what doesn't work.

How did you find this apartment?
[MW] The project was a competition that Jakob Steib's firm won. I only worked on the final push, but I already knew at the time that I really wanted this specific apartment. It was my absolute favorite apartment. One thing led to another, and we were able to buy it.

Have you made any adjustments?
[MW] Only minor ones: we had the double-folding door in the living room moved and narrowed, enlarged the bathroom a bit and changed the materials, and enclosed the coat rack—otherwise, we've really left everything as it was.

How long have you lived here?
[MW] Nine years. And we still like it a lot.

What do you particularly like?
[MW] It's a bright apartment. The various views of the mountains and the intersection, wherever something is going on. The windowsills, which are wide and set at a height that's practical, making them usable as shelf space, for instance. The way the rooms are marked off from one another and yet still hang together cohesively. The big windows with a lintel and a closed parapet that guarantee privacy despite the urban environment. The kitchen with the view into the distance and over the neighborhood. When we have guests over, they mostly sit on the windowsill at first, so if we're drinking aperitifs it feels like we're in a bar. I also like the high ceilings. That makes the room spacious. And one more thing: the nook.

What could be better?
[MW] A bigger nook for more storage space would be good. And a slightly larger entrance area would be great because of the two kids. Sometimes there are a lot of things lying around here ... But the apartment is basically well utilized.

What was it like to furnish the apartment?
[MW] We furnished it in our heads first, and then on the plan. It wasn't particularly difficult: we knew where the table would go and what room we wanted to use as the living room. Interestingly enough, our neighbors on the floor below us did exactly the opposite. So the apartment gives you a certain leeway. And there's a cozy corner.

Where is that?
[MW] That's typical of Jakob Steib's projects. In this apartment, it's there, where the sofa and the daybed are.

What is your favorite spot?
[MW] The dinner table. This is where the family gets together. Everyone also loves the rocking

chair in the oriel. Visitors sit there first. When my husband comes home in the evening, he sits there, and Nils reads his comic books there.

How do you use the balcony?
[MW] We use the balcony a lot, in both summer and winter. My husband loves to barbecue, even in the winter, when there's snow on the ground. The smoke dissipates well, and our neighbors have never complained, even though the balconies are very close to each other. I think the closed parapet is very nice, because it preserves our privacy. The balcony is also inset by half; that's practical too.

How do you move around when you first come home?
[MW] I usually go to the kitchen first. Or the dinner table.

"Everyone loves the rocking chair in the oriel. Visitors sit there first. When my husband comes home in the evening, he sits there, and Nils reads his comic books there."

Does the floor plan affect how you act?
[MW] Yes, I think it does. This apartment has a very open design. There aren't any hallway areas separating the living area from the sleeping area. When you come home, you're actually already in the middle of the apartment. That encourages communication. For instance, you can't sneak into the bedroom, you have to go through the kitchen and the dining room first. The bedrooms are accessible from the open areas, and I think that influences how a person lives.

Do you have any favorite furniture? Is there a story or a memory connected to it?
[MW] Definitely the Eames rocking chair. It fits in perfectly, and I got it as a farewell gift when I left Jakob Steib. I also really like our dinner table. The chairs are from Arne Jacobsen. They were my parents', and they were their first dining table chairs. They let me take them when I moved into a shared apartment. Oh, and there's also the Poulsen lamp. That has a great story. It came from a building that was supposed to be torn down and rebuilt by Jakob Steib. The owners wanted to throw the lights away. Jakob took all of them, and each of us in the office got two.

Do you feel at home here? And if so, why?
[MW] The apartment contributes a lot. I always look forward to coming home. We were also lucky with our neighbors, which is also important. I also like the neighborhood. Wipkingen is a good place for us. There's a lot going on, people know each other, it's vibrant, and there are a lot of things to do right around the corner.

4.8 James high-rise tenth floor

Lavish from the Foyer to the Small Apartment Itself

Christoph Schuepp,
architect

2.5 rooms
tenth floor
75 m²
Move-in date 2019
→ 2.2.2

A good design for a small apartment is challenging. This plan satisfies even our demands. The apartment is accessed through a spacious entryway. Three doors lead into the bathroom, the bedroom—accessed through a dressing room—and the living area with integrated kitchen. The enclosed balcony connects the living area to the private room, which, in turn, is connected to the bathroom. Various circulatory patterns are possible. From the bathtub, one sees the sky out over the balcony.

Our architectural inclinations take a step back to make room for a more personal atmosphere in the apartment.

In our original design, only the bathroom was given a colorful paint job. Further colors have been skillfully introduced into this apartment.

The ribbon windows afford an unencumbered breadth of view.

James high-rise tenth floor

Personal objects, pictures, and books portray a life and create ambiance!

James high-rise tenth floor 129

"When I'm alone, I keep all the doors open."

Christoph Schuepp

Who are you?
[CS] I'm an architect. I understand architecture holistically, from the draft to the execution.

How long have you lived here?
[CS] I moved my architecture firm into the third floor four years ago, and I moved into the apartment a year later. For a long time I tried to reconcile life and work. I only succeeded once I was able to rent a small space in this building and then, later, also a small apartment. It's the smallest, and there are four of them. A variety of different floor plans within one project is a specialty of SGGK's architects.

Why do you live and work here?
[CS] The James development was a household name to me, but I didn't make a point of looking here. In fact, I thought of a building on Zurich's Paul-Clairmont-Strasse that was built by the same company. But there were only big apartments there. In the end, I happened upon an ad.

What do you like about the apartment?
[CS] I particularly like that all the rooms are ten percent bigger than usual. It makes the apartment more lavish. I also like this particular plan.

What specifically do you mean by "lavish"?
[CS] It begins right in the foyer on the ground floor. And up here in the elevator area and the entrance to the apartment. You see a lot of projects where only the living room has generous proportions. But you have to be generous in the other rooms too. That creates a nice overall feel. That's exactly what they've done beautifully here.

What don't you like so much?
[CS] Mostly the execution. There are a lot of small technical flaws, particularly in the home technology. For instance, in the kitchen the range hood is a recirculating system, which I don't like. Or I think the sun protection could have been done better.

It looks like you had an easy time furnishing the apartment. It looks very consistent, as if your furniture had just been waiting for this apartment.
[CS] It's true, I didn't have much trouble furnishing it. I'm an expert at that too. Still, it was worth it to do a deep analysis. The position of the table is special here: I wanted a big table, and the way it's placed there, at a right angle to the facade, looks strange on the floor plan. But because there are also other things that are the same height, you don't notice it.

"I particularly like that all the rooms are ten percent bigger than usual. It makes the apartment more lavish."

Do you think of the room with the kitchen more as a kitchen or a living room?
[CS] It's actually a kitchen to me. I generally don't have much use for an eat-in kitchen. But here the kitchen is also a living room.

Do you like to cook? And do you like the kitchen?
[CS] I do like to cook. I would have given it a longer storage area and I wouldn't have installed a glass-ceramic stove. And why is the kitchen white higher up and gray below?

"I used kt.COLOR paints, which are unique and reflect different shades depending on the time of day."

Do you have a favorite spot?
[CS] Not really. But if I did, it would be the bathtub. Because I like to take baths, and I can open the sliding door and look out. That's very particular to this apartment. Really, I like it everywhere. Come to think of it, I even like being in the loggia in the winter.

What is your process when you come home?
[CS] There's no specific path. I come in through the entrance and go to the bathroom or the kitchen, either way.

Do you take advantage of the circulation option?
[CS] Yes, I like that option a lot. When I'm alone, I keep all the doors open. I don't need any doors. Sometimes that's different when I have visitors.

The colors in your apartment are striking. Why did you change the color scheme?
[CS] I've always wanted to do something with color. The previous tenant had painted over the original colors with one color, so I was able to carry out my own version. Working with color is exciting. There are surprises all the time. I used kt.COLOR paints, which are unique and reflect different shades depending on the time of day. I'm very happy with the results.

Do you have a favorite piece of furniture?
[CS] No.

Do you feel at home?
[CS] Yes. Because I like the qualities of the plan, the generous rooms, and the fact that you can see a lot from here. Also the fact that my office is so close. For me, there are two ideal living situations: a museum or a studio. My situation doesn't meet all of those criteria, but I feel good here nonetheless.

4.9　James high-rise　sixth floor

Trying Something New Now and Then for a Variety of Uses

Karin and Marc Briefer-Diezi,
interior designer and interior architect
with Mauriceand Lionel

4.5 rooms
sixth floor
123 m²
Move-in date 2012
→ 2.2.2

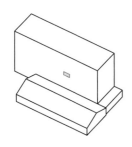

The living room was designed and built to have a cozy corner space for the living room suite. The sofa is positioned in an interesting way, with its back to the window.

The bathroom is also a tunnel washer and a corridor.

The recessed balcony functions as a sunroom, while simultaneously connecting the dining area with the master bedroom.

An apartment with many different circulatory possibilities. An especially wide entryway results from the placement of two doors next to each other.

We designed this kitchen with the image of the boss's glass-walled office in mind. It's thrust into the center of the plan, allowing the dining area to be arranged in various configurations and still be easily served.

"What I particularly like is the fluidity of the floor plan."

Karin Briefer-Diezi, Marc Briefer-Diezi

Who are you?
[MB] Karin plans interior furnishings, and I'm an interior architect. We work in a shared office with projects for residential and working environments. It's only ten minutes from here, which is ideal.

Why do you live here?
[KB] I was pregnant with our second child. We were living in a small two-and-a-half-room attic apartment without an elevator. So we were looking for a bigger apartment, and I also wanted a more comfortable life—with an elevator and a garage. We got a tip from an architect friend and we were lucky enough to get this apartment. [MB] We were familiar with SGGK, of course. We liked the idea of moving into a building designed by good architects. The first time we saw it, we were immediately struck by the interesting floor plans, the generous dimensions, the clever arrangement of the rooms, the openness, and the beautiful choice of materials. There's also another building by the same architect that's just as beautiful across the street.

What do you particularly like about the apartment?
[KB] The continuous floor plan with its morning and evening atmospheres. The sunsets are fantastic here. We take pictures of them and share them with our neighbors who don't have a western view. The colored walls and ceilings are also special. We never would have come up with a color scheme like that. [MB] What I particularly like is the fluidity of the floor plan. Also the ceiling height, which is higher than standard, and the little details, like the windowsills, the white plaster, the shadow gaps—you can see that the architects thought about everything.

What is it like living in a high-rise with children?
[KB] People always say that anywhere up to the sixth floor is fine for a family, because from there, you can still look down and communicate with the kids. Beyond that, it's difficult. I agree. Small kids who have to take the elevator—I have my doubts. The buzzer system is also difficult for kids.

What don't you like?
[KB] Also the buzzer system. But that's a detail. That and I miss having a balcony. [MB] Me too. We're not too fond of loggias. It's just the difference between having the open sky above you and stepping outside of the building or not. But I get that this building is a high-rise with a different concept from, for instance, the long building, with its big balconies.

What was it like to furnish this apartment?
[KB] We changed our minds a lot. The bedroom was once the rumpus room, the kids' rooms used to be our offices—the floor plan allows for all of that. That's great. [MB] A lot of apartments have one hallway with all the rooms arranged along it. How boring! We have various paths we can go through in this apartment. We had an easy time furnishing it. We have a lot of furniture, we also collect furniture and lend it to friends.

What is the heart of the apartment?
[KB] The dinner table is the center. [MB] Yeah, the dinner table. And the kitchen. We use those two rooms the most.

Do you have a cozy corner?
[KB] I mostly spend the evenings in my armchair reading the newspaper, while the boys play and Marc lies on the sofa.

What does the bedroom mean to you?
[KB] We sleep very well. But the bedroom isn't particularly important to us. [MB] We don't showcase it and we don't have any curtains. We use the room when we want to recuperate. We want the bedroom to be simply furnished and the bed to be comfortable.

How much value do you place on the bathroom?
[MB] It's an introverted space without any daylight. I like that. That way, you can move freely, without worrying that the neighbors can see. [KB] I think it's too small. We're not all bumping into each other yet, but our kids will be teenagers soon. One sink and one shower for four people—that's very tight. [MB] I definitely think it's still possible to switch things around again. Right now, there still isn't enough pressure to do it.

What is your routine when you come home?
[MB] I go straight to the kitchen, put down the shopping bag, and see who is around.

"Our kids can run around freely in the apartment, the various paths of the layout make for fluid patterns."

Does the floor plan affect how you act?
[MB] Of course. We often move through the house in a circle between the kitchen, the dinner table, and the living room. Our kids can run around freely in the apartment, the various paths of the layout make for fluid patterns. Thanks to its flexibility, the plan also allows us to use it in a variety of ways. We try out new things from time to time. We like that. It moves things forward. We really love how changeable our apartment is.

"The FC Zurich training facilities, where both boys play soccer, is right outside our door."

How is cooking? Is the kitchen set up in a practical way?
[KB] I used to really like to cook, but I've lost some of my enthusiasm due to the fact that the kids are picky. But I do the shopping, and I'll do the prep work. After that, Marc does most of the cooking. [MB] The kitchen is my workshop. Coming home, prepping, cooking: I like that. We're in the kitchen a lot. It gets a lot of use, and we've installed a wine refrigerator and various kitchen appliances.

Do you have a favorite piece of furniture?
[KB] Probably my Lehni side table. It's more like an exhibition piece, it almost seems curated. It always looks great, and it's constantly changing depending on the object that's added to it. [MB] My favorite piece of furniture is the sofa. It's leaving us after twenty years, unfortunately, and going to Karin's parents. I made that sofa myself. It can even convert into a bed. We bought a new one that's bigger and better fits the way we live now. I'm also a big fan of artificial light. It's important to me to that at night, the apartment is infused with a warm, atmospheric light. That's why we have a lot of different lights, mostly from Castiglioni.

What makes you feel at home here?
[KB] Our kids are growing up here. They have their friends. The neighbors in the building are good. I also used to organize a children's flea market, and I still have contacts and friends from that. I feel really comfortable here.
[MB] I like it too. The neighborhood has improved: it reached another milestone with the new buildings in the Koch precinct, the Letzigraben swimming pool is nearby, there are a lot of places to shop, the FC Zurich training facilities, where both boys play soccer, is right outside our door—we couldn't ask for much more. Hopefully we'll live here for a long time, unless we can snag ourselves a James penthouse apartment with a balcony …

"The bedroom was once the rumpus room, the kids' rooms used to be our offices—the floor plan allows for all of that. That's great."

One last question: Do the shared spaces, like the hall or the laundry, add to your sense of community here?
[KB] We mostly know people through our kids' school. [MB] There's a certain anonymity, but by now, we know a good two dozen people very well and others by sight, like people we see in the elevator. And yeah, it occurs to me that there's something else I'd like: a real common room.

4.10 Steinhofweg first floor

No Sooner Had We Stepped Inside the New, As-Yet Unfurnished Apartment Than We Felt At Home.

Jeannette and André Murer,
psychologist and architect
with Arno

4 rooms
first floor
98 m²
Move-in date 2015

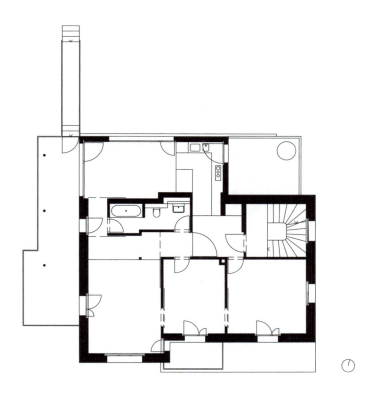
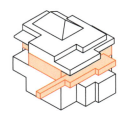

The plan is characterized by day- and nighttime configurations. Different spaces emerge according to the opening of different doors. Various circulatory possibilities arise.
At night and on Sundays, the doors are closed. Master bedroom, bath, and balcony can be joined together in a single spatial sequence. Whether this possibility is realized is up to the inhabitants.

Introduced by the renovation, an enfilade connects the rather small rooms so that the apartment seems larger than it is.

The kitchen and dining area were added on to the building. Like a sweater being darned, the little house was insulated and given a new facade of rough-sawn boards.

Thanks to an open corner, the garden gate can be used by cats as well!

James high-rise sixth floor

"There's something human about the dimensions."

Jeannette Murer, André Murer

How did you find this apartment?
[AM] I know about SGGK architects' buildings because of my job, of course. They've always fascinated me. Seven and a half years ago, I saw an announcement for this building, and it worked out. We lived in the top-floor apartment for the first six years. When our son Arno was born, we were able to move into the middle apartment, which had just become vacant.

What do you like about your apartment?
[JM] I think the colors are particularly nice. The first time I went into the unfurnished apartment, I immediately felt like it was home already. That was thrilling. A little bit of furniture is enough, and … [AM] … you feel at home. Personally, I was also interested in how the old floor plan had been transformed, how what used to be a closed structure became an open, permeable apartment. And of course the location. We're close to the city, but still in the country. That's a great thing about this house, which the architecture amplifies. For instance, the view on all sides, or the circulation options. We also really like the outside rooms. In the summer, they become the living room.

What don't you like as much?
What do you think doesn't work very well?
[AM] The sliding doors are impractical with small children. You can hear a lot through the walls, so we have to change how we do things so we don't wake our son up. Furnishing it is also a challenge. With the sliding doors and the big windows, there isn't much wall space. [JM] It takes a lot of strength to turn the doorknobs. And I also think the sliding doors are impractical.

How do you like the eggplant-colored window frames?
[AM] For me, they're like picture frames that capture the natural surroundings. I like that. [JM] Me too. You rarely see such dark window frames.

Where is your favorite spot?
[JM] Definitely the living room. I play with Arno there a lot. I spend a lot of time there.
[AM] For me, it's the dining room, with the big picture window. In the morning, when the sun shines in, that brings out the best in that room. It's also a bit separate from the rest of the apartment, which makes it ideal for the home office. I like working here.

What do you think is the heart of the apartment?
[AM] In the summer, definitely the balcony. It makes my stomach turn to think that we may have to move out of here someday because of space. Where are we going to find an apartment like this again?

"In the morning, when the sun shines in, that brings out the best in that room."

What does the bathroom mean to you?
[JM] It's too small to spend much time in there. But the colors are really nice. [AM] I like the loud colors too.

What is your routine when you come home?
[JM] First thing, I always go straight to the kitchen to put down the shopping bag. Then I take

care of Arno in the dining room or the living room. [AM] In the summer, I often go through the garden and over the bridge into the house. That way, I can see where my sweethearts are from the outside. It's like having a private entrance.

Do you use the internal circulation options?
[AM] Yes, especially with Arno. Sometimes there are also funny situations, like last week: Jeannette had called me, and I set off in one direction, and she went in the other, and then we changed direction almost simultaneously. In this fairly small apartment, it took a while for us to find one another.

How important is the kitchen?
[JM] I really like to cook. Unfortunately, I haven't had much time for it since Arno was born. [AM] It's fascinating that we actually never spend time with guests in the living room, always in the dining room. I think it's wonderful when you're cooking and can be part of the conversation at the same time.

Do you have a favorite piece of furniture?
[AM] My favorite piece of furniture is the folding chair. I worked in China for Ai Weiwei for a long time and in India at Studio Mumbai. The carpenters who I worked with there gave me this chair. They made it themselves.
[JM] My favorite is the sideboard in the living room. André picked out most of the furniture—he's more responsible for it.

One last question: Do you feel at home here? And if so, why?
[JM] I like it a lot: The way we've arranged the apartment, the colors, the floor plan, being close to the city, our colleagues and our families live nearby. And the neighborhood is very open. [AM] The size of the rooms also adds to the nice feel. There's something human about the dimensions.

"The first time I went into the unfurnished apartment, I immediately felt like it was home already."

4.11 Hirschi building maisonette

A Vibrant Home Is Made with Color, Dogs, and a Lot of Love

Daniela Anderhub and Maurizio D. Sacchet,
office manager und construction manager

5.5 rooms maisonette apartment
147 m²
Move-in date 2008

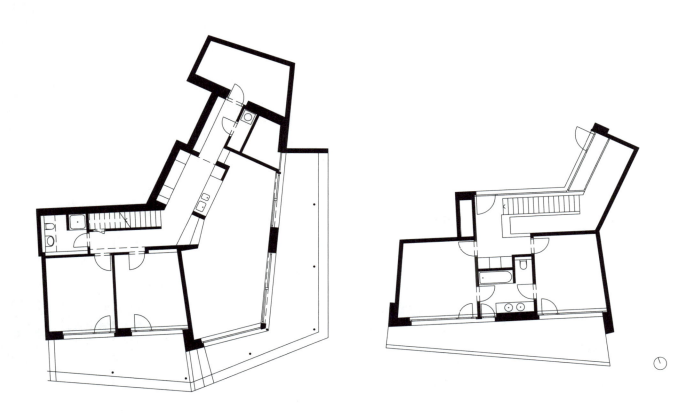
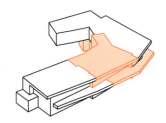

The steep hillside location and division of the rooms determine the design of this three-family home. This apartment is accessed through the shared patio and entered at bedroom level. The two-story stairwell becomes an entrance hall connecting to the kitchen. The living and dining area, three steps lower, thus has an especially high ceiling.

Hirschi building maisonette

The shared patio, with its "Mexican" color scheme, references the developer's familial ties to that country.

With its large opening onto the dining area, the kitchen becomes part of the connection to the stairwell.

Colorfully painted shafts bring daylight into the bathroom, which, due to the sloping hillside, lies at the rear of the building.

Diagonal sight-lines make the apartment feel like a house.

Hirschi building maisonette 169

"We wouldn't have had the confidence to use colors like these."

Daniela Anderhub, Maurizio D. Sacchet

Who are you and what was it about this apartment that caught your attention?
[DA] Fourteen years ago, we were looking for a new apartment. We found this one online and we were so excited that we grabbed it as soon as our application was approved. I work in real estate as an office manager. [MS] I'm a construction manager and I work in the same office, but I'm freelance.

Do you live here because of the architecture or the surrounding area?
[DA] At first, it was the architecture and the location, the fantastic view of the Alps. With today's dense construction, you can't take such an expansive vista for granted. And I enjoy the natural environment around here every day. We only fell for the area later.

Were you aware of the architecture firm that designed this house beforehand?
[MS] I was familiar with the James development in Zurich. [DA] No, but if we were looking for something else now or building something ourselves, we'd most likely go with these architects.

What do you particularly like about the apartment?
[MS] I think the room layout is great. The bathroom with the separate dressing room, everything is very well integrated. The spatial proportions are also right. The great use of materials with the bricks, the color scheme, the ceiling heights, the fact that the exposed concrete is painted. [DA] For us, as a two-person household with two dogs, it's the ideal apartment. I particularly like the atmosphere when I come home. I'm honestly grateful every day that I live here. [MS] The only thing that's missing is awnings. It gets very hot in the living room in the summer. The sun shines right in in the middle of the day. The porch doesn't do much to stop that. The windows are big, and the sun tends to fade our fabrics. Sometimes we roll down the wooden shutters, but then it's pitch dark.

What was it like to furnish this room?
[DA] We've been living together since we were thirty. Back then, we combined our households and we each brought things from our previous lives. That created a colorful mix that we think works. So we actually already had all the furniture we needed when we moved in here. The only thing that's new is the sofa. We planned out how we were going to furnish it first. That was helpful for me, because certain pieces of furniture are very important to me. I would have been upset if I couldn't find a place for them. I admit, the upstairs dressing room is definitely not perfectly furnished. But we already had the wardrobe and we didn't want to install a custom closet in a rented apartment.

What's your favorite spot?
[MS] The sofa. [DA] I have several, depending on the time of day and what I'm doing: the sofa early in the morning, because of the birdhouse. Then the chaise longue, but preferably in the middle of the day, when I'm reading or cuddling a bit with the dogs. I also like the kitchen a lot, and the balcony. I think every spot has its appeal.

What is the heart of the apartment?
[DA] The living and dining room, in conjunction with the kitchen.

Where do the two of you meet when you get home?
[MS] Here in the kitchen, of course. [DA] Yeah, because he's hungry and I'm usually in the kitchen already. [MS] When I come home a bit

on the early side, we often go to the upper balcony for an aperitif.

What does the bedroom mean to you?
[DA] It's an important place for me. It's a place of rest and a retreat. That's why it's also sparsely furnished. [MS] You can see Mount Rigi and Mount Pilatus from our bedroom. We enjoy that view a lot on weekends.

The bathroom?
[DA] That's also important to me. I wish it were twice as big. [MS] I prefer to shower downstairs and then use the upstairs bathroom after that.

What do you use more, the upstairs balcony or the outdoor space on the ground floor?
[MS] It depends on the time of day. In the morning, we're mostly downstairs, then we spend more time upstairs in the afternoon, enjoying the sun. [DA] I'm grateful for the beautiful, spacious outside areas. They mean a lot to me.

"You can see Mount Rigi and Mount Pilatus from our bedroom. We enjoy that view a lot on weekends."

What's your routine when you come home?
[MS] First I get changed and have a shower, then, as I said, I head to the kitchen. [DA] I usually come home with the groceries and put them down in the kitchen. Then I open the blinds, let the dogs out, put the groceries away, and make a tea or a coffee. Then I go upstairs and change.

Does the kitchen foster your love of cooking?
[DA] Yeah, I really like cooking. But there's not enough counter space when we have a lot of guests. Otherwise, it has everything you need. The kitchen is part of the living area, so I always make sure that it's clean. [MS] The kitchen is well designed considering the available space. I also like the two steps from the kitchen to the living and dining room, as well as how close it is to our guests when we're cooking.

How is it living with these colors?
[MS] Excellent. They have a presence, but they don't dominate, and they go really well together. [DA] I like them too. We've never had anything like that. We also probably wouldn't have had the confidence to use colors like these. They're a real joy.

They're Mexican colors. Is it a coincidence that your dogs are a Mexican breed?
[MS] Yes, that's really quite a funny coincidence!

Do you have a favorite piece of furniture?
[MS] The sofa, because it's so comfortable. And the antique armchair. I picked that out personally. Daniela wanted a different one, but I liked this one a lot. [DA] I have a lot of favorite pieces—like this sideboard. They're part of my life, and they've survived every move. I've looked after them.

What makes you feel at home here?
[MS] The two of us. [DA] Yeah, us as a couple. We complement each other well. We inspire each other. That's how a home is made. This apartment is an ideal framework that we've turned into something very personal with our belongings and furniture, but also with ourselves as people, our dogs, and a lot of love. For us, it's a privilege to be here. I've never lived in one place for so long. But a change will come at some point—you have to stay open.

Food for Architects
Volume 4: I Never Want to Have to Move

Published by: Steib Gmür Geschwentner Kyburz Partner
Introduction: Patrick Gmür
Interviews: Corinne Gasal
Lithography: Dieter Hall
Photography: Rita Palanikumar
Editor: Christoph Wieser
Translation: Hunter Bolin, Marc Hiatt and Joel Scott for
Gegensatz Translation Collective
Proofreading: Marc Hiatt and Joel Scott for Gegensatz Translation Collective
Design and layout: Sibylle Kanalz, Jürg Schönenberger, Nora Spaniol
Floor plan processing: Giuseppe Allegri
Image processing: Karin Prasser
 Photo credits: Rita Palanikumar, except for those by Georg Aerni p. 7 m., 9 m., 11 m.; Gonzalo Lozano Arce p. 174–179; Roger Frei p. 7 l., 7r., 8, 9 l., 9r., 10, 11; Dieter Hall p. 2–6
Printing and binding: DZA Druckerei zu Altenburg GmbH, Thuringia

© 2023 Steib Gmür Geschwentner Kyburz Partner and Park Books AG, Zurich
© for the texts: the authors

Park Books
Niederdorfstrasse 54
8001 Zurich
Switzerland
www.park-books.com

Park Books has received support from the Federal Office of Culture with a general subsidy for the years 2021–2024.

All rights reserved; no part of this publication may be reproduced, stored in a retrieval system or transmitted in any form or by any means, electronic, mechanical, photocopying, recording, or otherwise, without the prior written consent of the publisher.

ISBN 978-3-03860-360-3

This book is volume 4 of Food for Architects, a set of five volumes in a slipcase which are not available separately.

5

Five Courses for Four Friends

Steib Gmür Geschwentner Kyburz
A Well-Tended Conversation

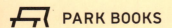

It's About Space!

Respecting, Fostering, and Appreciating
It takes space to make space. In our architecture firm, which has four partners and some thirty to forty staff members, this primarily means leaving space for ideas. Which is why we try to shape our everyday working environment in a way that leaves time to pursue ideas, both on our own and together. Although projects from major architects such as Le Corbusier, Mies van der Rohe, Frank Lloyd Wright, Alvar Aalto, or Álvaro Siza are often labeled as having sole creators, we know that architectural projects are always the result of challenging work undertaken as a team. We are four friends who enjoy designing, constructing, and building projects, either alone or together, but always with the unfailing support of our staff. We know our strengths, but we're also aware of our weaknesses. And we apply this knowledge on a daily basis.

When it comes to developing floor plans for apartments, our expertise in this field allows us to be quick and creative, and gives us the experience to deliver the goods. We are always happy to pass on our knowledge and also see ourselves as mentors. Both Matthias Kyburz and Michael Geschwentner were initially students and interns for Jakob Stein and Patrick Gmür. Today, they are both partners. Our most important goal is to share our knowledge with our staff. And to this end, we have structured our firm in a way that welcomes new partners.

Our organizational structure is simple and straightforward: everyone does everything! This blurring of boundaries certainly leads to more than the odd discussion and means that we always have to work out who's doing what. But this vagueness is actually the secret to the way we work together, as it gives everyone in our firm the space they need to be creative. Our partners also have space to follow their own pursuits. We have learned that we can only change our own actions, not those of our friends. The most important thing is mutual trust and the high level of appreciation we have for each other.

In our weekly management meetings and discussion sessions, we go over both our commissions and our working methods. We try to get to the bottom of any questions or issues we

We are four friends who enjoy designing, constructing, and building projects, either alone or together.

may have and to draw the relevant conclusions. At the same time, we are always looking for possible spaces that will open up room to maneuver in terms of design. We attempt to think through things that might seem impossible or illogical. We know that by working together, we will always land with our feet on the ground.

Starting in the Center
Alongside their organization, materialization, structure, and lines of sight, our apartment designs are above all centered around one idea: creating spaces. But the same old requirements, our knowledge of what the tenants will want, as well as legal requirements around accessibility often limit the scope of our desire to create spatial diversity when it comes to larger-scale apartment buildings. In addition, construction volumes are becoming increasingly large in order to boost their sustainability. What's more, a single stairwell with just a single lift is supposed to provide access to as many apartments as possible.

For this reason, we see the dark spaces at the center of these buildings as a design opportunity. Optimized floor plans can be supplemented with illuminated stairwells or other means of introducing light. We provide apartments on the top floor with private patios or rooftop terraces that are protected from prying eyes. In the apartments in the James development, for example, these spaces provide particularly stunning views of the city.

The Spatial Diversity of Interstitial Spaces
When possible, we try to sneak extra-high ceilings into our apartment designs. Which is why

We see the dark spaces at the center of these buildings as a design opportunity.

we often work with split-level solutions and design apartments that unfurl over multiple levels of a building. For the same reason, we are greatly interested in the typology of row houses. We have learned that in the interstitial spaces of a given building—for example between the various floors, in the corners of the building, or through melding together different typologies—it is often possible to open up new architectural and spatial concepts.

In line with this approach, in our Altwiesen building complex in the district of Schwamendigen in Zurich, we combined "row houses" with apartment buildings of up to seven stories into innovative volumes. We continued pursuing this approach on our Schweighof building project in Kriens, developing stacked row houses that were laid out differently depending on their position within the building. In addition, the overlying penthouses benefit from their position on the top floor, for example through skylights in the bathrooms and sheltered sun decks.

The Potential of Connections
It can sometimes happen that the allocation of space—along with the desired mix of apartments for a given project—leaves no room for spatial experiments. In one instance, the client threatened to cancel our contract if we came to them with one more staircase or split-level solution. In such cases, we try to find workarounds. In entry halls and stairwells, we look for alternative places for spatially interesting situations. Our "Goethe" staircase in one of the two apartment buildings for students and staff of the University Hospital Zurich, which serves as the central hub and meeting point of the building, is a good illustration of our approach in this regard.

Occasionally, we furnish buildings with generously sized stairwells, unified materials, or colorfully painted spaces with innovative lighting features, such as in the project on the Alte Landstrasse in Kloten, which provide these functional spaces with their own identity. The path from parking garage to doorstep thus becomes a spatial experience. Of course, we also try to keep the number of staircases and elevators in a given building to a minimum, supplementing them with covered walkways, *rues intérieures*, or connecting corridors. If these are able to be suffused with natural light, they cease to feel long and narrow.

Thanks to an additional emergency staircase, the spacious main stairwell in the Bombach housing complex in Zurich can also be used as a shared play area. In the replacement

In entry halls and stairwells, we look for alternative places for spatially interesting situations.

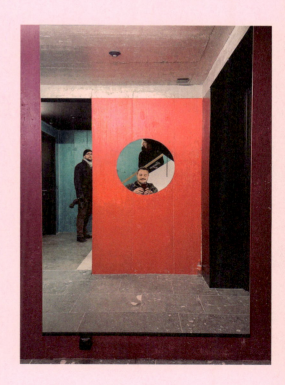

It's About Space! 9

Thanks to an additional emergency staircase, the stairwell can also be used as a shared play area.

buildings on Brüderhoferweg in Zurich, two stairwells share a single elevator. The two sections of the building are offset from one another by means of a split-level design, allowing them to be perfectly integrated into the surrounding landscape. Because of this split-level solution, the top-level apartments were able to be given one-and-a-half-story living rooms.

Better Together
In recent years, we have been able to provide work for between thirty and sixty staff members in various configurations. Naturally, we hope that this is something we will be able to continue to do. Our large team needs its daily "architectural fodder"—not just the gastronomic kind at our Friday lunches! What we mean by this is that we give our employees exciting, diverse, and instructive projects to work on. We know that without our team, we would neither be able to participate in competitions and tender processes nor plan and carry out our existing projects. The main takeaway here is that we all learn from each other!

The Steib Gmür Geschwentner Kyburz partnership was first founded as a legal entity three years ago, although some of us have been friends for over thirty years. Even though we sometimes operate in different constellations, we are constantly working together on some project or another. We knew that running an architecture firm with four partners would be demanding, but we still decided to take the leap. The pleasure of working together with friends is our biggest motivator. Architecture is about space in all its forms. The fact that we all grant each other the space we need is a key facet of how we approach our work. And the last of our five-volume series of books, which deals with the subject of apartment construction, thus focuses on creating these kinds of open spaces, along with other topics that bring people together—which of course includes food.

Patrick Gmür

We knew that running an architecture firm with four partners would be demanding, but we still decided to take the leap.

It's About Space!

Contents

Five Courses for Four Friends
A Well-Tended Conversation

"... go see a good architect." p.15

5.1	The Salad p.26
	Endive and Orange Salad with Pecorino and Candied Walnuts

5.2	The Soup p.32
	Pea and Ricotta Soup with Mint

5.3	The Appetizer p.38
	Spaghetti with Agretti and Anchovies

5.4	The Main Course p.58
	Osso Buco with Saffron Risotto

5.5	The Dessert p.64
	Panna Cotta eith Agar-Agar

"... go see a good architect."

Marrying the boss / In the shadow of the elders / Expertise versus presentation / Looking for a necktie in Finland / "It's only brutalism, but we like it" / The joy of a rude email / Communicating from a distance

a meal on an April evening...

Moderator and editor:
Gudrun Sachse

In the kitchen of the office on Flüelastrasse in Zurich, Petra Schlaefle is preparing a five-course meal. This modern kitchen contains a dishwasher, a combi-steamer, and a built-in oven—the works. A showroom kitchen, you could almost say, one that's ready for any culinary possibility. For the past two years, Petra has been a private chef for the architecture firm. She cooks to order. Next to the kitchen area is a long table. It's set with a white paper tablecloth, white crockery, and red-and-white-checkered napkins. Pencils lie next to the cutlery. But they're not standard pencils, as we'll soon find out. "Let's not sit next to each other," says Matthias Kyburz to Michael Geschwentner. "It's better to mix up the age groups." Each of the four partners place a bottle of wine at the end of the table. "Let's have an aperitif, then we can put the white wine back in the fridge," suggests Patrick Gmür, as he pulls out a cork with a pop. The men lean back against the windowsill and raise their glasses to a convivial evening. Jakob Steib asks, "Should I take off my scarf, or is it fine the way it is? It hides my wrinkled neck." Matthias Kyburz: "Maybe it's better to ask the photographer." Steib's scarf stays on, the silk fabric offering a pleasant warmth. Each partner finally finds a place to sit on one of the Moser chairs. Jakob Steib, whom everyone calls Joggi, is next to Matthias Kyburz, who sits opposite Patrick Gmür, who in turn is sitting by the counter next to Michael Geschwentner.

So you have lunch here at this table every Friday?
[Matthias] Yes, but it's usually a bigger gathering. On Fridays, the staff from the Wettingerwies office join us. There can be up to thirty people, so it can be a tight squeeze.
[Michael] The CO_2 levels are pretty high in here then.

The vegetarian lunch is written on the door every Friday

The CO$_2$ levels get pretty high in here.

"...go see a good architect." 17

We're at our best in plaid!

«Man fühlt sich am meisten als Schriftsteller, wenn man mit der Hand schreibt.»

"...go see a good architect."   19

Nobody ever sits next to me.

Is it compulsory for employees to eat together with the bosses each Friday?
Patrick You don't have to say that you'll be there, but you do have to say if you won't.
Michael It's sort of a hidden obligation.
Patrick It makes it easier for the chef to plan the meals.
Michael Patrick was the one who initiated the Friday lunch tradition.
Joggi We've had a kitchen for a long time in the Wettingerwies office. One of our employees, Nathalie, complained that there was no real place to eat here in the Flüelastrasse office, and asked if she could move back to the other office. So a year ago, we had a kitchen installed here too.

Is Nathalie still working with you?
Matthias Absolutely, now that we have a kitchen.
Patrick There's the famous example of the River Café in London, which was established by Ruth Rogers, the wife of Richard Rogers. She started off by making sandwiches for employees in the architecture firm, then set up a cafeteria. Today, everyone says it's one of the best Italian restaurants outside of Italy. The idea of eating together with other people has always appealed to me, and it has been well received by our employees, too.
Michael Everyone pays ten francs, including us. Apprentices and interns pay five francs. Guests pay twenty.

Does the office benefit from it?
Do your employees really want to eat together with their bosses on Fridays?
Matthias They value it. If Petra's not here, people even volunteer to cook for everyone.
Patrick People who are already working together on a project or share a workspace, tend to sit together anyway. The goal is not to have everyone at the table opening up and talking about their innermost feelings.
Joggi The four of us always have a Friday morning meeting, and we have an opportunity to compare notes then. So we don't need to sit together at the table for lunch afterwards.
Michael It's not a meeting in disguise. And it's good for new employees, it helps them to get to know people.

Do the spots next to you four get taken quickly—or do they stay empty?

Matthias We get pushed to the edges.
Joggi Nobody ever sits next to me.
Michael On field trips, nobody ever sits beside the teacher.
Joggi II always try to be as laid-back as possible so that people say, he's different when you talk to him one-on-one... I'm just kidding. The four of us always come toward the end of lunch. But it's not like the person next to me stands up and leaves as soon as I've sat down. It's a relaxed atmosphere.

Which one of you chose the menu for this evening?

Patrick The chef. I just had one request: that it include spaghetti or some other pasta. I also clarified beforehand that everyone likes what is being served today. I didn't check with you, Joggi, but Michael told me that you eat everything.
Joggi For me, pasta is very important. What I'm curious about today is how the agretti is cooked. Together in the water with the pasta, or is it steamed briefly beforehand? Petra? Oh, I see, just for two minutes in the water. I've gotten into cooking since I've been trying to lose weight. I like to cook something that can simmer away for hours, while I read something or wash the dishes in the meantime. I don't like having to rush around.
Matthias I only cook on weekends. Taking my time buying the ingredients in the morning and then spending all day preparing the food relaxes me.
Joggi Shopping is the first stage of cooking.

"...go see a good architect." 21

chilled pea & mint soup
*
new potatoes & asparagus with butter & herbs
*
strawberry tartlets

It's like eating at home—like in a big family! It does our team good!

"...go see a good architect." 23

"...go see a good architect."

5.1 The Salad

Endive and Orange Salad with Pecorino and Candied Walnuts

I've even had the privilege of looking after Patrick's two cats; that was a clear sign of trust.

Here comes the salad. Four partners means four opinions. Was the reason nobody chose today's menu to avoid arguments?

[Patrick] Things are much easier to bear when you're in a team. It also spreads the work around. You can talk about problems and develop strategies together. If a client starts making demands that we think are outrageous, we talk the situation through with each other and calm each other down, instead of going straight to a lawyer. When things are running smoothly, there's hardly anything to take care of, but when something doesn't pan out, being able to cushion the blow together is helpful.

Ideally, partners should be people you can depend on in a whole range of life situations. Is that the case for you guys?

[Matthias] I've even had the privilege of looking after Patrick's two cats; that was a clear sign he trusts me.

[Joggi] Our private lives and our work lives merge, but that doesn't mean that we go on vacation together. For our partners at home, that would be going too far.

Speaking of which: Matthias und Michael, if I may, it's a little like you've married your bosses.

Joggi, I've known you longer than I've known my current wife.

[Matthias] I've known Joggi the longest. He was my professor, then my boss—it has been an interesting process involving a degree of adjustment. Many young architects undergo these kinds of processes. Working together as architects is always an intimate process, which leads to you developing a relationship with each other. In the best-case scenario, the intern ends up becoming partner. It's not something that happens overnight, it can take a good twenty years. It needs time.

[Patrick] That kind of time allows trust to grow. Michael and I have also known each other for a very long time. The secret is to allow yourself some liberty. Take Joggi and me, for instance. The notion of us adapting to each other is hopeless; we just let ourselves be the way we are, and accept our differences.

[Joggi] Patrick and I never had a burning desire to set up an architecture firm together. We both worked in our own firms, and then we'd come together to work on individual projects. I noticed early on that Matthias was talented. I was always worried that he'd come to me one day and say that he was going to go out on his own. Luckily for us, he's content with things the way they are.

[Matthias] Well, first and foremost, I've heard the lamentations of colleagues who have set up their own firms. It's not an easy step to take. I felt privileged working here with Joggi and was able to participate in projects and competitions, so there was no reason for me to leave. Things were too good.

[Joggi] You always said that wasn't what you were looking for.

Would you say that in some sense, you're standing in the shadows of the older generation?

[Patrick] They say that an architect over the age of fifty-five is experienced, not old. If that's the case, then we would talk about standing in the shadow of experience. Under fifty-five, an architect can even be thought of as young.

[Michael] When I was getting to know Patrick, I went through a very similar process to Matthias and Joggi. When Patrick left the firm, I had to deal with things on my own. As a boss, I started seeing things from a different perspective. I kept asking myself: What would Patrick do? I drew on the years we'd spent working together, and also on the fact that his name, Gmür, was still in the firm's name. That kept me grounded. During those seven years, I learned to stand on my own two feet.

[Patrick] Joggi, I've known you longer than I've known my current wife.

[Joggi] I met you through Regula, your girlfriend at the time. Regula was working for my parents in the architecture firm back then.

[Patrick] That's right, she was an intern. My cousin, who started studying architecture together with you, was always telling me he knew an architect from Basel whose parents were also architects.

[Joggi] We invited her to dinner once and she asked if she could bring her boyfriend. That was you. You guys brought a little box of Sprüngli chocolates. It's funny, the things you remember…

I noticed early on that Matthias was talented.

I kept asking myself: What would Patrick do?

Also a collector of shoes: Michael

The Salad

As a boss, I started seeing things from a different perspective.

...ich habe zurückgerufen, aber dieser liebe Herr Kohler wusste nicht mehr, um was es ging....komischer Typ.

Steib Gmür Geschwentner Kyburz Partner AG
Architekten & Stadtplaner

The Salad 31

5.2 The Soup

Pea and Ricotta Soup with Mint

And now, you're sitting here together, enjoying pea and ricotta soup with mint. How lovely.

Patrick It was difficult for architects to set up their own firm in the early 1990s. Do you remember the Talwiesen competition? For us small firms, that was a big competition. Back then, we had five employees. Both of our firms got through to the second round of the tender process. Our two firms, and a third one too. Both of us were convinced that one of our firms would win, so we made a deal. No matter who placed first, the other would also be allowed to construct a building on the plot. Of course, the third firm won. But that was the beginning of our collaboration.

Joggi We became bigger because we merged. But we never wanted to become a really big firm. You only become really big when you release the handbrake and take on every project that comes your way. We were never driven by profit in that way…

Patrick We did things that were of interest to us, things we wanted to try out.

Joggi Petra, this is delicious.

The pencil is as important to an architect as a pipe wrench is to a plumber. You've even placed pencils next to the cutlery. Patrick has already gotten creative on the tablecloth…

Patrick That was a water stain. Now it's an eye.

We were never driven by profit in that way…

Forza Italia, fine footwear: Matthias

...we did things that were of interest to us, things we wanted to try out.

And to the side of it there's a cat. A beautifully drawn cat.

Patrick ...when we were at university, computers were just arriving on the scene, so we're rather old school. You don't actually need a pencil anymore these days. So we gift each new employee a soft-leaded pencil. Just like this one—they're a bit longer and sit better in your hand.

Michael I've acquired the habit of holding a pencil in my hand when I think. When I'm helping my son with math exercises at home, before long, I'll take out a pencil and explain something by sketching it out. It's automatic. A part of linguistic expression.

Patrick We mainly build apartments. And building apartments has a connection with the dimensions of the human body. How wide is a corridor, how high is a kitchen? If you're using a computer mouse and a cable for design, you lose the feel for dimensions, in my opinion.

Do the digital natives working with you share this view?

Michael They notice it when we point it out to them. And then they're surprised. Maybe it's just our point of view, but I strongly believe that you lose sight of dimensions when you're just zooming in and out on a screen. If a plan is coherent, you look at it and can see whether everything is correct without needing to measure it again.

Patrick We think with our hands. By drawing, I can tell if an apartment will work out. As we design, we mold everyday living into a layout to create the perfect arrangement.

Joggi On the other hand, digital natives can do things we can't. I see that with my son, who is very well-informed, but hardly ever reads. They've got other channels.

I've acquired the habit of holding a pencil in my hand when I think.

The Soup

Dwelling can be taken apart and put back together again every day.

5.3 The Appetizer

Spaghetti with Agretti and Anchovies

38

How about a little more wine to go with the appetizer? Each of you brought a bottle—I'm guessing from your own cellars at home.

[Joggi] I got mine from the Coop supermarket next door. It has a score of 99 points. I would pour it now, Patrick, to let it breathe. It should be good; it did cost over 30 francs, after all. The best wines aren't in the highest price category.

[Matthias] It was Patrick who requested we all bring a bottle. In summer I prefer white wine, in winter red.

[Patrick] I've been exploring white wine over the last two years.

[Joggi] It tastes a little bit like I expected. A good wine; it just needs to breathe more.

[Michael] I'm more of a beer drinker.

You all look very dapper. Did you dress up especially for this evening—or do you

It tastes a little bit like I expected.

always look like this, and is this how architects present themselves?

[Patrick] Finely checkered is my favorite pattern.

[Matthias] This is what I normally wear.

[Joggi] I wear this silk scarf when it's chilly outside. Today it was seven degrees Celsius. When I'm on a judging panel, I wear a necktie. I remember one Federation of Swiss Architects (FSA) expedition to Finland. We were invited to dinner by the Finnish Association of Architects and wearing a necktie was part of the dress code, but none of us had one with us. We spent a whole day looking for neckties. Even with the ties, you could hardly have called us overdressed. Things are different in Switzerland.

[Patrick] Years ago, architects wore dark neckties with a square end. Menswear specialist Hannes B. in Zurich always put checkered shirts aside for me. He always recommended a wide necktie, like those worn by Gilbert & George. The only problem for me is that I can't tie a knot.

[Joggi] At Arthur Rüegg's eightieth birthday, Jacques Herzog was telling us that Arthur also wore checkered shirts with knitted, square-end ties.

Cookbooks, one of our passions

Years ago, architects wore dark neckties with a square end.

Architects need to be able to present themselves and to speak about things articulately in a wide range of settings. What's more important: expertise or how you present yourself?
[Patrick] It's the combination that's important. An architect needs to be able to design, and be able to communicate their design to others. When I am on a judging panel and an architect can't express themselves during a presentation, I feel very sorry for them.
[Joggi] I'm nearly sixty-five and I still don't like giving presentations.
[Michael] That's funny. One time I asked you if you got nervous before presentations, and you said you don't.
[Joggi] Then you asked me at the wrong moment!
[Matthias] Probably after he gave the presentation.

Judging panels are becoming larger all the time, including all kinds of specialist to cover anything that might come up. To what extent does that change the architect's task?
[Joggi] Recently, a judging panel had to use three Doodle polls to set up a first meeting. It's true that the panels are growing. A lot is demanded of the architects, so the panels have to include experts.
[Michael] Often, you don't know who to address during the presentation, and that's challenging. In addition, having many experts can have an influence on the creative process. That can be an impediment.

What do you want to toast to?
[Michael] To friendship!
[Matthias] To the fact that we can all sit here and enjoy some delicious food.

Or to you four never running out of creativity?
[Patrick] We are in the happy position of being able to be selective about what we want to do. We make sure that we only take on projects that allow us to be creative.

[Matthias] When I think of colleagues in Italy, I see that we are pretty privileged here in Switzerland. Especially when it comes to building apartments. No one is interested in this field in Italy, it doesn't give you enough to do as an architect, and there are more constraints than in Switzerland.

[Michael] It's helpful to be an optimist when you're an architect. Sometimes, you can become exasperated with certain topics. It's important to get to the core of the task. That's where my inner optimist comes through, when I get to that moment that inspires me. Searching for a solution is perhaps a little more difficult than it used to be, but you always find a way. Maybe you need to move the cellar into the apartment itself, or need to rethink the connective elements. It might sound trivial, but a lot can come out of simple ideas. But it also takes hard work and perseverance.

[Matthias] Optimism is a vital part of the job. You could also call it naivety. But not letting yourself be hindered by too much knowledge is no bad thing.

[Joggi] It's also important to note that we didn't always have it easy. We have had a few setbacks, that's for sure. And thank goodness for that—it means we still have the freedom to be naive. We've been lucky, but things could have gone the other way, and that would be frustrating because then you have to take on projects that become stressful. We've had these kinds of projects time and again, but as the years have gone by, we've been able to free ourselves of them.

[Patrick] Dwelling spaces can be dismantled and rearranged in new ways. A bathtub in the kitchen. A cellar inside an apartment is not counted as a room. Wide doors to let more light in. The interesting thing is that many ideas aren't immediately obvious.

Competitions haven't actually been around for that long in Switzerland...

[Joggi] They didn't emerge until the 1990s. Before that, firms received commissions directly. Competitions were just for school buildings or art museums, if anything. In Basel, Carl Fingerhuth was the one who established the culture of competitions more broadly. Following Basel's example, one city passed the

Our daily spaghetti…

The Appetizer

torch to the next. Fingerhuth also made sure to enable young architects to implement their ideas. Those who benefitted included Jacques Herzog and Pierre de Meuron, as well as Roger Diener. Soon enough, every head of urban planning was saying that they wanted to do things the same way as Fingerhuth in Basel. It's great, and we're envied for it abroad.

But the end product is often quite mainstream, a substitute for reliable values. What about the value of ideas?
[Patrick] It's of no use when a judging panel pushes through a project that the investor

I'd be the drummer. And Joggi would be on bass.

doesn't understand at all. The vacancy rate for apartments in Zurich is 0.0 percent. In that context, as an architect, you get a sense of what's wanted and know it will be difficult to introduce innovative ideas in a competition that will actually be rewarded. The zeitgeist always plays some kind of a role in architecture. You can try to resist it, but you won't be able to. Today, for instance, all younger architects use color in competitions.
[Michael] The way something should be presented, which projects have won—all this information spreads at lightning speed. As soon as an idea becomes mainstream, it's already over. There's much more pressure these days, images are omnipresent and are shared around in forums and magazines. Prevailing opinions are formed by a select few. Then you know that if you stick to those ideas, you're on the safe side. As a young architect back then, I saw how you guys tried to move away from all this, whether consciously or unconsciously. At least, that's how it appeared to me. It was interesting.
[Joggi] There's no recipe for coming up with ideas. Having said that, many ideas come about from our discussions. Every single idea needs to be examined, and then you have to say, okay, that one is impossible to realize. Good ideas are not always innovative, but combine one element with another: for example, where we have to move the cellars upstairs, because we only want to build one basement level. It's a succession of logical considerations. Something might look like an idea in the end, but it was actually the result of a logical path.
[Michael] ...and the ideas don't always solve the problem.
[Patrick] When I'm on judging panels, I am of course happy when I don't have to look at the same thing all the time. It's only when something new is presented that we have interesting discussions; then it becomes a matter of getting the other judges excited about the concept. It's difficult when a colleague you respect prefers a different project. Then, considerations other than architecture come into play, and we have to ask questions such as: Is it politically feasible, does the city have a mayor with the will to push through this kind of project, or can they forget about re-election if they do so?

[Joggi] Often, judges are presented with projects whose aerodynamic design is purely for effect. It takes experience to identify these. They're dangerous.

What inspired you most recently, for instance during a vacation?
[Patrick] I'm trying to think of where I was…
[Joggi] Yes, where were you?
[Patrick] Ah yes, my wife had a visiting professorship in St. Louis in the US Midwest. From there, we visited cities that I would otherwise have never discovered. For instance, in St. Louis, Missouri, Gyo Obata and his firm designed buildings that I wasn't familiar with, but are still hugely impressive some fifty years later. My focus is on Modernism, on Le Corbusier and what followed, Louis Kahn, and how things continued after his time. For example, I stand in front of a Methodist church and see a porch in a design that I have never seen before. Just like memories of eating in my grandmother's kitchen, I can remember it later with total clarity. I won't implement the design at a later stage, but let it flow into my own work, in whatever form. I need this kind of visual inspiration.
[Michael] I look at architecture when I'm on vacation, but I am also keen to hear what my partners have to say, and then come up with my own ideas. Four people means there is a lot of input. The way your own perception of familiar things changes over the course of your life is also exciting. How the effect changes as you get older. It's just like music. The piece remains the same, but as you yourself change, it sounds different every time.

Matthias would be the lead singer.

What kind of a band would you guys form, Michael?
[Patrick] James Last…
[Michael] Could we all be in one band? Why not. A loud one, preferably. Matthias would be the lead singer.
[Matthias] I can't sing.

The Appetizer

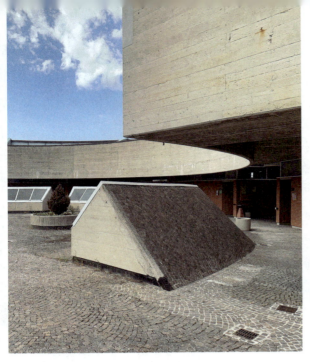

44

We're gatherers and hunters! We fill up the tank when we travel.

The Appetizer 45

[Michael] Patrick, then. I'd be the drummer. And Joggi would be on bass.
[Joggi] I'm not musical, I can't sing or dance either. The kind of music I love others call corny. If my musical taste left its mark on my architectural designs, I'd always come last in competitions.
[Matthias] You're just not mainstream.
[Michael] I think our music would go in the punk direction. There's an existential urgency about punk, a lack of fear about making mistakes. I have a playlist that I'm continuously adding to. It's similar to collecting architectural prints. At the moment, Hank Williams is at the top of the playlist, something I never could have imagined five years ago.

You're just not mainstream.

[Matthias] He's finally made it to the top.
[Michael] You'd be the dancer, you'd hog the limelight.
[Matthias] Out of all the things that you've mentioned, I'd probably be able to do that the best. My sense of rhythm is pretty good.
[Michael] You can express yourself through dance.
[Patrick] I've got a few possible band names! "Michi and the Concrete Crew" or "Aalto and Mies's Meanies." Our song would be called: "Here come the iron layers." Maybe at the start, we'd just do covers of famous songs, something like "It's only brutalism, but we like it!" or even more contemporary, "Knock on Wood." Or, we could call ourselves "The Archinauts." Our first album would be *Lost in Space*.

If you're not in harmony, what happens then?
[Joggi] That passes soon enough.

How do you deal with conflict?
[Joggi] Could we have a bit more water? Matthias, I see you've taken off your scarf.
[Matthias] It's gotten a little warmer in here now…
[Joggi] That's alright for you, you don't have an old neck…
[Michael] I'll tell you what I do: I go home and listen to music really loud. After that, everything's okay. Having a good foundation is crucial. That's how I feel about it. You trust each other and are generous with each other. It's necessary.
[Patrick] When one of us has a good idea, that person is responsible for it in the firm.

Fit as a gym shoe: Patrick

Our first album would be *Lost in Space*.

The Appetizer

That allows us to avoid a lot of conflicts. But there are various kinds of differences. We're always good at hammering out the details. And anyway, I'm aware that if there's something that you all don't like, I can't change your mind, and I just have to come to terms with that.

Matthias So Michael goes home—epitomizing the idea of taking a step back and rethinking things. Generally, this doesn't take long, and misunderstandings are always followed by optimism.

What does it mean to you when you encounter setbacks?

Patrick That's easy: if we don't win a competition, it's the judges' fault, because they didn't understand the design.

Michael That's true.

Patrick Losing more than winning is part and parcel of our job, but also, it's good to remember that losing is more instructive, and is a way to progress. Now and then, you have to concede that someone else had better ideas. It's something you just have to admit, if not entirely without envy.

Joggi It's important to be big enough to accept defeat and congratulate the winner. There is nothing more unpleasant than winning and having the feeling that everyone else is against you. If you're runner-up, you could say something like, well, for a winning project like this, I'm happy I came second. Coming second is thankless anyway. In my opinion, the feeling of being the best is the worst trait that an architect can have. It won't get you anywhere. Or saying that the judges are to blame.

Patrick, Joggi is contradicting what you said. What do you say to that?

Patrick Yes, Joggi's right, of course, you have to work through the emotions on your own.

Matthias We still always have opportunities to take part in new competitions. Post-competition is pre-competition.

Joggi That's your motto.

Patrick But it's always a big disappointment.

Michael Enormous.

Matthias Judging panels often have a certain dynamic. There are no guarantees—only that architects lose more often than they win.

Michael You invest so much in the process: money, time, ideas. But we're not keeping a tally on the office wall.

Patrick We do, however, keep a list of judges that we haven't won with yet. A "hit list."

Maybe I should cut that part out, before you do later.

Patrick Leave it in, it's fine.

Joggi You run into certain people again and again. But afterward, you're back to everyday life, and you need to keep your strength for everyday life.

Your job is not just about ideas, innovation, and competitions: it also involves a lot of administration. And that's not diminishing at all.

Joggi I sometimes ask myself if things really were always better in the past. Every point in time has its easy and challenging aspects. Change can be seen as something positive. Maybe it's simply more all-encompassing these days. Years ago, you would see skiers in competitions wearing sponsorship beanies with the words "Use oil heating." Who would

There are no guarantees—only that architects lose more often than they win.

wear something like that today? There are also topics that younger generations are more involved with than older generations. When it comes to sustainability, we've had to step out of our comfort zone. I don't belong to the generation who automatically think about sustainability with every idea—I am open to it, but I can't just go along with it without thinking. A different generation is already questioning whether or not to create new buildings and thinking about how to utilize existing ones. In my view, it's a welcome trend.

Digitalization is changing the landscape as radically as industrialization once did. Is it a curse or a blessing, Joggi?

Joggi Neither. It is what it is. A situation. A kid who starts playing soccer at three years of age handles the ball differently to an eighteen-year-old starting out in the sport.

Michael I'm hopeful for the new generation. For us, it's more difficult, because we are between two worlds. It would be nice if digital advance-

The Appetizer   49

Competitions are our daily work-out—but we know that it's just as important to catch your breath.

The Appetizer 51

ments would encourage people to be more daring, but for many, they're just a tool to provide even more protection.

You're referring to BIM: building information modeling?

Joggi BIM is already on the way out.

Matthias It arrived on the scene five years ago to a lot of fanfare. It wasn't really able to take root in these parts, though. Interestingly, a lot of institutions started using BIM, but gave up on it pretty quickly. Evidently it didn't work as people had hoped. The goal was that BIM could be used throughout the entire project cycle, from planning and construction through to facility operation.

Michael BIM involves an enormous volume of data, which gives the false impression of accuracy. You are no longer able to observe certain issues from the necessary distance. The main problem with BIM is that you need to be much too precise at an early design stage. Another difficulty is that people who are only skilled at using this one instrument, but not others, can excel at BIM. I find that to be a challenge. Nevertheless, we have built using BIM.

Patrick Working on a project using BIM involves a colossal effort, not only on the part of the architect, but also the building management. We have also participated in these kinds of competitions. Recently one for 300 apartments. Mapping a building with 100,000 elements is extremely complex. Out of the blue, we received feedback querying why we had included 900 bathrooms. Apparently, building shafts were counted as toilets by the calculation. Everyone involved thought they had done things correctly—but something was amiss with the outcome.

Michael Ultimately, it's just a competition. The competition should really be about coming up with an idea, a good idea, not talking about the number of bathrooms. That wastes a lot of time, and means there's less time for thinking about the actual idea. And that's what it leads to—that's what I meant.

Matthias We're not opposed to BIM per se. If we have been commissioned to use it, sure, it's doable. But we don't take an active interest in it.

You're reminding me a little of the dinosaurs right now…

Patrick For me, the future, and our future as a firm, has nothing to do with BIM. It has more to do with what Joggi said earlier: we should be asking ourselves whether we're up-to-date in terms of sustainability. We know that we're experiencing climate change. And we could have started dealing with it differently in our building designs years ago. But we didn't. The smart thing would be to work together on such topics with younger firms that have the right know-how, but not the commissions. Recently, I was involved in a competition where some colleagues submitted a building made of straw. Gosh, that's pretty bold, I thought, when only two years ago they submitted a concrete building. I've been thinking a lot about that. Would I also submit a straw building, or throw my plan out the window at the first sign of resistance? I'm not sure.

Sustainability is a new language.

Matthias | I also think that the issue of sustainability will affect us much more than BIM.
Joggi | I can already see that with my students. When, for instance, I suggest using three-ply panels, they say: absolutely not. It's as if someone has forgotten to use gender-neutral language. As if I'm not as up-to-date as I'd like to be. Sustainability is a new language. The question of space will not be as relevant in the future as it is now. Architects will be asking different questions instead. Even if I'm interested in the topic, other generations will be at the forefront.
Patrick | I think we were very clever with our design for the apartment building in Wettswil.
Michael | We *can* be like that, now and again.
Patrick | Experience helps us adapt solutions and develop a logic. The sustainability expert was really delighted with our design for that.
Michael | He was really surprised that this old firm could come up with it.

We keep a hit list.

The Appetizer   53

The Appetizer

Our team makes many things much easier to bear.

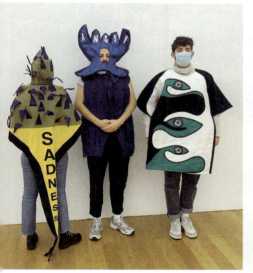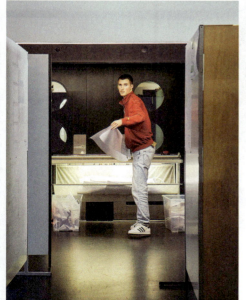

The Appetizer 57

5.4 The Main Course

Osso Buco with Saffron Risotto

Not far from the kitchen where we are eating, and have just been served the main course of osso buco, is your model room, where you craft the models for competitions.
Michael Where we *construct* them.
Patrick We are a serious firm. We don't do craft, and we don't play around with things.
Joggi We aren't artists, either.

Are the models made by hand or using a 3D printer?
Michael Ouch.
Matthias We've discussed that several times.
Patrick If we wanted to try 3D, one of us would have to say, ok, let's do it that way. But no one has said that yet. Plus, we would need somebody who knows how to use the printer. And if that person isn't here, we have a problem.
Matthias We even discussed a budget for it.
Patrick When I accompanied my wife to St. Louis, I had a look around the university and at the students' working environment, too. Their workspaces reminded me of the NASA control center. Each workspace had a good eight screens and two laser printers. Whatever they drew was printed in 3D right away. All you could hear was the whirring of the printers. It

We don't do craft, and we don't play around. We aren't artists, either.

was intriguing. Although I do wonder whether they are really necessary. I was amazed at how good they were at using them.
Joggi It's a tool that's similar to CAD. I've got an old program that I learned fifteen years ago. For projects, I always work with a staff member who I supervise and who then maps things out in 3D. Then I decide which solution is better.
Michael It ultimately depends on what you need the model for, and in what context it is used. For urban planning, for instance, you can make quicker progress using conventional tools and polystyrene than with a 3D printer. Also, the project and the model develop in parallel. It's a process. I like the directness of a handmade model. If the model is required solely for the presentation, we have it laser cut externally. We send the data to a specialist, and by the afternoon, a package with the blocks has arrived and we can begin assembling them.

I'm asking these questions because I'm interested in how an established firm such as yours deals with the way that things change over time…
Joggi When, as a large firm, you start bringing in new concepts, you pay dearly for it. I saw that happen to my father. When he starting using CAD, he had two employees who oversaw everything, because they were the only ones who could use it. It became a chokepoint.
Michael A tool is only ever as useful as the person who operates it. And that person requires skill.
Matthias Before, it was all about the technical pen, now it's 3D. They're just tools. You need to be skilled at the job. You need to be able to implement your ideas.
Michael The fact that several things come

together here may make the job more complex, but it also makes it more exciting.

[Patrick] Our firm has more of a conventional approach. Frank Gehry used software developed for the aviation industry early on in his designs. In the future, there are going to be innovations that we can't even imagine today. Maybe that's why we build apartments, because it's conventional: you have a kid's room that's twelve square meters, a bedroom that's fourteen square meters. The combinations for residential construction are different to the designs for a Guggenheim Museum in Bilbao. You could say we're a little old-fashioned.

Who wants to live in a badly designed apartment?

[Joggi] The ideas of the residents are also important. Say you're living in a loft apartment, and then you meet a new partner who has a child. How can you keep living in that space? Someone I know put up a tent in the living room. As a kid's room.

Why is it necessary to build high-quality apartments?

[Michael] Who wants to live in a badly designed apartment?

[Patrick] Someone who lives in a well-designed home becomes an architect. Or on the other hand, they could become an architect precisely because they don't live in a well-designed apartment. In all seriousness, though, we think that when a museum is not well designed, it doesn't matter to visitors. They just won't go to the museum. However, an apartment will be in use for 100 years. It is our responsibility to design it so that the residents feel comfortable there. If you're in pain, you go to the doctor...

[Joggi] ...and they then say: you're living in a badly designed apartment.

[Matthias] ...you should go see a good architect.

[Patrick] Just like the doctor, our responsibility lies in putting our expertise into practice. That's what drives me. We usually complete between 20 and 300 apartments per project. And I think we're very good at what we do. Throughout the years, we've developed a feel for developing ideal solutions for apartments and floor plans.

[Joggi] We operate on the principle that we build apartments well. But maybe, one day, people will be critical of our floor plans. I don't think that good apartments make for better people. There are many wonderful people who grew up in small, cramped apartments, and were not as privileged as us, who grew up in houses.

[Matthias] I grew up in a very cramped apartment.

[Michael] Me too.

[Matthias] I wasn't familiar with a double door until I was twenty years old. There were four of us living in a ninety-square-meter apartment. My childhood bedroom measured nine square

I still live in a pretty small space today.

meters. It's didn't do me any harm. Although now, I appreciate being able to live in a bigger place.

Joggi Perceiving an apartment as being good is similar to how you engage with wine. It is a slow process, a process of raising awareness. It doesn't have to be a big apartment, but it should have a well-designed floor plan. The space needs to be right. Others are of the opinion that an apartment should be sustainable, which is correct too.

Matthias I still live in a pretty small space today. There are two of us living in a seventy-five-square-meter apartment.

Have you all been to Matthias's home?
Patrick I've been there. I had to see what kind of place I was bringing my cats to.
Matthias They missed your patio.
Patrick But then you got up and played with them every day. I'm still suffering the consequences of that.

The Main Course   61

We like to work—on the weekends, too—to potter around, search for something, and try things out.

The Main Course 63

5.5   The Dessert

Panna Cotta with Agar Agar

The art lies in creating your own world within those four walls.

We've already reached dessert: panna cotta made with agar agar and decorated with violets.

[Matthias] Have you all already eaten the flowers?

[Michael] Yes. I've eaten flowers many times, and lots of things that grow in the garden. We didn't have money as kids to buy ice cream, but we had apples and pears from our neighbor's garden.

[Joggi] Are they from your garden, Petra? It's really delicious, this dessert.

[Michael] Joggi, do you really think that architecture doesn't make people happy?

[Joggi] Sometimes I'm watching a movie where the action takes place in an unsightly environment, with engines, old cars in front of the door, stuff like that, and I catch myself thinking that there's some form of beauty there. Things can always be considered from a different perspective.

[Patrick] The exciting thing about apartment living is that tastes in home decor have changed over centuries. A dwelling is more than just a floor plan. It includes furnishings, silverware, glasses. This is how worlds are created. Matthias, I thought your apartment was a wonderful space, not cramped. I think I'm the only one of us who has been at all of your homes.

[Joggi] It's fascinating when there's a patterned vinyl cloth on the table in an apartment and it looks good. If everything was simply beautiful and in good taste, it would be boring. The art lies in creating your own world within those

Hand-sewn and very British: Joggi

Ninety-five percent of the time, it's me that turns off the lights and locks up.

four walls. A world that other people would not expect. Good apartments are the ones that offer the space for people to create their own worlds. Architecture should simply facilitate these worlds.

Do you think a living space influences the resident?

[Joggi] There is an interplay. They shape each other until everything is the way it should be.

[Michael] As architects, we start thinking about furnishings when we begin to sketch. We see that the kitchen table should be in the center, the chair should be in a certain position to make it easier to open the refrigerator, and so on. The resident should get the impression that everything fits together and that someone thought about them when designing the apartment. It's as if we're communicating with the resident from a distance. To say to them, this is how you can live, this is a basis for arranging things the way you want.

Patrick My wife and I built a place for ourselves, a vacation home. It has just been completed. Being able to do that was fantastic. The building we renovated is a seventeenth-century parsonage. Working with the existing spaces has been challenging. Some are so small that we had to design new tables for them, because conventional tables are too big.

Michael I grew up in a tiny apartment in Heerbrugg, which was only designed in theory, rather than practice. It was a government-subsidized apartment. Our hallway was so narrow you could barely walk through it. The kitchen offered exactly enough space for an eighty-centimeter-long table, where the four of us would sit. In all the apartments I've lived in since, it was compulsory for me to have the same kind of table. The main question I always had about decor was where I would put the table. The apartment where I live with my family today is not small, but I still prefer to sit at a table that's eighty centimeters in length. I've brought this aspect of living from my childhood with me.

Patrick is not the only one who has been creative on the tablecloth, I see that you have been too, Michael. Your drawing looks a little like the person sitting opposite you. Is that Joggi?

Michael When we were talking about BIM a while back, this man appeared on the cloth while I was thinking, but it's not Joggi.

How do you relax in your free time?

Joggi All I know is that I need more time these days to relax and unwind. I also don't sleep well, which gets me thinking about annoying stuff. That last, curtly written email that was cc'd to everyone; I go over things like that again and again in my head when I'm lying in bed. There are some people who, rather insidiously, send these kinds of emails on a Friday evening, right before the weekend. That's why I've stopped looking at my emails after midday on a Friday.

Patrick I tend to enjoy that situation.

Getting a rude email?

Michael Then they'll get a rude one back from Patrick.

Patrick I don't really have any issues with that. I tell myself that it's better to react than sit something out. I walk to the office and walk back home in the evenings. When I still have to process something related to work, I take a detour to think. I don't want to bother my partner about work stuff, she's an architect herself and already has enough to think about. I can only change myself, not other people. That Buddhistic wisdom is something I learned when I got older.

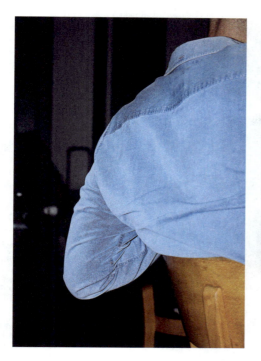
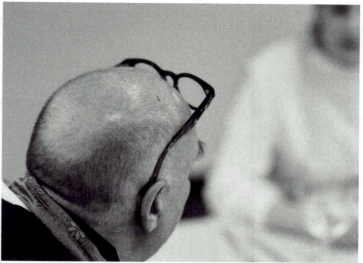

[Joggi] Interestingly, everyone at the table here has a partner who is also an architect. I'm the only one who doesn't, and I see that as a good thing. If I complain about things, I get a matter-of-fact reply from my partner, they might suggest that I shouldn't have gone through official channels, or something similar. A different perspective is helpful for me.

The architectural profession can be challenging for a relationship. That's certainly the case if you take the job seriously and are passionate about it.

[Patrick] It's also not always good to be cooped up together all the time.

Do you prefer to be in the office or at home?

[Joggi] I love being at home. I like being able to eat together with my family.
[Patrick] I like being in the office. To busy myself with something, without any stress. Try out something new. Just for my own personal satisfaction.
[Joggi] I write judge's reports in the office. At home, I don't work.
[Matthias] I like working from home.
[Michael] I actually don't like working from home so much, apart from tasks that aren't so taxing, such as writing texts.

Who's the last one to turn off the lights in the office?

[Matthias] Ninety-five percent of the time, it's me that turns off the lights and locks up. But it's never really that late. I'm usually home by 8:30.
[Joggi] While I'm usually the first one there in the morning. I get in at 7:30 a.m., pop in quickly so that all the employees can see that I'm there, and then I go out again to read the newspaper. I'm back at my desk at 8:45 a.m. That's when I'm actually in the office. I'm on the go a lot, for instance giving lectures, or participating in judging panels.

You guys didn't drink much during our conversation.

[Joggi] I had two glasses of wine. I don't drink more than that generally.
[Matthias] I'm thinking about tomorrow. We've got to be back in the office.
[Joggi] I need to fast for a blood test tomorrow morning.
[Patrick] I drink when there's something there to drink. And I eat when there's something to eat.

Which course was your favorite?

[Michael] Everything was excellent.
[Joggi] It was, but one thing stood out for me: the spaghetti with... what was it?
[Patrick] ...and the chili pepper, it was chili, right?
[Matthias] Anchovies.

The Dessert   67

Matthias Kyburz   Patrick Gmür

Michael Geschwentner   Jakob Steib

The Dessert   69

SGGK Partners

Jakob Steib (born 1959)
studied at ETH Zurich. In 1983, he was awarded a scholarship to attend the Harvard Graduate School of Design in Cambridge, Massachusetts, USA. From 1986 to 1989 he worked as an assistant to Prof. Arthur Rüegg at ETH Zurich, and in 1994 as a teaching assistant. Since 1997, he has been Professor of Design and Construction at the Zurich University of Applied Sciences (ZHAW) in Winterthur. He founded his own architectural firm in Zurich (JSA) in 1987. From 2000 to 2009, he also ran a firm together with Patrick Gmür (GSA), and from 2009 one with Michael Geschwentner (SGA), both in Zurich. Since 1995 he has served on judging panels and as an expert advisor in Switzerland and Germany, and is also a member of the FSA.
In 2020, he founded the firm Steib Gmür Geschwentner Kyburz Architekten (SGGK) in Zurich together with Patrick Gmür, Michael Geschwentner, and Matthias Kyburz.

Patrick Gmür (born 1961)
studied at ETH Zurich, and from 1989 to 2009 ran his own architectural firm in Zurich (PGA), until 1998 together with Regula Lüscher Gmür (GLG). From 2000 to 2009, he ran another Zurich-based firm together with Jakob Steib (GSA). From 2009 to 2016, he was director of the Zurich City Planning Office. From 2016 to 2019, he was co-proprietor of Gmür & Geschwentner Architekten + Stadtplaner (GGAS). He has held various teaching positions, including as a guest professor in Vienna in 2017 and in St. Louis, Missouri, USA in 2019. From 2005 to 2008, he was head of the Institute of Architecture at the University of Applied Sciences Northwestern Switzerland (FHNW). He has also served on a number of judging panels, as chairman of the Stuttgart Design Advisory Board, has given lectures at home and abroad, and is a member of the FSA.
In 2020, he founded the firm Steib Gmür Geschwentner Kyburz Architekten (SGGK) in Zurich with Jakob Steib, Michael Geschwentner, and Matthias Kyburz.

Michael Geschwentner (born 1971)
studied at ETH Zurich. He completed internships at Burkhalter & Sumi Architekten, Zurich, and at Leslie Gill Architect, New York, USA. From 1998 to 2006, he worked at Gmür Lüscher Gmür Architekten (GLG) and Patrick Gmür Architekten (PGA) in Zurich. He received a travel scholarship from the Ernst Schindler Foundation in 2001. From 2009 to 2016 he was a proprietor of Gmür & Geschwentner Architekten (GGA), and from 2009 to 2016 he was co-proprietor of Steib & Geschwentner Architekten (SGA) in Zurich with Jakob Steib. From 2016 to 2019, he was a co-proprietor of Gmür & Geschwentner Architekten + Stadtplaner (GGAS). He has also served on judging panels and is a member of the FSA. In 2020, he founded the Steib Gmür Geschwentner Kyburz Architekten (SGGK) firm in Zurich with Jakob Steib, Patrick Gmür, and Matthias Kyburz.

Matthias Kyburz (born 1979)
completed an apprenticeship as a draftsman and studied at the Zurich University of Applied Sciences (ZHAW) in Winterthur. In 2002, he completed an internship at the office of Jakob Steib, Zurich, and did a semester abroad at the University of the Arts in Berlin under Prof. Adolf Krischanitz in 2003. He has worked as an architect since 2005. From 2013, he was part of the management group at Jakob Steib Architekten (JSA), and from 2010 was an employee and part of the management at Steib & Geschwentner Architekten (SGA), both in Zurich. In 2020, he founded the firm Steib Gmür Geschwentner Kyburz Architekten (SGGK) in Zurich with Jakob Steib, Patrick Gmür, and Michael Geschwentner.

Current Members of Staff

Ömer Acar

Viktoria Kelderer

Luna Theer

Domenico Desumma

Paola Falconi

Aleksandra Ćurčin

Emil Schaad

Tita Campino

Isidor Escobar

Fiona Endres

Natalie Bachmann

Marina Kuhn

Nicolò Suzani

Annsophie Vogt

Marc Paessens

Lua Gmür

Vivian Bonzel

Nora Spaniol

Jürg Schönenberger

Peter Roesch

Claudia Häfeli

Carlos Craveiro

Caroline Schartz

Simone Liner

Sven Ledermann

Scarlett-Rose Strub

Laura Scheerer

Maja Pantelić

Lucas Bellomo

Sophie Guilleux

Former Members of Staff 2008–2023

Salvatore Agostinelli, Katja Albiez, Cristina Alén Mendes, Emina Alitovic, Giuseppe Allegri, David Altinger, Oliver Altorfer, Aline Amore, Tsering Anodunkhartsang, Jarolim Antal, Veit Auch, Stefania Bacskay, Christa Baldinger, Hansi Bargeld, Susanne Bartholomé, Nicola Baviera, Silvia Benelli, Lorena Bernasconi, Misia Bernasconi, Isabel Bernhard, Sybille Besson, Christoph Bieri, Roman Birrer, Laura Bissegger, Manuel Blum, Eveline Blunschi, Sabina Bogacz, Lelia Bollinger, Seraina Bollinger, Manuela Borges, Emil Brechenmacher, Sandy Brunner, Nico Brunschweiler, Lea Bucher, Nicole Bucher, Thomas Bucher, David Büeler, Timo Bullmann, Silvia Burgermeister, Lukas Burkart, Michal Bzdziuch, Britta Callsen, Barbara Campolongo, Daiana Camastra, Christiano Catenzaro, Anna Caviezel, Sonja Christen, Lorella Civale, Suzanne Coleman, Marta Da Costa, Miley Cyrus, Ileana Dan, Nils de Buhr, Laura de Capitani, Nicole Deiss, Eliane Della Gola Bigliotti, Ricardo Dias, Adrian Dominguez Valido, Ole Drescher, Daniel Düsentrieb, Silke Ebner, Ralph Edelmann, Bruno Eggenschwiler, Susana Elias, Ralph Edelmann, Jule Eppler, Manuel Federer, Lukas Felleisen, Cristiano Ferreira, Madleina Fischer, Patrick Fischer, Corinna Flad, Isabel Frehner, Roland Frei, René Frey, Sven Fricker, Andreas Frössler, Olivia Furrer, Kate Gannon, Alejandra Garcia Sahelices, Corinne Gasal, Ingrid Gentry-Schmidt, Tina Gernet, Giovanni Girotto, Gabriel Gmür, Benian Göncüoglu, Daniela Gonzalez, Natalia Gorgol, Eric Gösswald, Sonja Grigo, Eva Gröbly-Prenci, Michel Gübeli, Pascale Guignard, Miguel Guimaraes , Maya Gunz, Daniel Gutzwiller, Erling Haaland, Safia Hachemi, Lena Hagen, Demjan Haller, Christina Hamminger, Susan Held, Mariken Helle, Thea Helle, Elena Helmreich, Sabine Herzog, Florian Hoch, Esther Hodel, Anette Höller, Moritz Hörnle, Hilke Horsthemke, Ali Hossaini, Teresa Huber, Fredi Humorlos, Eldina Husic, Charlotte Hustinx, Corinne Huwyler, Maria Imbach, Mirjam Imgrüth, Natalia Irazustabarrena, Verena Jacob, Katharina Janz, Anique Jaquier, Aline Jean, Andrea Jeger, Sabrina Joye, Attila Jung, Tryfonas Kalogiannis, Gabriela Kappeler, Daniel Kapr, Veronika Karl, Fabian Kaufmann, Andreas Keiser, Alma Kelderer, Carmen Keller, Isabel Kern, Aresu Khoshy, Sabina Kickhofel Näf, Patrick Knock, Nils Knodel, Silvia Kobel, Gaby Köhler, Anastasia König, Simon Kramer Vrscaj, Simon Krauss, Patrick Knock, Anna Kübler, Thomas Küpper, Jochen Lambmann, Adhika Lang, Julia Lang, Danai Laskari, Anssi Lauttia, Renate Lavater, Quentin Le Normant, Sandro Lehnherr, Oliver Leu, Laetitia Lietha, Gonzalo Lozano Arce, Gianmarco Maina, Michael Malnatti, Michèle Mambourg, Kelly Man, Ana Sofia Mateus, Felix Matschke, John McEnroe, Lionel Messi, Timo Meyer, Franziska Moog, Linda Müller, Michelle Müller, Lorenz Müller, Ricardo Nader, Barbara Neff, Tuyet Nguyen, Manuel Niggli, Patrick Nock, Livia Notarangelo, Sophie Oberst, Lisa Obertautsch, Segun Ogunsola, Xemein Oiartzabal Goñi, Barbara Ott, Roberto Outumuro, Giani Pardini, Silvana Perner, Fahny Pesenti, Bojan Petrovic, Michael Pfister, Aiste Plentaite, Natalie Pomer, Lukas Prestele, Corinne Previtali, Alberto Quiñones, Leon Raithel, Valton Rexha, Iliana Rieger, Elisa Rimoldi, Christina Ringelmann, Susanne Ristic, Fabienne Roth, Kesha Rüeger, Thomas Rujbr, Frida Ruppe, Barbara Ruppeiner, Kylie Russnaik, Karolina Sadomska, Pedro Santos, Stéphanie Savio, Laura Schäfer, Johnny Rotten, Anja Schaffner, Eva Schaub, Mario Scheinecker, Matthias Scherer, Eva Schiess, Sandro Schmid, Johanna Schmücker, Michèle Schneble Säuberli, Florian Schrenk, Peter Schuberth, Leart Sejdiu, Marta Shtipkova-Michael, Meltem Simsek, Marta Sobral Brito Saraiva de Costa, Lyn Sorgfältig, Kevin Sorglos, Stefan Spichty, Barbara Spirig, Linn Echo Stählin, Manca Starmann, Lara Steger, Lyle Stemper, Katharina Stepien, Laura Stock, Kerstin Stoffers, Sonja Strickmann, Jasna Strukelj, Sergio Suárez, Thomas Summermatter, Taylor Swift, Bernadett Széles, Zita Széplaki, Nayanatara Tampi, Simon Thurnherr, Samuel Tobler, Valeria Tosa, Gian Trachsler, Ines Trenner, Louise Tusch, Michael Ursprung, Barbara Verbost, Rémy Voisard, Martina Vogel, Johanna von der Lage, Martin von der Ropp, Angela Waibel, Sabina Walker, Barbara Waltert, Monika Walther Lisa Wawrzyniak, Gabriela Weber, Lenka Weinzettlovà, Andreas Weiz, Sidonia Wiesmann, Cheryl Wigger, Christine Wilkening, Rebecca Will, Astrid Wirth, Andrea Wolfer, Sebastian Worm, Nimm Aber Reichlich, Marie-Luise Wunder , Tanja Wurmitzer, Saskia Wyss, Katharina Wyss, Sandra Wyss, Hanspeter Wyss, Myrto Xopapa, Forever Young, Laura Zachmann, Jan Zangerl, Albin Zeitgeist, Stephanie Zgraggen, Jing Zhao, Robert Zimmermann, Armon Zimmermann, Johanna Zinnecker, Dominik Ziswiler, Annick Zucchetti, Sarah Züger, Caesar Zumthor, Chiara Zunino

A heartfelt thank-you!

With her expertly posed questions, Gudrun Sachse guided us through the evening with a five-course dinner and did a tremendous job of editing our conversation afterward. Photographer Markus Bertschi documented the dinner with a series of felicitous photographs. We thank them from the bottom of our hearts! Petra Schlaefle not only devised and cooked the five-course meal for this volume, she also whips up marvelous menus of "architect's fodder" every Friday at our office canteen.

It's rare that we get a chance to meet the people that end up living in the buildings we design. For this reason, we are particularly delighted that the fourth volume provides a glimpse of what everyday life is like in some of our apartments. We would like to extend our sincere gratitude to all the residents who opened their doors and showed us how they furnished their apartments, and who provided such cogent answers in the interviews. With her impeccable eye for detail, Rita Palanikumar photographed the eleven apartments, while Corinne Gasal conducted the interviews with the residents; to them both, our sincere appreciation. For years we have followed and admired the work of Zurich artist Dieter Hall, and we have long been fascinated by the idiosyncratic visions in his paintings. We are honored that he has provided us with three images that are perfect for the opening credits. Thank you, Dieter!

The core labors of our slipcase are found in volume three, which features vivid descriptions of apartment floor plans we've designed over the years. Hilke Horsthemke, Cristina Alén Mendes, Paloma Romero, Anna Caviezel, Lukas Felleisen, as well as Lyle Stemper drew and furnished all these floor plans—and many more—with scrupulousness, patience, and unfaltering concentration. Giuseppe Allegri coordinated the work, helped draw up the floor plans, and was also responsible for ensuring the uniform presentation of the sixty-five project overviews. We owe them all a great big thank-you. We would also like to thank the heroes of our everyday kitchen. These are Mischa Käser, the admired chef of the Restaurant Italia in Zurich, Anna Pearson, author of the cookbook Pasta, the legendary Richard Kägi (who cooks better than he plays tennis), as well as the cooks and authors of the cookbooks who created the spaghetti recipes we selected: Marianne Kaltenbach, Marcella Hazan, and Ruth Rogers and Rose Gray of the River Café in London.

Architecture is teamwork. That's exactly what it takes to write, illustrate, lay out, and take photographs for a book—or in our case, five books. "Teamwork makes the dream work!" The saying is as simple as it is true and appropriate.

A book project of this scope required some digging into our huge photo collection and some contact with former employees. There were also associated administrative tasks. Our heartfelt thanks go to Laura Scheerer and Maja Pantelic for undertaking this work.

As you can see in the five volumes, over the years we have had many opportunities to have our buildings documented by professional photographers. For this we thank Georg Aerni, Roger Frei, Menga von Sprecher, Beat Schweizer, and Zeljko Gataric. Your photographs make our buildings all the better! The same goes for the many architectural models that we study again and again. To mention them all here would exceed the scope of this closing note. Your works deserve our respect.

Sibylle Kanalz, Nora Spaniol, and Jürg Schönenberger designed and laid out the five books and provided the different contents with a unified form. We appreciate their dedication and hard work. Merci beaucoup pour tout! Jürg was a driving force behind the many threads that made up this work and tied them together miraculously. He also coordinated the entire project. He always kept the bigger picture in mind and, above all, kept his cool. We are endlessly grateful for his efforts.

We would like to thank Christoph Wieser for the essential discussions regarding the content, as well as for collating, correcting, editing, and improving the texts. We like his story about our office.

Thomas Kramer from Park Books supported us from the very first conversation we had together. He encouraged us to pursue this path. His trust has sustained us. To him and his team—grazie mille per tutto!

As an architectural firm, we depend on our clients. Without their trust in our ideas and designs for our residential buildings, we would not have been able to fill these pages with content. Their support—even if we sometimes take a little detour—as well as their patience is most precious to us. Thank you!

Our deepest thanks go to our former and current members of staff. Without all of you, our office would not exist. Each of these plans represents your contributions. Your patience, enthusiasm, and shared laughter are indispensable! Peter Roesch's outsider perspective is equally invaluable to us. He has worked by our side for many years.

Finally, I would like to personally thank my partners Joggi, Michael, and Matthias for their generosity and above all their friendship and constant support for this book project. Our office demands indefatigable commitment from us. The unconditional solicitude of Karin, Simone, Luca, and Annette means the world to me!

Patrick Gmür

Contributors

Markus Bertschi (born 1970), photographer
First trained as a photographer, before working as a freelance photographic assistant in Zurich and New York. Since 2001, he has been self-employed as a photographer in Zurich. He works for companies and magazines at home and abroad in the fields of portrait photography, advertising, photojournalism, architecture, and editorial photography. He is a member of the 13PHOTO agency. He has owned and operated the online gallery Weissgrad Edition since 2021. He was head of examinations at the Swiss Photo Club Photography Program from 2016 to 2022, and since 2023 has served as the expert assessor for the photography examinations at the EFZ.

Sibylle Kanalz (born 1976), designer
She trained as a lithographer at Tamedia and completed a Diploma of Typographic Design in St. Gallen. She has been responsible for art direction and customer-facing graphic design and graphic design for the media at Facts Magazin (1998–2002) and Effact AG (2002–2005) and worked as art director and senior designer at Crafft Kommunikation AG in Zurich. Further training in digital and interactive design, After Effects, and CAS in digital typography UX/UI at ZHdK. From 2021–2023 collaborations with various partners. Freelance since 2021.

Rita Palanikumar, freelance photographer
She studied photography at the École supérieure d'arts appliqués in Vevey. She co-founded and is a board member of 13PHOTO – Agentur für Fotografie. She has received various awards and shown work at numerous exhibitions at home and abroad. Selected publications include Freilager Zürich (Park Books, 2016), A Life with Art and Artists, Trix and Robert Haussmann in conversation with Dieter Schwarz (Edition Patrick Frey, 2021). Her focus is on architecture, interior design, portraiture, and photojournalism for organizations such as Schauspielhaus Zürich, USM, Linck Keramik, Das Magazin, The Weekender, and Hochparterre.

Gudrun Sachse (born 1972), moderation and text
Is an art and architectural historian and journalist. She studied in Zurich, Bern, and Paris. Sachse held a position at Sotheby's in Zurich, in addition to working as an author and editor for various Swiss and international media outlets. Her focus is on global sociopolitical issues, and producing features, conversations, and stories for prominent magazines and books. From 2005 to 2019 she was editor at the monthly magazine Folio for the Neue Zürcher Zeitung (NZZ). She has been a lecturer and consultant at the Swiss School of Journalism MAZ, moderator, and author of the NZZ-Folio column "Wer wohnt da?" (Who Lives There?). Since 2019, she has worked as an independent journalist and entrepreneur.

Petra Schlaefle (born 1964), cook
Her home in Zurich is filled with hundreds of cookbooks that she flips through every day. Since the COVID-19 pandemic, the chef and interior stylist has worked as a private chef for private individuals and businesses. She works on call. For the fifty-nine-year-old, every single moment in the kitchen brings pleasure; from the texture of an onion to the consistency of kohlrabi. And this enjoyment is not only experienced by Petra herself, but by those she cooks for too. Every Friday for the last one and a half years, she has cooked in the architecture office in Flüelastrasse, Zurich, where she serves a three-course meal. She finds the architects to be "fairly easy to please." There's only one person in the office who is lactose intolerant, so she prepares a sauce without cream for him.

Christoph Wieser (born 1967), editing
Is an architectural theorist, lecturer, and writer. He studied at ETH Zurich and Lausanne, earning a doctorate in 2005. From 2003 to 2009 he was editor of the magazine werk, bauen + wohnen. Since 2006, he has been a lecturer at various Swiss universities of applied sciences, and since 2013 at the University of Applied Sciences Northwestern Switzerland (FHNW) in Muttenz. From 2009 to 2013 he was head of the Center (later the Institute) of Constructive Design at the Zurich University of Applied Sciences (ZHAW) in Winterthur. Since 2015, he has worked as a consultant in the field of monument preservation.

Food for Architects
Volume 5: Five Courses for Four Friends

Published by: Steib Gmür Geschwentner Kyburz Partner
Introduction: Patrick Gmür
Moderation and text: Gudrun Sachse
Photography: Markus Bertschi
Editor: Christoph Wieser
Translation: Hunter Bolin, Ryan Eyers and Gráinne Toomey for Gegensatz Translation Collective
Proofreading: Marc Hiatt and Joel Scott for Gegensatz Translation Collective
Design and layout: Sibylle Kanalz, Jürg Schönenberger, Nora Spaniol
Image processing: Karin Prasser
Photo credits: Steib Gmür Geschwentner Kyburz, except for those by 360 360̸ p. 50, 51; Georg Aerni p. 9 m.; Berrel Krautler Architekten GmbH p. 50, 51; Markus Bertschi p. 14, 15, 16, 17, 19 t. r., 20, 21, 24–29, 32–35, 38–43, 52–55, 58–61, 64–69; various others, including Rita Palanikumar p. 22, 30, 31, 56, 57; Roger Frei p. 10 b.; Zeljko Gataric p. 9 t. l.; Nightnurse Images AG p. 50, 51; Onur Ozman GmbH p. 51; Rita Palanikumar p. 62, 63; Beat Schweizer p. 9 b. l., 10 t. r.; Studio Blomen p. 50, 51; Studio Maleta p. 51; Studio Miskeljin p. 50; Zuend p. 51
Printing and binding: DZA Druckerei zu Altenburg GmbH, Thuringia

© 2023 Steib Gmür Geschwentner Kyburz Partner and Park Books AG, Zurich
© for the texts: the authors

Park Books
Niederdorfstrasse 54
8001 Zurich
Switzerland
www.park-books.com

Park Books has received support from the Federal Office of Culture with a general subsidy for the years 2021–2024.

All rights reserved; no part of this publication may be reproduced, stored in a retrieval system or transmitted in any form or by any means, electronic, mechanical, photocopying, recording, or otherwise, without the prior written consent of the publisher.

ISBN 978-3-03860-360-3

This book is volume 5 of Food for Architects, a set of five volumes in a slipcase which are not available separately.